Essentials of Generative AI

Takeshi Okadome

Essentials of Generative AI

Takeshi Okadome
School of Science and Technology
Kwansei Gakuin University
Sanda, Hyogo, Japan

ISBN 978-981-96-0028-1   ISBN 978-981-96-0029-8 (eBook)
https://doi.org/10.1007/978-981-96-0029-8

© The Editor(s) (if applicable) and The Author(s), under exclusive license to Springer Nature Singapore Pte Ltd. 2025

This work is subject to copyright. All rights are solely and exclusively licensed by the Publisher, whether the whole or part of the material is concerned, specifically the rights of translation, reprinting, reuse of illustrations, recitation, broadcasting, reproduction on microfilms or in any other physical way, and transmission or information storage and retrieval, electronic adaptation, computer software, or by similar or dissimilar methodology now known or hereafter developed.
The use of general descriptive names, registered names, trademarks, service marks, etc. in this publication does not imply, even in the absence of a specific statement, that such names are exempt from the relevant protective laws and regulations and therefore free for general use.
The publisher, the authors and the editors are safe to assume that the advice and information in this book are believed to be true and accurate at the date of publication. Neither the publisher nor the authors or the editors give a warranty, expressed or implied, with respect to the material contained herein or for any errors or omissions that may have been made. The publisher remains neutral with regard to jurisdictional claims in published maps and institutional affiliations.

This Springer imprint is published by the registered company Springer Nature Singapore Pte Ltd.
The registered company address is: 152 Beach Road, #21-01/04 Gateway East, Singapore 189721, Singapore

If disposing of this product, please recycle the paper.

Preface

This book primarily serves as a companion for researchers or graduate students in machine learning, aiming to help them understand the essence of generative AI and lay the groundwork for advancing their own research. In March 2024, the author published a Japanese textbook on deep learning aimed at second to third-year undergraduate students. The textbook aims for students to understand generative AI while also introducing a wide range of topics in deep learning beyond generative AI. This book, in contrast, focuses specifically on generative AI.

In this book, Part I explains the foundational technologies and architectures that support the realization of generative models. It covers evolved and deepened elements, word embeddings as a representative example of representation learning, and the Transformer as a network foundation, along with its underlying attention mechanism. Reinforcement learning, which became essential for elevating large-scale language models to language generation models, is also discussed in detail, focusing on essential aspects.

Part II deals with language generation. It starts by elucidating language models and introduces large-scale language models with broad applications as the foundational architecture of language processing, further discussing language generation models as their evolution. Though not common terminology, in this book, models such as ChatGPT and Llama 2, which are large-scale language models fine-tuned using reinforcement learning, are referred to as generative language models.

Part III addresses image generation, discussing variational autoencoders and the remarkable diffusion models. Additionally, it explains GANs (Generative Adversarial Networks). Although GANs pose challenges due to unstable learning, their conceptual framework is widely applicable, especially Wasserstein GAN seems suitable for introducing optimal transport distance, which is utilized in various scenarios.

Typesetting in LaTeX and the creation of figures were assisted by Keiko Horiguchi, the secretary of the Faculty of Engineering at Kwansei Gakuin University. I appreciate her support.

Sanda, Japan Takeshi Okadome
February 2025

Contents

Part I Basis

1   Introduction 3
  1.1   Fundamentals of Neural Networks 3
      1.1.1   Forward Computation: Neural Network
              as a Function 4
      1.1.2   Neural Network Learning 6
  1.2   Matrix Representation of Neural Networks 17
  1.3   The Development of Deep Learning and Its Factors 20
  1.4   Appendix 21
      1.4.1   Proof of the Backpropagation Formula 21

2   Fundamental Technologies Supporting Deep Learning 23
  2.1   Enhancement of Stochastic Gradient Descent 23
      2.1.1   Momentum Stochastic Gradient Descent
              (Momentum Method) 24
      2.1.2   Adaptive Adjustment of Learning Rate 26
      2.1.3   Momentum Method + Adaptive Learning Rate 28
  2.2   Dealing with the Gradient Vanishing/Diverging Problem 28
      2.2.1   ReLU Function 29
  2.3   Residual Connection 30
  2.4   Normalization of Activations 32
      2.4.1   Necessity of Normalization 32
      2.4.2   Batch Normalization 32
      2.4.3   Layer Normalization 35
      2.4.4   Instance Normalization 36
      2.4.5   Group Normalization 37
  2.5   Appendix 37
      2.5.1   Convergence Rate of Gradient Descent 37
      2.5.2   Completeness of ReLU Functions 39
      2.5.3   Subdifferential 44

3 RNN: Recurrent Neural Network 45
3.1 Architecture and Computation of RNN 45
3.2 Learning in RNNs 48

4 Autoencoder 51
4.1 Overview of Autoencoders 51
4.2 Architecture of Autoencoders 51
4.3 Training Autoencoders 52
4.4 Properties of Autoencoders 54

5 Word Embedding 55
5.1 Vector Representations of Words 55
5.2 Word2Vec 57
5.3 Learning in Word2Vec 58
    5.3.1 CBOW 58
    5.3.2 Skip-Gram 60
    5.3.3 Negative Sampling 62
5.4 Obtaining Embeddings 63

6 Transformer 65
6.1 Attention 65
6.2 Transformer 71
    6.2.1 Multi-head Attention 71
    6.2.2 Transformer 72

7 Reinforcement Learning 81
7.1 Problem Setting 81
7.2 Q-Learning and DQN 86
7.3 Policy Gradient Methods and Their Extensions 91
7.4 Appendix 96
    7.4.1 Proof of Policy Gradient Theorem 96

Part II Generative Language Model

8 Language Generation 101
8.1 Language Model 101
8.2 RNN Language Model 106
8.3 Sequence-to-Sequence Models 108

9 Large-Scale Language Models 117
9.1 BERT 117
9.2 GPT 120
9.3 Towards Generative Language Models 121
9.4 Generative Language Models 124
    9.4.1 Basics of RLHF 124
    9.4.2 Direct Preference Optimization 131
    9.4.3 Challenges of Generative Language Models 133

	9.5	Appendix	134
		9.5.1 Example of Labeler Ranking in Data Creation for InstructGPT	134
		9.5.2 Derivation of the Policy $\pi(y \mid x)$ that Maximizes the Objective Function of RLHF	135

Part III Generative Image Model

10 Variational Autoencoder 139
    10.1 Introduction 139
    10.2 Structure of Variational Autoencoders 139
    10.3 Variational Lower Bound 141
    10.4 Learning of Variational Autoencoders 143
        10.4.1 Training of Variational Autoencoders 143
        10.4.2 Why Maximizing Variational Lower Bound? 146
    10.5 Features of VAE 147
        10.5.1 VAE as a Generative Model 147
        10.5.2 Operations in Latent Space 147
    10.6 Appendix 149
        10.6.1 Computation of $\mathbb{KL}(q_\phi(\mathbf{z} \mid \mathbf{x}) \parallel p(\mathbf{z}))$ 149
        10.6.2 Proof of Decomposition Formula of the Likelihood 151

11 Diffusion Model 153
    11.1 Overview of Diffusion Model 153
    11.2 Markov Process (Markov Chain) 153
        11.2.1 Origin of the Diffusion Model 154
    11.3 Formulation of Diffusion Model 155
    11.4 Learning of Diffusion Models 157
        11.4.1 Variational Upper Bound 158
        11.4.2 Temporal Decomposition of Variational Upper Bound 160
    11.5 Implementation of Diffusion Models 166
        11.5.1 Stable Diffusion 167
    11.6 Appendix 169
        11.6.1 Equivalence of Definitions for Markov Processes 169
        11.6.2 Markov Property of the Inverse Process 171
        11.6.3 Derivation of Diffusion Equation from a Markov Chain 171
        11.6.4 Time-Wise Decomposition of Variational Upper Bound 173
        11.6.5 Distribution of $\mathbf{x}_{t-1}$ Conditioned on $\mathbf{x}_0$ and $\mathbf{x}_t$ 174
        11.6.6 KL Divergence Between Gaussian Distributions 176

12 GAN: Generative Adversarial Network 177
12.1 Basics of GAN 177
12.2 Development of GANs 183
12.2.1 PGGAN and Conditional GAN 183
12.2.2 Wasserstein GAN 185

Appendix A: Basic Terminology of Optimization Problems 195

Appendix B: Kullback-Leibler Divergence 199

Appendix C: Sampling from Gaussian Distributions 205

Appendix D: Enlargement of Image Size 209

Appendix E: Strong Duality in Linear Programming 217

References 225

Index 229

Notation

- ≡ denotes that the left-hand side is defined by the right-hand side. For example, $n! \equiv n \cdot (n-1)!$, $n > 1$, means that $n!$ is defined by $n \cdot (n-1)!$ for $n > 1$.
- Italic lowercase letters (e.g., x) represent scalars.
- Roman bold lowercase letters (e.g., $\mathbf{x}$) represent column vectors. The superscript T attached to a vector (or matrix) denotes transpose, for example, $\mathbf{x}^\mathrm{T}$ represents a row vector.
- Under this notation, the usual inner product (dot product) of two vectors $\mathbf{x}$ and $\mathbf{y}$ is denoted by $\mathbf{x}^\mathrm{T}\mathbf{y}$. Of course, $\mathbf{x}^\mathrm{T}\mathbf{y} = \mathbf{y}^\mathrm{T}\mathbf{x}$ holds.
- For a vector $\mathbf{x}$, $\|\mathbf{x}\|$ denotes its norm (magnitude), defined as $\|\mathbf{x}\| \equiv \sqrt{\mathbf{x}^\mathrm{T}\mathbf{x}}$.
- Roman bold uppercase letters (e.g., $\mathbf{M}$) represent matrices. Particularly, $\mathbf{I}$ denotes the identity matrix. Also, $\mathbf{M}^\mathrm{T}$ represents the transpose of $\mathbf{M}$.
- (a, b) represents an open interval, while $[a, b]$ represents a closed interval. For example, the coordinates of a point on a 2-dimensional plane with x coordinate a and y coordinate b can also be denoted as (a, b).
- Component representation of a row vector is denoted without commas as $(a_1 \cdots a_D)$.
- For N D-dimensional vectors of observations $\mathbf{x}_1, \ldots, \mathbf{x}_N$, $\mathbf{X}$ represents the set $\{\mathbf{x}_1, \ldots, \mathbf{x}_N\}$. $\mathbf{X}$ may also represent a matrix where the i-th column is $\mathbf{x}_i$ or its transpose.
- General sets other than sets of observations are represented by italic uppercase letters (e.g., S). Specifically, the set of all real numbers is denoted by R, and the set of all D-dimensional real vectors is denoted by R^D. The set of data, however, is denoted by $\mathcal{D}$.
- Scalar-valued functions are represented in italic font (e.g., $f(\mathbf{x})$). Also, vector-valued functions are represented in bold font (e.g., $\boldsymbol{\phi}(\mathbf{x})$ and $\mathbf{f}(\mathbf{x})$). The logistic sigmoid function is denoted as $\sigma(x)$, and the softmax function is denoted as $\boldsymbol{\sigma}(\mathbf{x})$.
- $\mathcal{N}(\mathbf{x}|\boldsymbol{\mu}, \boldsymbol{\Sigma})$ denotes a Gaussian distribution with mean $\boldsymbol{\mu}$ and covariance matrix $\boldsymbol{\Sigma}$.
- $\mathbb{KL}(p(\mathbf{x})\|q(\mathbf{x}))$ represents the Kullback-Leibler divergence (KL divergence) between probability distributions $p(\mathbf{x})$ and $q(\mathbf{x})$.

- The minimum value of a function on the set S is denoted as $\min_{\mathbf{x} \in S} f(\mathbf{x})$. The minimum of a function on S is denoted as $\arg\min_{\mathbf{x} \in S} f(\mathbf{x})$. Also, the maximum value of a function on S is denoted as $\max_{\mathbf{x} \in S} f(\mathbf{x})$. The maximum of a function on S is denoted as $\arg\max_{\mathbf{x} \in S} f(\mathbf{x})$ (for basic terminologies of the optimization problem, see Appendix A at the end of the book).

Part I
Basis

Chapter 1
Introduction

We begin by summarizing the basics of neural networks.

1.1 Fundamentals of Neural Networks

A *neural network* is a mathematical model that simplifies the mechanism and function of the brain, which consists of numerous neurons and axons connecting these neurons. Through learning, it becomes capable of performing various computations.

Figure 1.1 depicts the structure of a neural network called a 3-layer perceptron, consisting of *units* and *links* connecting these units.

Each link in the network has a different weight. The cluster of units arranged on the far left is called the *input layer*, the cluster in the middle is called the *hidden layer* (also known as the *middle layer* or *intermediate layer*), and the group of units arranged on the far right is referred to as the *output layer*. A neural network computes a specific function $\mathbf{F}$. That is, it receives a vector $\mathbf{x}$ as input at the input layer and outputs a vector $\mathbf{y} = \mathbf{F}(\mathbf{x})$ at the output layer. The hidden layer performs simple computations based on the information transmitted through the links from the input layer and passes the results to the output layer via the links.

A neural network with one or more hidden layers is called a *multi-layer perceptron*. Particularly, a multi-layer perceptron with a deep structure (having a large number of layers) is referred to as a *deep neural network*. *Deep learning* refers to the framework of machine learning that utilizes deep neural networks (DNNs).

In this section, we review the fundamental aspects of computation and learning performed by neural networks, focusing on a 3-layer perceptron. The computation and learning in neural networks with two or more hidden layers are essentially the same as those in a 3-layer perceptron. In a 3-layer perceptron, there are links between all units in the input layer and the hidden layer, and between all units in the hidden

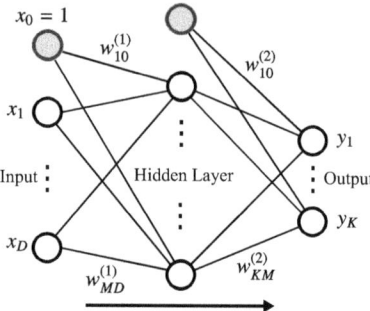

Fig. 1.1 Diagram of a neural network structure called a 3-layer perceptron. It consists of layers: input layer, hidden layer, and output layer, each represented by clusters of units depicted by circles, connected by links. Links are lines representing connections between units in each layer, with associated real numbers called weights. Gray units are dummy units with no input and a fixed output of 1

layer and the output layer, with the weights of these links being independent. In a layer, each unit is connected to all the units in the preceding layer, and if the weights of these links are independent, the layer is called *fully connected*.

Note that neural networks with different weights or different structures (such as the number of hidden layers and the total number of units) essentially compute different functions. Conversely, by changing the weights and structure, various functions can be represented within the framework of neural networks.

1.1.1 Forward Computation: Neural Network as a Function

We illustrate the computations performed at each layer concretely.

Input layer. The input layer consists of units equal to the dimensionality D of the input vector **x**. The i-th unit receives the i-th component x_i of **x**. Each unit i transmits the product of the input x_i and the weight of the link, through the links extending to all units in the hidden layer. That is, unit j in the hidden layer receives the product of the weight $w_{ji}^{(1)}$ of the link from unit i in the input layer and x_i.

Hidden layer (middle layer). Each unit j in the hidden layer takes the sum $\sum_{i=1}^{D} w_{ji}^{(1)} x_i$ received from each unit in the input layer, where $w_{ji}^{(1)}$ denotes the weight of the link, and adds a term called the *bias parameter* $w_{j0}^{(1)}$, resulting in an *activation* u_j. This activation is defined as

$$u_j = \sum_{i=1}^{D} w_{ji}^{(1)} x_i + w_{j0}^{(1)}, \quad j = 1, \ldots, M,$$

1.1 Fundamentals of Neural Networks

where M represents the number of units in the hidden layer excluding those related to the bias parameter. Then, the *activation function* f_1 is applied to u_j to obtain

$$z_j = f_1(u_j), \quad j = 1, \ldots, M.$$

Furthermore, the product of z_j and the weight $w_{kj}^{(2)}$ of the outgoing link is transmitted to all units in the output layer.

Output layer. The units in the output layer correspond to the dimensionality K of the output vector $\mathbf{y}$. Each unit k in the output layer receives the product $z_j w_{kj}^{(2)}$ from each unit in the hidden layer. These products are summed up, adding the bias parameter $w_{k0}^{(2)}$, to compute the activation u_k

$$u_k = \sum_{j=1}^{M} w_{kj}^{(2)} z_j + w_{k0}^{(2)}, \quad k = 1, \ldots, K.$$

Then, the activation function f_2 is applied to u_k to obtain the output y_k

$$y_k = f_2(u_k), \quad k = 1, \ldots, K.$$

In the case of regression, K units in the output layer output each component of the output vector. For binary classification (where $K = 1$), the output layer consists of a single unit that typically outputs the probability of belonging to one class. When $K > 1$, indicating multiple units in the output layer, each unit outputs the result (probability) of a binary classification independently. For example, in an image classification task with two classes, unit 1 might output the probability of being a car or not, while unit 2 might output the probability of being an airplane or not. For multi-class classification (K classes), each unit typically outputs the probability of belonging to one of the K classes. For instance, in an image classification task with K classes, unit 1 might output the probability of being a car, unit 2 might output the probability of being an airplane, and so forth, up to unit K which would output the probability of being a bicycle.

When expressing the input-output functions of the 3-layer perceptron mentioned above, it can be written as follows:

$$y_k(\mathbf{x}) = f_2 \left(\sum_{j=1}^{M} w_{kj}^{(2)} f_1 \left(\sum_{i=1}^{D} w_{ji}^{(1)} x_i + w_{j0}^{(1)} \right) + w_{k0}^{(2)} \right), \quad k = 1, \ldots, K. \quad (1.1.1)$$

In relatively shallow multi-layer perceptrons, commonly used activation functions in the hidden layers include the differentiable logistic sigmoid function

$$\sigma(x) \equiv \frac{1}{1 + \exp(-x)}$$

and the hyperbolic tangent function

$$\tanh(x) \equiv \frac{e^x - e^{-x}}{e^x + e^{-x}}.$$

In deep learning with a large number of hidden layers, we usually use the rectified linear unit (ReLU) function:

$$\text{ReLU}(x) \equiv \begin{cases} 0, & x < 0, \\ x, & x \geq 0. \end{cases}$$

Although ReLU is continuous, it is not differentiable at the origin. ReLU is extensively employed to mitigate the issue of vanishing gradients during weight learning, as discussed in detail in Sect. 2.2 of Chap. 2.

Furthermore, for the activation function used in the output layer, in regression tasks, we commonly use the identity function. In classification tasks, to represent class probabilities:

- for binary classification, we typically use the logistic sigmoid function, and
- for multi-class classification, we commonly use the *softmax function* that is a vector-valued function defined by

$$\sigma(\mathbf{x}) \equiv \text{softmax}(\mathbf{x}) \equiv \left(\frac{\exp(x_1)}{\sum_{j=1}^{K} \exp(x_j)} \quad \frac{\exp(x_2)}{\sum_{j=1}^{K} \exp(x_j)} \quad \cdots \quad \frac{\exp(x_K)}{\sum_{j=1}^{K} \exp(x_j)} \right)^{\text{T}},$$

where $\mathbf{x} = (x_1 \cdots x_K)^{\text{T}}$ is a K-dimensional vector variable. That is, the softmax function is used to produce a probability distribution over the K classes.

1.1.2 Neural Network Learning

We denote the vector that collects all the weights in the neural network as $\mathbf{w}$. In a 3-layer neural network, $\mathbf{w}$ is a vector consisting of all the components $w_{ji}^{(1)}$ and $w_{kj}^{(2)}$ in Eq. (1.1.1). Similar to linear regression models and logistic sigmoid regression models, learning in a neural network involves determining the weights $\mathbf{w}$ given the provided data. The learning process of a neural network aims to minimize the error with respect to the given data. We outline commonly used errors in neural network learning. Below, we explicitly express the function computed by the neural network as depending on the weights and denote it as $\mathbf{y}(\mathbf{x}, \mathbf{w})$. This is a vector, where the k-th component corresponds to the output of the k-th unit in the neural network's output layer. We also represent the data as

$$\mathcal{D} = \{(\mathbf{x}_1, \mathbf{t}_1), \ldots, (\mathbf{x}_N, \mathbf{t}_N)\},$$

1.1 Fundamentals of Neural Networks

where the labels t_n provided correspond to the target variable values for the input x_n. In regression tasks, t_n is a K-dimensional real vector. For binary classification with K classes, t_n is a K-dimensional vector with elements of 0 or 1. In K-class classification, $\mathbf{t}_n = (t_{n1} \cdots t_{nK})^T$ is a K-dimensional *one-hot representation (vector)*, where only one component, from t_{n1} to t_{nK}, takes the value 1, and the rest are 0: $t_{ni} \in \{0, 1\}$,

$$\sum_{i=1}^{K} t_{ni} = 1.$$

1.1.2.1 Error Function (Loss Function)

Firstly, in regression, the *error function* (the *loss function*, more precisely, the *empirical loss function*)[1] commonly used is the simplest squared error, defined as

$$E(\mathbf{w}) = \frac{1}{2} \sum_{n=1}^{N} \|\mathbf{y}(\mathbf{x}_n, \mathbf{w}) - \mathbf{t}_n\|^2.$$

In simple binary classification tasks, similar to classification using generalized linear models, neural networks also deal with target variables t that take on either 0 or 1. When $t = 1$, it represents class C_1, and when $t = 0$, it represents class C_2. As mentioned earlier, in classification tasks, we commonly use the logistic sigmoid function as the activation function for the output units. Particularly, for simple binary classification, a neural network has only one output unit. The output $y(\mathbf{x}, \mathbf{w})$ is interpreted as representing the probability $p(C_1 \mid \mathbf{x})$, and $p(C_2 \mid \mathbf{x})$ is given by $1 - y(\mathbf{x}, \mathbf{w})$. The conditional probability of the target variable t given the input $\mathbf{x}$, therefore, can be represented by a Bernoulli distribution

$$p(t \mid \mathbf{x}, \mathbf{w}) = y(\mathbf{x}, \mathbf{w})^t \{1 - y(\mathbf{x}, \mathbf{w})\}^{1-t}.$$

For independent and identically distributed data $\mathcal{D} = \{(\mathbf{x}_1, t_1), \ldots, (\mathbf{x}_N, t_N)\}$, the likelihood function is

$$\prod_{n=1}^{N} y(\mathbf{x}_n, \mathbf{w})^{t_n} \{1 - y(\mathbf{x}_n, \mathbf{w})\}^{1-t_n}.$$

By taking the negative logarithm of this, we have the following cross-entropy error function as the loss function:

$$E(\mathbf{w}) = -\sum_{n=1}^{N} \{t_n \ln y_n + (1 - t_n) \ln(1 - y_n)\},$$

---

[1] In the following chapters, we often refer to the term "error function" simply as "loss."

where $y_n = y(\mathbf{x}_n, \mathbf{w})$.

In the case of K different binary classifications, a neural network consists of an output layer with K units, each with a logistic sigmoid activation function. The k-th unit in the output layer outputs $y_k(\mathbf{x}, \mathbf{w})$, which can be interpreted as the probability that the target variable (class label) t_k takes the value 1 given the input $\mathbf{x}$. Assuming that the K target variables t_k, $k = 1, \ldots, K$, are independent, the conditional distribution of the target variable $\mathbf{t} = (t_1 \cdots t_K)^{\mathrm{T}}$ given the input $\mathbf{x}$ is

$$p(\mathbf{t} \mid \mathbf{x}, \mathbf{w}) = \prod_{k=1}^{K} y_k(\mathbf{x}, \mathbf{w})^{t_k} \{1 - y_k(\mathbf{x}, \mathbf{w})\}^{1-t_k}.$$

Hence, assuming independent and identically distributed data $\mathcal{D} = \{(\mathbf{x}_1, \mathbf{t}_1), \ldots, (\mathbf{x}_N, \mathbf{t}_N)\}$, where $\mathbf{t}_n = (t_{n1} \cdots t_{nk})^{\mathrm{T}}$, the likelihood function is

$$\prod_{n=1}^{N} \prod_{k=1}^{K} y_k(\mathbf{x}_n, \mathbf{w})^{t_{nk}} \{1 - y_k(\mathbf{x}_n, \mathbf{w})\}^{1-t_{nk}}.$$

Taking the negative logarithm of this yields the cross-entropy error function:

$$E(\mathbf{w}) = -\sum_{n=1}^{N} \sum_{k=1}^{K} \{t_{nk} \ln y_{nk} + (1 - t_{nk}) \ln(1 - y_{nk})\},$$

where $y_{nk} = y_k(\mathbf{x}_n, \mathbf{w})$.

Finally, we consider multi-class classification for K different classes. In this scenario, a neural network has an output layer consisting of K units. For a given input $\mathbf{x}$, the target variable (class label) $\mathbf{t}$ is represented as a one-hot vector, where only one component, from t_1 to t_K, takes the value 1, and the rest are 0. The activation function for the output layer units is typically the softmax function. The output of the k-th unit in the output layer, denoted as $y_k(\mathbf{x}, \mathbf{w})$, can be interpreted as $p(t_k = 1 \mid \mathbf{x})$ (although to compute the softmax function, the activations of all units in the output layer are needed, not just the k-th unit). In this case, the loss function is the cross-entropy error function:

$$E(\mathbf{w}) = -\sum_{n=1}^{N} \sum_{k=1}^{K} t_{nk} \ln y_k(\mathbf{x}_n, \mathbf{w}).$$

1.1.2.2 Learning Parameters

For given data $\mathcal{D}$, the weight $\mathbf{w}^*$ that minimizes the error function $E(\mathbf{w})$ mentioned in the previous section is the desired weight. There are many methods known to find the extremum of a function without using gradients. When gradient information is available, it is generally more efficient to utilize it to find the extremum. In the context of neural network learning, we commonly use the gradient of the error function

1.1 Fundamentals of Neural Networks

$\nabla E(\mathbf{w})$. In principle, at the $\mathbf{w}^*$ that minimizes the error function $E(\mathbf{w})$, the derivative of $E(\mathbf{w})$ with respect to $\mathbf{w}$, that is, the gradient $\nabla E(\mathbf{w})\big|_{\mathbf{w}=\mathbf{w}^*}$ [2] becomes $\mathbf{0}$. The error function, however, takes a complex form with respect to the weight, which is a high-dimensional vector, and it is not straightforward to solve the equation $\nabla E(\mathbf{w}) = \mathbf{0}$ to obtain $\mathbf{w}^*$ in a simple form.

Thus, we usually use gradient descent methods or stochastic gradient descent methods. Particularly a stochastic gradient descent method called *mini-batch learning* is advantageous for acceleration in parallel computing environments. In mini-batch learning, we select a small number of data points from the training data, for example randomly, to form a mini-batch, and repeatedly adjust the weights using gradient descent on each mini-batch. The size of the mini-batches is typically varied, for example randomly, within the range of 10 to 100. For each mini-batch, in the case of regression, we minimize the mean squared error for the data in the mini-batch:

$$E_{mb}(\mathbf{w}) = \frac{1}{B} \sum_{i=1}^{B} \|\mathbf{y}(\mathbf{x}_i, \mathbf{w}) - \mathbf{t}_i\|^2,$$

where B is the size of the mini-batch.[3] That is, starting from an initial weight $\mathbf{w}_0$ determined, for example, by randomization, we update the weight $\mathbf{w}^{(\tau)}$ to $\mathbf{w}^{(\tau+1)}$ as follows:

$$\mathbf{w}^{(\tau+1)} = \mathbf{w}^{(\tau)} - \eta \nabla E_{mb}(\mathbf{w})\big|_{\mathbf{w}=\mathbf{w}^{(\tau)}},$$

where η is a small constant (learning rate). We perform this weight update for each mini-batch and continue until the error no longer changes. We define one complete coverage of the entire dataset as one *epoch*, and we refer to the number of epochs repeated as the *epoch count*. Furthermore, we can easily parallelize the computation of the gradient $\nabla E_{mb}(\mathbf{w})$ as we can compute it independently for each data point. In computing environments with parallelization capabilities such as GPUs, using appropriately sized mini-batches becomes advantageous.

To complicate matters, since $E(\mathbf{w})$ is a non-linear function of $\mathbf{w}^*$, there exist multiple $\mathbf{w}$ values, aside from the minimizing $\mathbf{w}^*$, that satisfy $\nabla E(\mathbf{w}) = \mathbf{0}$ (see Fig. 1.2). Hence, even if $\hat{\mathbf{w}}$ is obtained through stochastic gradient descent, it may not necessarily be the optimum solution. In practical terms, $\hat{\mathbf{w}}$ obtained need not be the optimal solution; it suffices for $\hat{\mathbf{w}}$ to sufficiently reduce the error. To find such $\hat{\mathbf{w}}$, we perform the stochastic gradient descent multiple times, starting from different initial values $\mathbf{w}_0$, and we adopt the weight that yields the minimum error among these iterations.

Now, in methods that utilize gradients to find the optimal solution, we need to compute the gradient $\nabla E(\mathbf{w})$ repeatedly. Fast computation of $\nabla E(\mathbf{w})$, therefore, is crucial. Historically, the rapid computation of gradients, called backpropagation, was discovered, which made neural network learning practical, and the same applies to

---

[2] $\nabla E(\mathbf{w})\big|_{\mathbf{w}=\mathbf{w}^*}$ represents the value (vector) of the gradient $\nabla E(\mathbf{w})$ at $\mathbf{w}=\mathbf{w}^*$.
[3] Note that since the size of each mini-batch varies, we divide the squared error by the batch size.

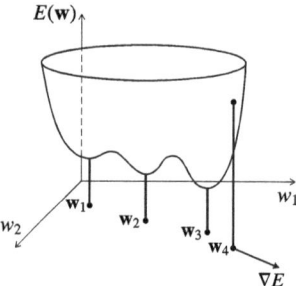

Fig. 1.2 Representation of the error function $E(\mathbf{w})$ as a surface in weight space. Generally, there are multiple extremal points, and the gradient $\nabla E(\mathbf{w})$ is a vector orthogonal to the contour surfaces of the error function in weight space. At extremal points, the gradient $\nabla E(\mathbf{w})$ becomes $\mathbf{0}$

modern deep learning. Before introducing backpropagation in the next section, let us mention that the computational complexity can become significant with simple gradient computations.

The gradient $\nabla E(\mathbf{w})$ is a vector formed by taking partial derivatives of $E(\mathbf{w})$ with respect to each component w_{ji} of the weight vector $\mathbf{w}$. That is,

$$\nabla E(\mathbf{w}) = \left(\frac{\partial E(\mathbf{w})}{\partial w_{11}} \frac{\partial E(\mathbf{w})}{\partial w_{21}} \cdots \frac{\partial E(\mathbf{w})}{\partial w_{ji}} \cdots \frac{\partial E(\mathbf{w})}{\partial w_{MK}} \right)^{\mathrm{T}}.$$

Consider a 3-layer perceptron for 10-class classification of an image consisting of 100 pixels vertically and 100 pixels horizontally. The input layer of the perceptron consists of 10,000 units (100 × 100 = 10,000 pixels), and the output layer consists of 10 units corresponding to the number of classes. For simplicity, assuming the hidden layer also consists of 10,000 units like the input layer, the total number of weights is 1,000,000,000 (1 billion), i.e., 10,000 × 10,000 × 10. Thus, the gradient $\nabla E(\mathbf{w})$ is also a vector of 1 billion dimensions. For each iteration of the optimization calculation using stochastic gradient descent as described in the previous section, we need to perform such a large number of partial derivative computations.

The partial derivative $\frac{\partial E(\mathbf{w})}{\partial w_{ji}}$ represents the ratio (in the limit) of the change in $E(\mathbf{w})$ with a slight variation in w_{ji} while keeping the values of other weights fixed. We elaborate on this further. For instance, in the case of error $E_{mb}(\mathbf{w})$ in mini-batch learning, it is the sum of errors between the output and the correct labels for each of the B data points within the mini-batch. Thus, a straightforward method to compute $\frac{\partial E_{mb}(\mathbf{w})}{\partial w_{ji}}$ following the definition of partial derivatives would involve (1) firstly, computing the total error $E_{mb}(\mathbf{w})$ when the mini-batch of B data points is input to the neural network, (2) then, for each weight w_{ji}, making a slight alteration one at a time and calculating the total error $E_{mb}(\mathbf{w} + \Delta w_{ji})$ when the same mini-batch of data points is input, and (3) finally, finding the difference $E_{mb}(\mathbf{w} + \Delta w_{ji}) - E_{mb}(\mathbf{w})$.

1.1 Fundamentals of Neural Networks

To estimate the computational complexity of this naive gradient computation method, we count the number of multiplications involved in the activation calculations per unit. Since there are only connections between units in adjacent layers, the number of weights is usually much larger than the number of units. Thus, counting multiplications related to weights is sufficient. We denote the total number of weights as W. For each learning data point,

- W multiplications are required for computing the error $E_n(\mathbf{w})$ and
- for each weight w_{ji}, W multiplications are necessary for computing the error $E_n(\mathbf{w} + \Delta w_{ji})$.

Since we need similar calculations for all W weights, the total number of multiplications per learning data point is roughly estimated as $W + W^2$. In the case of a 3-layer perceptron for 10-class classification of an image, where W is 1 billion, the number of multiplications becomes on the order of 10^{18}, which is the square of 1 billion.

1.1.2.3 Backpropagation of Errors

In this section, we consider stochastic gradient descent, where we compute the error function value for each piece of training data $\mathbf{w}$, and update $\mathbf{w}$ accordingly. Thus, we handle the error $E(\mathbf{w})$ (or simply E) for a single pair of training data $\mathbf{x}_n$ and $\mathbf{t}_n$, dropping the subscript n for simplicity. Although we here discuss the error E_n for each individual training data, in mini-batch learning, for instance, the gradient for each mini-batch is the average of gradients for the data within the mini-batch:

$$\frac{\partial E_{mb}}{\partial w_{ji}} = \frac{1}{B} \sum_{n=1}^{B} \frac{\partial E_n}{\partial w_{ji}},$$

where B is the number of data points in the mini-batch.

Backpropagation of errors is used to compute the gradient of the error function. In this process, a quantity called "error" δ_j is utilized for each unit j. Specifically, for units j and i connected by a weight w_{ji}, the "error" δ_j multiplied by the output z_i of unit i, i.e., $\delta_j z_i$, becomes the component of the gradient $\frac{\partial E(\mathbf{w})}{\partial w_{ji}}$. The error $\delta_k = y_k - t_k$ of the output y_k with respect to the input $\mathbf{x}$ is treated as the "error" of unit k in the output layer. This error is propagated backward from the output layer to the input layer and the error of a unit in the previous layer is computed using the errors of units in the following layer. We formalize the calculation of gradients using error backpropagation below.

The *error* for unit j, denoted as δ_j, is defined by

$$\delta_j \equiv \frac{\partial E}{\partial u_j}, \tag{1.1.2}$$

where u_j represents the activation of unit j. We will address the formal aspects of this definition later. Based on this definition, we demonstrate that the error δ_k for units in the output layer is $y_k - t_k$. Recall first that the activation of output unit k, when introducing a fixed output of 1 for the hidden layer unit 0 ($z_0 = 1$) and incorporating the bias into the sum, is given by

$$u_k = \sum_{j=0}^{M} w_{kj}^{(2)} z_j, \quad k = 1, \ldots, K$$

and the output is

$$y_k = f_2(u_k), \quad k = 1, \ldots, K.$$

When dealing with regression, assuming the identity function as the activation function f_2 for the output units, we have

$$y_k = u_k, \quad k = 1, \ldots, K.$$

Furthermore, assuming the squared error function as the loss function, we have

$$E(\mathbf{w}) = \frac{1}{2} \sum_{k=1}^{K} (y_k - t_k)^2 = \frac{1}{2} \sum_{k=1}^{K} (u_k - t_k)^2.$$

We obtain, therefore,

$$\frac{\partial E}{\partial u_k} = u_k - t_k = y_k - t_k.$$

Even in classification, if we use the logistic sigmoid function as the activation function for the output units and the cross-entropy error function:

$$E(\mathbf{w}) = -\sum_{k=1}^{K} \{t_k \ln y_k + (1 - t_k) \ln(1 - y_k)\}, \quad y_k = \sigma(u_k),$$

as the loss function, then, using $\sigma'(u_k) = \sigma(u_k)(1 - \sigma(u_k)) = y_k(1 - y_k)$, we have

$$\frac{\partial E}{\partial u_k} = \frac{\partial E}{\partial y_k} \frac{\partial y_k}{\partial u_k} = -\left(\frac{t_k}{y_k} - \frac{1 - t_k}{1 - y_k}\right) y_k(1 - y_k)$$
$$= -t_k(1 - y_k) + (1 - t_k) y_k = y_k - t_k.$$

Similarly, in the case of multi-class classification, if we assume the softmax function as the activation function for the output units and cross-entropy error function as the loss function, we can also show that $\delta_k = y_k - t_k$ for output unit k. Now we

1.1 Fundamentals of Neural Networks

understand that δ holds the meaning of error for output layer units.[4] Thus, we refer to δ as the error for units in other layers as well.

Now, we show that, using the error δ_j for unit j, we can easily compute the components of the gradient. The component of the gradient $\dfrac{\partial E}{\partial w_{ji}}$ represents the rate of change of E when only the weight w_{ji}, linking unit i to unit j, is slightly varied while keeping other weights fixed. In the computation of the error function E, the appearance of w_{ji} is solely through the activation u_j of unit j, given by

$$u_j = w_{j1}z_1 + w_{j2}z_2 + \cdots + w_{ji}z_i + \cdots + w_{jI}z_I. \tag{1.1.3}$$

Thus, the change in E with respect to the change in w_{ji} is determined by the change in activation u_j. In other words, with other weights fixed, u_j can be seen as a function of w_{ji}, denoted as $u_j = u_j(w_{ji})$, and the error function can be regarded as a composite function $E(u_j(w_{ji}))$. Hence, by the chain rule for composite functions,

$$\frac{\partial E}{\partial w_{ji}} = \frac{\partial E}{\partial u_j} \frac{\partial u_j}{\partial w_{ji}} \tag{1.1.4}$$

holds. From Eq. (1.1.3), we have

$$\frac{\partial u_j}{\partial w_{ji}} = z_i.$$

Using the definition of the error for unit j in Eqs. (1.1.2) and (1.1.4), we conclude

$$\frac{\partial E}{\partial w_{ji}} = \delta_j z_i. \tag{1.1.5}$$

Thus, the component of the gradient is obtained simply by multiplying the error δ of the unit and the output z of the input-side unit connected to that unit.

Each unit's output z is obtained during the forward calculation of a neural network by inputting the input $\mathbf{x}$. Furthermore, if we denote the output of unit k in the output layer as y_k, the error of each unit δ is efficiently calculated step by step starting from the error δ_k of the output layer's unit k, in the backward calculation towards the input layer. That is, we have

$$\delta_j = f'(u_j) \sum_{l=1}^{L} w_{k_l j} \delta_{k_l}, \tag{1.1.6}$$

where the sum is taken over all units connected to unit j on the output side (see Fig. 1.3).

---

[4] Note, however, that depending on the choice of an error function (and an activation function), $\delta_k = y_k - t_k$ may not hold true for output layer units. We will address this later in this section.

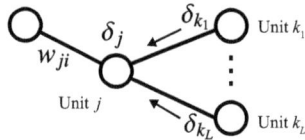

Fig. 1.3 Error backpropagation. The error δ_j of unit j becomes a weighted sum of errors of units connected to the output side

This formula is called the *error backpropagation formula* or the *backpropagation formula*. The proof of this formula is provided in the appendix at the end of this chapter. As shown in Fig. 1.3, the value of unit error δ is obtained by propagating δ backward from units on the output side. By starting from the error δ_k of the output layer's unit k and applying the backpropagation formula (1.1.6) towards the input side, we can calculate the error δ of all units.

We summarize the calculation of gradients. When representing the activation function by f, we can outline the process as follows.

1. Input the training data $\mathbf{x}_n$ into the neural network and calculate the activations $u_j = \sum_i w_{ji} z_i$ and outputs $z_j = f(u_j)$ for all units in the forward direction.
2. Calculate the error δ_k of the output layer unit k using $\dfrac{\partial E}{\partial u_k}$. (As mentioned in the text, for example, when using a squared error function as the error function and an identity function as the activation function for output layer units, $\delta_k = y_k - t_k$.)
3. Use the error backpropagation formula (1.1.6) to propagate the errors of units backward and calculate the errors δ_j of all units. Note that the error of the input layer is irrelevant to gradient calculation and thus unnecessary.
4. Compute the gradient $\dfrac{\partial E}{\partial w_{ji}} = \delta_j z_i$.

1.1.2.4 Note on Errors

As mentioned earlier in a footnote, it is not always the case that $\delta_k = y_k - t_k$ holds for output layer unit k. When the target variable distribution is taken from a distribution called the exponential family and the error function is determined by the log-likelihood determined by that distribution, and when the activation function of the output layer is taken to be a function called the canonical link function for that distribution, then $\delta_k = y_k - t_k$ is known to hold.

For example, in cases where a squared error function and an identity function are used, or when a cross-entropy error function and a logistic sigmoid function are used, $\delta_k = y_k - t_k$ holds. However, in cases where this is not true, for instance, when the error function $E(\mathbf{w})$ is defined as the entropy function (not the cross-entropy function) of the output y_k:

1.1 Fundamentals of Neural Networks

$$-\sum_k \{y_k \ln y_k + (1 - y_k) \ln(1 - y_k)\}$$

and the activation function is the logistic sigmoid function $\sigma(u_k)$, then the error δ_k of the output unit k is given by

$$\delta_k = \frac{\partial E}{\partial u_k} = \sigma(u_k)(1 - \sigma(u_k)) \ln\left(\frac{1 - y_k}{y_k}\right).$$

The errors given by this equation for all units in the output layer serve as the starting point for backpropagation.

1.1.2.5 Computing Gradients of Functions

More generally, using the backpropagation technique, we can calculate the gradients of a function $g(\mathbf{w}) = g(\mathbf{y}(\mathbf{w}, \mathbf{x}))$ with respect to its weights $\mathbf{w}$, where $\mathbf{x}$ is an input to the neural network and $\mathbf{y}$ its output for $\mathbf{x}$. For this purpose, for instance, assume that the activation function of the output layer is chosen to be the identity function. Then, the derivatives of $g(\mathbf{y})$ with respect to the outputs $\mathbf{y}$ of the output layer can be propagated backward as the "errors."

From the chain rule of composite functions, we have

$$\frac{\partial g(\mathbf{y})}{\partial u_i} = \frac{\partial g(\mathbf{y})}{\partial y_i} \frac{\partial y_i}{\partial u_i},$$

where y_i is the output of output layer unit i and u_i is its activation. Thus, in general, if we can compute $\frac{\partial g(\mathbf{y})}{\partial y_i}$ and $\frac{\partial y_i}{\partial u_i}$, we can calculate $\frac{\partial g(\mathbf{y})}{\partial u_i}$. Usually, we can simply obtain $\frac{\partial y_i}{\partial u_i}$. This is because

$$\frac{\partial y_i}{\partial u_i} = \frac{\partial f(u_i)}{\partial u_i}$$

holds because of $y_i = f(u_i)$, where $f(u_i)$ is an activation function of unit i. For example, if f is the logistic sigmoid function, we have

$$\frac{\partial y_i}{\partial u_i} = y_i(1 - y_i)$$

and if f is the softmax function, we have

$$\frac{\partial y_i}{\partial u_i} = y_i - y_i^2.$$

Thus, using backpropagation, where this $\frac{\partial g(\mathbf{y})}{\partial u_i}$ is considered as the "error," we can compute the "error" of each unit. We can, therefore, obtain the gradients of $g(\mathbf{y})$ with respect to $\mathbf{w}$ by multiplying the output of each unit with its "error." To prove this, it suffices to replace $E(\mathbf{w})$ with $g(\mathbf{w})$ in the pathway for obtaining the gradient of the error function $E(\mathbf{w})$ via backpropagation.

The gradient calculation of functions using error backpropagation is utilized in many neural network trainings, such as policy gradient methods in reinforcement learning and training of variational autoencoders, which we will introduce in later chapters.

1.1.2.6 Computing the Jacobian Matrix

We can also use backpropagation to calculate the Jacobian matrix, whose the (k, i) element is given by the derivatives of the network output y_k with respect to the input x_i:

$$J_{ki} \equiv \frac{\partial y_k}{\partial x_i},$$

where each such derivative is evaluated with all other inputs held fixed. First, by using (1.1.3), we write the element J_{ki} in the form

$$J_{ki} = \frac{\partial y_k}{\partial x_i} = \sum_j \frac{\partial y_k}{\partial u_j} \frac{\partial u_j}{\partial x_i} = \sum_j w_{ji} \frac{\partial y_k}{\partial u_j}, \quad (1.1.7)$$

where u_j is the activation of unit j to which the input unit i sends connections and the sum runs over all such units j. To determine the derivatives $\frac{\partial y_k}{\partial u_j}$, we can write down a recursive backpropagation formula:

$$\frac{\partial y_k}{\partial u_j} = \sum_l \frac{\partial y_k}{\partial u_l} \frac{\partial u_l}{\partial u_j} = f'(u_j) \sum_l w_{lj} \frac{\partial y_k}{\partial u_l}, \quad (1.1.8)$$

where the sum runs over all units l to which unit j sends connections and f is its activation function.[5] If we use the identity function at each output unit, then we have

$$\frac{\partial y_k}{\partial u_l} = \begin{cases} 1, & l = k, \\ 0, & l \neq k, \end{cases} \quad (1.1.9)$$

whereas for the sigmoidal activation function, we have

---

[5] Note that we have $u_l = f(\sum_i w_{li} u_i)$, where the sum runs over all units i which send connections to unit l. Thus, we obtain $\frac{\partial u_l}{\partial u_j} = f'(u_j) w_{lj}$.

1.2 Matrix Representation of Neural Networks

$$\frac{\partial y_k}{\partial u_l} = \begin{cases} \sigma'(u_k), \\ 0, \quad l \neq k. \end{cases} \quad (1.1.10)$$

We can summarize the procedure for calculating the Jacobian matrix as follows. First, compute the activations of all units in the hidden and output layers of the neural network for the input vector. Next, for each row k of the Jacobian matrix, corresponding to the output unit k, backpropagate the derivatives $\frac{\partial y_k}{\partial u_j}$ using the recursive formula (1.1.8), beginning with (1.1.9) or (1.1.10), for all of the hidden units. Finally, use Eq. (1.1.7) to obtain the elements of the Jacobian matrix.

1.2 Matrix Representation of Neural Networks

In this section, we represent the computation and learning of DNNs (deep neural networks) using matrices. That is, we express the unit's activation u, output z, link weights w, and activation function f as matrices grouped by mini-batch and layer, and we represent the bias b, which does not depend on the mini-batch, as a vector grouped by layer. Matrix representation of computations contributes to simplifying the representation. Furthermore, it is crucial in realizing and implementing the computations.

In the following, we represent mini-batches and activations in matrix form (see Fig. 1.4), where we consider the input layer as the first layer and the output layer as the L-th layer.

Mini-batch: Let $\mathbf{X} = (\mathbf{x}_1 \cdots \mathbf{x}_N)$ be the mini-batch of inputs, and $\mathbf{Y} = (\mathbf{y}_1 \cdots \mathbf{y}_N)$ be the corresponding outputs for $\mathbf{X}$, where $\mathbf{y}_n$ represents the output of the neural network for input $\mathbf{x}_n$.

Activation: Let $\mathbf{U}^{(l)}$ be a matrix containing the activations $u_{jn}^{(l)}$ of units in layer l. The j-th row of matrix $\mathbf{U}^{(l)}$ corresponds to the j-th unit, and the n-th column

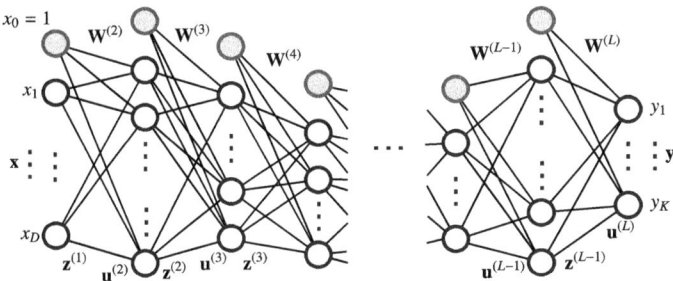

Fig. 1.4 Matrix representation of a neural network

corresponds to the n-th mini-batch data. Representing the activations of layer l for input $\mathbf{x}_n$ as $\mathbf{u}_n^{(l)}$ in vector form, we have $\mathbf{U}^{(l)} = (\mathbf{u}_1^{(l)} \cdots \mathbf{u}_N^{(l)})$.

Activation function: Let $\mathbf{f}^{(l)}(\mathbf{U}^{(l)})$ be a matrix, where the (j, n) entry represents the value of the activation function $f^{(l)}(u_{jn}^{(l)})$ for the component $u_{jn}^{(l)}$ of $\mathbf{U}^{(l)}$.

Output: Let $\mathbf{Z}^{(l)}$ be a matrix containing the outputs $z_{jn}^{(l)}$ of units in layer l. Similar to activations, the j-th row of matrix $\mathbf{Z}^{(l)}$ corresponds to the j-th unit, and the n-th column corresponds to the n-th mini-batch data. Representing the outputs of layer l for input $\mathbf{x}_n$ as $\mathbf{z}_n^{(l)}$ in vector form, we have $\mathbf{Z}^{(l)} = (\mathbf{z}_1^{(l)} \cdots \mathbf{z}_N^{(l)})$.

Weight: Let $\mathbf{W}^{(l)}$ be a matrix where the (j, i) entry represents the weight $w_{ji}^{(l)}$ of the link between unit i in layer $l-1$ and unit j in layer l.

Bias: Let $\mathbf{b}^{(l)}$ be a vector containing the biases $w_{j0}^{(l)}$ for units in layer l.

Using the notation provided, we can express the forward computation as follows. The following expressions can be easily verified by directly computing them using the element representation of matrices and vectors. For the relationship between the activation of unit j in layer l and the output of unit i in layer $l-1$:

$$u_j^{(l)} = \sum_{i=1}^{D} w_{ji}^{(l)} z_i^{(l-1)} + w_{j0}^{(l)},$$

we can summarize it as

$$\mathbf{U}^{(l)} = \mathbf{W}^{(l)} \mathbf{Z}^{(l-1)} + \mathbf{b}^{(l)} \mathbf{1}_N^{\mathrm{T}},$$

where $\mathbf{1}_N$ is an N-dimensional vector with all components being 1, i.e., $(1\ 1\ \cdots\ 1)^{\mathrm{T}}$. Similarly, for the output of unit j in layer l

$$z_j^{(l)} = f^{(l)}(u_j^{(l)}), \quad 1 < l < L, \quad z_j^{(1)} = x_j, \quad z_k^{(L)} = y_k,$$

we can express it as

$$\mathbf{Z}^{(l)} = \mathbf{f}^{(l)}(\mathbf{U}^{(l)}), \quad 1 < l < L, \quad \mathbf{Z}^{(1)} = \mathbf{X}, \quad \mathbf{Z}^{(L)} = \mathbf{Y}.$$

Next, we express the backpropagation calculation using matrix representation (see Fig. 1.3). The formula for backpropagation states that for unit j, the error δ_j is given by

$$\delta_j = f'(u_j) \sum_{l=1}^{L} w_{k_l j} \delta_{k_l},$$

where the summation is taken over units directly connected to unit j on the output side. To represent this in matrix form, we introduce the following matrix $\Delta^{(l)}$.

Error: Let $\Delta^{(l)}$ be a matrix, where the (j, n) entry represents the error $\delta_{jn}^{(l)}$. The j-th row of this matrix corresponds to the j-th unit in layer l, and the n-th column corresponds to the n-th data $\mathbf{x}_n$ in the mini-batch. We denote the error of layer l for data $\mathbf{x}_n$ as a vector $\boldsymbol{\delta}_n^{(l)}$, then $\Delta^{(l)} = (\boldsymbol{\delta}_1^{(l)} \cdots \boldsymbol{\delta}_N^{(l)})$.

1.2 Matrix Representation of Neural Networks

Then, the backpropagation can be summarized as

$$\Delta^{(l)} = \mathbf{f}^{(l)'}(\mathbf{U}^{(l)}) \odot (\mathbf{W}^{(l+1)\mathrm{T}}\Delta^{(l+1)}), \quad (1.2.1)$$

where $\odot$ denotes the Hadamard product (element-wise multiplication) of matrices, and $\mathbf{f}^{(l)'}(\mathbf{U}^{(l)})$ is a matrix with the (j, n) entry being the derivative of the activation function $f'(u_{jn}^{(l)})$ with respect to each component $u_{jn}^{(l)}$ of $\mathbf{U}^{(l)}$.

Let us denote all the weights as $\mathbf{W} = (\mathbf{W}^{(1)} \cdots \mathbf{W}^{(L)})$,[6] and let the loss function (error function) with respect to the mini-batch be $E(\mathbf{W})$. The loss for one data point $\mathbf{x}_n$ in the mini-batch is denoted as $E_n(\mathbf{W})$ then we can express $E(\mathbf{W})$ as

$$E(\mathbf{W}) = \frac{1}{N} \sum_{n=1}^{N} E_n(\mathbf{W}).$$

For simplicity, we denote $E(\mathbf{W})$ as E and $E_n(\mathbf{W})$ as E_n, and often drop the explicit reference to $\mathbf{W}$.

Now, the gradient of one weight w_{ji} (and one bias $b_j = w_{j0}$) with respect to the loss function E is given by

$$\frac{\partial E}{\partial w_{ji}} = \delta_j z_i, \quad \frac{\partial E}{\partial b_j} = \delta_j \times 1.$$

Thus, by introducing the following matrix and vector,

Gradient with respect to weights: $\partial \mathbf{W}^{(l)}$, where the (j, i) entry represents the derivative of E with respect to $w_{ji}^{(l)}$, and

Gradient with respect to biases: $\partial \mathbf{b}^{(l)}$, where the j-th entry represents the derivative of E with respect to $w_{j0}^{(l)}$,

the gradients can be summarized as

$$\partial \mathbf{W}^{(l)} = \frac{1}{N} \Delta^{(l)} \mathbf{Z}^{(l-1)\mathrm{T}},$$

$$\partial \mathbf{b}^{(l)} = \frac{1}{N} \Delta^{(l)} \mathbf{1}_N.$$

Also, the update equations for gradient descent can be summarized as

$$\mathbf{W}^{(l)} \leftarrow \mathbf{W}^{(l)} - \eta \cdot \partial \mathbf{W}^{(l)},$$

$$\mathbf{b}^{(l)} \leftarrow \mathbf{b}^{(l)} - \eta \cdot \partial \mathbf{b}^{(l)},$$

where η is the learning rate.

---

[6] Matrix $\mathbf{W}^{(1)}$ is a dummy.

1.3 The Development of Deep Learning and Its Factors

As demonstrated in the appendix of Chap. 2, in perceptrons with one or more hidden layers, neural networks can approximate "any" function with arbitrary precision as the number of units in the hidden layers increases to the limit. A vast amount of data is, however, required for learning. This is because the number of parameters is proportional to the square of the number of units in the hidden layers. In contrast, Deep Neural Networks (DNNs) restrain the number of units in the hidden layers and reduce the number of parameters in proportion to the number of units by deepening the layers. Additionally, by utilizing large amounts of unlabeled data, it is possible to capture input features at each layer and compactly represent them (representation learning), leading to a "quantitative to qualitative transition," or it could be said that "quantity itself becomes quality." Thus, deep learning has surpassed humans in tasks such as image and language generation.

The transition from quantity to quality did not simply occur because a large amount of data accumulated; rather, it involved the evolution and deepening of key technologies in neural networks. Examples include the advancement of stochastic gradient descent, adoption of the ReLU function as an activation function, residual connections, and activation normalization. We will describe these topics in Chap. 2. Moreover, the active adoption of learning strategies utilizing large amounts of unlabeled data was another significant factor in enhancing quality. Specifically, this includes representation learning, which captures input features at each layer, retraining of pre-trained DNNs in similar domains (transfer learning), and the learning of models to generate complex data (generative models).

Representation learning is designed to capture input features and represent them compactly at each layer. When the calculation from input to hidden layer is denoted as

$$F : \mathbf{R}^M \to \mathbf{R}^D,$$

the input space $\mathbf{R}^M$, even as a Euclidean space, does not inherently provide meaningful interpretations for inner products or distances between elements concerning the task at hand. For example, consider the one-hot representation of words, where only one component takes the value 1, and the rest are 0. In contrast, the embedding space $\mathbf{R}^D$, for instance in Euclidean space, provides meaning for inner products or distances between elements. Word embedding representations, which will be described in Chap. 5, are a typical example of this. Deep learning acquires such representations from data without relying on labels.

Transfer learning refers to the framework of utilizing knowledge acquired to solve one task for learning to solve another task. In transfer learning, a common strategy involves learning representation from a large amount of data, for example, using the output of a DNN up to the final fully connected layer as a feature extractor, and then training only the fully connected layer for the target task. Additionally, distinguishing from transfer learning, *fine-tuning* refers to the process of using the weights of a pre-trained DNN as initial weights and retraining them for the target task. When the purpose is transfer learning or fine-tuning, the training of the original task for the DNN is referred to as *pre-training*. Large-scale language models, which will be described in Chap. 9, are typical examples of those which are trained in these learning strategies.

1.4 Appendix

1.4.1 Proof of the Backpropagation Formula

First, let us recall the concept of composite functions and the differentiation rule, the chain rule. Suppose z is a function of two variables y_1 and y_2, i.e., $z(y_1, y_2)$, and y_1 and y_2 are functions of two variables x_1 and x_2, denoted as $y_1(x_1, x_2)$ and $y_2(x_1, x_2)$, respectively. Then, the composite function, $z(x_1, x_2) = z(y_1(x_1, x_2), y_2(x_1, x_2))$, is a function of x_1 and x_2. In this case, the following equations hold:

$$\frac{\partial z}{\partial x_1} = \frac{\partial z}{\partial y_1}\frac{\partial y_1}{\partial x_1} + \frac{\partial z}{\partial y_2}\frac{\partial y_2}{\partial x_1},$$
$$\frac{\partial z}{\partial x_2} = \frac{\partial z}{\partial y_1}\frac{\partial y_1}{\partial x_2} + \frac{\partial z}{\partial y_2}\frac{\partial y_2}{\partial x_2}.$$

The chain rule similarly applies to the differentiation of composite functions with more than two variables.

Now, in the context of neural networks, the error function E is a function of the outputs y_k of the output layer units, which in turn are functions of the weights $\mathbf{w}$. The output y_k is a function of the activation $u_k^{(L)}$ of the units in the output layer. Furthermore, $u_k^{(L)}$ is a function of the activations $u_j^{(L-1)}$ of all the units j in the previous layer. In general, the activation $u_j^{(l)}$ of a unit j in the l-th layer is a function of all the units' activations $u_1^{(l-1)}, \ldots, u_{M_{l-1}}^{(l-1)}$ in the preceding layer $l-1$:

$$u_1^{(l)}(u_1^{(l-1)}, \ldots, u_{M_{l-1}}^{(l-1)}), \ldots, u_{M_l}^{(l)}(u_1^{(l-1)}, \ldots, u_{M_{l-1}}^{(l-1)}).$$

This implies that the error function E can be viewed as a function of the activations of the units in the l-th layer.

Based on the above preparation, we represent the error $\delta_j = \dfrac{\partial E}{\partial u_j}$ recursively. As mentioned earlier, the partial derivative with respect to the variable u_j means considering the change in error when only u_j is slightly varied while keeping the activations of all other units in the same layer, except for unit j, fixed. Since the activations of the units in the subsequent layers depend on u_j, by the chain rule, we have

$$\delta_j = \frac{\partial E}{\partial u_j} = \sum_{l=1}^{L} \frac{\partial E}{\partial u_{k_l}} \frac{\partial u_{k_l}}{\partial u_j}, \qquad (1.4.1)$$

where the sum is taken over all units connected to the output side of unit j (see Fig. 1.3).

Using $u_{k_l} = \sum_j w_{k_l j} z_j$ and $z_j = f(u_j)$ with the activation function f, and substituting $\delta_{k_l} = \dfrac{\partial E}{\partial u_{k_l}}$ into Eq. (1.4.1), we obtain

$$\delta_j = f'(u_j) \sum_{l=1}^{L} w_{k_l j} \delta_{k_l}.$$

This is what we wanted to show.

Chapter 2
Fundamental Technologies Supporting Deep Learning

Simply deepening neural networks leads to several challenges in learning. First and foremost, in the optimization computations of neural networks with many parameters, we cannot use efficient optimization methods utilizing second-order differentials such as Newton's method. Moreover, when using activation functions such as the logistic sigmoid function or the hyperbolic tangent function, problems such as gradient vanishing or exploding, attributed to the depth of the layers, are known to occur, hindering the progress of learning. Furthermore, there are problems of restricted computation and representation, where relationships between inputs that are temporally or spatially distant cannot be captured effectively.

To overcome the challenges during learning, improvements in stochastic gradient descent optimization have been made. These improvements include the introduction of momentum (akin to "momentum" in physics) and adaptive adjustment of the learning rate. Addressing the issue of gradient vanishing/exploding involves adopting the ReLU function (or its variants) as the activation function, introducing residual connections, and normalizing the output of layers. Regarding inference-time problems, attention mechanisms have been introduced to overcome restricted computation and representation. We begin with an explanation of the improvements in stochastic gradient descent optimization.

2.1 Enhancement of Stochastic Gradient Descent

In the learning of Deep Neural Networks (DNNs), weight updates are typically performed per mini-batch. In the following, thus, learning is conducted on a mini-batch basis.

2.1.1 Momentum Stochastic Gradient Descent (Momentum Method)

Let $\mathbf{w}_t$ denote the weights at time t. Define the *momentum* $\mathbf{v}_t$ at time t as

$$\mathbf{v}_t \equiv \mathbf{w}_t - \mathbf{w}_{t-1}.$$

The update rule for stochastic gradient descent with learning rate η

$$\mathbf{w}_{t+1} = \mathbf{w}_t - \eta \nabla E(\mathbf{w}_t).$$

Incorporating momentum into this, the *momentum stochastic gradient descent* method (or *Momentum method*) [31] is defined as

$$\mathbf{w}_{t+1} = \mathbf{w}_t - \eta \nabla E(\mathbf{w}_t) + \mu \mathbf{v}_t, \tag{2.1.1}$$

where η (learning rate) and μ (0.5 to 0.9) are hyperparameters. As evident from this equation, the modification of weights incorporates momentum, reflecting the momentum of the previous update, thus making it a momentum-aware gradient descent method.

We discuss some properties of the Momentum method. First, from the equations $\mathbf{v}_{t+1} = \mathbf{w}_{t+1} - \mathbf{w}_t$ and $\mathbf{w}_{t+1} = \mathbf{w}_t - \eta \nabla E(\mathbf{w}_t) + \mu \mathbf{v}_t$, we obtain

$$\mathbf{v}_{t+1} = \mu \mathbf{v}_t - \eta \nabla E(\mathbf{w}_t).$$

With setting $\mu = 1$, we can consider $-\eta \nabla E(\mathbf{w}_t)$ as the correction term for the modification amount of weights. Furthermore, setting $\mathbf{v}_0 = \mathbf{0}$, we have

$$\mathbf{v}_t = -\eta \cdot (\mu^{t-1} \nabla E(\mathbf{w}_0) + \mu^{t-2} \nabla E(\mathbf{w}_1) + \cdots + \nabla E(\mathbf{w}_{t-1})). \tag{2.1.2}$$

Thus, we can see the modification amount of weights as a weighted average of past modification amounts.

Due to the properties of the Momentum method, it is expected to converge faster when the error function exhibits a deep, elongated, and flat valley shape. In other words, for error functions with such deep, elongated, and flat valleys, the convergence of the Momentum method is anticipated to be faster. Specifically, for error functions with deep, elongated, and flat valleys, in gradient descent, if the trajectory deviates even slightly from the valley floor, a large gradient in the direction perpendicular to the valley is generated. Consequently, with each update, the weights are adjusted in a direction perpendicular to the valley. As a result, the trajectory zigzags, and it struggles to reach the local minima, as illustrated in Fig. 2.1a. This behavior slows down the convergence of gradient descent.

In contrast, with the Momentum method, the correction in the direction perpendicular to the valley is averaged and tends towards $\mathbf{0}$ (see Fig. 2.1b). This property

2.1 Enhancement of Stochastic Gradient Descent

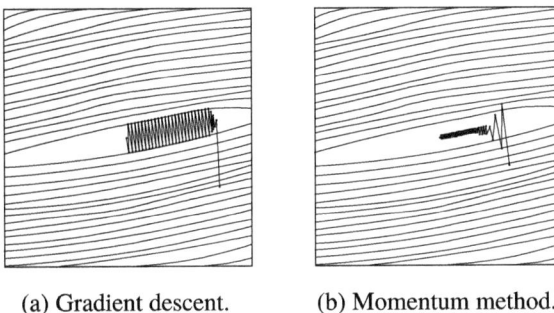

(a) Gradient descent. (b) Momentum method.

Fig. 2.1 When the error function exhibits a deep, elongated, and flat valley. **a** In gradient descent, deviating slightly from the valley floor leads to a large gradient perpendicular to the valley, causing the weights to be updated in a direction perpendicular to the valley with each iteration. **b** In the Momentum method, the correction in the direction perpendicular to the valley is averaged and tends towards **0**.

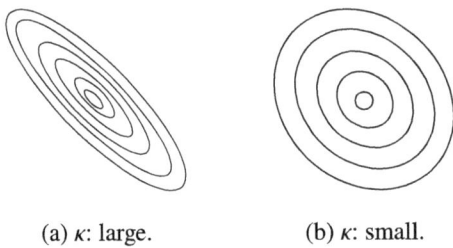

(a) κ: large. (b) κ: small.

Fig. 2.2 Difference in the shape of the error function due to the difference in the condition number κ of the Hessian matrix. The ellipsoids represent the contours of the quadratic approximation of the error function

enables the Momentum method to navigate through such valleys more efficiently and converge faster compared to standard gradient descent.

We quantitatively evaluate the above qualitative analysis by approximating the error function in the vicinity of the extremum with a quadratic function. That is, we evaluate the speed of convergence using the convergence rate, which is the rate at which the error decreases per update. The contours of the quadratic approximation form ellipsoids, and the ratio of the maximum eigenvalue λ_D to the minimum eigenvalue λ_1 of the Hessian matrix (the condition number of the Hessian matrix)

$$\kappa = \frac{\lambda_D}{\lambda_1} \geq 1$$

indicates how flattened the ellipsoid is, and thus how elongated the valley is (see Fig. 2.2a, b).

As shown in the appendix at the end of this chapter, the convergence rate of gradient descent is $\frac{\kappa - 1}{\kappa + 1}$, while the convergence rate of the Momentum method is

$\frac{\sqrt{\kappa}-1}{\sqrt{\kappa}+1}$. Thus, we can understand that the error decreases faster with the Momentum method compared to gradient descent.

2.1.2 Adaptive Adjustment of Learning Rate

In the most basic form of gradient descent update equation

$$\mathbf{w}_{t+1} = \mathbf{w}_t - \eta \nabla E(\mathbf{w}_t),$$

the learning rate η remains a constant, causing a phenomenon where the value of the update does not change as the updates progress. Thus, manual adjustment of the learning rate based on the progress of learning has often been practiced, requiring expertise for appropriate tuning. Consequently, techniques have been developed to adaptively adjust the learning rate based on the state of the updates. Here, we introduce representative methods for adaptive adjustment of the learning rate, namely AdaGrad, RMSProp, and Adadelta.

In the following, the increment of $\mathbf{w}_t$ at time t for one update is denoted as

$$\Delta \mathbf{w}_t = \mathbf{w}_{t+1} - \mathbf{w}_t$$

and the i-th component of $\Delta \mathbf{w}_t$ is denoted as Δw_{ti}. Additionally, the gradient of the error function is represented as $\mathbf{g}_t$. That is,

$$\mathbf{g}_t \equiv \nabla E(\mathbf{w}_t)$$

and the i-th component of $\mathbf{g}_t$ is denoted as g_{ti}. AdaGrad, RMSProp, and Adadelta, all fundamentally depart from using a constant learning rate η independent of components, as in basic gradient descent, and instead adopt a strategy to adjust it for each component. Specifically, they utilize a parameter ε (also referred to as the *learning rate*) to scale the "second moment" of g_{ti}. This allows components with historically large gradients to have a modest learning rate, while components with consistently small gradients tend to have larger learning rates over time.

Firstly, *AdaGrad* [8] defines the i-th component of the increment for one update as

$$\Delta w_{ti} = -\frac{\varepsilon}{\sqrt{\sum_{\tau=1}^{t} g_{\tau i}^2 + \epsilon}} g_{ti}, \qquad (2.1.3)$$

2.1 Enhancement of Stochastic Gradient Descent

where ε is the learning rate, which is divided by the square root of the sum of squares of gradients from the beginning of learning up to the current time t (plus ϵ).[1] The drawback of AdaGrad is that as learning progresses, the sum of squares of gradients increases, causing the update magnitude Δw_{ti} to approach zero. Additionally, the parameter ϵ in the denominator needs to be determined from the data.

In *RMSProp* [16], the i-th component of the update increment is given by

$$\Delta w_{ti} = -\frac{\varepsilon}{\sqrt{m_{ti}^{(g)} + \epsilon}} g_{ti}, \quad (2.1.4)$$

where $m_{ti}^{(g)}$ is defined using a constant γ such that $0 < \gamma < 1$ recursively as

$$m_{ti}^{(g)} = \gamma \cdot m_{t-1,i}^{(g)} + (1-\gamma) g_{ti}^2 \quad (2.1.5)$$

representing a weighted moving average of the squares of gradients up to that point, termed as the moving average of squared gradients (of the i-th component) at time t. By dividing the learning rate ε by the square root of this moving average (plus ϵ), RMSProp overcomes the drawback of AdaGrad. Similar to AdaGrad, however, the parameter ϵ in the denominator needs to be determined from the data.

Adadelta [54] provides the i-th component of the update increment as follows:

$$\Delta w_{ti} = -\frac{\sqrt{m_{ti}^{(\Delta w)}}}{\sqrt{m_{ti}^{(g)} + \epsilon}} g_{ti}, \quad (2.1.6)$$

where $m_{ti}^{(g)}$ is the moving average of the squares of gradients as defined in Eq. (2.1.5), and $m_{ti}^{(\Delta w)}$ is the moving average of the squares of update increments defined using a constant γ' such that $0 < \gamma' < 1$:

$$m_{ti}^{(\Delta w)} = \gamma' \cdot m_{t-1,i}^{(\Delta w)} + (1-\gamma') \Delta w_{ti}^2.$$

In this method, by dividing by the square root of the moving average of the squares of gradients (plus ϵ), the physical units (virtual) of parameters and update increments are aligned, and the parameter ϵ in the denominator can be a small arbitrary value without needing to be determined from the data.

---

[1] A small constant ϵ is added to avoid division by zero.

2.1.3 Momentum Method + Adaptive Learning Rate

We introduce *Adam* [20], a method that combines both the Momentum method and adaptive learning rate adjustment. In Adam, the i-th component of the update increment for one update is given by

$$\Delta w_{ti} = -\frac{\varepsilon}{\sqrt{\hat{g}_{ti}} + \epsilon} \hat{v}_{ti}, \tag{2.1.7}$$

where

$$\hat{g}_{ti} \equiv \frac{m_{ti}^{(g)}}{1 - \gamma^t}, \quad \hat{v}_{ti} \equiv \frac{m_{ti}^{(v)}}{1 - \mu^t}$$

and

$$m_{ti}^{(g)} = \gamma \cdot m_{t-1, i}^{(g)} + (1 - \gamma) g_{ti}^2$$

represents the moving average of the squared gradients, while $m_{ti}^{(v)}$ is defined as

$$m_{ti}^{(v)} = \mu \cdot m_{t-1, i}^{(v)} + (1 - \mu) g_{ti}$$

representing the moving average of the gradients. Here, γ and μ are constants such that $0 < \gamma, \mu < 1$. If we recall that, in the Momentum method, a momentum is a weighted average of past gradients multiplied by the negative of the learning rate (Eq. (2.1.2)), then, we see that $m_{ti}^{(v)}$ (also, $\hat{v}_{ti}$) corresponds to the i-th component of the momentum. Additionally, ϵ appears outside the square root in the denominator on the right-hand side, which is merely a historical convention and not essential.

Adam incorporates both the Momentum method and adaptive learning rate adjustment, providing robustness against variations in the learning rate ε. As long as ε is within a certain range, Adam tends to converge, leading to stable and consistent results in optimization tasks.

2.2 Dealing with the Gradient Vanishing/Diverging Problem

The formula for backpropagation is linear with respect to the error Δ. Therefore, during backpropagation of errors from output to input, if the weights are large, the error grows rapidly and diverges, whereas if the weights are small, the error rapidly diminishes and collapses to $\mathbf{0}$. Particularly,

$$\begin{aligned}\Delta^{(l-2)} &= \mathbf{f}^{(l-2)'}(\mathbf{U}^{(l-2)}) \odot (\mathbf{W}^{(l-1)\mathrm{T}} \Delta^{(l-1)}) \\ &= \mathbf{f}^{(l-2)'}(\mathbf{U}^{(l-2)}) \odot (\mathbf{W}^{(l-1)\mathrm{T}} (\mathbf{f}^{(l-1)'}(\mathbf{U}^{(l-1)}) \odot (\mathbf{W}^{(l)\mathrm{T}} \Delta^{(l)})))\end{aligned}$$

2.2 Dealing with the Gradient Vanishing/Diverging Problem

as seen from the transformation above, the error propagated from the output layer to the input layer involves factors of

$$\mathbf{f}^{(L)\prime}, \mathbf{f}^{(L-1)\prime}, \ldots, \mathbf{f}^{(2)\prime}, \mathbf{f}^{(1)\prime}.$$

Thus, when using activation functions such as the logistic sigmoid function or the hyperbolic tangent function, since the absolute values of $\mathbf{f}^{(l)\prime}$ components are less than 1, the components of errors in layers close to the input layer are likely to become nearly zero, depending on the weights. Consequently, the learning process may stagnate. To address this issue, methods such as adopting the ReLU function (or similar functions), introducing skip connections, and normalizing the activity of units have been employed. Below, we explain each of these in turn.

2.2.1 ReLU Function

We list the properties that an activation function should have to achieve stable learning in deep learning.

1. First, the activation function must be non-linear. Non-linearity is necessary to represent general functions other than linear functions. Furthermore, the completeness of the activation function is required. That is, the activation function must be able to sufficiently approximate a wide range of functions, including discontinuous functions, through composition and linear combinations.
2. Next, scale preservation is crucial. Because the activation function is applied repeatedly for each layer in the hierarchy, if the values taken by the activation function become extremely large, they diverge, and if they approach zero, they collapse to zero. To avoid this phenomenon, scale preservation, where the function values are of the same order of magnitude as the independent variable, is necessary.
3. Furthermore, differentiability is required. This is necessary for optimization calculations. Also, just like function values, extreme values of derivatives lead to divergence when too large and collapse to zero when approaching zero, so having appropriate magnitudes is desirable.

The *ReLU function* [10, 13, 29]

$$\text{ReLU}(x) = \begin{cases} x, & 0 \leq x, \\ 0, & x < 0 \end{cases}$$

possesses all these desirable properties and is simple (see Fig. 2.3). As shown in the appendix at the end of this chapter, by increasing the units of hidden layers using the non-linear ReLU function as the activation function, neural networks can represent any piecewise linear function. Since a wide range of functions, including

Fig. 2.3 ReLU function

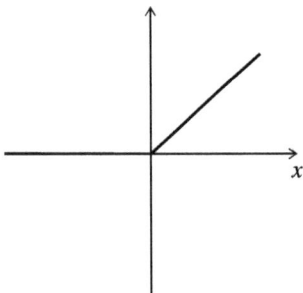

discontinuous functions, can be approximated by piecewise linear functions, the ReLU function is complete in that sense. For inputs 0 or $x > 0$, the function values are simply preserved as 0 or x, respectively, so the scale is naturally preserved. The differentiability[2] is also evident from

$$\text{ReLU}'(x) = \begin{cases} 1, & 0 \leq x, \\ 0, & x < 0. \end{cases}$$

2.3 Residual Connection

Residual connection[3] is a method where links are created to bypass several layers, and the output that has passed through the layers without bypassing is added (see Fig. 2.4). Residual connections are observed to prevent the vanishing gradient problem in error backpropagation and to alleviate the information loss in forward pass (due to traversing through multiple layers).

In a residual connection, let **z** be the input to the bypassed part, $\mathbf{y} = \mathbf{f}(\mathbf{z})$ be the output of the bypassed part, and **z′** be the output of the residual connection. Then, it is expressed as

$$\mathbf{z}' = \mathbf{f}(\mathbf{z}) + \mathbf{z}.$$

This equation can be transformed into $\mathbf{z}' - \mathbf{z} = \mathbf{f}(\mathbf{z})$, which represents the "residual," the correction amount for the input **z**. The bypassed part can be seen as predicting this correction amount.

---

[2] Strictly speaking, the ReLU function is not differentiable at $x = 0$ and differentiable elsewhere. However, there exists a subdifferential at $x = 0$, which is the interval [0, 1], so it is acceptable to assign the derivative value of the ReLU function at $x = 0$ as 1. For more information on subdifferential, refer to the appendix at the end of this chapter.

[3] Originally proposed by [38]. In deep learning, see [14].

2.3 Residual Connection

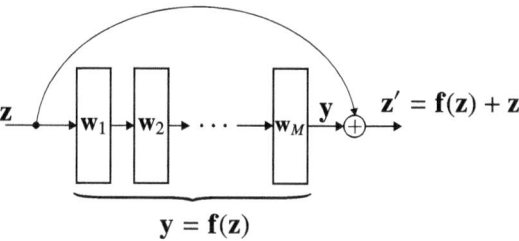

Fig. 2.4 Residual connection

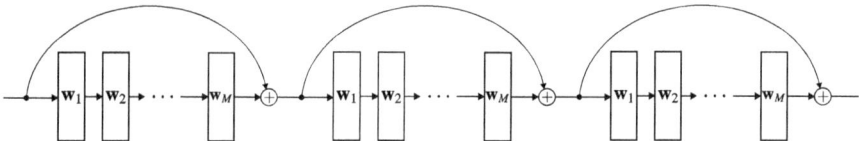

Fig. 2.5 Stacking of residual blocks

A network consisting of layers bypassed by skip connections is called a *residual block*. Additionally, the bypassed route is referred to as a *skip connection*. Normally, multiple residual blocks are stacked together (see Fig. 2.5).

We can consider the utility of residual connections in several aspects. One of them is the effect of avoiding vanishing gradients. This can be observed from the fact that the error stems from considering $\mathbf{z}$ as the activity of the residual block and $\mathbf{z}'$ as the activity of the subsequent residual block:

$$\frac{\partial E}{\partial \mathbf{z}} = \left(\frac{\partial \mathbf{z}'}{\partial \mathbf{z}^T}\right)^T \frac{\partial E}{\partial \mathbf{z}'} = \left(\frac{\partial (\mathbf{z} + \mathbf{f}(\mathbf{z}))}{\partial \mathbf{z}^T}\right)^T \frac{\partial E}{\partial \mathbf{z}'}$$

$$= \left(\mathbf{I} + \frac{\partial \mathbf{f}(\mathbf{z})}{\partial \mathbf{z}^T}\right)^T \frac{\partial E}{\partial \mathbf{z}'} = \frac{\partial E}{\partial \mathbf{z}'} + \left(\frac{\partial \mathbf{f}(\mathbf{z})}{\partial \mathbf{z}^T}\right)^T \frac{\partial E}{\partial \mathbf{z}'}.$$

From this, it can be confirmed that the error in the input block is obtained by adding $\left(\frac{\partial \mathbf{f}(\mathbf{z})}{\partial \mathbf{z}^T}\right)^T \frac{\partial E}{\partial \mathbf{z}'}$ to the error of the output block.

Additionally, residual connections contribute to the robustness of computations. In a deep network without residual connections, if the computation in any layer results in **0**, the overall computation also becomes **0**. With skip connections, however, even if the computation in a layer within the residual block becomes **0**, the overall computation does not necessarily become **0**.

Furthermore, residual connections enable the realization of bottleneck layers that preserve information. A *bottleneck* is a technique where the size is reduced in the channel or spatial directions, costly computations are performed, and then the size is restored (see Chap. 4). Generally, it is known that information is lost when a

2.4 Normalization of Activations

2.4.1 Necessity of Normalization

In multidimensional quantities, such as pairs like height and weight, the components are often heterogeneous. Generally, not only in neural networks but also in other contexts, it is known that learning efficiency decreases with multidimensional quantities **u** where the magnitudes and variations differ for each component. For example, in simple gradient descent, the learning rate may be appropriate for one component but inappropriate for others, which often happens. Even when adjusting the learning rate adaptively, it may not fully compensate for the decrease in learning efficiency. Additionally, in the case of multidimensional quantities **u** consisting of the same sign (e.g., all positive), the learning efficiency deteriorates because only searches in the same direction are performed for each component. This occurs because when the data has the same sign, the sign of the gradients with respect to the weights connected to a single unit will be consistent for all components.

In deep learning, uneven input and output across units can hinder learning. Thus, several methods have been proposed to normalize the activities of units. In this section, we describe batch normalization, layer normalization, instance normalization, and group normalization. We begin with batch normalization.

2.4.2 Batch Normalization

Normalizing the activity of units for each mini-batch is called *batch normalization* [18]. We elaborate on this below. Let $\mathbf{X} = \{\mathbf{x}_1, \ldots, \mathbf{x}_N\}$, where $\mathbf{x}_N = (x_{1n} \cdots x_{Dn})^{\mathrm{T}}$ represents a mini-batch, and let $u_{jn}^{(l)}$ denote the activity of unit j in layer l for data $\mathbf{x}_n$. The mean of activities in the mini-batch is given by

$$\mu_j^{(l)} = \frac{1}{N} \sum_{n=1}^{N} u_{jn}^{(l)},$$

and the variance is

$$(\sigma_j^{(l)})^2 = \frac{1}{N} \sum_{n=1}^{N} (u_{jn}^{(l)} - \mu_j^{(l)})^2.$$

2.4 Normalization of Activations

Using these, during training, batch normalization transforms the activity $u_{jn}^{(l)}$ of unit j in layer l for data $\mathbf{x}_n$ as follows:

$$\hat{u}_{jn}^{(l)} = \frac{u_{jn}^{(l)} - \mu_j^{(l)}}{\sqrt{(\sigma_j^{(l)})^2 + \epsilon}},$$

and further applies a linear transformation

$$\tilde{u}_{jn}^{(l)} = \gamma_j^{(l)} \hat{u}_{jn}^{(l)} + \beta_j^{(l)}$$

to obtain the activity of unit j for data $\mathbf{x}_n$. Here, $\gamma_j^{(l)}$ and $\beta_j^{(l)}$ are parameters learned during training. This linear transformation is applied to enhance the expressive power since normalization alone imposes significant constraints on representation.

During inference, batch normalization normalizes the activity of unit j in layer l for input $\mathbf{x}$ using the exponentially weighted moving averages[4] of $\mu_j^{(l)}$, $(\sigma_j^{(l)})^2$, $\gamma_j^{(l)}$, and $\beta_j^{(l)}$ obtained during training.

In the foregoing, we have proceeded with the discussion ignoring channels. Generally, in image processing, color images are usually represented as three "images" of RGB. Correspondingly, in neural networks dealing with color images, the input is divided into three "images" of RGB, each referred to as a channel and, thus, an input layer has three channels. Likewise, each layer consists of multiple channels and, in the calculation of the activation of each layer, the outputs of the channels from the previous layer are summed for each corresponding unit's activation, squashing the channel information before passing it through the activation function. The output is then convolved with multiple filters, resulting in multiple channels again. Below, we discuss batch normalization taking into account channels. Before that, we summarize the tensor notation necessary for introducing channels.

Tensor Notation in Neural Networks

In Sect. 1.2, we introduced matrices to represent activities and outputs of units for each layer and mini-batch collectively. Below, we introduce *tensors* to collectively handle layers, mini-batches, and channels. Intuitively, if vectors are arrays of components aligned along a line, and matrices are arrays of components arranged 2-dimensionally on a plane, then tensors introduced here are arrays of components arranged 3-dimensionally in space. In terms of array terminologies in programming languages, vectors are 1-dimensional arrays, matrices are 2-dimensional arrays, and

---

[4] Suppose the mini-batch is used T times during training, and let A denote a quantity learned during training, with A_t representing its value at the t-th training iteration. The *exponential moving average* of A is calculated as

$$\frac{A_T + \alpha A_{T-1} + \alpha^2 A_{T-2} + \cdots + \alpha^{T-1} A_1}{1 + \alpha + \alpha^2 + \cdots + \alpha^{T-1}},$$

where $0 < \alpha < 1$. In batch normalization, we set α to $1/2$.

tensors are 3-dimensional arrays. Below are the tensor representations of activities, weights, and other components.

Activity $\mathbf{U}^{(l)}$ is a tensor consisting of activities u_{jnc} of units in layer l, where j denotes the unit, n denotes the data in the mini-batch, and c corresponds to the channel.

Activation function $\mathbf{f}^{(l)}(\mathbf{U}^{(l)})$ is a tensor where the (j, n, c) component represents the activation function value $f^{(l)}(u_{jnc})$ for the component u_{jnc} of $\mathbf{U}^{(l)}$.

Output $\mathbf{Z}^{(l)}$ is a tensor consisting of outputs z_{jnc} of units in layer l, where the row j represents the j-th unit, column n represents the n-th data in the mini-batch, and c corresponds to the channel.

In multi-channel batch normalization, normalization is performed for each channel. Let c denote the channel, and (M, N, C) denote the shape of the tensor. Also, let $u_{jnc}^{(l)}$ represent the activity of unit j in channel c of layer l for data $\mathbf{x}_n$. The mean of activities in the mini-batch and for units in layer l is computed channel-wise as follows:

$$\mu_c^{(l)} = \frac{1}{NM} \sum_{n=1}^{N} \sum_{j=1}^{M} u_{jnc}^{(l)}.$$

The variance is computed as

$$(\sigma_c^{(l)})^2 = \frac{1}{NM} \sum_{n=1}^{N} \sum_{j=1}^{M} (u_{jnc}^{(l)} - \mu_c^{(l)})^2.$$

Using these, the activity $u_{jnc}^{(l)}$ of unit j in channel c for data $\mathbf{x}_n$ is normalized as follows:

$$\tilde{u}_{jnc}^{(l)} = \gamma_{jc}^{(l)} \frac{u_{jnc}^{(l)} - \mu_c^{(l)}}{\sqrt{(\sigma_c^{(l)})^2 + \epsilon}} + \beta_{jc}^{(l)}, \quad c = 1, \ldots, C$$

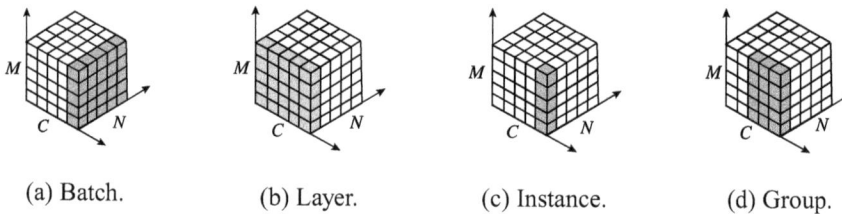

(a) Batch. (b) Layer. (c) Instance. (d) Group.

Fig. 2.6 Visualization of activation normalization. Each figure represents a different normalization technique, where the light gray area indicates the treated batch, layer, instance, or group. Channel (C), layer (M), and mini-batch (N) are represented on the three axes, showing how each normalization treats them as a collective unit

2.4 Normalization of Activations

Fig. 2.7 Convergence to flatter solutions facilitated by batch normalization

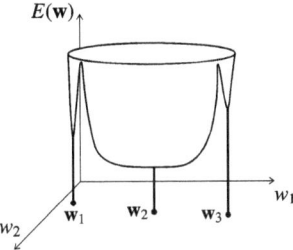

(see Fig. 2.6a). Note that in the case of multiple channels, we calculate the mean and variance along the layer direction and we apply the same normalization to all units in the same layer.

The benefits of batch normalization include improved learning efficiency and enhanced generalization performance due to convergence to flatter solutions (see Fig. 2.7). The drawbacks and constraints of batch normalization are as follows.

- Different values of normalization parameters μ_j and σ_j^2 during training and inference stages may lead to varying network behavior between these stages for the same input.
- When the mini-batch size is small, the variability in the estimated values of μ_j and σ_j^2 increases, leading to a diminished effect of normalization.
- When using activation functions such as logistic sigmoid or softmax, where the absolute magnitude of activations is crucial, normalization should be avoided.
- Additionally, in networks with loop connections such as recurrent neural networks (RNNs), where information passes through the same layer multiple times, the values of mean and variance may vary significantly with each pass, making batch normalization challenging to apply.

Now that we have covered batch normalization, let us move on to layer normalization. For simplicity, we will drop the index n representing the mini-batch data $\mathbf{x}_n$ in the following discussion.

2.4.3 Layer Normalization

Layer normalization (also known as *layer-wise normalization*) [2] is a normalization technique used in the blocks of Transformers, as detailed in Chap. 6. In layer normalization, the activation of units is normalized within each layer for each data point (see Fig. 2.6b). In the case of multiple channels, we calculate the mean and variance along the channel direction and we apply the same normalization to all channels. Specifically, in layer normalization, for each data point $\mathbf{x}$, the mean and variance of activations for each unit in channel c of layer l are computed as follows:

$$\mu^{(l)} = \frac{1}{MC}\sum_{j=1}^{M}\sum_{c=1}^{C} u_{jc}^{(l)}$$

and

$$(\sigma^{(l)})^2 = \frac{1}{MC}\sum_{j=1}^{M}\sum_{c=1}^{C}(u_{jc}^{(l)} - \mu^{(l)})^2.$$

Then, the activations of each unit $u_{jc}^{(l)}$ in channel c of layer l are normalized and linearly transformed as

$$\tilde{u}_{jc}^{(l)} = \gamma_j^{(l)} \frac{u_{jc}^{(l)} - \mu^{(l)}}{\sqrt{(\sigma^{(l)})^2 + \epsilon}} + \beta_j^{(l)}.$$

The layer normalization parameters $\gamma_j^{(l)}$ and $\beta_j^{(l)}$ are learned during training along with other model parameters, allowing the network to adaptively adjust the scale and bias of the normalized activations. This helps the network capture more complex patterns in the data.

2.4.4 Instance Normalization

Instance normalization [45] normalizes the activation of each unit within the data and channel at a given layer (see Fig. 2.6c). Specifically, for each data **x**, the mean and variance of activations across the layer for each channel c of layer l are computed as follows:

$$\mu_c^{(l)} = \frac{1}{M}\sum_{j=1}^{M} u_{jc}^{(l)},$$

$$(\sigma_c^{(l)})^2 = \frac{1}{M}\sum_{j=1}^{M}(u_{jc}^{(l)} - \mu_c^{(l)})^2.$$

Then, the normalization and linear transformation are applied as follows:

$$\tilde{u}_{jc}^{(l)} = \gamma_{jc}^{(l)} \frac{u_{jc}^{(l)} - \mu_c^{(l)}}{\sqrt{(\sigma_c^{(l)})^2 + \epsilon}} + \beta_{jc}^{(l)}.$$

2.4.5 Group Normalization

Group normalization [53] divides channels into several groups and normalizes the activation of each unit within the channel groups and data (see Fig. 2.6d). In group normalization, for each data **x**, the mean and variance of activations across the layer for each channel group C_g of layer l are computed as follows:

$$\mu_{C_g}^{(l)} = \frac{1}{M \cdot |C_g|} \sum_{j=1}^{M} \sum_{c \in C_g} u_{jc}^{(l)},$$

$$(\sigma_{C_g}^{(l)})^2 = \frac{1}{M \cdot |C_g|} \sum_{j=1}^{M} \sum_{c \in C_g} (u_{jc}^{(l)} - \mu_{C_g}^{(l)})^2.$$

Then, the normalization and linear transformation are applied as follows.

$$\tilde{u}_{jc}^{(l)} = \gamma_{C_g}^{(l)} \frac{u_{jc}^{(l)} - \mu_{C_g}^{(l)}}{\sqrt{(\sigma_{C_g}^{(l)})^2 + \epsilon}} + \beta_{C_g}^{(l)}.$$

By considering the specific characteristics of data, models, and hardware constraints, we can select the most appropriate normalization technique. For example, we use batch normalization for large batches, fast training, and networks like CNNs. We use layer normalization for RNNs, Transformers, or when batch size is small or variable. Also, we use instance normalization for tasks focused on individual sample statistics. We use group normalization for small batches or when we need a balance between batch-based and layer-based normalization, especially in computer vision tasks.

2.5 Appendix

2.5.1 Convergence Rate of Gradient Descent

We approximate the error function as follows:

$$E(\mathbf{w}) \approx E_0 + \mathbf{w}^T \mathbf{b} + \frac{1}{2} \mathbf{w}^T \mathbf{H} \mathbf{w},$$

where E_0 is a constant, **b** is a constant vector, and **H** is the Hessian matrix of E. Setting the gradient of this expression to zero, we obtain the equation

$$\nabla E \approx \mathbf{b} + \mathbf{H}\mathbf{w} = \mathbf{0}.$$

Solving this equation, we find the minimum solution $\mathbf{w}^*$ for the second-order approximation. That is,

$$-\mathbf{H}\mathbf{w}^* = \mathbf{b} \Leftrightarrow \mathbf{w}^* = -\mathbf{H}^{-1}\mathbf{b}. \tag{2.5.1}$$

We diagonalize the Hessian matrix $\mathbf{H}$. That is,

$$\mathbf{H} = \mathbf{U}\mathbf{\Lambda}\mathbf{U}^{\mathrm{T}} \Leftrightarrow \mathbf{U}^{\mathrm{T}}\mathbf{H} = \mathbf{\Lambda}\mathbf{U}^{\mathrm{T}}, \tag{2.5.2}$$

where $\mathbf{U}$ is an orthogonal matrix formed by stacking the eigenvectors of $\mathbf{H}$, and $\mathbf{\Lambda}$ is a diagonal matrix with the eigenvalues λ_i of $\mathbf{H}$ as its diagonal elements.

Under the second-order approximation, the update equation for gradient descent is given by

$$\mathbf{w}_{t+1} = \mathbf{w}_t - \eta \cdot (\mathbf{b} + \mathbf{H}\mathbf{w}_t).$$

Multiplying both sides of the equation by $\mathbf{U}^{\mathrm{T}}$ and utilizing Eqs. (2.5.1) and (2.5.2), we have

$$\mathbf{U}^{\mathrm{T}}\mathbf{w}_{t+1} = \mathbf{U}^{\mathrm{T}}\mathbf{w}_t - \eta \cdot (\mathbf{U}^{\mathrm{T}}\mathbf{b} + \mathbf{U}^{\mathrm{T}}\mathbf{H}\mathbf{w}_t) = \mathbf{U}^{\mathrm{T}}\mathbf{w}_t - \eta \cdot (-\mathbf{U}^{\mathrm{T}}\mathbf{H}\mathbf{w}^* + \mathbf{U}^{\mathrm{T}}\mathbf{H}\mathbf{w}_t)$$
$$= \mathbf{U}^{\mathrm{T}}\mathbf{w}_t - \eta \cdot (-\mathbf{\Lambda}\mathbf{U}^{\mathrm{T}}\mathbf{w}^* + \mathbf{\Lambda}\mathbf{U}^{\mathrm{T}}\mathbf{w}_t).$$

Subtracting $\mathbf{U}^{\mathrm{T}}\mathbf{w}^*$ from both sides and defining $\hat{\mathbf{w}}_t$ as

$$\hat{\mathbf{w}}_t = \mathbf{U}^{\mathrm{T}}(\mathbf{w}_t - \mathbf{w}^*), \tag{2.5.3}$$

we obtain

$$\hat{\mathbf{w}}_{t+1} = \hat{\mathbf{w}}_t - \eta \cdot \mathbf{\Lambda}\hat{\mathbf{w}}_t.$$

The i-th component of this equation is given by

$$\hat{w}_{t+1,i} = \hat{w}_{ti} - \eta \lambda_i \hat{w}_{ti} = (1 - \eta \lambda_i)\hat{w}_{ti} = (1 - \eta \lambda_i)^{t+1}\hat{w}_{0i}.$$

Using this and Eq. (2.5.3), we have

$$\mathbf{w}_t - \mathbf{w}^* = \mathbf{U}\hat{\mathbf{w}}_t = \sum_{i=1}^{D} \hat{w}_{0i}(1 - \eta \lambda_i)^t \mathbf{u}_i,$$

where $\mathbf{u}_i$ is a column vector of $\mathbf{U}$. Hence,

$$\|\mathbf{w}_t - \mathbf{w}^*\| = \left\|\sum_{i=1}^{D} \hat{w}_{0i}(1 - \eta \lambda_i)^t \mathbf{u}_i\right\| \leq \sum_{i=1}^{D} |\hat{w}_{0i}| \cdot |1 - \eta \lambda_i|^t \cdot \|\mathbf{u}_i\| \leq M \sum_{i=1}^{D} |1 - \eta \lambda_i|^t,$$

2.5 Appendix

where $M = \sup_i |\hat{w}_{0i}| \cdot \|\mathbf{u}_i\|$.

Taking $\eta > 0$ small enough, we have $|1 - \eta\lambda_i| < 1$. Thus, when t becomes large, the right-hand side is determined by the largest term. In the following, we seek the learning rate η that minimizes the above equation and determine the convergence rate at that learning rate. Since $|1 - \eta\lambda_i|$ is maximized at either the smallest eigenvalue λ_1 or the largest eigenvalue λ_D, the desired learning rate is given by

$$\eta^* = \arg\min_\eta \max\{|1 - \eta\lambda_1|, |1 - \eta\lambda_D|\}.$$

The minimum of the larger of the expressions $|1 - \eta\lambda_1|$ and $|1 - \eta\lambda_D|$ in this equation is achieved when

$$1 - \eta\lambda_1 = -(1 - \eta\lambda_D)$$

holds. At this point, we have

$$\eta^* = \frac{2}{\lambda_1 + \lambda_D}.$$

Thus, since for each update in the gradient descent method, the error of each component decreases by a factor of $1 - \eta^*\lambda_i$, the convergence rate is given by

$$1 - \eta^*\lambda_D = 1 - \frac{2}{\lambda_1 + \lambda_D}\lambda_D = \frac{\kappa - 1}{\kappa + 1},$$

where $\kappa \equiv \dfrac{\lambda_D}{\lambda_1}$.

2.5.2 Completeness of ReLU Functions

Increasing the units in the hidden layer with ReLU activation function allows a neural network to represent any piecewise linear function. We demonstrate this for the case of a single variable. Let a be a non-zero constant. Then, for any point ξ on the x-axis, the function shown in Fig. 2.8

$$\phi_\xi(x) \equiv \begin{cases} 0, & x < \xi, \\ ax - a\xi, & \xi \leq x \end{cases}$$

can be realized with the network depicted in Fig. 2.9. Here, the input layer includes a bias unit and another unit that outputs the input as it is. The hidden and output layers each consist of one unit, with ReLU and identity activation functions, respectively. Using the function $\phi_\xi(x)$, we define the function $\psi_{\xi_1, \xi_2}(x)$ for any $\xi_1 < \xi_2$ as

$$\psi_{\xi_1,\xi_2}(x) \equiv \phi_{\xi_1}(x) - \phi_{\xi_2}(x) = \begin{cases} 0, & x < \xi_1, \\ ax - a\xi_1, & \xi_1 \le x \le \xi_2, \\ a\xi_2 - a\xi_1, & \xi_2 < x \end{cases}$$

(see Fig. 2.10). This function can be realized with the network shown in Fig. 2.11. Here, the activation function for the hidden layer is ReLU, and for the output layer unit, it is the identity function. Let us represent this network as depicted in Fig. 2.12.

Here, if we keep $a\xi_2 - a\xi_1 = b$ constant and let ξ_2 approach $\xi = \xi_1$, and increase the slope a (or decrease a if it is negative), $\psi_{\xi_1,\xi_2}(x)$ approximates a step function

$$S_{b,\xi}(x) = \begin{cases} 0, & x < \xi, \\ b, & \xi \le x \end{cases}$$

(see Fig. 2.13). We can represent this discontinuous function with the network depicted in Fig. 2.14.

Similarly, the function shown in Fig. 2.15

$$\phi_\xi^-(x) \equiv \begin{cases} -ax + a\xi, & x < \xi, \\ 0, & \xi \le x \end{cases}$$

can be realized with the network depicted in Fig. 2.16.

Using the function $\phi_\xi^-(x)$, define

$$\psi_{\xi_1,\xi_2}^-(x) \equiv \phi_{\xi_2}^-(x) - \phi_{\xi_1}^-(x) = \begin{cases} -a\xi_1 + a\xi_2, & x < \xi_1, \\ -ax + a\xi_2, & \xi_1 \le x \le \xi_2, \\ 0, & \xi_2 < x. \end{cases}$$

Then, keeping $a\xi_2 - a\xi_1 = b$ constant, as ξ_2 approaches ξ_1 and a becomes large (or small if a is negative), $\psi_{\xi_1,\xi_2}^-(x)$ approximates the step function

$$S_{b,\xi}^-(x) = \begin{cases} b, & x < \xi, \\ 0, & \xi \le x, \end{cases}$$

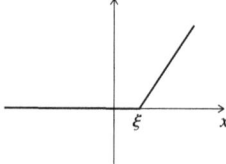

Fig. 2.8 Function $\phi_\xi(x) \equiv 0 \ (x < \xi), \quad ax - a\xi \ (\xi \le x)$

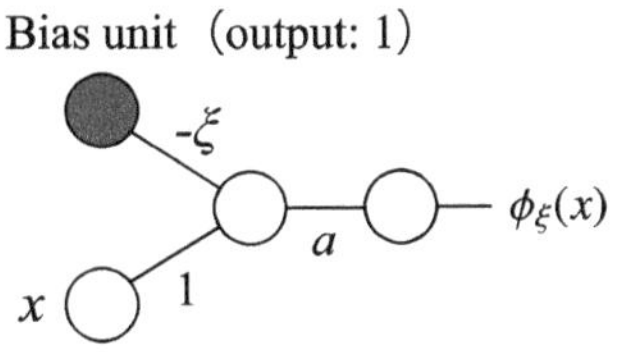

2.5 Appendix

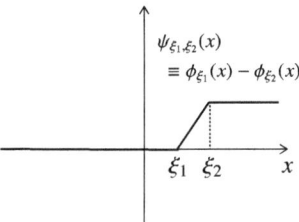

Fig. 2.9 Network to compute function $\phi_\xi(x)$. Units in the input layer output the input as is, while the activation function for the hidden layer is ReLU and identity for the output layer unit

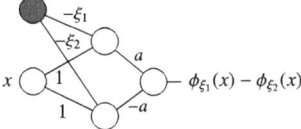

Fig. 2.10 Function $\psi_{\xi_1, \xi_2}(x) \equiv \phi_{\xi_1}(x) - \phi_{\xi_2}(x)$

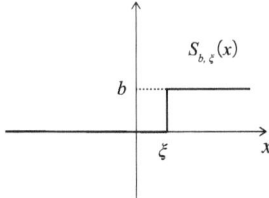

Fig. 2.11 Network to compute function $\psi_{\xi_1, \xi_2}(x)$. The activation function for the hidden layer is ReLU, and for the output layer unit, it is identity

$$-\boxed{S_l}-$$
$$\xi_1, \xi_2$$

Fig. 2.12 Abbreviated notation for the network shown in Fig. 2.11

$$S_{b,\xi}(x)$$

Fig. 2.13 Step function rising from 0 to b at $x = \xi$.

where $a\xi_2 - a\xi_1 = b$ (see Fig. 2.17). This approximation can be represented by the network depicted in Fig. 2.18.

Now, we consider a "line segment function" which includes one line segment

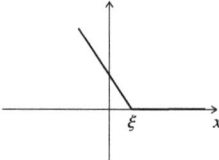

Fig. 2.14 Simplified representation of the network approximating a step function rising from 0 to b at $x = \xi$

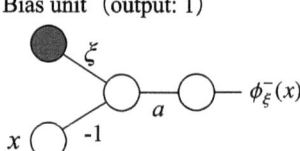

Fig. 2.15 Function $\phi_\xi^-(x) \equiv -ax + a\xi \ (x < \xi), \ 0 \ (\xi \leq x)$

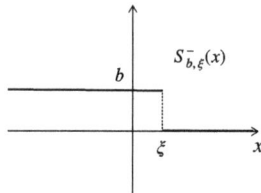

Fig. 2.16 Network computing the function $\phi_\xi^-(x)$. The input layer units output the input as it is, the activation function of the hidden layer is ReLU, and the activation function of the output layer unit is the identity function

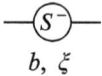

Fig. 2.17 Step function that falls from b to 0 at $x = \xi$

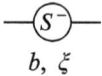

Fig. 2.18 Abbreviated representation of the network approximating the function that falls from b to 0 at $x = \xi$

$$y(x) = \begin{cases} ax + c, & \xi_1 < x \leq \xi_2, \\ 0, & x \leq \xi_1, \ \xi_2 < x, \end{cases}$$

where c is a constant, and $b_1 = a\xi_1 + c$, $b_2 = a\xi_2 + c$ (see Fig. 2.19). This "line segment function" can be expressed as

2.5 Appendix

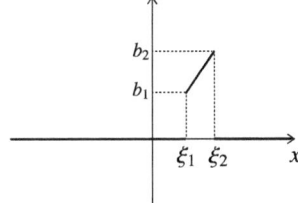

Fig. 2.19 Function that coincides with the straight line $ax + c$ over the interval $[\xi_1, \xi_2]$ and takes the value 0 elsewhere

Fig. 2.20 Neural network realizing a function that coincides with the straight line $ax + c$ over the interval $[\xi_1, \xi_2]$ and takes the value 0 elsewhere

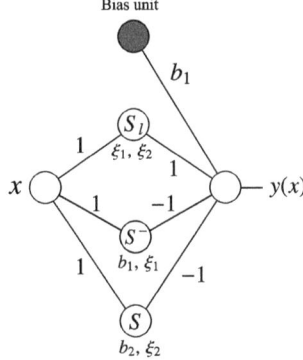

Fig. 2.21 Neural network for computing a piecewise linear curve

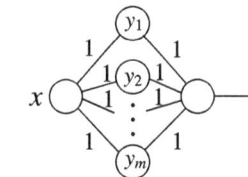

$$\psi_{\xi_1, \xi_2}(x) + b_1 - S^-_{b_1, \xi_1}(x) - S_{b_2, \xi_2}(x) \qquad (2.5.4)$$

and the network approximating it is illustrated in Fig. 2.20. We refer to this network as a "line segment unit" and denote it as y.

Finally, suppose we are given a piecewise linear curve composed of line segments $y_1(x), \ldots, y_m(x)$. We construct a neural network as depicted in Fig. 2.21, comprising a single input unit and a single output unit. We arrange the line segment units y_i, each connected to the input unit, in parallel, and connect the outputs of y_i to the output unit. Assume that all link weights are set to 1. Then, this neural network computes the piecewise linear curve consisting of the segments $y_1(x), \ldots, y_m(x)$.

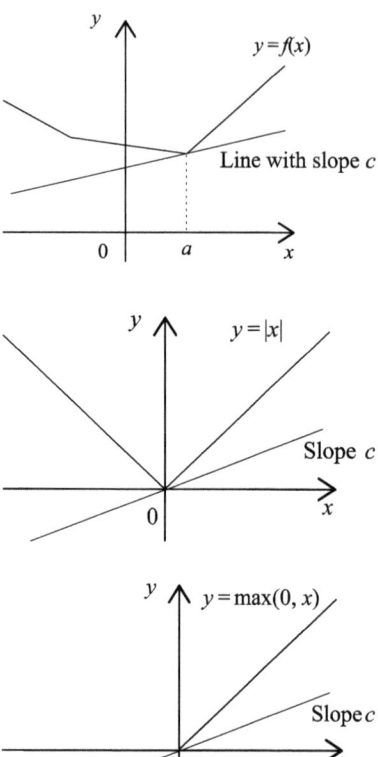

Fig. 2.22 Subdifferential. Generally, the subdifferential is represented by intervals, where the slopes denoted by c in the figure are elements of the subdifferential

Fig. 2.23 The subdifferential of the function $f(x) = |x|$ at $x = 0$ is the interval $[-1, 1]$, where the slopes denoted by c in the figure are elements of the subdifferential

Fig. 2.24 The subdifferential of the function $f(x) = \max(0, x)$ at $x = 0$ is the interval $[0, 1]$, where the slopes denoted by c in the figure are elements of the subdifferential

2.5.3 Subdifferential

The *subdifferential* of a convex function $f(x)$ at $x = a$ is defined as the set of c satisfying

$$f(x) \geq f(a) + c \cdot (x - a)$$

for $x = a$ (see Fig. 2.22). It is denoted as

$$\{c \in \mathbf{R} \mid f(x) \geq f(a) + c \cdot (x - a)\}.$$

Let us consider some examples. For the function $f(x) = |x|$, the subdifferential at $x = 0$ is the interval $[-1, 1]$ (see Fig. 2.23).

For $f(x) = \max(0, x)$, the subdifferential at $x = 0$ is the interval $[0, 1]$ (see Fig. 2.24).

Note that in optimization, points where the subdifferential of the objective function includes 0 are candidates for extreme values. This is evident from the definition of subdifferential or by observing the examples above.

Chapter 3
RNN: Recurrent Neural Network

3.1 Architecture and Computation of RNN

Sequential data such as financial data, audio data, and weather data cannot be handled by ordinary neural networks. While the number of units in the input and output layers of ordinary neural networks is fixed, sequential data varies in both input length and output length depending on the input. The *recurrent neural network* (*RNN*) [9, 23] is a neural network that processes sequential data, with several variants. While large-scale language models and generative language models based on Transformers are not directly related to RNNs, comparing them with RNN-based language models (RNN language models) highlights the distinguishing features of large-scale language models (and generative language models). In this chapter, with an understanding of RNN language models in mind, we explain the simplest form of RNN structure and the learning process of RNNs.

RNNs receive sequential data (typically sequences of vectors) $\mathbf{x}^1, \ldots, \mathbf{x}^T$ one at a time.[1] Figure 3.1 illustrates an RNN with scalar sequences as input and output, where both the input and output layers consist of a single unit, and there are two units in the hidden layer. From the input layer to the hidden layer, and from the hidden layer to the output layer, there are links similar to those in a standard neural network (dashed arrows in Fig. 3.1). Additionally, there are links between units in the hidden layer (solid arrows in Fig. 3.1). The activation of the output layer, $w_4 z^t + w_5 z'^t$ (and its output), follows the same pattern as a standard neural network. The activation of hidden unit 1, however, is $u^t = w_1 x^t + w_2 z^{t-1} + w_3 z'^{t-1}$, and its output is $z^t = f(u^t)$, where $w_2 z^{t-1} + w_3 z'^{t-1}$ represents the weighted sum of outputs from the previous time step's hidden units.

In the following, for simplicity, we represent the input layer, hidden layer, and output layer collectively as single rectangles, as shown in Fig. 3.2. Furthermore, we represent the links between layers as single arrows, as depicted in Fig. 3.3. In this

---

[1] In this section, we use superscripts as indices for sequences of random variables. When there are multiple sentences to distinguish them, we use subscript indices. Thus, we here use superscript indices for indexing the sequence.

Fig. 3.1 An example of a recurrent neural network. In this example, the input and output layers consist of a single unit each, and there are two units in the hidden layer

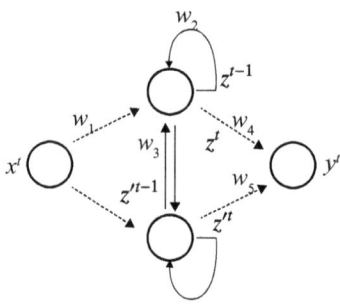

figure, $\mathbf{W}_x$, $\mathbf{W}_y$, and $\mathbf{W}_z$ are matrices where the (i, j) element represents the weight of the link from unit j to unit i. The outputs of the layers are depicted inside the rectangles.

In an RNN, one input (vector) is fed into the network at each time step. If we arrange the components of the RNN in a figure (vertically) in chronological order, we obtain the diagram illustrated in Fig. 3.4, which is the so-called time-unrolled representation of the RNN. Considering the time-unrolled RNN, the input sequences $\mathbf{x}^1, \ldots, \mathbf{x}^T$ are simultaneously fed into the input layer (bottom layer in the diagram), and the outputs are also produced simultaneously from the output layer (top layer in the diagram). The computations performed are as follows.

$$\mathbf{z}^0 = \mathbf{0}, \quad \text{Input to the hidden layer at time step 0,}$$
$$\mathbf{u}^t = \mathbf{W}_x \mathbf{x}^t + \mathbf{W}_z \mathbf{z}^{t-1}, \quad \text{Hidden layer activation,}$$
$$\mathbf{z}^t = \mathbf{f}(\mathbf{u}^t), \quad \text{Output of the hidden layer,}$$
$$\mathbf{y}^t = \mathbf{W}_y \mathbf{z}^t, \quad \text{Output of the output layer,}$$

Fig. 3.2 Simplified diagram of an RNN. The input layer, hidden layer, and output layer are represented as single rectangles

Fig. 3.3 Simplified diagram of an RNN. Links between layers are represented as single arrows

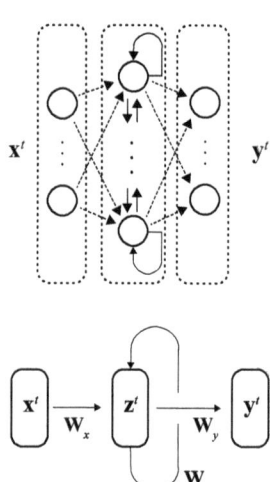

3.1 Architecture and Computation of RNN

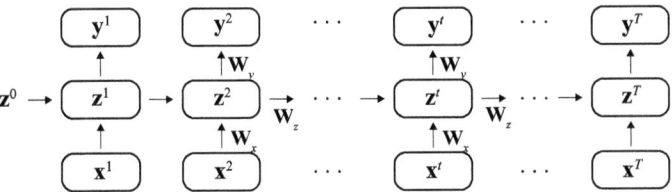

Fig. 3.4 Time-unrolled representation of an RNN

where biases are incorporated into $\mathbf{W}_x$ and $\mathbf{W}_y$, and $\mathbf{f}$ is the activation function of the hidden layer (which is assumed to be the identity function for the output layer). Note that weights (and biases) are shared in the time-unrolled network. That is, weights of links from the input layer to the hidden layer, weights of links between hidden layers, and weights of links from the hidden layer to the output layer are all shared across time steps, respectively.

The RNN architecture we have seen so far has only one hidden layer. We can extend this to a multi-layered hidden structure, which is illustrated in Fig. 3.5. Note that the figure represents the time-unrolled configuration. The multi-layered hidden structure enhances the expressive power of the model by increasing the number of basis functions. The computation for an RNN with K hidden layers is as follows:

$$\mathbf{z}_k^0 = \mathbf{0}, \quad \mathbf{z}_0^t = \mathbf{x}^t,$$ Input to the k-th hidden layer at time step 0,
$$\mathbf{u}_k^t = \mathbf{W}_z^{(k)} \mathbf{z}_{k-1}^t + \mathbf{W}_{zk} \mathbf{z}_k^{t-1},$$ Activation of the k-th hidden layer,
$$\mathbf{W}_z^{(1)} = \mathbf{W}_x,$$
$$\mathbf{z}_k^t = \mathbf{f}(\mathbf{u}_k^t),$$ Output of the k-th hidden layer,
$$\mathbf{y}^t = \mathbf{W}_y \mathbf{z}_K^t,$$ Output of the output layer.

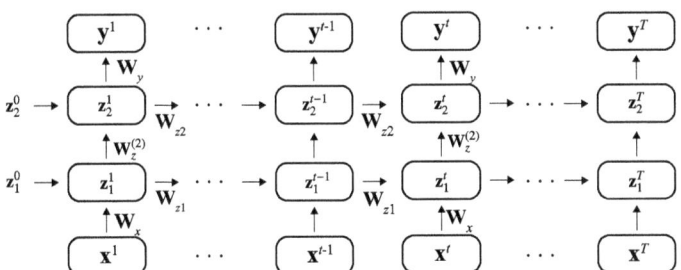

Fig. 3.5 Time-unrolled multi-layer RNN

In this setup, $\mathbf{W}_z^{(k)}$ denotes the weight matrix connecting the $(k-1)$-th and k-th hidden layers, for the k-th hidden layer, and $\mathbf{W}_{zk}$ denotes the weight matrix for the k-th hidden layer. The input to the first hidden layer at each time step t is the input $\mathbf{x}^t$, and the output of the last hidden layer $\mathbf{z}_K^t$ is fed into the output layer to produce the output $\mathbf{y}^t$.

In the training of RNNs (see the next section), the phenomenon of vanishing gradients occurs, where gradients become extremely close to zero for long sequences, halting the learning process. Specifically, in RNNs, typically, the hyperbolic tangent function is used as the activation function f for hidden layers, and its derivative satisfies $0 < f'(u) < 1$. Consequently, in the backpropagation of errors between hidden layers, as $t \to \infty$, the term δ_i^1 approaches zero, given by

$$f'(u_{\hat{i}}) \ldots f'(u_{i'}^t) f'(u_i^{t+1}) \to 0.$$

Note that even when using the ReLU function as the activation function f, it is not possible to completely prevent the vanishing gradients. Additionally, in some cases, gradient explosions can occur for long sequences.

3.2 Learning in RNNs

Several methods are known for learning in RNNs. In this section, we will explain one of them, *backpropagation through time* (BPTT) [51]. In RNN learning, the minimization of the error function also employs stochastic gradient descent. Thus, we need to compute the error for each unit. Backpropagation through time in RNNs is essentially the same as error backpropagation in conventional neural networks. That is, as illustrated in Fig. 3.6, considering an RNN unfolded in time, the error δ^t is propagated backward in time. We will now examine this process in detail.

Note, first, that in an RNN unfolded in time, as shown in Fig. 3.7, the weights (and biases) are shared. That is, for all $t = 1, \ldots, T$, the weights $\mathbf{W}_x$, $\mathbf{W}_y$, and $\mathbf{W}_z$ are shared.

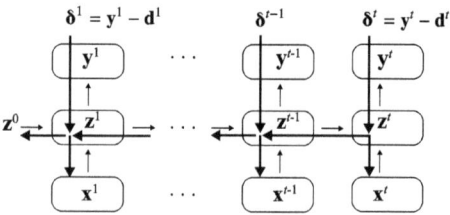

Fig. 3.6 Backpropagation through time (BPTT)

3.2 Learning in RNNs

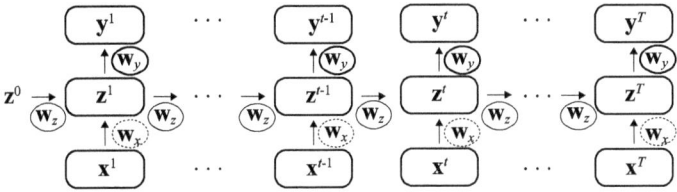

Fig. 3.7 Weight sharing (and bias sharing) in RNNs

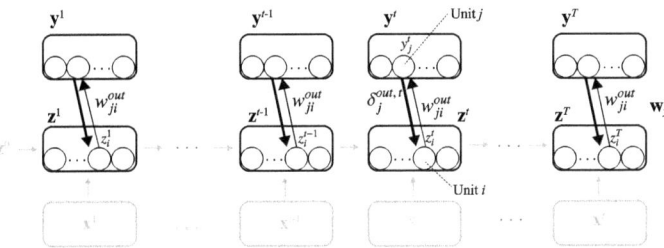

Fig. 3.8 Error propagation: from output layer to hidden layer

We start by computing the gradient of the output layer. As depicted in Fig. 3.8, at time t, let the error of output unit j be denoted by $\delta_j^{out,t}$, and let the output of hidden unit i be z_i^t. Since the weights w_{ji}^{out} between units i and j are shared across time steps, the gradient between the output layer and the hidden layer is the sum over time, given by

$$\frac{\partial E(\mathbf{w})}{\partial w_{ji}^{out}} = \sum_{t=1}^{T} \delta_j^{out,t} z_i^t.$$

Next, we determine the error of the hidden layer (see Fig. 3.9). At time t, the hidden unit i receives errors $\delta_{\hat{i}}^{t+1}$ from each unit $\hat{i}$ in the hidden layer at time $t+1$, and errors $\delta_j^{out,t}$ from each unit j in the output layer at time t (see Fig. 3.10). Taking this into account, according to the error propagation formula, the error of hidden unit i at time t is given by

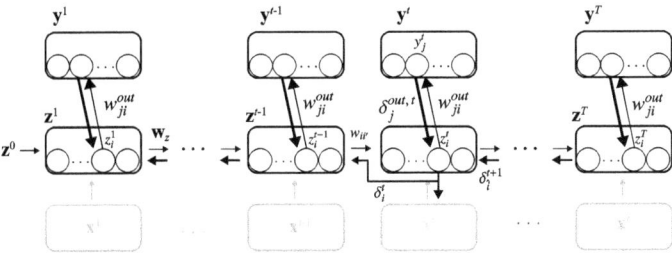

Fig. 3.9 Error propagation: within hidden layer

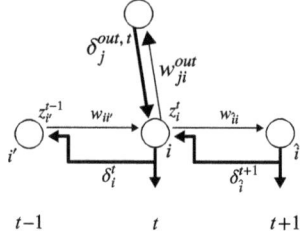

Fig. 3.10 Detailed error propagation: within hidden layer

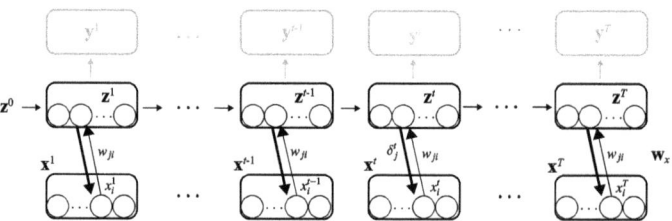

Fig. 3.11 Error propagation: from hidden layer to input layer

$$\delta_i^t = f'(u_i^t) \left(\sum_j w_{ji}^{out} \delta_j^{out,t} + \sum_{\hat{i}} w_{\hat{i}i} \delta_{\hat{i}}^{t+1} \right), \tag{3.2.1}$$

where u_i^t represents the activation of hidden unit i at time t, and f is its activation function. Using this equation, we can compute the errors sequentially from $t = T$ to $t = 1$. Note that $\delta_i^{T+1} = 0$. Thus, the gradient between hidden layers is

$$\frac{\partial E(\mathbf{w})}{\partial w_{ii'}} = \sum_{t=1}^{T} \delta_i^t z_{i'}^{t-1}.$$

Similarly, the gradient between the hidden layer and the input layer is computed as follows (as shown in Fig. 3.11). Let δ_j^t denote the error of hidden unit j at time t. Since the weights w_{ji} between input unit i and hidden unit j are shared across time steps, the gradient is again the sum over time, given by

$$\frac{\partial E(\mathbf{w})}{\partial w_{ji}} = \sum_{t=1}^{T} \delta_j^t x_i^t,$$

where the error δ_j^t is given by Eq. (3.2.1). With this, all gradients have been computed.

Chapter 4
Autoencoder

4.1 Overview of Autoencoders

An *autoencoder* (AE) is a type of artificial neural network used to learn efficient representations of data, typically for the purpose of dimensionality reduction or feature learning [15]. It consists of two main parts:

Encoder. This part compresses the input data into a smaller representation. It takes the input data and maps it to a lower-dimensional latent space. The encoder can be seen as a function $\mathbf{h} = \mathbf{f}(\mathbf{x})$, where $\mathbf{x}$ is the input data, and $\mathbf{h}$ is the latent space representation.

Decoder. This part reconstructs the data from the lower-dimensional representation back to its original form. It takes the compressed data and attempts to restore it to the original input data. The decoder can be seen as a function $\hat{\mathbf{x}} = \mathbf{g}(\mathbf{h})$, where $\hat{\mathbf{x}}$ is the reconstructed data.

The autoencoder is trained to minimize the difference between the input data and the reconstructed data. This difference is often measured using a loss function, such as mean squared error. Although there are several variants of autoencoders designed for specific purposes, we describe the most basic autoencoder.

4.2 Architecture of Autoencoders

We consider a 3-layer neural network shaped like an hourglass as shown in Fig. 4.1. Denoting the input represented at the input layer as $\mathbf{x}$, the output $\mathbf{z}$ of the middle (hidden) layer units can be expressed as

$$\mathbf{z} = \mathbf{f}_e(\mathbf{W}\mathbf{x} + \mathbf{b}),$$

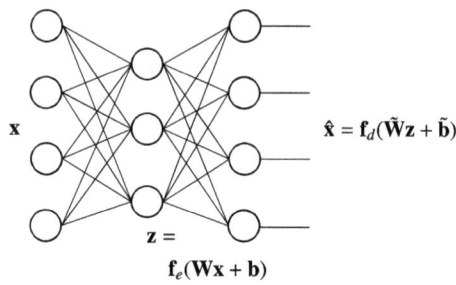

Fig. 4.1 Autoencoder. It has an hourglass shape, with a narrow middle. The output is trained to replicate the input

where $\mathbf{W}$ is a matrix whose (i, j)-th element represents the weight from input unit j to middle layer unit i, $\mathbf{b}$ is a vector concatenating biases for the middle layer units, and $\mathbf{f}_e(\mathbf{x})$ is a function whose value is a vector formed by concatenating the outputs $f_e(\mathbf{x})$ of the middle layer units. Similarly, the output of the output layer units, utilizing the output $\mathbf{z}$ of the middle layer units, is expressed as

$$\hat{\mathbf{x}} = \mathbf{f}_d(\tilde{\mathbf{W}}\mathbf{z} + \tilde{\mathbf{b}}),$$

where $\tilde{\mathbf{W}}$ is a matrix whose (i, j)-th element represents the weight from middle layer unit j to output layer unit i, $\tilde{\mathbf{b}}$ is a vector concatenating biases for the output layer units, and $\mathbf{f}_d(\mathbf{x})$ is a function whose value is a vector formed by concatenating the outputs $f_d(\mathbf{x})$ of the output layer units.

This hourglass-shaped neural network first converts the input $\mathbf{x}$ into $\mathbf{z}$, and then performs a transformation to bring $\mathbf{z}$ back into the same space as the input $\mathbf{x}$. Combining these two transformations, the transformation from input $\mathbf{x}$ to output $\hat{\mathbf{x}}$ can be written as

$$\hat{\mathbf{x}}(\mathbf{x}) = \mathbf{f}_d(\tilde{\mathbf{W}}\mathbf{f}_e(\mathbf{W}\mathbf{x} + \mathbf{b}) + \tilde{\mathbf{b}}).$$

The activation function $\mathbf{f}_e$ of the middle layer in the autoencoder can be any nonlinear function, but commonly, we use functions like the logistic sigmoid function. We choose the output function $\mathbf{f}_d$ of the output layer depending on the type of input to ensure that the input $\mathbf{x}$ becomes the output itself as described in the next section.

4.3 Training Autoencoders

In this type of neural network architecture, the weights are learned such that the output $\hat{\mathbf{x}}$ for input $\mathbf{x}$ closely resembles the original input $\mathbf{x}$. Considering the output $\mathbf{z}$ of the middle layer when $\mathbf{x}$ is input to the trained neural network, since the number of units in the middle layer is smaller than that of the input and output layers, the output of the middle layer serves as a compressed representation of the given input

4.3 Training Autoencoders

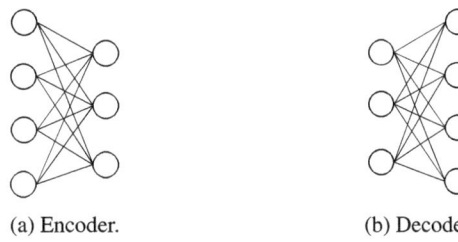

Fig. 4.2 Encoder and decoder realized by a 2-layer neural network

(a) Encoder. (b) Decoder.

information. Thus, **z** for input **x** is considered as the *code* of **x**, and the initial transformation $\mathbf{z} = \mathbf{f}_e(\mathbf{W}\mathbf{x} + \mathbf{b})$ is called *encoding*. Additionally, the latter transformation $\hat{\mathbf{x}} = \mathbf{f}_d(\tilde{\mathbf{W}}\mathbf{z} + \tilde{\mathbf{b}})$ is called *decoding*.

Generally, a neural network that encodes the input and then decodes it, aiming to faithfully reproduce the original input, is called an *autoencoder*. Furthermore, the neural network that performs encoding is called an *encoder*, while the one that performs decoding is called a *decoder*. In the autoencoder shown in Fig. 4.1, the half from the center to the input side constitutes the encoder (Fig. 4.2a), while the other half constitutes the decoder (Fig. 4.2b).

For weight learning, we select an appropriate error function based on the type of input to measure the similarity between **x** and $\hat{\mathbf{x}}$. Specifically, if the components of input **x** are real numbers, we choose the identity mapping as the activation function $\mathbf{f}_d$ and the squared error function as the error function:

$$E(\mathbf{w}) = \sum_{n=1}^{N} \|\mathbf{x}_n - \hat{\mathbf{x}}(\mathbf{x}_n)\|^2,$$

where **w** is a vector concatenating all the components of weights and biases in the neural network. Moreover, if the components of **x** are binary values (0 and 1), we use the logistic sigmoid function for $\mathbf{f}_d$ and the cross-entropy error function:

$$E(\mathbf{w}) = -\sum_{n=1}^{N}\sum_{i=1}^{D}\{x_i \ln \hat{x}_i(\mathbf{x}) + (1 - x_i)\ln(1 - \hat{x}_i(\mathbf{x}))\},$$

where D is the dimension of **x**, and x_i and $\hat{x}_i(\mathbf{x})$ represent the i-th component of **x** and $\hat{\mathbf{x}}(\mathbf{x})$, respectively. During the training of the autoencoder, the goal is to find the parameters **w** that minimize the above error function. Since there are no explicit target labels in the training data, this learning process is considered *unsupervised learning*.

4.4 Properties of Autoencoders

In autoencoders, we focus on the weights and biases of the middle layer of the neural network after training, particularly because these parameters are referred to as *features* that represent the data. The computation of the output **z** of the units in the middle layer involves the multiplication of the matrix **W** and **x**, where this product comprises the calculation of the dot product between each row vector of **W** and **x**. In other words, this calculation extracts the components of **x** along the directions of each row vector of **W**.

The purpose of an autoencoder is to learn such features, thereby obtaining a compressed representation **z** of the input **x**. In autoencoders, due to the smaller number of units in the middle layer, there may be information that cannot be represented, which could be represented at the input layer. In some cases, for example, for input **x** containing noise, it is possible to obtain a representation **z** with the noise removed. Thus, in tasks such as classification using classifiers like support vector machines or 3-layer perceptrons, it may improve performance to use **z** for learning rather than using **x** as input.

The autoencoders introduced in this section consist of encoder and decoder, each implemented with a 2-layer neural network. As an extension, we can consider autoencoders with both encoder and decoder consisting of more layers. Generally, learning in multi-layer neural networks can be challenging due to issues such as the vanishing gradient problem, where gradients approach zero during training. Similarly, when training multi-layer autoencoders, similar problems arise. To address these issues, skip connections are introduced between layers at the same level of the encoder and decoder. Methods such as greedy layer-wise pre-training or training with neural networks initialized using greedy layer-wise pre-training have been devised. These methods aim to mitigate the challenges associated with learning in multi-layer architectures.

Chapter 5
Word Embedding

5.1 Vector Representations of Words

Word embedding (also known as *word vector representation*) is a technique where words are represented as vectors in real vector space, as shown in Fig. 5.1. This representation transforms natural language processing, which has been traditionally studied and developed as symbolic processing, into a domain handled by neural networks.

Neural networks are also employed to convert symbolic words into real vectors, a transformation achieved through learning from extensive corpora (databases of text). This process represents a prominent example of *representation learning*.

One of the crucial properties of word embedding is that semantically similar words tend to be positioned close to each other in the embedding space (see Fig. 5.2). Another important property is the ability to perform operations with vectors. Operations with vectors are feasible, which is also significant.[1] For instance, in Fig. 5.2, if we denote $v(w)$ as the embedding of word w, then

$$v(\texttt{queen}) - v(\texttt{king}) \approx v(\texttt{woman}) - v(\texttt{man})$$

holds true, where both sides represent vectors interpreted as "`female`" from the perspective of "`male`." Consequently,

$$v(\texttt{queen}) \approx v(\texttt{king}) + (v(\texttt{woman}) - v(\texttt{man}))$$

---

[1] Operations with embeddings (vectors) are carried out after normalizing (with norm 1) all embeddings involved. Generally, embeddings obtained through learning, as described later, are not normalized.

Fig. 5.1 Example of word embedding

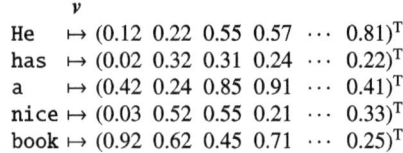

Fig. 5.2 Word embeddings in embedding space. Embeddings of semantically similar words are positioned close to each other in the embedding space

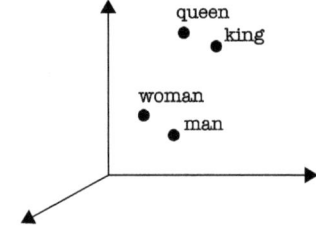

also holds. Similarly,

$$v(\text{France}) - v(\text{Italy}) \approx v(\text{Paris}) - v(\text{Rome}),$$
$$v(\text{France}) + v(\text{Capital}) \approx v(\text{Paris})$$

approximately hold. These relationships suggest that embeddings capture the meaning of words. Figure 5.3 provides a more intuitive image of the meanings captured by embeddings, with a few more words included.

As mentioned earlier, word embedding is obtained through representation learning. In representation learning for words, the fundamental concept is the *distributional hypothesis*. This hypothesis suggests that the meaning of a word is determined by the surrounding words (context) in a sentence or text (see Fig. 5.4). In word representation learning, the architecture and learning strategies of the network are based on this distributional hypothesis.

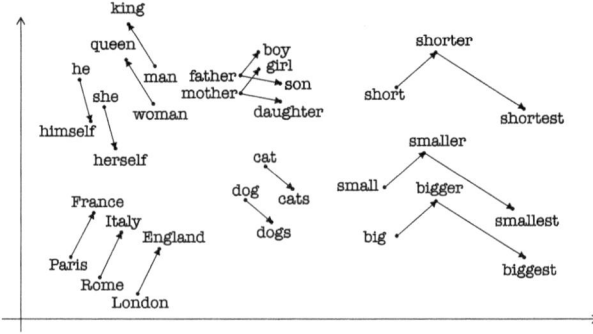

Fig. 5.3 Image: word embeddings

Fig. 5.4 Distributional hypothesis of words

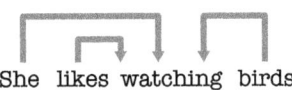

In the following sections, we will explain Word2Vec, which was one of the earliest methods to achieve word embedding through learning.

5.2 Word2Vec

Word2Vec [26] is a method based on the distributional hypothesis that utilizes context information to compress high-dimensional one-hot vectors of words into low-dimensional vectors in an embedding space. Word2Vec achieves this dimensionality reduction through learning from extensive corpora (text data). The learning process in Word2Vec roughly follows the framework of an encoder and a decoder. While a typical encoder and decoder aim to compress and reconstruct information so that the output of the decoder resembles the input to the encoder, Word2Vec utilizes contextual information, i.e., surrounding words, to compress information. We describe the details of it below.

Consider a word s that is represented in a one-hot encoding $\mathbf{x}_s$ and denote the embedding of s by $\mathbf{v}_s$. Then, in Word2Vec, we obtain $\mathbf{v}_s$ by multiplying $\mathbf{x}_s$ with a *embedding matrix* $\mathbf{W}$ as follows:

$$\mathbf{v}_s^\mathrm{T} = \mathbf{x}_s^\mathrm{T} \mathbf{W}.$$

That is, if the k-th component of the one-hot encoding $\mathbf{x}_s$ is 1, then the k-th row of $\mathbf{W}$ becomes $\mathbf{v}_s^\mathrm{T}$. For example,

$$(0\ 0\ 1\ 0\ \cdots\ 0) \begin{pmatrix} 0.12 & 0.22 & 0.55 & \cdots & 0.81 \\ 0.02 & 0.32 & 0.31 & \cdots & 0.22 \\ 0.42 & 0.24 & 0.85 & \cdots & 0.41 \\ 0.33 & 0.12 & 0.86 & \cdots & 0.89 \\ & & \vdots & & \\ 0.92 & 0.62 & 0.45 & \cdots & 0.25 \end{pmatrix} = (0.42\ 0.24\ 0.85\ \cdots\ 0.41).$$

Assuming there are V words in total, denoted as $s_1, s_2, \ldots, s_V$, the embedding matrix $\mathbf{W}$ is

$$\mathbf{W} = \begin{pmatrix} \mathbf{v}_{s_1}^\mathrm{T} \\ \mathbf{v}_{s_2}^\mathrm{T} \\ \vdots \\ \mathbf{v}_{s_V}^\mathrm{T} \end{pmatrix}.$$

The computation described in Word2Vec is realized by a neural network with an embedding layer directly linked to the input layer. The (k, i) element of the embedding matrix $\mathbf{W}$ represents the weight of the link connecting the k-th unit of the input layer to the i-th unit of the hidden layer. As we will explain shortly, the embedding matrix is determined by learning from data.

5.3 Learning in Word2Vec

Word2Vec offers two learning models: Continuous Bag-Of-Words (CBOW) and Skip-gram. We start by explaining CBOW.

5.3.1 CBOW

CBOW (Continuous Bag-Of-Words) aims to predict (guess) a word s_i based on the context vector $\mathbf{v}_c$ created from the one-hot representations $\mathbf{x}_{-m}, \ldots, \mathbf{x}_{-2}, \mathbf{x}_{-1}, \mathbf{x}_{+1}, \mathbf{x}_{+2}, \ldots, \mathbf{x}_{+n}$ of the words $s_{-m}, \ldots, s_{-2}, s_{-1}, s_{+1}, s_{+2}, \ldots, s_{+n}$ that appear before and after s in the sentence

$$s_{-M}, s_{-M+1}, \ldots, s_{-2}, s_{-1}, s, s_{+1}, s_{+2}, \ldots, s_{+N}.$$

In CBOW, the order of appearance of words in the context (preceding and following consecutive words) is disregarded. Hence, it is termed "Continuous Bag-Of-Words" in the field of natural language processing, where "bag" is akin to the mathematical concept of a "set."

For example, in the sentence "I have a habit of drinking tea at noon," we predict the word "tea" by considering the two words before and after it:

$$\boxed{\text{of}}\ \boxed{\text{drinking}}\ \boxed{X}\ \boxed{\text{at}}\ \boxed{\text{noon}},$$

where we refer to the target word "tea" as X. We will use two types of embeddings for each word s: $\mathbf{v}$ and $\mathbf{v}'$. The typical embedding for s will be denoted by $\mathbf{v}$, while $\mathbf{v}'$ will represent a vector for "reconstruction" called the *context vector*. We explain the detail of learning by considering two words before and after the target word, similar to this example. Let $\mathbf{v}_{-2}, \mathbf{v}_{-1}, \mathbf{v}_{+1}, \mathbf{v}_{+2}$ denote the embeddings of the words $s_{-2}, s_{-1}, s_{+1}, s_{+2}$, respectively. We calculate their average

$$\mathbf{v}_c = \frac{1}{4}(\mathbf{v}_{-2} + \mathbf{v}_{-1} + \mathbf{v}_{+1} + \mathbf{v}_{+2}).$$

Using $\mathbf{v}_c$ and the context vector $\mathbf{v}'$, we define the probability of the occurrence of s conditioned on the two words before and after it as follows:

5.3 Learning in Word2Vec

$$P(s \mid s_{-2}, s_{-1}, s_{+1}, s_{+2}) \equiv \frac{\exp \mathbf{v}_c^T \mathbf{v}'}{\sum_{i=1}^{V} \exp \mathbf{v}_c^T \mathbf{v}'_i},$$

where $\mathbf{v}'_i$ represents the context vector of the i-th word in the sequence of all words, and V is the total number of words.

In CBOW, the embedding representations are determined such that the conditional probability of occurrence, conditioned on the context, is maximized for every word appearing in the corpus. In other words, the embeddings are chosen to maximize the similarity between the context vector $\mathbf{v}'$ and the average vector $\mathbf{v}_c$. This ensures that in the embedding space, the representations of words that have similar meanings (i.e., appear in similar contexts) are close to each other. For instance, the words "`tea`" and "`coffee`" often appear in similar contexts, such as in sentences like "`He drinks a cup of tea every morning`" or "`He drinks a cup of coffee every morning.`" In these sentences, the context vectors for "`tea`" and "`coffee`" are likely to be similar, which reflects their semantic similarity in the embedding space.

Figure 5.5 illustrates the implementation of a CBOW neural network that predicts from two words before and after a given word.

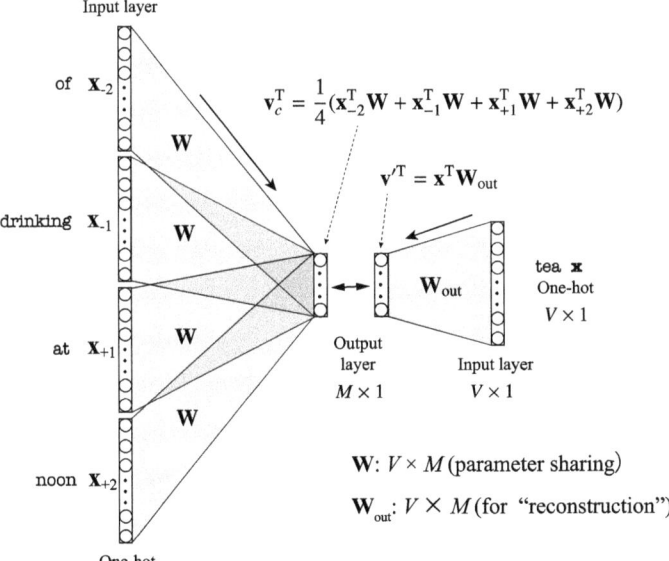

Fig. 5.5 CBOW. Illustration of a neural network implementing CBOW, which predicts a single word from its surrounding two words each. Comparison is made between the actual occurrences in the corpus and the probabilities (word occurrences) output by CBOW, and weights (embedding matrix and "reconstruction" matrix) are learned to minimize loss

The neural network implementing CBOW consists of two layers: an encoder and a decoder. The encoder, with its weight matrix denoted as $\mathbf{W}$, transforms the one-hot representations $\mathbf{x}_i$ of several words s_i surrounding a word s into their respective embeddings $\mathbf{v}_i$, and outputs their average $\mathbf{v}_c$. The decoder "recovers" the one-hot representation $\mathbf{x}$ of word s from its context vector $\mathbf{v}'$. In practice, $\mathbf{v}'$ is derived from $\mathbf{x}$ by computing $\mathbf{v}'^T = \mathbf{x}^T \mathbf{W}_{\text{out}}$, where $\mathbf{W}_{\text{out}}$ is the weight matrix.

To achieve the most accurate predictions possible, learning in CBOW involves finding the weights (embedding matrix and reconstruction matrix) of the neural network that minimize the negative log-likelihood. Specifically, in the case of predicting from two words before and after (context size equals four), if we denote the sequence of words in the corpus as $s_{-1}, s_0, s_1, \ldots, s_T, s_{T+1}, s_{T+2}$, then the loss function to minimize is

$$L = -\frac{1}{T} \sum_{t=1}^{T} \ln P(s_t \mid s_{t-2}, s_{t-1}, s_{t+1}, s_{t+2}).$$

This involves finding $\mathbf{W}$ and $\mathbf{W}_{\text{out}}$ that minimize this loss function.

5.3.2 Skip-Gram

Next, we explain Skip-gram. Skip-gram is a model that predicts surrounding words $s_{-m}, \ldots, s_{-2}, s_{-1}, s, s_{+1}, s_{+2}, \ldots, s_{+n}$ within a sentence

$$s_{-M}, s_{-M+1}, \ldots, s_{-2}, s_{-1}, s, s_{+1}, s_{+2}, \ldots, s_{+N}$$

from the one-hot representation $\mathbf{x}_s$ of the word s. In the example sentence mentioned above, "I have a habit of drinking tea at noon," the words surrounding "tea," excluding two words before and after, are "of," "drinking," "at," and "noon," and the model predicts them from "tea."

Skip-gram introduces two types of embedding representations, $\mathbf{v}$ and $\mathbf{v}'$, for a word s, similar to CBOW. The typical embedding for word s is denoted by $\mathbf{v}$, while $\mathbf{v}'$ represents the context vector. Let $\mathbf{v}$ be the embedding for word s, and let $\mathbf{v}'_{-2}, \mathbf{v}'_{-1}, \mathbf{v}'_{+1}, \mathbf{v}'_{+2}$ be the context vectors for the preceding and following words $s_{-2}, s_{-1}, s_{+1}, s_{+2}$, respectively, conditioned on the word s. We define the joint probability of two preceding and two following words conditioned on the word s as follows:

$$P(s_{-2}, s_{-1}, s_{+1}, s_{+2} \mid s) \equiv \frac{(\exp \mathbf{v}^T \mathbf{v}'_{-2})(\exp \mathbf{v}^T \mathbf{v}'_{-1})(\exp \mathbf{v}^T \mathbf{v}'_{+1})(\exp \mathbf{v}^T \mathbf{v}'_{+2})}{(\sum_{i=1}^{V} \exp \mathbf{v}^T \mathbf{v}'_i)^4}.$$

For each word appearing in the corpus, Skip-gram determines the embedding representation such that the joint probability of the context words conditioned on the word is maximized.

5.3 Learning in Word2Vec

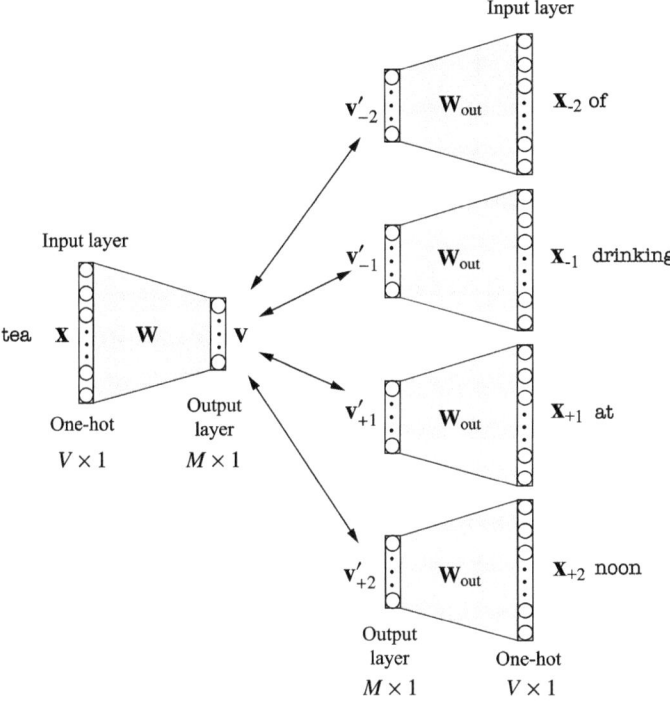

Fig. 5.6 Skip-gram. This illustrates an example of predicting two preceding and two following words of a single word from its embedding. The correctness in the corpus is compared with the probabilities of occurrence output by Skip-gram, and the weights (embedding matrix and "reconstruction" matrix) are learned to minimize loss

The neural network that implements Skip-gram, as shown in Fig. 5.6, consists of a decoder for each word forming the context and a single encoder, both of which are 2-layer neural networks. The encoder, with weight matrix $\mathbf{W}$, computes the embedding from the one-hot representation $\mathbf{x}$ of the word s as $\mathbf{v}^T = \mathbf{x}^T \mathbf{W}$. The decoder "reconstructs" the one-hot representations $\mathbf{x}_i$ of some preceding and following words s_i from their context vectors $\mathbf{v}'_i$. In practice, this is done by computing $\mathbf{v}'^T_i = \mathbf{x}^T_i \mathbf{W}_{\text{out}}$ in the reverse direction, where $\mathbf{W}_{\text{out}}$ is a weight matrix.

In Skip-gram, the weight matrices are determined by learning to make predictions as accurate as possible. Specifically, we aim to minimize the loss (when predicting two preceding and two following words), given by

$$L = -\frac{1}{T}\sum_{t=1}^{T}\{\ln P(s_{t-2}|s_t) + \ln P(s_{t-1}|s_t) + \ln P(s_{t+1}|s_t) + \ln P(s_{t+2}|s_t)\},$$

where we seek $\mathbf{W}$ and $\mathbf{W}_{\text{out}}$ that minimize this loss. In Skip-gram, weight sharing in the decoder and the independence assumption of the joint probabilities of preceding and following words correspond to the bag-of-words model, where the order of words is ignored. Moreover, keeping the weights of the decoder separate from those of the encoder contributes to enhancing expressiveness.

5.3.3 Negative Sampling

Both CBOW and Skip-gram require a normalization constant in the denominator of the loss function, given by $\sum_{i=1}^{V} \exp \mathbf{v}^T \mathbf{v}'_i$, which involves computing the sum of all words in the corpus. Since this value varies for each word in the corpus, it is impractical to compute it every time. Thus, an approximation called *negative sampling* is employed. In the following, we discuss its application in the context of Skip-gram.

First, we use the logistic sigmoid function to probabilize the similarity (dot product) in such a way that the probability of the correct word is high, while the probability of other words is low, approximating the loss. However, since there are a vast number of words apart from the correct ones, we represent them as an expectation over the distribution of all words. For simplicity, we write down the approximate loss for predicting the surrounding words of a single word s:

$$\begin{aligned} L &\approx -\sum_{\mathbf{v}' \in V'} \ln \sigma(\mathbf{v}^T \mathbf{v}') - \mathbb{E}_{\mathbf{v}' \sim p(\mathbf{v}')}[\ln(1 - \sigma(\mathbf{v}^T \mathbf{v}'))] \\ &= -\sum_{\mathbf{v}' \in V'} \ln \sigma(\mathbf{v}^T \mathbf{v}') - \mathbb{E}_{\mathbf{v}' \sim p(\mathbf{v}')}[\ln(\sigma(-\mathbf{v}^T \mathbf{v}'))], \end{aligned}$$

where V' is the set of some surrounding context words of the word s, and $p(\mathbf{v})$ is the distribution of word embeddings. Note that we used $1 - \sigma(x) = \sigma(-x)$. Furthermore, we replace the term of expectation with K samples $\mathbf{v}'_k$ from the distribution $p(\mathbf{v})$:

$$L \approx -\sum_{\mathbf{v}' \in V'} \ln \sigma(\mathbf{v}^T \mathbf{v}') - \frac{1}{K} \sum_{k=1}^{K} \ln \sigma(-\mathbf{v}^T \mathbf{v}'_k).$$

The number of samples K depends on the size of the corpus, typically ranging from 2 to 5 for large corpora and from 5 to 20 for small corpora.

The critical point here is the distribution $p(\mathbf{v})$. While various distributions could be considered, Word2Vec employs the word occurrence frequency $c(s)$ in the training corpus. Specifically, the formula

$$p(\mathbf{v}) = \frac{c(s)^{\frac{3}{4}}}{\sum_{s' \in V} c(s')^{\frac{3}{4}}}$$

Fig. 5.7 Using the encoder, embeddings for words can be obtained from their one-hot representations

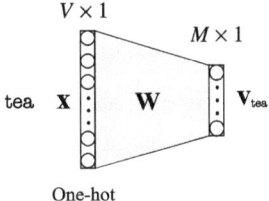

is used. By raising the occurrence frequency to the power of 3/4, relatively high-frequency words such as articles like "a" or "the" are less likely to be chosen, while low-frequency words, which are often crucial for prediction, are more likely to be selected.

In the original loss minimization, we are solving a multi-class classification problem where each word is treated as a separate class. Thus, the softmax function is used, and the calculation of its normalization constant is required. In contrast, in loss minimization with negative sampling, we treat it as a binary classification problem: the correct word versus all other words. We apply logistic regression in this case.

5.4 Obtaining Embeddings

Once trained with CBOW or Skip-gram, we can use the trained encoder to obtain embeddings for words represented in one-hot encoding (see Fig. 5.7).

Note that in Word2Vec training, we do not need for labeling the corpus. Thus, vast corpora, such as web pages, can be easily used. One drawback of Word2Vec embeddings is that they may assign a single vector even to polysemous words. For example, the word "bat" in the sentences "He swung the bat and hit a home run" (noun meaning a piece of sports equipment used in baseball) and "The bat flew silently through the night sky" (noun meaning a flying mammal) would receive the same embedding despite having different meanings.

Chapter 6
Transformer

Fully connected neural networks and CNNs (convolutional neural networks) struggle with capturing relationships between spatially distant elements in inputs, such as determining the identity of objects far apart in a single image. Similarly, RNNs dealing with time-series data find it challenging to capture relationships between input elements that are temporally distant. To address the difficulty of capturing relationships between distant input elements, an attention mechanism was initially introduced in language models based on RNNs to extract relationships between words located at distant positions.

The Transformer [46] is a deep neural network that incorporates attention mechanisms. In terms of neural networks, it can be used in various ways through learning. What distinguishes the Transformer is its utilization of attention mechanisms, which represent relationships between distant components in input data such as sequential data or image data as vectors, actively leveraging them. The Transformer adopts unsupervised learning strategies for tasks like prediction and interpolation on unlabeled data and achieves high accuracy in tasks such as language generation, translation, and image classification by further conducting task-specific learning. The Transformer has become an indispensable component of large-scale language models, serving as a fundamental network mechanism.

6.1 Attention

The primary components that govern the taste of coffee are known to be chlorogenic acid (acidity), caffeine (bitterness), tannin (astringency), and sugar (sweetness). We here assume that the composition of these components varies for each type of coffee bean. In other words, each type of bean contains chlorogenic acid, caffeine, tannin, and sugar in proportions specific to the bean variety, which can be represented as a 4-dimensional vector.

Let us say there was a coffee bean, labeled as Q, which you previously enjoyed but were not sure about its origin. You brought back the beans and had them analyzed, revealing its composition to be $\mathbf{q}$ (a 4-dimensional vector). Currently, you have five types of coffee beans: Mocha, Brazil, Mandheling, Kilimanjaro, and Guatemala, each with compositions $\mathbf{z}_1$, $\mathbf{z}_2$, $\mathbf{z}_3$, $\mathbf{z}_4$, and $\mathbf{z}_5$, respectively (each a 4-dimensional vector). Now, you want to create a new blend from these five types of coffee beans, taking into account the similarity of taste between type Q and each of these five types.

In the attention mechanism, we define the similarity between the normative coffee bean Q's component vector $\mathbf{q}$ and the component vector $\mathbf{z}_i$ of the coffee beans at hand as their inner product $\mathbf{q}^T \mathbf{z}_i$. Then, we normalize these inner products and use the normalized inner products as the blending ratios to mix the five types of beans and create a new blend.

More generally, consider that there are N types of coffee beans available, each represented by a vector expressing its composition: $\mathbf{z}_1, \mathbf{z}_2, \ldots, \mathbf{z}_N$. We refer to the collection of these vectors as the "source" and denote it as $\mathbf{Z} = (\mathbf{z}_1\ \mathbf{z}_2\ \cdots\ \mathbf{z}_N)^T$, represented as a matrix (or its transpose). Additionally, we denote the component vector of a particular type of coffee bean (the normative bean) as $\mathbf{q}$, which we call the "target." We aim to create a new blend from the N types of source beans, considering their similarity to the target bean. For this blending process, we first compute what we call "relatedness vectors" as follows:

$$\mathbf{r}^T = \mathbf{q}^T \mathbf{Z}^T = \left(\mathbf{q}^T \mathbf{z}_1\ \mathbf{q}^T \mathbf{z}_2\ \cdots\ \mathbf{q}^T \mathbf{z}_N \right).$$

Note that when there is no ambiguity, we may also refer to the vector $\mathbf{z}_i$ as a "source."

Here, we introduce the softmax function with temperature scaling, which adds temperature scaling to the softmax function

$$\sigma_T(\mathbf{x}) \equiv \sigma(\mathbf{x}/T) = \text{softmax}(\mathbf{x}/T)$$

$$= \left(\frac{\exp(x_1/T)}{\sum_{j=1}^{K} \exp(x_j/T)}\ \frac{\exp(x_2/T)}{\sum_{j=1}^{K} \exp(x_j/T)}\ \cdots\ \frac{\exp(x_K/T)}{\sum_{j=1}^{K} \exp(x_j/T)} \right)^T.$$

This function divides the input components by the hyperparameter T. The temperature T controls the emphasis on the maximum component when it is small and smooths out the output when it is large (see Fig. 6.1). In the following discussion in this chapter, $\sigma(\mathbf{x}^T)$ and $\sigma_T(\mathbf{x}^T)$ are considered as row vectors.

Now, considering the relatedness vector

$$\mathbf{r}^T = \left(\mathbf{q}^T \mathbf{z}_1\ \mathbf{q}^T \mathbf{z}_2\ \cdots\ \mathbf{q}^T \mathbf{z}_N \right)$$

6.1 Attention

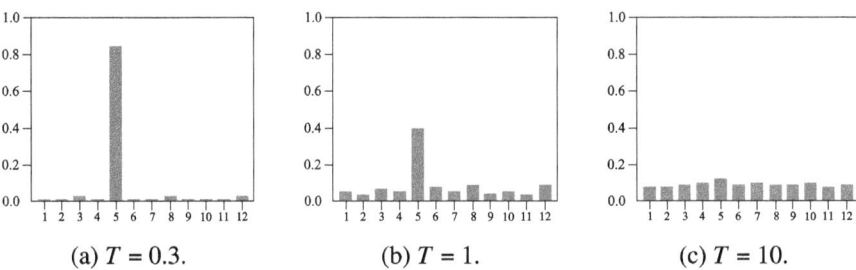

Fig. 6.1 Softmax function with temperature scaling. The parameter T represents "temperature"

passed through the softmax function with temperature scaling, we have the normalized vector

$$(a_1 \cdots a_N) = \sigma_T(\mathbf{r}^T) = \sigma_T\left((\mathbf{q}^T\mathbf{z}_1 \; \mathbf{q}^T\mathbf{z}_2 \; \cdots \; \mathbf{q}^T\mathbf{z}_N)\right)$$
$$= \sigma\left((\mathbf{q}^T\mathbf{z}_1/T \; \mathbf{q}^T\mathbf{z}_2/T \; \cdots \; \mathbf{q}^T\mathbf{z}_N/T)\right).$$

In this case, by choosing the value of temperature T, we can emphasize the source beans that are most similar (have large inner products) to $\mathbf{q}$, or conversely, each source bean can be equally considered.

Furthermore, taking a_i as weights, we compute the weighted average of the sources. That is, starting from the normalized (probabilized)

$$(a_1 \cdots a_N) = \sigma\left((\mathbf{q}^T\mathbf{z}_1/T \; \mathbf{q}^T\mathbf{z}_2/T \; \cdots \; \mathbf{q}^T\mathbf{z}_N/T)\right),$$

we take the weighted sum of the source vectors using these weights and obtain

$$\mathbf{c} = \sum_{i=1}^{N} a_i \mathbf{z}_i.$$

This represents the desired composition of the newly created blend.

Building upon the example provided, we formally define an attention mechanism. Suppose we want to express the degree of relevance of $\mathbf{z}_1, \cdots, \mathbf{z}_N$ to a target $\mathbf{q}$. We call $\mathbf{q} \in \mathbf{R}^D$ the *target* (or *query*), and $\mathbf{Z} = (\mathbf{z}_1 \cdots \mathbf{z}_N)^T$, $\mathbf{z}_i \in \mathbf{R}^D$, the *sources*. The magnitude of the relationship between the target $\mathbf{q}$ and the sources $\mathbf{Z}$ is represented by a single vector (attention). We refer to the following steps as an *attention mechanism* [3, 24].[1]

1. Extract the magnitude of the relationship (relevance) between the target $\mathbf{q}$ and the sources $\mathbf{Z}$:

$$\mathbf{r}^T = (r_1 \cdots r_N), \quad r_i = r(\mathbf{q}, \mathbf{z}_i),$$

---

[1] Reference [3] does not explicitly use the term "attention."

where $r(\mathbf{q}, \mathbf{z}_i)$ represents a function expressing the relationship between $\mathbf{q}$ and $\mathbf{z}_i$.
2. Normalize (probabilize) the relevance:

$$(a_1 \cdots a_N) = \sigma(\mathbf{r}^T) = \sigma((r_1 \cdots r_N)),$$

where the temperature parameter is embedded in the function r, and a typical softmax function is used.
3. Aggregate the information of the sources $\mathbf{Z}$ into a single vector based on their relevance to the target $\mathbf{q}$:

$$\mathbf{c}^T = \sum_{i=1}^{N} a_i \mathbf{z}_i^T.$$

We call this vector $\mathbf{c}$ the *attention*[2] for $\mathbf{Z}$ with respect to $\mathbf{q}$. Additionally, we refer to $\mathbf{r}$ as the *relatedness vector* for $\mathbf{Z}$ with respect to $\mathbf{q}$.

We can view the attention $\mathbf{c}$ as a reconstruction of the target $\mathbf{q}$ using a set of sources $\mathbf{z}_1, \ldots, \mathbf{z}_M$, taking into account their relevance (similarity). Conversely, we can also see $\mathbf{c}$ as a vector that compresses the information of the set of sources $\mathbf{z}_1, \ldots, \mathbf{z}_M$ based on their relevance (similarity) to the target $\mathbf{q}$.

In neural networks, attention mechanisms, especially self-attention mechanisms as will be discussed later, typically represent relationships between parts of the input (targets) and "distant" parts (sources) using attention vectors. For example, in images, self-attention might be used to relate one part of the image to another, or in language, self-attention could relate one word to the rest of the words in a sentence. Attention mechanisms are not limited to relationships between input elements; they can also be used to extract relationships between the information represented by a particular unit (target) and the information represented by a group of units (sources). We can utilize attention vectors representing relationships as additional information for tasks such as classification or data generation, serving as reinforcement to other information.

Furthermore, the attention obtained from the function representing relevance can vary. The inner product used in the example of coffee bean blending is a representative example of such a function

$$r(\mathbf{z}, \mathbf{q}) = \frac{\mathbf{z}^T \mathbf{q}}{\sqrt{D}},$$

where D is the dimension of the vectors $\mathbf{q}$ and $\mathbf{z}$. In this function, $\sqrt{D}$ acts as a temperature parameter for the temperature-scaled softmax function, easing the polarization of the softmax function's output to 0 and 1. Attention using the inner product as the function representing relevance is called *dot product attention*. Another

---

[2] The term "attention" often refers to the attention mechanism, thus calling the vector $\mathbf{c}$ attention might not be conventional. To eliminate ambiguity, in this book, we distinguish between attention mechanism and attention, and we refer to the vector $\mathbf{c}$ as attention.

function representing relevance, which enhances the representational power of the inner product using a weight matrix $\mathbf{W}$ ($D \times D$), is given by

$$r(\mathbf{z}, \mathbf{q}) = \frac{\mathbf{z}^T \mathbf{W} \mathbf{q}}{\sqrt{D}},$$

where $\mathbf{W}$ is determined during learning along with the network's weights. This attention mechanism is called *multiplicative attention*. Moreover, attention using the function

$$r(\mathbf{z}, \mathbf{q}) = \text{ReLU}\left(\mathbf{w}^T \begin{pmatrix} \mathbf{z} \\ \mathbf{q} \end{pmatrix}\right)$$

is called *additive attention*. Here, $\mathbf{w}$ is a 2-dimensional vector determined during learning along with the network's weights. All of the aforementioned functions representing relevance are defined based on the components (contents) of vectors. Thus, we refer attention using these functions as *content-based attention*.

In addition to content-based attention, we use *position-based attention*. Instead of using $\mathbf{z}$, position-based attention uses only $\mathbf{q}$ to compute the normalized relevance vector as

$$(a_1 \cdots a_N) = \sigma(\mathbf{W}\mathbf{q}),$$

where $\mathbf{W}$ is a matrix of size $N \times D$, also determined during learning along with the network's weights.

In a neural network, to incorporate attention, such as with dot product attention, we cannot realize simply as a linear combination of weights and unit outputs. Instead, we need a mechanism to compute the inner product between the outputs of units representing the target and the units representing the source.

Now, to increase the expressive power of attention, we will extend the attention mechanism in several steps, leading to the introduction of the Transformer. First, we allow the sources to be represented as pairs of keys and values. That is, we represent the target as $\mathbf{q} \in \mathbf{R}^D$, and the sources are split into matrices of *keys* and *values*:

keys: a matrix $\mathbf{K} = (\mathbf{k}_1 \cdots \mathbf{k}_N)^T$, where $\mathbf{k}_i \in \mathbf{R}^D$,
values: a matrix $\mathbf{V} = (\mathbf{v}_1 \cdots \mathbf{v}_N)^T$, where $\mathbf{v}_i \in \mathbf{R}^D$.

Here, each key $\mathbf{k}_i$ is associated with a value $\mathbf{v}_i$. In this case, the relationship between the target and each key is represented by the relatedness vector

$$\mathbf{r}^T = (r_1 \cdots r_N), \quad r_i = r(\mathbf{q}, \mathbf{k}_i).$$

Furthermore, we normalize the relatedness vector to obtain

$$(a_1 \cdots a_N) = \sigma(\mathbf{r}^T) = \sigma((r_1 \cdots r_N)).$$

Then, we compute the attention **c** by weighting the values corresponding to the keys with the normalized relatedness vector components and taking the sum. That is,

$$\mathbf{c}^T = \sum_{i=1}^{N} a_i \mathbf{v}_i^T.$$

By representing the sources as pairs of keys and values, we increase the expressive power of attention. Additionally, splitting the sources into keys and values is important for the proper functioning of the self-attention mechanism to be introduced later. Hereafter, for simplicity when no confusion arises, we refer to the matrix $\mathbf{K}$ as keys and the matrix $\mathbf{V}$ as values.

Next, we extend the attention mechanism to allow for multiple targets. In the example of coffee bean blending, this corresponds to having multiple reference beans (norms), and from a set of N available beans, creating blends similar to each of the M reference beans. First, let $\mathbf{q}_i$, $i = 1, \ldots, M$, be the targets, and arrange them into a matrix $\mathbf{Q} = (\mathbf{q}_1 \cdots \mathbf{q}_M)^T$, where $\mathbf{q}_i \in \mathbf{R}^D$. For each target $\mathbf{q}_i$, $i = 1, \ldots, M$, the relatedness between $\mathbf{q}_i$ and the list of keys is represented by the vector

$$\mathbf{r}_i^T = (r_{i1} \cdots r_{iN}), \quad r_{ij} = r(\mathbf{q}_i, \mathbf{k}_j).$$

We normalize this relatedness vector to obtain

$$(a_{i1} \cdots a_{iN}) = \sigma(\mathbf{r}_i^T) = \sigma((r_{i1} \cdots r_{iN})).$$

Using these components as weights, we compute a weighted sum of the values corresponding to the keys to obtain a single vector of attention $\mathbf{c}_i$

$$\mathbf{c}_i^T = \sum_{j=1}^{N} a_{ij} \mathbf{v}_j^T, \quad i = 1, \ldots, M.$$

In other words, we obtain attention for each of the M targets, resulting in a total of M attention vectors. Hereafter, for simplicity when no confusion arises, we refer to the matrix $\mathbf{Q}$ as targets.

We can represent the attention mechanism using matrices by expressing the relatedness function as the dot product $r(\mathbf{z}, \mathbf{q}) = \dfrac{\mathbf{z}^T \mathbf{q}}{\sqrt{D}}$. The relatedness vector for the target $\mathbf{q}_i$ can be written as

$$\mathbf{r}_i^T = (r_{i1} \cdots r_{iN}) = \left(\frac{\mathbf{k}_1^T \mathbf{q}_i}{\sqrt{D}} \cdots \frac{\mathbf{k}_N^T \mathbf{q}_i}{\sqrt{D}} \right) = \left(\frac{\mathbf{q}_i^T \mathbf{k}_1}{\sqrt{D}} \cdots \frac{\mathbf{q}_i^T \mathbf{k}_N}{\sqrt{D}} \right)$$

$$= \frac{\mathbf{q}_i^T (\mathbf{k}_1 \cdots \mathbf{k}_N)}{\sqrt{D}} = \frac{\mathbf{q}_i^T \mathbf{K}^T}{\sqrt{D}}.$$

Thus, the normalized relatedness vector becomes

6.2 Transformer

$$(a_{i1} \cdots a_{iN}) = \sigma(\mathbf{r}_i^T) = \sigma\left(\frac{\mathbf{q}_i^T \mathbf{K}^T}{\sqrt{D}}\right).$$

Using this notation, the attention for the target $\mathbf{q}_i$ can be expressed as

$$\mathbf{c}_i^T = \sum_{j=1}^N a_{ij} \mathbf{v}_j^T = (a_{i1} \cdots a_{iN}) \begin{pmatrix} \mathbf{v}_1^T \\ \vdots \\ \mathbf{v}_N^T \end{pmatrix} = \sigma\left(\frac{\mathbf{q}_i^T \mathbf{K}^T}{\sqrt{D}}\right) \mathbf{V}.$$

Furthermore, compactly representing the attention by the attention matrix $\mathbf{C} = (\mathbf{c}_1 \cdots \mathbf{c}_M)^T$ and incorporating the target matrix $\mathbf{Q} = (\mathbf{q}_1 \cdots \mathbf{q}_M)^T$, we obtain

$$\mathbf{C} = \begin{pmatrix} \mathbf{c}_1^T \\ \vdots \\ \mathbf{c}_M^T \end{pmatrix} = \begin{pmatrix} a_{11} & \cdots & a_{1N} \\ a_{21} & \cdots & a_{2N} \\ & \vdots & \\ a_{M1} & \cdots & a_{MN} \end{pmatrix} \begin{pmatrix} \mathbf{v}_1^T \\ \vdots \\ \mathbf{v}_N^T \end{pmatrix} = \begin{pmatrix} \sigma\left(\frac{\mathbf{q}_1^T \mathbf{K}^T}{\sqrt{D}}\right) \\ \vdots \\ \sigma\left(\frac{\mathbf{q}_M^T \mathbf{K}^T}{\sqrt{D}}\right) \end{pmatrix} \mathbf{V}$$

$$= \sigma\left(\frac{\mathbf{Q}\mathbf{K}^T}{\sqrt{D}}\right) \mathbf{V}.$$

6.2 Transformer

6.2.1 Multi-head Attention

To arrive at the Transformer, we need further extension of the attention mechanism, known as multi-head attention. Firstly, we introduce the attention function. As before, let the target be $\mathbf{Q} = (\mathbf{q}_1 \cdots \mathbf{q}_M)^T$, where $\mathbf{q}_i \in \mathbf{R}^D$, and the keys be $\mathbf{K} = (\mathbf{k}_1 \cdots \mathbf{k}_N)^T$, where $\mathbf{k}_j \in \mathbf{R}^D$, and the values be $\mathbf{V} = (\mathbf{v}_1 \cdots \mathbf{v}_N)^T$, where $\mathbf{v}_j \in \mathbf{R}^D$. What has been described as $\mathbf{c}_i$ so far, we denote as $\mathbf{h}_i$, and we define the matrix of $\mathbf{h}_i$ as $\mathbf{H} = (\mathbf{h}_1 \cdots \mathbf{h}_M)^T$, where $\mathbf{h}_i \in \mathbf{R}^D$. Treating $\mathbf{Q}$, $\mathbf{K}$, $\mathbf{V}$ as independent variables and attention as the value, we define a function called *attention function* as

$$\mathcal{A}(\mathbf{Q}, \mathbf{K}, \mathbf{V}) \equiv \sigma\left(\frac{\mathbf{Q}\mathbf{K}^T}{\sqrt{D}}\right) \mathbf{V}.$$

That is,

$$\mathbf{H} = \begin{pmatrix} \mathbf{h}_1^T \\ \vdots \\ \mathbf{h}_M^T \end{pmatrix} = \mathcal{A}(\mathbf{Q}, \mathbf{K}, \mathbf{V}).$$

Next, we introduce weights for the D-dimensional vectors of the target, keys, and values and linearly transform them into D' dimensions. Specifically, let $\mathbf{W}^Q$, $\mathbf{W}^K$, $\mathbf{W}^V$ be $D \times D'$ matrices, and transform $\mathbf{Q}$, $\mathbf{K}$, $\mathbf{V}$ into $\mathbf{QW}^Q$, $\mathbf{KW}^K$, $\mathbf{VW}^V$, respectively. With this transformation, attention becomes

$$\mathbf{H} = \begin{pmatrix} \mathbf{h}_1^\mathrm{T} \\ \vdots \\ \mathbf{h}_M^\mathrm{T} \end{pmatrix} = \mathcal{A}(\mathbf{QW}^Q, \mathbf{KW}^K, \mathbf{VW}^V).$$

At this point, $\mathbf{H}$ becomes an $M \times D'$ matrix. Typically, D is greater than D'.

With the preparations made above, we proceed to multi-head attention mechanism. We introduce multiple sets of weights for both the target and keys-values pairs. Let us denote these weight matrices as

$$\mathbf{W}_1^Q, \ldots, \mathbf{W}_H^Q, \mathbf{W}_1^K, \ldots, \mathbf{W}_H^K, \mathbf{W}_1^V, \ldots, \mathbf{W}_H^V.$$

Using these weight matrices, we compute multiple attentions as follows:

$$\mathbf{H}_h = \mathcal{A}(\mathbf{QW}_h^Q, \mathbf{KW}_h^K, \mathbf{VW}_h^V), \quad h = 1, \ldots, H.$$

Furthermore, we concatenate these $\mathbf{H}_1, \ldots, \mathbf{H}_H$ matrices to form a new matrix and then linearly transform this concatenated matrix using weight $\mathbf{W}^O$ to aggregate information into an $M \times D$ matrix

$$\mathcal{A}^M(\mathbf{Q}, \mathbf{K}, \mathbf{V}) \equiv (\mathbf{H}_1 \cdots \mathbf{H}_H)\mathbf{W}^O.$$

This is called *multi-head attention*. At this point, $(\mathbf{H}_1 \cdots \mathbf{H}_H)$ is an $M \times D'H$ matrix, $\mathbf{W}^O$ is a $D'H \times D$ matrix, and $\mathcal{A}^M(\mathbf{Q}, \mathbf{K}, \mathbf{V})$ is an $M \times D$ matrix. The weights mentioned here are determined through training. Typically, multi-head attention involves splitting the D-dimensional vectors of the target, keys, and values into H sets of vectors. In this case, we have $D' = D/H$. The significance of multi-head attention, where D-dimensional vectors are split into H vectors, will become clear later in the section on self-attention. Here, note that the expressiveness increases by separately linearly transforming the vectors of the target, keys, and values using different matrices.

6.2.2 Transformer

Finally, we have reached a point where we can explain the Transformer. First, in Fig. 6.2, we show the *Transformer block*, referred to simply as "block" hereafter, which is a constituent element of the Transformer. It consists of multi-head attention

6.2 Transformer

Fig. 6.2 Transformer block: constituent elements and information flow in the Transformer

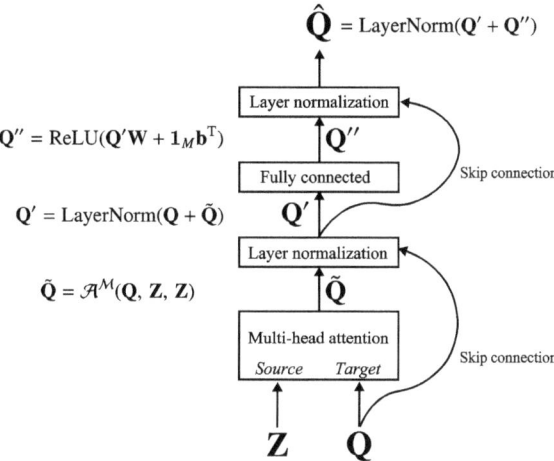

mechanism, skip connections, and fully connected layers, with layer normalization being applied in intermediate layers.

Calculations within the block are performed token-wise. That is, *token*[3] refers to one target, one source (key-value), and the intermediate layer's output collectively.

The detailed calculations within the block are as follows (refer to Fig. 6.2).

1. Firstly, we compute the multi-head attention. The source is essentially $\mathbf{Z} = \mathbf{K} = \mathbf{V}$, and $\tilde{\mathbf{Q}} = \mathcal{A}^M(\mathbf{Q}, \mathbf{Z}, \mathbf{Z})$.
2. We apply layer normalization $\mathbf{Q}' = \text{LayerNorm}(\mathbf{Q} + \tilde{\mathbf{Q}})$ to the multi-head attention and information from skip connections. Here, the layer normalization parameters β and γ are shared across tokens.
3. Next, we pass it through a fully connected layer to obtain $\mathbf{Q}'' = \text{ReLU}(\mathbf{Q}'\mathbf{W} + \mathbf{1}_M \mathbf{b}^T)$.
4. Additionally, we apply layer normalization $\hat{\mathbf{Q}} = \text{LayerNorm}(\mathbf{Q}' + \mathbf{Q}'')$ to the information from skip connections. Here again, the layer normalization parameters β and γ are shared across tokens.

As described in Sect. 2.4.3, the layer normalization parameters γ and β are learned during training along with other model parameters, allowing the network to adaptively adjust the scale and bias of the normalized activations. This helps the network capture more complex patterns in the data.

In particular, the attention mechanism where the source and target are the same is called *self-attention* (Fig. 6.3). Mathematically, considering the source and target as

---

[3] In general, a token is the smallest unit of data that the model processes. In a language processing model, a token can be a word, a subword, or even a character. Tokens are the result of breaking down the input text into manageable pieces that the model can understand and work with. For example, in the sentence "The cat sat on the mat," the tokens might be individual words: ["The," "cat," "sat," "on," "the," "mat"]. Sometimes, the tokens could be, however, subwords or morphemes, such as ["The," "ca," "t," "sat," "on," "the," "mat"].

Fig. 6.3 Self-attention

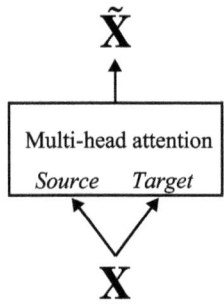

$$\mathbf{X} = \begin{pmatrix} \mathbf{x}_1^T \\ \vdots \\ \mathbf{x}_M^T \end{pmatrix},$$

we express self-attention as

$$\tilde{\mathbf{X}} = \begin{pmatrix} \tilde{\mathbf{x}}_1^T \\ \vdots \\ \tilde{\mathbf{x}}_M^T \end{pmatrix} = \mathcal{A}^M(\mathbf{X}, \mathbf{X}, \mathbf{X}),$$

where

$$\mathcal{A}^M(\mathbf{Q}, \mathbf{K}, \mathbf{V}) \equiv (\mathbf{H}_1 \cdots \mathbf{H}_H) \mathbf{W}^O,$$
$$\mathbf{H}_h = \mathcal{A}(\mathbf{Q}\mathbf{W}_h^Q, \mathbf{K}\mathbf{W}_h^K, \mathbf{V}\mathbf{W}_h^V), \quad h = 1, \ldots, H.$$

Note that, generally, the self-attention $\tilde{\mathbf{X}}$ of $\mathbf{X}$ also consists of M attention vectors $\tilde{\mathbf{x}}_1, \ldots, \tilde{\mathbf{x}}_M$, if $\mathbf{X}$ consists of M vectors $\mathbf{x}_1, \ldots, \mathbf{x}_M$.

By utilizing self-attention, we can construct new feature vectors in a set of vectors by referencing information within the set. However, in a simple (single-head) self-attention mechanism where the source is not split into keys and values, the dot product between a vector and itself becomes significantly larger than the dot product between the vector and other vectors, and thus, the weight between the vector and itself approaches 1, rendering self-attention meaningless. We can avoid this problem by splitting the source into keys and values and adopting multi-head attention. This is because splitting the source and using multi-head attention result in applying separate linear transformations to each split vector.

Additionally, typically, these linear transformation matrices are learned during training. Thus, if the loss is minimized by matrices that emphasize relationships

6.2 Transformer

Fig. 6.4 Transformer block utilizing multi-head self-attention

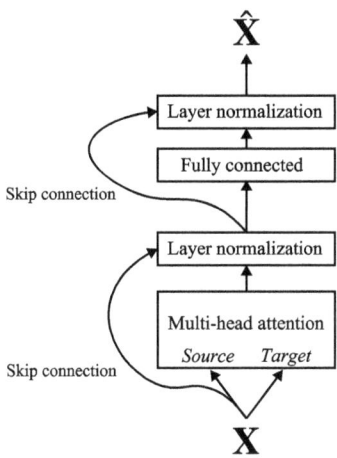

between distant elements, the resulting attention mechanism can capture relationships between these distant elements. The Transformer utilizes self-attention to create new feature vectors that consider relationships between elements of the input. Figure 6.4 illustrates a Transformer block using multi-head self-attention.

Now, we discuss the Transformer. The *Transformer* typically consists of a network composed of stacked encoders and decoders, each of which employs self-attention on the input blocks (Fig. 6.5). In the encoder-decoder architecture, multiple blocks are stacked together. In the decoder, however, an additional extension block is inserted between self-attention and fully connected layers. This extension block utilizes a (cross) multi-head attention mechanism that takes information from the encoder blocks as the source and targets the output of the self-attention (Fig. 6.6).

To describe the structure of the Transformer in more detail, we need to explain positional encoding. The Transformer often deals with 1-dimensional sequential data or 2-dimensional spatial data as input. For example, in the case of sequential data, as illustrated in Fig. 6.7, the initial block receives the sequential data in parallel.

In such data, positional information across the entire input is often crucial. For instance, in natural language processing, the positional information of words within the sentence itself carries meaning in addition to the relationships between words in a sentence. Thus, in the Transformer, positional information of each component of the input is encoded explicitly and added as part of the input. Specifically, the positional information of each component of the input is represented by vectors of the same dimension as the dimension of the input space, and these positional encoding vectors are input alongside the input vectors into the attention mechanism.

We can consider several methods to encode positions into vectors of the same dimension as the embedding space. One simple approach is to use the sequence order directly, such as $1, 2, \ldots, T$, as the first component of a D-dimensional vector. With this encoding, however, only the first component holds special significance, while the rest are all zeros. In embeddings like word embeddings, it is generally not

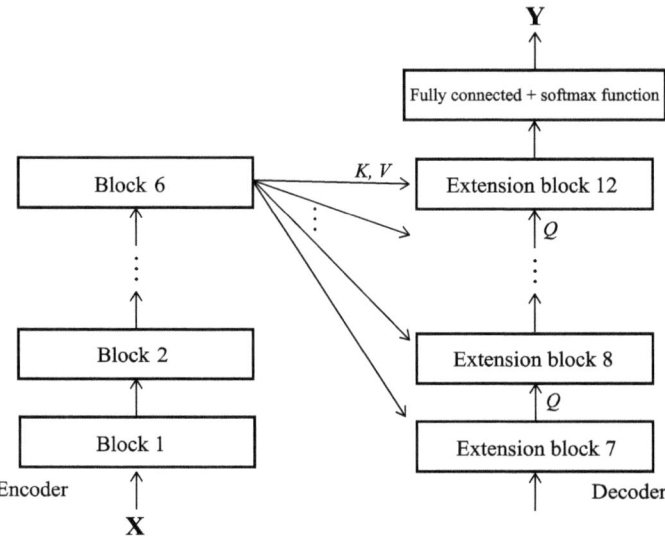

Blocks 7 to 12 of the decoder consist of extension blocks that include a cross-multi-head attention mechanism.

Fig. 6.5 A simplified representation of the Transformer. The Transformer consists of encoders and decoders, each composed of multiple (usually 6) self-attention blocks connected in series

Fig. 6.6 The extension block. This block, present in the decoder of the Transformer, incorporates a cross-attention mechanism that takes information from the encoder blocks as the source and targets the output of multi-head (self) attention

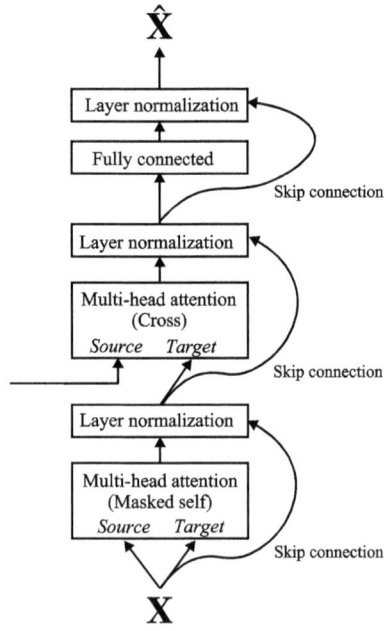

6.2 Transformer

Fig. 6.7 Input to the encoder of the Transformer processing sequential data

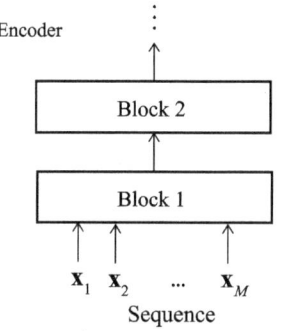

the case that specific components are always zero. Thus, for positional encoding, we would like an encoding that effectively utilizes all components of the D-dimensional vector, rather than such a simplistic approach.

Here, we introduce a positional encoding using trigonometric functions, specifically sin and cos, for discrete 1-dimensional input (i.e., the position of the i-th component is i). In this encoding, we define $\mathbf{p}_i$ as the positional encoding vector when i represents the position of input components, and D represents the dimension of the input vector

$$\mathbf{p}_i = (p_1 \ p_2 \ \cdots \ p_{2j-1} \ p_{2j} \ \cdots \ p_D)^\mathrm{T},$$

where

$$p_{2j-1} = \cos\left(\frac{i}{10000^{\frac{2j}{D}}}\right), \quad p_{2j} = \sin\left(\frac{i}{10000^{\frac{2j}{D}}}\right).$$

The choice of 10000 in the denominator is arbitrary; it could be any sufficiently large number compared to the encoding dimension, typically about one order of magnitude larger. With this encoding, for $i \neq i'$, in most cases, $\mathbf{p}_i \neq \mathbf{p}_{i'}$, making $\mathbf{p}_i$ and $\mathbf{p}_{i'}$ distinct encodings. Additionally, when i and i' are close, $\mathbf{p}_i$ and $\mathbf{p}_{i'}$ also become close due to the continuity of sin and cos functions.

To illustrate the phase (angle), let us consider an encoding dimension $D = 500$ and 100 input components. For $j = 1$ to 250 and $i = 1$ to 100, $\dfrac{i}{10000^{\frac{2j}{D}}}$ satisfies

$$i > \frac{i}{10000^{\frac{2j}{D}}} \geq \frac{i}{10000} \geq \frac{1}{10000}.$$

Furthermore, for larger j, the phase difference between $i+1$ and i becomes significantly small, with p_{2j-1} decreasing monotonically and p_{2j} increasing monotonically.

Note that the norm of the positional encoding vector using this encoding is

$$\|\mathbf{p}_i\| = \sqrt{\frac{D}{2}},$$

which is the same for all positional encodings. Additionally, we can view this positional encoding as an approximation of the discrete Fourier transform of the one-hot function $f_i(j) \equiv \delta_{ij}$, where δ_{ij} is the Kronecker delta:

$$\delta_{ij} = \begin{cases} 1, & j = i, \\ 0, & j \neq i, \end{cases}$$

which means that the positional encoding vector $\mathbf{p}_i$ is approximately composed of the "Fourier components" of position i [22].

For the input sequences $\mathbf{x}_1, \mathbf{x}_2, ..., \mathbf{x}_M$, where the encoding of $\mathbf{x}_i$ is denoted as $\mathbf{v}_i = \mathbf{W}\mathbf{x}_i$, we use the following as the input to the Transformer (as shown in Fig. 6.8):

$$\sqrt{D}\mathbf{v}_1 + \mathbf{p}_1, \sqrt{D}\mathbf{v}_2 + \mathbf{p}_2, ..., \sqrt{D}\mathbf{v}_M + \mathbf{p}_M.$$

Generally, when considering encoding operations, we usually normalize encodings. Thus, we multiply $\mathbf{v}$ by $\sqrt{D}$ to normalize it to be of the same order of magnitude as the positional encoding $\mathbf{p}$. We can view the input to the Transformer, $\sqrt{D}\mathbf{v} + \mathbf{p}$, as a translation of the input embedding $\mathbf{v}$ (scaled by a constant). Thus, we can assume that there exists a subspace for each input element's position (as shown in Fig. 6.9).

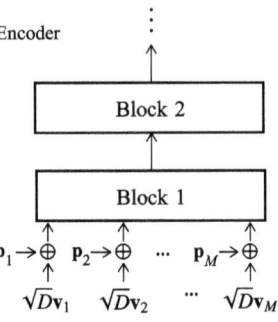

Fig. 6.8 Input to the first block of the encoder in the Transformer for processing sequential data. Embeddings of elements (e.g., words) and their positional encodings are summed and inputted

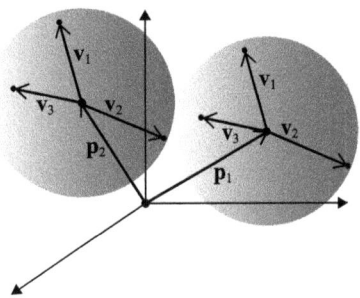

Fig. 6.9 Subspaces of input elements. There exists a subspace for each position of the input element

6.2 Transformer

Sometimes, we also concatenate $\mathbf{v}_i$ and $\mathbf{p}_i$ and use the resulting vector $(\sqrt{D}\mathbf{v}_i^T\ \mathbf{p}_i^T)^T$ as the input to the self-attention mechanism.

The following is a detailed explanation of the Transformer architecture shown in Fig. 6.10, which is designed for processing sequential data such as language sentences.

- The input consists of a sequence of elements (labeled as "Input" in the encoder). Unlike RNNs, where elements are input sequentially from the beginning, in the Transformer, the sequence of elements is input all at once. Thus, the input is taken as a fixed-length sequence, and for shorter sequences, a special symbol is inserted at the end of the sequence. The output depends on the task. For tasks like language translation, the output is generated by predicting one element at each time step, starting from the first element of the transformed sequence. For subsequent parts

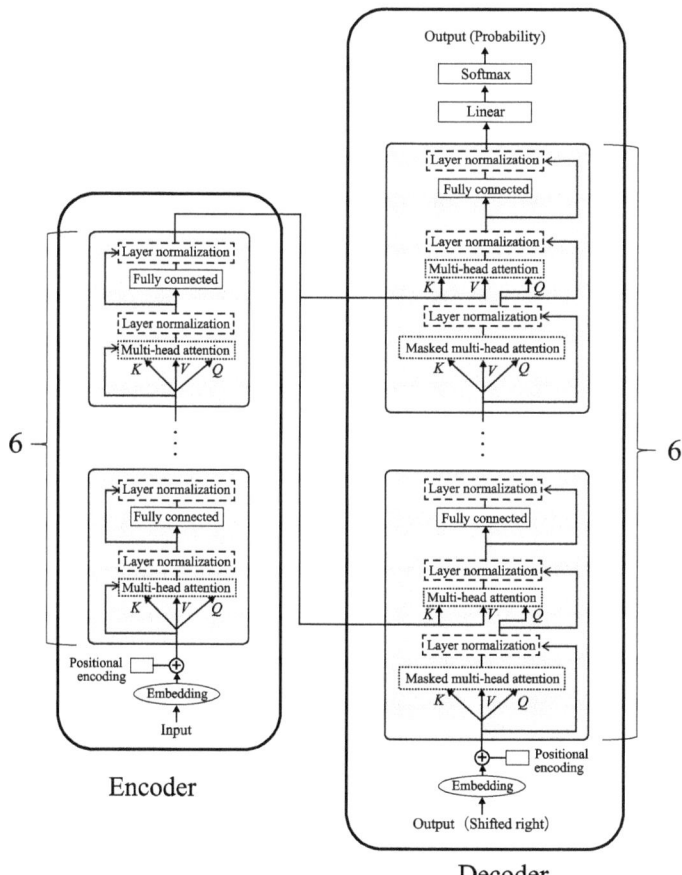

Fig. 6.10 Details of the Transformer architecture. Based on Fig. 1 of [46]

of the input sequence, the output is simply the prediction for that part labeled as "Output (Probability)" in the decoder.
- Both the encoder and decoder have positional encodings added. Each consists of six stacked blocks, although the structure of these blocks slightly differs between the encoder and decoder.
- In the encoder, the input is processed to output vectors representing features of the input, such as relationships between distant elements. These output vectors serve as inputs to the multi-head attention mechanism within the six blocks of the decoder.
- The "input" to the decoder consists of the output (shifted right). This means that the input to the decoder for predicting a particular element includes the embedding representation (with softmax function applied for calculating the probability) of the previously predicted elements up to that point, excluding the last element of the input to the encoder. Thus, the decoder utilizes its previous predictions as additional input information.
- Unlike traditional sequence models that generate tokens one by one, the Transformer can process sequences in parallel. This applies equally to the decoder as well. That is, in the Transformer decoder, the entire input sequence, including future tokens, is provided simultaneously.
- The decoder blocks include a mechanism called *masked multi-head attention*, which is a form of attention mechanism where certain input elements (words in the case of language sentences) are masked, preventing the calculation of attention towards subsequent elements. By using masked attention, the model ensures that even though computations are parallelized, each position only attends to appropriate past positions. This mechanism is essential both during inference and during training for tasks like sequence translation to prevent referencing future transformation results, ensuring the model infers and learns in a causal manner. Masked attention allows the Transformer to leverage parallel computation while maintaining the necessary sequential dependencies in the decoding process.

As evident from the above structure, the Transformer is a deep neural network incorporating attention mechanisms. In terms of neural networks, we can use it in various ways through learning. In particular, the Transformer utilizes attention mechanisms to represent relationships between distant components in input data, such as sequential or image data, as vectors, actively leveraging them. Through training, it achieves high accuracy in tasks such as language generation, translation, and image classification by allowing predictions and interpolations of input data. In Chap. 8, we will provide a detailed discussion on language generation.

Chapter 7
Reinforcement Learning

The field of reinforcement learning encompasses a wide range of theoretical frameworks and learning methods, making it impossible for the author to comprehensively cover them all. The main focus of this chapter is to outline the backbone of reinforcement learning, with a focus on the aspects necessary for understanding generative language AI.

7.1 Problem Setting

We start with an example where reinforcement learning is applied. Consider a manufacturing company that aims to significantly increase sales in the long term. To simplify the problem, we assume that sales depend on the overall purchasing intention of individuals (i.e., societal purchasing intention), and this purchasing intention changes based on the release of new products or whether the company runs commercials. For instance, if no new products have been released for a long time, purchasing intention naturally decreases. Running commercials often increases purchasing intention, but there are cases where it does not, and higher sales are not guaranteed. The challenge here is to determine the timing of introducing new products and running commercials to maximize long-term sales. For the sake of simplicity, however, we will disregard the cost associated with running commercials, although it is acknowledged that there are costs involved.

In response to this challenge, reinforcement learning involves trial and error, especially in the beginning stages. It starts by introducing new products and observing their effects (how purchasing intention and profit change) or running commercials and observing their effects, thus accumulating experience. This accumulation of experience constitutes learning, and as a result of this learning (though it may take time), reinforcement learning can provide optimal actions, such as whether to introduce new products or take no action, at any given point in time.

We introduce the concepts necessary for the formulation of reinforcement learning based on the example provided above. Firstly, regarding purchasing intention, there are two possible *states* that it can take: high or low. At each time point, purchasing intention is assumed to be in one of these states. Decisions such as whether to introduce new products, run commercials, or take no action are *actions* that the company (referred to as an *agent* in reinforcement learning) can take depending on the current state of societal purchasing intention. For example, if the agent introduces new products when purchasing intention is low, there might be a high probability that purchasing intention will increase in the next time step. Conversely, if it takes no action when purchasing intention is low, there might be a high probability that purchasing intention will remain low in the next time step. The probability of transitioning to the next state conditioned on the current state and action is called the *state transition probability*.

Moreover, in any given state, when the agent takes a certain action, it obtains some form of sales revenue. In reinforcement learning, this is referred to as *reward*. Particularly, the reward obtained at that moment is called *immediate reward*, and the sum of immediate rewards from time t until the end is called *cumulative reward*. Lastly, a *policy* is a guideline that determines the action to be taken in the current situation. Reinforcement learning aims to acquire the optimal policy.

Let us generalize the concepts introduced above. We consider a finite set of elements called *states*, denoted by S. In the previous example, the set S consists of two elements representing high and low purchasing intentions: $S = \{\text{high}, \text{low}\}$. We assume that time t is discretized. The variable representing the state at time t is denoted by S_t, which is generally a random variable. Moreover, a sequence of random variables $S_0, S_1, S_2, \ldots, S_T$ is called a *stochastic process*.

We denote a finite set of elements called *actions* by $\mathcal{A}$. In the previous example, there are three actions: introducing a new product, running a commercial, or taking no action, represented as $\mathcal{A} = \{\text{new}, \text{com}, \text{non}\}$. The variable representing the action at time t is denoted by A_t, which is also generally a random variable.

In reinforcement learning, we assume that the state at the next time step is probabilistically determined based on the current state-action pair. The probability of transitioning from the current state and action to the (next) state, conditioned on the current state and action, is called the *state transition probability*, denoted as $p(s'|s, a)$, where s' is the next state, s is the current state, and a is the action. For example,

- in any state, if no action is taken, there tends to be a decrease in purchasing intention,
- when purchasing intention is low, introducing a new product tends to increase purchasing intention, and
- when purchasing intention is low, running a commercial tends to increase purchasing intention.

7.1 Problem Setting

These regularities in the "environment" in which the agent operates reflect in the probabilities of state transitions influenced by actions.

As a consequence of taking an action, the value obtained at that moment is termed *immediate reward*. Note, however, that this immediate reward can sometimes be negative, reflecting losses incurred. We denote the immediate reward obtained at time t as R_t. The immediate reward is assumed to be uniquely determined by a *reward function* $g(s, a)$ of state s and action a, which brings us to

$$R_t = g(S_t, A_t).$$

Note that R_t is a random variable because S_t and A_t are random variables. Let us obtain the immediate reward R_t at time t. Then, we represent its value at time 0 by the *discounted present value*:

$$R_t \gamma^t, \quad 0 < \gamma < 1,$$

where the constant γ is referred to as the *discount factor*. When we intend to prioritize the present value over uncertain future values, we adopt the discounted present value. Generally, the discounted present value is also a random variable.

The sum of immediate rewards over time is termed *cumulative reward*. We can categorize cumulative rewards into two types: undiscounted cumulative reward and discounted cumulative reward. *Undiscounted cumulative reward* represents the sum of immediate rewards without discounting:

$$C_t = \sum_{k=0}^{(T-1)-t} R_{t+k}.$$

Discounted cumulative reward, on the other hand, represents the sum of immediate rewards discounted by their present value:

$$C_t = \sum_{k=0}^{(T-1)-t} R_{t+k} \gamma^k, \quad 0 < \gamma < 1.$$

In this text, when referring to cumulative reward without specification, we typically refer to discounted cumulative reward. Generally, cumulative rewards are random variables.

In any given state s, the probability of taking a particular action is termed *policy* (or *action policy*). In other words, a policy is represented by a conditional probability distribution:

$$\pi(a \mid s) = P(A_t = a \mid S_t = s).$$

Reinforcement learning involves taking actions either through trial and error or following some guidelines. The outcomes of these actions (rewards) are accumulated,

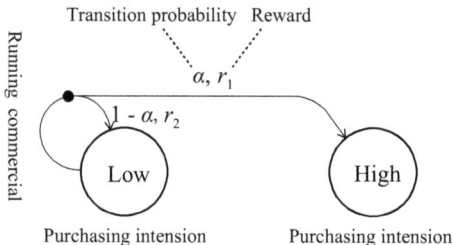

Fig. 7.1 A part of the state transition diagram. Circles represent states, arrows represent actions taken in those states, and each arrow is accompanied by transition probabilities and rewards. Black dots represent branches in the arrows

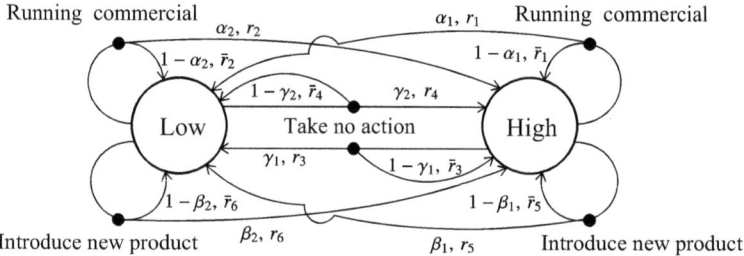

Fig. 7.2 An example of a Markov decision process depicted in a state transition diagram. There are two states: "low" and "high," and three possible actions in each state: "run commercial," "introduce new product," and "take no action"

and the accumulated rewards are used as an evaluation function to determine the policy's maximization.

We can represent the relationship among states, actions, transition probabilities, and rewards, as defined above, in a state transition diagram. Figure 7.1 depicts a portion of the state transition diagram to be shown shortly. In this diagram, circles represent states, arrows represent actions taken in those states, and each arrow is accompanied by transition probabilities and rewards. Additionally, black dots represent branches in the arrows.

Figure 7.2 depicts the complete state transition diagram for the example of maximizing sales for the manufacturing company. From this state transition diagram, it is evident that the distribution of the next state s_{t+1} conditioned on the current state s_t and action a_t becomes independent of the states and actions before time t. In other words, the distribution of the state s_{t+1} at time $t + 1$ is determined by the state s_t at time t and the action a_t taken at that time. A probability process where the state at time t is determined by the current state s_t and action a_t in this way is called a *Markov decision process* (MDP). Reinforcement learning deals with Markov decision processes.

7.1 Problem Setting

In reinforcement learning, the objective is to determine a policy such that the (discounted or undiscounted) expected cumulative reward from time $t = 0$ to the end (T) serves as the evaluation function and is maximized. For the case of discounted cumulative reward, we can express the evaluation function as[1]

$$\mathbb{E}[C_0] = \mathbb{E}\left[\sum_{t=0}^{T-1} R_t \gamma^t\right], \quad 0 < \gamma < 1. \tag{7.1.1}$$

This evaluation function prioritizes the present value and reflects the diminishing value over time. For example, in tasks where the goal is to reach a destination as quickly as possible, such as in a maze, the value of this evaluation function increases as the goal is reached sooner. Thus, adopting this evaluation function can be effective in such scenarios.

In reinforcement learning, a series of transitions involving taking action a in the current state s, transitioning to a new state, receiving a reward r, and updating the policy π is repeated for a predetermined number of iterations, starting from an appropriate initial state. This sequence of transitions (sequence of states, actions, and rewards) is referred to as an *episode*. The goal of reinforcement learning is to find a policy that maximizes the cumulative reward over episodes. This involves iterating through episodes multiple times to find the policy that maximizes cumulative reward, as illustrated by the following example episodes.

Episode 1 $\{s_0, a_0, r_0, \ldots, s_{T-1}, a_{T-1}, r_{T-1}, s_T\}$,
Episode 2 $\{s'_0, a'_0, r'_0, \ldots, s'_{T'-1}, a'_{T'-1}, r'_{T'-1}, s'_{T'}\}$,

$$\vdots$$

Episode n $\{s^*_0, a^*_0, r^*_0, \ldots, s^*_{T^*-1}, a^*_{T^*-1}, r^*_{T^*-1}, s^*_{T^*}\}$.

Note that the ending time T varies for each episode in general. Through repeating iterations of episodes, we aim to discover the policy that maximizes cumulative reward.

In general, in reinforcement learning, the sets of states and actions are assumed to be known, but information about the environment other than that is typically not available at the start of learning. For example, probabilities of increasing purchase intention when introducing a new product in a state of low purchase intention are initially unknown. At least initially, the state transition probabilities:

---

[1] The expected value is taken over the joint probability of $S_0, A_0, \ldots, S_{T-1}, A_{T-1}$. Also, exactly, the evaluation function is defined by

$$\mathbb{E}\left[\lim_{T \to \infty} C_0\right] = \mathbb{E}\left[\lim_{T \to \infty} \sum_{t=0}^{T-1} R_t \gamma^t\right], \quad 0 < \gamma < 1.$$

In this section, for simplicity, letting T be sufficiently large, we ignore the limit as T approaches infinity.

$$p(s' \mid s, a) = P(S_{t+1} = s' \mid S_t = s, A_t = a)$$

are unknown. Additionally, the reward function $g(s, a)$ is also unknown. If this environmental information (state transition probabilities and reward function) were known, finding the episodes that optimize the evaluation function would be a computational problem rather than a learning problem. In reinforcement learning, we assume that, for each state s, the immediate reward r obtained by taking action a and the next state s' are observable. By taking actions and accumulating this information while exploring, we discover optimal policies over time.

In situations where there is minimal environmental information, the approach to policy determination is broadly categorized into two main methods. One approach is to introduce a utility function with actions (and states) as independent variables, selecting actions that yield higher utility values. Specifically, the utility is often represented by the expected value of rewards (Q-function), and the strategy is to continuously select actions that maximize this utility function. An exemplary method based on this approach is called *Q-learning*, where the solution to the equation that the Q-function satisfies is estimated through accumulating experiences. Furthermore, there is a deep learning version of Q-learning known as *Deep Q-Network (DQN)*.

Another approach is to directly represent policies using neural networks or generalized linear models. An exemplary learning method based on this approach is to assume a distribution family for the policy π and then determine the policy that maximizes the evaluation function using gradient descent. This method is known as *policy gradient methods*. We have a method based on this approach named *trust region policy optimization (TRPO)*, which is an extension of the policy gradient method. Furthermore, there is an improved version called *proximal policy optimization (PPO)*, which is a further enhancement of TRPO.

We will explain these methods below, starting with Q-learning.

7.2 Q-Learning and DQN

At time 0, taking action a in state s and then continuing to act under policy π, the expected value of the cumulative reward, denoted as

$$Q^\pi(s, a) \equiv \mathbb{E}^\pi[C_0 \mid S_0 = s, A_0 = a]$$

7.2 Q-Learning and DQN

is called the *action-value function*, or the *Q-function*. The action-value function depends on the policy π by definition.[2] As the name suggests, the action-value function represents the value of taking action a in state s under policy π.

In particular, when considering a policy of "continuously taking actions that maximize the action-value function in each state," we call the action-value function under that policy the *optimal action-value function*. This is expressed recursively as the policy refers to the action-value function. Thus, formally, letting $S_t = s$ and $A_t = a$, where t is an arbitrary time, $s \in \mathcal{S}$, and $a \in \mathcal{A}$, we define the optimal action-value function $Q(s, a)$ by the following recursive equation:

$$Q(s, a) = g(s, a) + \gamma \cdot \mathbb{E}_{S'}[\max_{a' \in \mathcal{A}} Q(S', a')], \qquad (7.2.1)$$

where $S' = S_{t+1}$ (a random variable). That is, $Q(s, a)$ represents the expected value of discounted cumulative rewards when choosing action a in state s at time t, followed by the optimal action in the next state $s' \in S'$. This value is the sum of the immediate reward at time t, $g(s, a)$, and the expected cumulative reward over the next state s' maximized with respect to the action a, multiplied by γ. This is a type of equation called the *Bellman equation*. In Q-learning, we adopt a policy that chooses the action a that maximizes $Q(s, a)$ at each step instead of finding a policy that maximizes the evaluation function (7.1.1).

Here, we make several observations about the optimal action-value function.

1. The optimal action-value function $Q(s, a)$ is a function, so its value must be determined for any pair (s, a). Specifically, the function $Q(s, a)$ represents the expected cumulative reward when starting from an arbitrary initial action from state s and taking the optimal action from the next step onwards.
2. Acting to maximize the function $Q(s, a)$ implies choosing actions that maximize the expected cumulative reward. This entails selecting a policy deterministically rather than probabilistically. That is, we have

$$\pi(a^* \mid s) = 1, \quad a^* = \arg\max_{a \in \mathcal{A}} Q(s, a). \qquad (7.2.2)$$

3. If environmental information (transition probabilities and reward function) is known, we can, in principle, obtain the policy that maximizes the function $Q(s, a)$ by solving the Bellman equation using dynamic programming.

---

[2] Expressing the action-value function using the definition of expectation yields

$$\begin{aligned} Q^\pi(s, a) &\equiv \mathbb{E}^\pi[C_0 \mid S_0 = s, A_0 = a] \\ &= g(s, a) + \sum_{k=1} \gamma^k \sum_{(s', a')} P(S_k = s', A_k = a') g(s', a') \\ &= g(s, a) + \sum_{k=1} \gamma^k \sum_{(s', a')} \pi(a' \mid s') P(S_k = s') g(s', a'). \end{aligned}$$

Because the transition probabilities $P(S_k = s')$ are generally unknown even with a fixed policy π, the action-value function $Q^\pi(s, a)$ is also unknown in general.

Now, solving the Bellman equation (7.2.1) would determine the desired policy as given by Eq. (7.2.2). We cannot, however, directly solve Eq. (7.2.1), since the environmental information (transition probabilities and reward function) is unknown. Thus, we approximate the Bellman equation (7.2.1) through repeated experiences. Using samples (episodes)

$$s_0, a_0, r_0, \ldots, s_{t-1}, a_{t-1}, r_{t-1}, s_t, \ldots$$

and assuming that the expectation can be approximated by averaging over many experiences, we derive an approximate equation without the expectation term. That is, we have

$$Q(s, a) = g(s, a) + \gamma \max_{a' \in \mathcal{A}} Q(s', a'). \tag{7.2.3}$$

We then iteratively compute the solution to this equation through repeated calculations. This is the idea behind *Q-learning* [47, 48].

We formalize Q-learning. First, we introduce the fundamental equation of Q-learning and the method to determine $Q(s, a)$ using this equation. By multiplying the approximate equation (7.2.3) by a constant (sequence) α_t, where $0 < \alpha_t < 1$, and adding the left and right sides of the identity

$$(1 - \alpha_t)Q(s, a) = (1 - \alpha_t)Q(s, a),$$

we obtain

$$Q(s, a) = (1 - \alpha_t)Q(s, a) + \alpha_t(g(s, a) + \gamma \max_{a' \in \mathcal{A}} Q(s', a')).$$

Rearranging the right-hand side by α_t, we obtain

$$Q(s, a) = Q(s, a) + \alpha_t(g(s, a) + \gamma \max_{a' \in \mathcal{A}} Q(s', a') - Q(s, a)), \tag{7.2.4}$$

for $Q(s, a)$. Starting from an appropriately chosen pair (s, a) and its initial value of $Q(s, a)$, we replace the left-hand side of Eq. (7.2.4) with the value of the right-hand side iteratively until convergence. (If the sequence α_t satisfies certain conditions, convergence to the true solution is guaranteed.) Additionally, $g(s, a)$ and s' are obtained from samples. Note, however, that the determination of the function $Q(s, a)$ requires to compute the above for all pairs (s, a).

Choosing pairs (s, a) in a predetermined order or completely randomly for computation leads to poor learning efficiency. In Q-learning, one solution to this is to randomly select pairs (s, a) in some cases, while in other cases, select pairs (s, a) that maximize the value of $Q(s, a)$ during computation. Summarizing the above, we present the algorithm for Q-learning below.

The input initializes all $Q(s, a)$ to be 0 (or some random values) for all (s, a). Additionally, T represents the maximum number of steps taken in one episode (a

7.2 Q-Learning and DQN

positive integer), and ε, where $0 < \varepsilon < 1$, indicates the degree of randomness in selecting actions.

We repeat the following steps for each episode until a certain number of times or until Q no longer improves.

1. First, determine the initial state s and set $t = 0$.
2. Keeping s fixed,

   (a) With probability ε, randomly select the pair (s, a) (not greedy).
   (b) With probability $1 - \varepsilon$, determine the pair (s, a) where $Q(s, a)$ is maximized (greedy).

3. Let s' be the state resulting from action a, and update $Q(s, a)$ using the equation

$$Q(s, a) \leftarrow Q(s, a) + \alpha_t \cdot (g(s, a) + \gamma \max_{a' \in \mathcal{A}} Q(s', a') - Q(s, a)).$$

4. Update $s \leftarrow s'$. If $t = T$, proceed to the next episode; otherwise, set $t = t + 1$ and go back to step 2.

We provide some additional clarification regarding the Q-learning algorithm. In Step 2, suppose we always choose option (b) while progressing. This means we are advancing the learning based on the achievements made so far. In other words, we are always selecting the option that maximizes the previously formed evaluation function, thus continually advancing the learning by selecting the action that maximizes the learned value function. Such a learning strategy is called *greedy*. In the Q-learning algorithm, we set ε as a constant. When ε is small, it implies a greedy exploration (utilization of the evaluation function), while a large ε indicates a broader range of exploration. This type of exploration strategy is called ε-*greedy*. In ε-greedy exploration, setting $\varepsilon = 1$ means selecting states completely at random, leading to inefficient exploration as it explores even unimportant regions equally. On the other hand, setting $\varepsilon = 0$ means always acting greedily, resulting in repeatedly selecting the same action and hindering learning progress.

The above constitutes the basics of Q-learning. As evident from the Q-learning algorithm presented earlier, Q-learning suffers from the issue of overly broad exploration. Essentially, it necessitates maintaining the optimal action-value function Q for all combinations of states and actions. In games like chess or Go, this would mean exploring even improbable board positions, which might not contribute meaningfully to the learning process. Furthermore, Q-learning fundamentally deals with discrete states. Of course, it is possible to discretize continuous variables by dividing them into intervals. For instance, however, dividing the interval $(0, 1)$ into 100 intervals would result in 100^{10} states if there were 10 variables (a 10-dimensional space). Learning in such a vast state space would be practically infeasible.

Using a neural network enables handling high-dimensional data and allows learning in cases where the state is represented by continuous variables or data such as images. Particularly, a method for approximating the action-value function Q using a deep neural network for reinforcement learning is called *Deep Q-Network* [28]

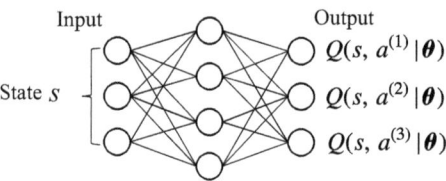

Fig. 7.3 DQN (Deep Q-Network). The input is the state, and the output is the approximate value of Q for the input state and each action. For simplicity, a neural network consisting of three layers is shown

(DQN; see Fig. 7.3). The input of this deep neural network is the state s, and the output is the approximation of the value function for each action given the state s:

$$Q(s, a^{(1)} | \theta), \ldots, Q(s, a^{(|\mathcal{A}|)} | \theta),$$

where θ represents the weights of the deep neural network.

The objective of learning in DQN is to make the approximation $Q(s, a)$ by $Q(s, a | \theta)$ satisfy

$$Q(s, a | \theta) = g(s, a) + \gamma \max_{a' \in \mathcal{A}} Q(s', a' | \theta).$$

To achieve this objective, DQN sets the loss as follows. When we take action a in state s and receive reward $g(s, a)$, during learning, we compute $Q(s', a' | \theta)$ for all a', and by using $\max Q(s', a' | \theta)$, we can obtain

$$g(s, a) + \gamma \max_{a' \in \mathcal{A}} Q(s', a' | \theta).$$

This is considered to be closer to the true value $Q(s, a)$ as more experience is accumulated. Thus, using $g(s, a) + \gamma \max_{a' \in \mathcal{A}} Q(s', a' | \theta)$ as the target data and $Q(s, a | \theta)$ as the predicted value, we define the loss for one action as the squared error:

$$E(\theta) = \frac{1}{2} \left(Q(s, a | \theta) - (g(s, a) + \gamma \max_{a' \in \mathcal{A}} Q(s', a' | \theta)) \right)^2.$$

By differentiating (varying) the loss with respect to the predicted value $Q(s, a | \theta)$, we obtain

$$\frac{\partial E}{\partial Q(s, a | \theta)} = Q(s, a | \theta) - (g(s, a) + \gamma \max_{a' \in \mathcal{A}} Q(s', a' | \theta)).$$

Backpropagating this error, we can compute $\frac{\partial E}{\partial \theta}$, and by using stochastic gradient descent, we can find the optimal solution for θ.

7.3 Policy Gradient Methods and Their Extensions

As it stands, however, learning would be inefficient and unstable. Thus, we typically employ the following enhancements to address efficiency and instability.

1. *Experience replay.* We store records of actions and randomly sample from them to form mini-batches for learning. By using this method, we can utilize each action for learning multiple times. Mixing past experiences contributes to stabilization.
2. *Gradient clipping.* We ensure that the absolute value of the slope of the error function does not exceed a certain threshold. For example, if the threshold is set to 1, instead of using $E = (\hat{y} - y)^2$ (where $\hat{y}$ is the predicted value and y is the target value), we use

$$E = \begin{cases} (\hat{y} - y)^2, & |\hat{y} - y| \leq 1, \\ |\hat{y} - y|, & |\hat{y} - y| > 1. \end{cases}$$

This method prevents the gradient $\partial E / \partial \hat{y}$ from becoming too large.

In Q-learning and its deep learning version, Deep Q-Network (DQN), when actions are continuous, the approach to approximating the action-value function faces difficulty in computing the arg max involved in action selection and update equations. The policy gradient methods, introduced next, aim to overcome this limitation.

7.3 Policy Gradient Methods and Their Extensions

We consider approximating the policy using a neural network. This is called representing the policy by a model. In particular, policy gradient methods assume a distribution family for the policy π and use gradient ascent to maximize the objective function to determine the policy. This section introduces policy gradient methods and their extensions.

In the previous section, we defined the action-value function (Q-function). Similar to that, we here introduce another function called the value function (V-function). The *value function (V-function)* is defined as the expected total cumulative reward starting at time 0, being in state s, and then continuing to act under policy π:

$$V^\pi(s) \equiv \mathbb{E}^\pi[C_0 \mid S_0 = s].$$

This function represents the value of state s and, like the Q-function, depends on policy π. As evident from their definitions, we have the following relationship between the Q-function and the V-function:

$$\sum_{a \in \mathcal{A}} \pi(a \mid s) Q^\pi(s, a) = V^\pi(s).$$

Furthermore, from the Q-function and the V-function, we define the *advantage function* as follows:
$$A^\pi(s, a) \equiv Q^\pi(s, a) - V^\pi(s).$$

Intuitively, this function[3] represents the value of the action alone. Thus, by updating the policy such that the probability of selecting actions with positive advantage function values increases, and the probability of selecting actions with negative advantage function values decreases, we expect the policy to improve.

Now, we consider learning a stochastic policy model regulated by policy parameters $\theta \in \mathbb{R}^d$:
$$\pi_\theta : \mathcal{A} \times \mathcal{S} \to [0, 1].$$

For such models, a Gaussian policy model is representative for continuous distributions:
$$\pi_\theta(a \mid s) \equiv \frac{1}{\sqrt{2\pi}\sigma(s;\theta)} \exp\left(-\frac{(a - \mu(s;\theta))^2}{2\sigma(s;\theta)^2}\right),$$

where $\mu(\cdot;\theta)$ and $\sigma(\cdot;\theta)$ are represented as outputs of deep neural networks with parameters θ (weights). For discrete distributions, it is common to use the output of a deep neural network with parameters θ as the distribution itself. For example, if p_i represents the probability of occurrence of word w_i, the policy is represented by the output of a neural network:
$$(p_1 \; p_2 \; \cdots \; p_{|V|})^\mathrm{T},$$

which is usually the value of the softmax function, where $|V|$ is the total number of words. Generally, representing policies using models is effective when the action space is high-dimensional or continuous because we can directly use the probability distribution of the action conditioned on the state variable.

To learn the policy, we consider the following objective function, *average reward* (undiscounted):
$$f_\infty(\theta) \equiv \lim_{T \to \infty} \mathbb{E}^\pi \left[\frac{1}{T}\sum_{t=0}^{T-1} g(S_t, A_t)\right].$$

This objective function represents the expected average reward over an infinite horizon, where $g(S_t, A_t)$ denotes the immediate reward at time t.

To learn the optimal policy by maximizing the objective function, we need update equations for policy evaluation and policy improvement, which update the policy model characterized by parameters θ. We define the update equation for the parameter θ as follows:
$$\theta := \theta + \alpha_t \nabla_\theta f_\infty(\theta), \tag{7.3.1}$$

---

[3] Like the Q-function, the value function and the advantage function are generally unknown.

7.3 Policy Gradient Methods and Their Extensions

where $\alpha_t > 0$ is a constant (sequence).[4] If we can compute the gradient $\nabla_\theta f_\infty(\theta)$, we can use this update equation to learn the policy. Learning the policy using the update Eq. (7.3.1) is called *policy gradient methods* [43]. In practice, we can compute $\nabla_\theta f_\infty(\theta)$ under the assumptions of stationarity and ergodicity with respect to the state distribution, which are described shortly.

In the following, we assume stationarity and ergodicity with respect to the state distribution. Specifically, letting $p_\infty^\pi(s)$ be the probability distribution of states in the limit as $T \to \infty$ under the policy π, for the Markov decision process under consideration, we make the following assumptions.

1. The distribution $p_\infty^\pi(s)$ is *stationary*, meaning

$$p_\infty^\pi(s') = \sum_{s \in S} \sum_{a \in \mathcal{A}} p(s' \mid s, a) \pi(a \mid s) p_\infty^\pi(s)$$

and there exists only one such distribution.

2. For a function $h : S \times \mathcal{A} \to \mathbb{R}$, with respect to the policy π and the distribution $p_\infty^\pi(s)$, the *ergodicity*

$$\mathbb{E}_{\pi(a \mid s) p_\infty^\pi(s)}[h(s, a)] = \lim_{T \to \infty} \frac{1}{T} \sum_{t=0}^{T-1} h(S_t = s, A_t = a)$$

holds. This is important for approximate computation through sampling.

Under these two assumptions, we can demonstrate to compute $\nabla_\theta f_\infty(\theta)$. First, we present the policy gradient theorem (We show a proof of the policy gradient theorem in Appendix in this chapter).

Policy gradient theorem.
Under the assumption of the stationary distribution $p_\infty^{\pi_\theta}(s)$, the policy gradient of the average reward is given by

$$\nabla_\theta f_\infty(\theta) = \sum_{s \in S} \sum_{a \in \mathcal{A}} p_\infty^{\pi_\theta}(s) \pi_\theta(a \mid s) \nabla_\theta \ln \pi_\theta(a \mid s)(Q_\infty^{\pi_\theta}(s, a) - b(s)) \quad (7.3.2)$$
$$= \mathbb{E}^{\pi_\theta}[\nabla_\theta \ln \pi_\theta(a \mid s)(Q_\infty^{\pi_\theta}(s, a) - b(s))],$$

where $b(s)$ is a function of the state, called the *baseline function*.

Typically, we use the estimated value function $V(s)$ as the baseline function. Also, we call

$$Q_\infty^{\pi_\theta}(s, a) \equiv \sum_{t=0}^{\infty} \mathbb{E}^{\pi_\theta}[R_t - f_\infty(\theta) \mid S_0 = s, A_0 = a]$$

---

[4] In this Eq. (7.3.1), we maximize the objective function, so it is an update by addition rather than subtraction (which would be for minimizing a loss).

the *differential action-value function*, which redefines the action-value function (since the sum diverges without discounting, we subtract the average reward).

Before exploring the specific (approximate) calculation of gradients, we express Eq. (7.3.2) using the advantage function. When using the value function as the baseline function, we can write the gradient as

$$\nabla_\theta f_\infty(\theta) = \sum_{s \in \mathcal{S}} \sum_{a \in \mathcal{A}} p_\infty^{\pi_\theta}(s) \pi_\theta(a \mid s) \nabla_\theta \ln \pi_\theta(a \mid s) A_\infty^{\pi_\theta}(s, a)$$

$$= \mathbb{E}^{\pi_\theta}[\nabla_\theta \ln \pi_\theta(a \mid s) A_\infty^{\pi_\theta}(s, a)].$$

In other words, $Q_\infty^{\pi_\theta}(s, a) - b(s)$ is represented by the advantage function:

$$A_\infty^{\pi_\theta}(s, a) = Q_\infty^{\pi_\theta}(s, a) - V_\infty^{\pi_\theta}(s),$$

where

$$V_\infty^{\pi_\theta}(s) = \sum_{a \in \mathcal{A}} \pi_\theta(a \mid s) Q_\infty^{\pi_\theta}(s, a).$$

The purpose of using the advantage function as the baseline function is to standardize the mean of the weights $Q_\infty^{\pi_\theta}(s, a) - b(s)$ of the weighted gradients $\nabla_\theta \ln \pi_\theta(a \mid s)(Q_\infty^{\pi_\theta}(s, a) - b(s))$ to zero.

Using Eq. (7.3.2), we can compute the gradients $\nabla_\theta \ln \pi_\theta(a_t \mid s_t)$ via error backpropagation, because the (log of) policy $\ln \pi_\theta(a_t \mid s_t)$ is a function of the output of a neural network (see Sect. 1.1.2.5). Furthermore, we can approximate the expectation of Eq. (7.3.2) using the *REINFORCE method* [12, 52]. That is, by assuming ergodicity for policy π_θ and $p_\infty^{\pi_\theta}(s)$:

$$\mathbb{E}_{\pi_\theta(a \mid s) p_\infty^{\pi_\theta}(s)}[h(s, a)] = \lim_{T \to \infty} \frac{1}{T} \sum_{t=0}^{T-1} h(S_t = s, A_t = a),$$

where h is a mapping from $\mathcal{S} \times \mathcal{A}$ to $\mathbf{R}$, Eq. (7.3.2) yields

$$\nabla_\theta f_\infty(\theta) = \lim_{T \to \infty} \frac{1}{T} \sum_{t=0}^{T-1} \nabla_\theta \ln \pi_\theta(a_t \mid s_t) A_\infty^{\pi_\theta}(s_t, a_t)$$

for an episode sampled by policy π_θ:

$$\{s_0, a_0, r_0, \ldots, s_{T-1}, a_{T-1}, r_{T-1}, s_T\}^5. \tag{7.3.3}$$

Thus, we have

$$\nabla_\theta f_\infty(\theta) \approx \frac{1}{T} \sum_{t=0}^{T-1} \nabla_\theta \ln \pi_\theta(a_t \mid s_t) A_\infty^{\pi_\theta}(s_t, a_t).$$

7.3 Policy Gradient Methods and Their Extensions

In practical calculations using the REINFORCE method, we use several additional approximations. Specifically, for an episode (7.3.3), we use the following approximations.

1. For the sample approximation of $Q_\infty^{\pi_\theta}$, the return c_t is utilized as follows:

$$c_t = \sum_{k=t}^{T-1} r_k, \quad t = 0, \ldots, T-1.$$

2. Using $b(s_t)$ as the estimated value of the mean reward, the update equation for policy parameters is formulated as

$$\theta := \theta + \alpha_t \frac{1}{T} \sum_{t=0}^{T-1} (c_t - b(s_t)) \nabla_\theta \ln \pi_\theta(s_t, a_t),$$

where α_t is a constant. This is equivalent to approximating the advantage function as $A_\infty^{\pi_\theta}(s, a) \approx \hat{A}_t(s_t, a_t) \equiv c_t - b(s_t)$.

In Eq. (7.3.2) of the policy gradient theorem, $\ln \pi_\theta(a \mid s)$ represents the log-likelihood, and $\nabla_\theta \ln \pi_\theta(a \mid s)$ represents its gradient (referred to as the score function). The (log) policy gradient $\nabla_\theta \ln \pi_\theta(a \mid s)$ points towards the direction where the log-likelihood is maximized for the state-action pair (s, a). On the other hand, since we want to emphasize likelihood for state-action pairs (s, a) with higher action values, we adjust the parameter updates by weighting the score function with action values. This adjustment allows us to give more importance to state-action pairs with higher action values.

In policy gradient methods, gradients often become excessively large during policy updates. To address this issue, we use methods that constrain the magnitude of policy updates. Two representative methods are trust region policy optimization (TRPO) and proximal policy optimization (PPO). We briefly introduce these methods. For simplicity, we drop the limit symbol ∞ in the descriptions below. Additionally, we denote the sum: $\frac{1}{T} \sum_{t=0}^{T-1} x_t$ as $\hat{\mathbb{E}}_t[x_t]$. Under this notation, the gradient of the objective function in policy gradient methods is given by

$$\nabla_\theta f(\theta) = \hat{\mathbb{E}}_t[\nabla_\theta \ln \pi_\theta(a_t \mid s_t) \hat{A}_t],$$

where $\hat{A}_t \equiv A^{\pi_\theta}(s_t, a_t)$. This gradient corresponds to the gradient of the following objective function:

$$f(\theta) = \hat{\mathbb{E}}_t[\ln \pi_\theta(a_t \mid s_t) \hat{A}_t].$$

First, we discuss the *trust region policy optimization (TRPO)* method [39], which maximizes the objective function:

$$\hat{\mathbb{E}}_t \left[\frac{\pi_\theta(a_t \mid s_t)}{\pi_{\theta_{\text{old}}}(a_t \mid s_t)} \hat{A}_t - \beta \cdot \mathbb{KL}(\pi_\theta(\cdot \mid s_t) \parallel \pi_{\theta_{\text{old}}}(\cdot \mid s_t)) \right],$$

where β is a constant and θ_{old} represents the parameters before the update, and $\mathbb{KL}(p(z) \parallel q(z))$ is the KL divergence[5] between probability distributions $p(z)$ and $q(z)$. As evident from this objective function, TRPO introduces the KL divergence between the policy before and after the update as a regularization term to control the magnitude of updates. Experimental results have shown that the optimal value of β varies depending on the problem, and even within the same problem, the optimal value of β may change during the learning process.

In the *proximal policy optimization (PPO)* method [40], large changes are directly restricted by "clipping." Specifically, PPO updates the parameter by maximizing the objective function:

$$\hat{\mathbb{E}}_t \left[\min(r_t(\theta) \hat{A}_t, \text{clip}(r_t(\theta), 1 - \epsilon, 1 + \epsilon) \hat{A}_t) \right],$$

where ϵ is a hyperparameter,

$$\text{clip}(x, a, b) = \begin{cases} a, & x \leq a, \\ x, & a < x \leq b, \\ b, & b < x, \end{cases}$$

and

$$r_t(\theta) \equiv \frac{\pi_\theta(a_t \mid s_t)}{\pi_{\theta_{\text{old}}}(a_t \mid s_t)},$$

with $r_t(\theta_{\text{old}}) = 1$, where θ_{old} represents the parameters before the update.

7.4 Appendix

7.4.1 Proof of Policy Gradient Theorem

In this appendix, we show a proof of policy gradient theorem. Considering that the policy $\pi_\theta(a \mid s)$ and the state transition probability $p(s' \mid s, a)$ are fixed, we can transform the differential action-value function into the following recursive expression:

---

[5] For KL divergence, see Appendix B in the appendix at the end of the book.

7.4 Appendix

$$Q_\infty^{\pi_\theta}(s, a) = g(s, a) - f_\infty(\theta) + \sum_{t=1}^{\infty} \mathbb{E}^{\pi_\theta}[R_t - f_\infty(\theta) \mid S_0 = s, A_0 = a]$$

$$= g(s, a) - f_\infty(\theta) + \sum_{s' \in S} p(s' \mid s, a) \sum_{a' \in \mathcal{A}} \pi_\theta(a' \mid s') Q_\infty^{\pi_\theta}(s', a').$$

By taking the gradient with respect to θ on both sides of this equation and using the partial differentiation of $\ln \pi_\theta$ with respect to θ, which gives

$$\pi_\theta(a' \mid s') \nabla_\theta \ln \pi_\theta(a' \mid s') = \nabla_\theta \pi_\theta(a' \mid s'),$$

we obtain

$$\nabla_\theta f_\infty(\theta) = -\nabla_\theta Q_\infty^{\pi_\theta}(s, a)$$
$$+ \sum_{s' \in S} \sum_{a' \in \mathcal{A}} p(s' \mid s, a) \pi_\theta(a' \mid s') (\nabla_\theta \ln \pi_\theta(a' \mid s') Q_\infty^{\pi_\theta}(s', a') + \nabla_\theta Q_\infty^{\pi_\theta}(s', a')).$$

(7.4.1)

Since the average reward depends only on θ and $\sum_{s \in S} \sum_{a \in \mathcal{A}} p_\infty^{\pi_\theta}(s) \pi_\theta(a \mid s) = 1$, we note that

$$\sum_{s \in S} \sum_{a \in \mathcal{A}} p_\infty^{\pi_\theta}(s) \pi_\theta(a \mid s) \nabla_\theta f_\infty(\theta) = \nabla_\theta f_\infty(\theta) \sum_{s \in S} \sum_{a \in \mathcal{A}} p_\infty^{\pi_\theta}(s) \pi_\theta(a \mid s)$$
$$= \nabla_\theta f_\infty(\theta).$$

From this and Eq. (7.4.1), we have

$$\nabla_\theta f_\infty(\theta) = \sum_{s \in S} \sum_{a \in \mathcal{A}} p_\infty^{\pi_\theta}(s) \pi_\theta(a \mid s) \Big\{ - \nabla_\theta Q_\infty^{\pi_\theta}(s, a)$$
$$+ \sum_{s' \in S} \sum_{a' \in \mathcal{A}} p(s' \mid s, a) \pi_\theta(a' \mid s')(\nabla_\theta \ln \pi_\theta(a' \mid s') Q_\infty^{\pi_\theta}(s', a') + \nabla_\theta Q_\infty^{\pi_\theta}(s', a')) \Big\}.$$

Removing the parentheses with the distributive property, we have

$$\nabla_\theta f_\infty(\theta) = - \sum_{s \in S} \sum_{a \in \mathcal{A}} p_\infty^{\pi_\theta}(s) \pi_\theta(a \mid s) \nabla_\theta Q_\infty^{\pi_\theta}(s, a)$$
$$+ \sum_{s' \in S} \sum_{a' \in \mathcal{A}} \sum_{s \in S} \sum_{a \in \mathcal{A}} p(s' \mid s, a) \pi_\theta(a' \mid s') p_\infty^{\pi_\theta}(s) \pi_\theta(a \mid s)$$
$$\times (\nabla_\theta \ln \pi_\theta(a' \mid s') Q_\infty^{\pi_\theta}(s', a') + \nabla_\theta Q_\infty^{\pi_\theta}(s', a'))$$
$$= - \sum_{s \in S} \sum_{a \in \mathcal{A}} p_\infty^{\pi_\theta}(s) \pi_\theta(a \mid s) \nabla_\theta Q_\infty^{\pi_\theta}(s, a)$$
$$+ \sum_{s' \in S} \sum_{a' \in \mathcal{A}} \pi_\theta(a' \mid s') \left(\nabla_\theta \ln \pi_\theta(a' \mid s') Q_\infty^{\pi_\theta}(s', a') + \nabla_\theta Q_\infty^{\pi_\theta}(s', a') \right)$$
$$\times \sum_{s \in S} \sum_{a \in \mathcal{A}} p(s' \mid s, a) p_\infty^{\pi_\theta}(s) \pi_\theta(a \mid s)$$

$$= -\sum_{s \in S} \sum_{a \in \mathcal{A}} p_\infty^{\pi_\theta}(s) \pi_\theta(a \mid s) \nabla_\theta Q_\infty^{\pi_\theta}(s, a)$$

$$+ \sum_{s' \in S} \sum_{a' \in \mathcal{A}} \pi_\theta(a' \mid s') \left(\nabla_\theta \ln \pi_\theta(a' \mid s') Q_\infty^{\pi_\theta}(s', a') + \nabla_\theta Q_\infty^{\pi_\theta}(s', a') \right) \times p_\infty^{\pi_\theta}(s')$$

$$= -\sum_{s \in S} \sum_{a \in \mathcal{A}} p_\infty^{\pi_\theta}(s) \pi_\theta(a \mid s) \nabla_\theta Q_\infty^{\pi_\theta}(s, a)$$

$$+ \sum_{s' \in S} \sum_{a' \in \mathcal{A}} \pi_\theta(a' \mid s') \nabla_\theta \ln \pi_\theta(a' \mid s') Q_\infty^{\pi_\theta}(s', a') \times p_\infty^{\pi_\theta}(s')$$

$$+ \sum_{s' \in S} \sum_{a' \in \mathcal{A}} \pi_\theta(a' \mid s') \nabla_\theta Q_\infty^{\pi_\theta}(s', a') \times p_\infty^{\pi_\theta}(s')$$

$$= \sum_{s \in S} \sum_{a \in \mathcal{A}} p_\infty^{\pi_\theta}(s) \pi_\theta(a \mid s) \nabla_\theta \ln \pi_\theta(a \mid s) Q_\infty^{\pi_\theta}(s, a).$$

The second equality is derived by factoring out terms that are independent of (s', a'), the third equality is due to the assumption of stationarity for π_θ: $p_\infty^{\pi_\theta}(s') = \sum_{s \in S} \sum_{a \in \mathcal{A}} p(s' \mid s, a) \pi_\theta(a \mid s) p_\infty^{\pi_\theta}(s)$, and the last equality holds because the first and third terms cancel each other out. For any baseline function $b(s)$, the following holds:

$$\sum_{a \in \mathcal{A}} \pi_\theta(a \mid s) \nabla_\theta \ln \pi_\theta(a \mid s) b(s) = \sum_{a \in \mathcal{A}} \nabla_\theta \pi_\theta(a \mid s) b(s) = b(s) \nabla_\theta \left\{ \sum_{a \in \mathcal{A}} \pi_\theta(a \mid s) \right\} = b(s) \nabla_\theta 1 = \mathbf{0}.$$

Hence, we have

$$\nabla_\theta f_\infty(\theta) = \sum_{s \in S} \sum_{a \in \mathcal{A}} p_\infty^{\pi_\theta}(s) \pi_\theta(a \mid s) \nabla_\theta \ln \pi_\theta(a \mid s) \left(Q_\infty^{\pi_\theta}(s, a) - b(s) \right).$$

This concludes the proof.

Part II
Generative Language Model

Chapter 8
Language Generation

The topic of this chapter is generative language models (generative language AI). To this end, we first explain what a language model is and briefly introduce a language model using RNN as a specific example (RNN language model). Furthermore, we introduce a sequence-to-sequence model with an encoder and decoder consisting of RNNs, equipped with attention mechanisms, and then develop it into a sequence-to-sequence model using Transformers. In the next chapter, we present large-scale language models, and finally, we explain generative language models. The reasons for following such a procedure include the following.

1. We can gain a better understanding of the characteristics of large-scale language models by comparing them with RNN language models.
2. We can encounter specific examples of the application of attention mechanisms.
3. We can understand specific applications and features of Transformers. We can also clarify the positioning of large-scale language models.

8.1 Language Model

A language model is a model of the probability of generating a sentence. For example, for the sentence "John saw Mary," we can express the joint probability of composing the words in the sentence as

$$P(\text{John, saw, Mary}).$$

Similarly, for the sentence "The capital of Italy is Rome," we can define the joint probability of the sentence as

$$P(\text{The, capital, of, Italy, is, Rome}).$$

Language models have various applications such as determining the likelihood of sentences generated by a system and predicting and generating words, sentences, and paragraphs.

Using a language model, particularly, enables the prediction of words, i.e., predicting the next word (the word following a given text). For example, for the phrase "The capital of Italy is," considering candidate words, we can represent the joint probabilities as follows:

$$P(\text{The, capital, of, Italy, is, Tokyo}) = 0.0000043,$$
$$P(\text{The, capital, of, Italy, is, Paris}) = 0.0000082,$$
$$\vdots$$
$$P(\text{The, capital, of, Italy, is, Rome}) = 0.0000103.$$

Among these probabilities, we can choose the word with the maximum probability, which in this example is "Rome." In other words, we have

$$y^* = \arg\max_{y \in V} P(\text{The, capital, of, Italy, is}, y),$$

where V is the set of all candidate words.

We represent joint probability as the product of conditional probabilities from the beginning of the sentence (denoted by the special symbol "BOS") to each word sequentially. That is,

$$P(y_1, \ldots, y_T) = P(y_1 \mid \text{BOS}) P(y_2 \mid \text{BOS}, y_1) \cdots P(y_T \mid \text{BOS}, y_1, \ldots, y_{T-1})$$

holds. Using this notation based on the product of conditional probabilities, an example of predicting the continuation of the preceding text is as follows:

$$P(\text{The, capital, of, Italy, is}, y)$$
$$= P(\text{The} \mid \text{BOS}) \cdots P(\text{is} \mid \text{BOS}, \ldots, \text{Italy}) P(y \mid \text{BOS}, \ldots, \text{is}).$$

In this equation, excluding the last factor on the right-hand side

$$P(\text{The} \mid \text{BOS}) \cdots P(\text{is} \mid \text{BOS}, \ldots, \text{Italy})$$

is a constant unrelated to y. Thus, we have

$$y^* = \arg\max_{y \in V} P(\text{The, capital, of, Italy, is}, y)$$
$$= \arg\max_{y \in V} P(y \mid \text{The, capital, of, Italy, is}).$$

We formalize the language model a bit more. Consider a sequence of random variables taking values as words or word embeddings: X_t, where $t = 1, \ldots, T$, given

8.1 Language Model

by
$$X_1, X_2, \ldots, X_T.$$

In this context, we will encounter random variables such as Y_t, S_t, X_t, etc. For simplicity, we omit the random variable when referring to the realization x_t of X_t. For example, instead of

$$P(X_t = x_t \mid X_1 = x_1, \ldots, X_{t-1} = x_{t-1}),$$

we write
$$P(x_t \mid x_1, \ldots, x_{t-1}).$$

As realizations of random variables, y_t, s_t, $\mathbf{x}_t$, etc., will appear.

We introduce a special symbol $y_0 = \text{BOS}$ at the beginning and another special symbol $y_{T+1} = \text{EOS}$ at the end of the word sequence $y_1, \ldots, y_T$, forming the sequence $\mathbf{Y}$:

$$\mathbf{Y} = y_0, y_1, \ldots, y_T, y_{T+1}.$$

Since $y_0 = \text{BOS}$ has a generation probability of 1, we can express the generation probability of the sequence $\mathbf{Y}$ using the definition of conditional probability as

$$P(\mathbf{Y}) = \prod_{t=1}^{T+1} P(y_t \mid \mathbf{Y}_{0:t-1}), \tag{8.1.1}$$

where $\mathbf{Y}_{0:t-1}$ represents the subsequence $y_0, y_1, \ldots, y_{t-1}$. From this equation, clearly, achieving a good language model relies on accurately modeling the conditional probability $P(y_t \mid \mathbf{Y}_{0:t-1})$.

In this chapter, as good language models, we introduce language models based on Transformers, particularly large-scale language models and their development into generative language models. Before Transformers, several methods for modeling the conditional probability $P(y_t \mid \mathbf{Y}_{0:t-1})$ have been studied. We mention some representative examples.

1. Direct estimation of conditional probability from corpora. This method suffers from the problem of *data sparsity*, where the number of data points for long conditional sequences rapidly decreases.
2. N-gram methods approximate the conditional probability's condition as

$$P(y_t \mid y_0, \ldots, y_{t-1}) \approx P(y_t \mid y_{t-n+1}, \ldots, y_{t-1}),$$

   predicting based on the preceding $n - 1$ words. While this method partially addresses the data sparsity problem, it fails to capture relationships between distant words.
3. Methods utilizing neural networks designed for sequence processing, such as a recurrent neural network (RNN) or a long short-term memory (LSTM). These

methods face issues like vanishing gradients during training and an inability to capture relationships between distant words.

Among these methods, in this chapter, we briefly introduce the language model using RNN (RNN language model). Before diving into its explanation, we briefly discuss the beginning and end of sentences and look at the algorithm for generating sentences given a language model.

Using BOS (beginning of sentence) as the starting symbol and EOS (end of sentence) as the ending symbol, we denote the 0-th position of a sentence consisting of a sequence of T words as BOS and the $(T + 1)$-th position as EOS. For example, the word sequence:

"has a good tool"

is a natural order in English text, whereas

"BOS has a good tool EOS"

is considered as a single sentence. Thus, the latter has a lower probability of being generated compared to the former. Henceforth, unless stated otherwise, we assume that BOS is at the beginning and EOS is at the end of a sentence.

In general, the generation of sentences (or texts) using a language model is achieved by predicting one word at a time from the beginning of the sentence in order to maximize the probability of the generated sentence. This process involves predicting a new word from the previously predicted word sequence based on conditioned probabilities. Using a greedy search algorithm, which always selects the word with the highest probability at each step, may not result in the highest probability for the generated sentence (the joint probability of the words constituting the sentence).

On the other hand, maintaining the probabilities of all words at each step of prediction and selecting each word to maximize the probability of the entire sentence leads to an exponentially increasing computational complexity with the length of the sentence. Thus, it becomes infeasible to find the sentence with the highest probability. A compromise between these approaches is the beam search method, which maintains the top k candidates with high conditional probabilities and explores word sequences to maximize the probability of the sentence. This method strikes a balance between considering all possibilities and computational efficiency.

Both greedy search and beam search approaches, by selecting the word or sentence with the maximum probability, tend to generate the same output for a given input text or sentence when predicting subsequent text. In many applications, however, rather than determining a unique sentence, we need diverse outputs. To achieve diverse predictions, in the case of greedy search, we can sample words according to their probability distribution instead of always selecting the word with the highest probability. Similarly, in the case of beam search, sampling sentences according to their probability distribution can lead to diverse predictions. We provide a bit more detailed explanation about greedy search and beam search.

8.1 Language Model

We denote the word sequence generated up to time $t-1$ starting from BOS at time 0 as
$$\tilde{\mathbf{Y}}_{t-1} = \text{BOS}, \tilde{y}_1, \tilde{y}_2, \ldots, \tilde{y}_{t-1}.$$

The *greedy search* approach selects the word $\tilde{y}_t$ at each time step t (where $t > 0$) until EOS is generated by maximizing the conditional probability:
$$P(y_t \mid \tilde{\mathbf{Y}}_{t-1}).$$

That is, at each step t, we have
$$\tilde{y}_t = \arg\max_{y_t \in V} P(y_t \mid \tilde{\mathbf{Y}}_{t-1}),$$

where V is the set of all words.

In greedy search, the generated sentence may not have the highest probability. We explain this using an example. Consider two-word sentences consisting of only the words "papa" and "mama," and suppose the conditional probabilities are as follows:

$$P(\text{papa} \mid \text{BOS}) = 0.4, \quad P(\text{mama} \mid \text{BOS}) = 0.6,$$
$$P(\text{papa} \mid \text{BOS, papa}) = 0.9, \quad P(\text{mama} \mid \text{BOS, papa}) = 0.1,$$
$$P(\text{papa} \mid \text{BOS, mama}) = 0.45, \quad P(\text{mama} \mid \text{BOS, mama}) = 0.55,$$
$$P(\text{EOS} \mid \text{BOS}, x, y) = 1.0, \quad x, y \text{ are either papa or mama}.$$

In greedy search, "mama" is initially chosen. Then, "mama" is chosen again, resulting in the generated sentence
$$\text{BOS mama mama EOS}$$
with a probability of $0.6 \times 0.55 = 0.33$. However, the sentence with the highest joint probability is
$$\text{BOS papa papa EOS}$$
with a probability of $0.4 \times 0.9 = 0.36$. The choice of word at each step depends on the words chosen in the past, leading to this discrepancy.

To generate the sentence (word sequence) with the highest probability, we might consider maintaining the conditional probabilities of all words at each prediction step and then identifying the word sequence that maximizes the probability according to Eq. (8.1.1). This approach would, however, require maintaining the conditional probabilities of all words, resulting in a computational complexity of the order $|V|^l$, where $|V|$ is the total number of words in the vocabulary and l is the length of the sentence. Thus, in practice, it is not feasible to compute the sentence with the highest probability using this method due to its exponential computational complexity.

Beam search maintains only the top k words (referred to as the *beam width*) with the highest conditional probabilities:

Fig. 8.1 Illustration of beam search method. At each time step t, select the top k words with the highest conditional probability $P(y_t | \tilde{\mathbf{Y}}_{t-1})$ (in this illustration, $k = 2$) and maintain only those. The numbers above the arrows represent $P(y_t | \tilde{\mathbf{Y}}_{t-1})$

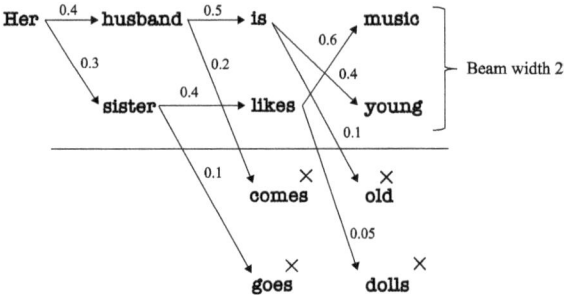

$$P(y_t | \tilde{\mathbf{Y}}_{t-1})$$

at each time step t, rather than keeping the probabilities for all words. It constructs a word sequence using only these maintained words in order to maximize the joint probability of the sentence (see Fig. 8.1). Beam search avoids computational explosion by limiting the number of words considered at each step.

Now, we transition to discussing the RNN language model.

8.2 RNN Language Model

We call the language model utilizing RNN the *RNN language model* [25]. As depicted in Fig. 8.2, the RNN language model takes input as the one-hot representation of token (word) sequences and outputs the probability of the next token conditioned on the preceding inputs, using an RNN. By predicting one step ahead, it learns from large unlabeled corpora.

Fig. 8.2 A segment of the RNN language model. Outputs the prediction (probability of all tokens) for the next token

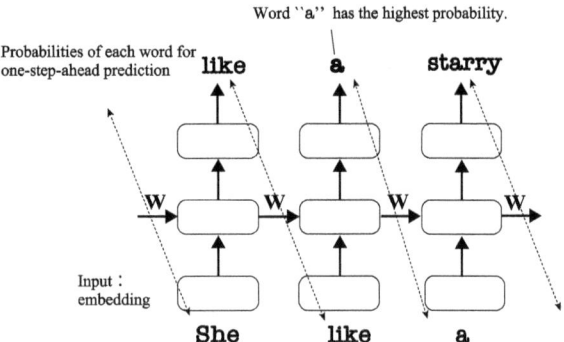

8.2 RNN Language Model

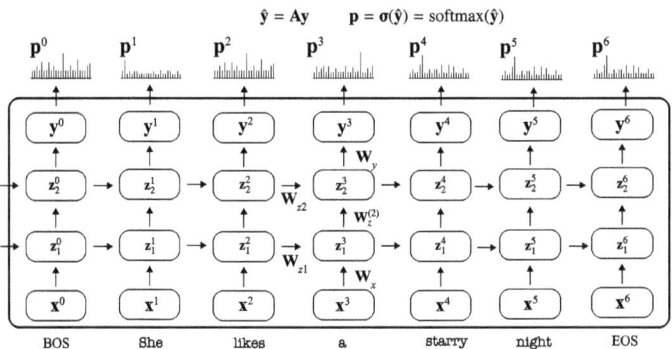

Fig. 8.3 In the RNN language model, the one-hot representation s of the words composing a sentence is transformed into embeddings **x**, which serve as inputs. The output layer units produce a vector **y** of embedding dimensions. This vector is then linearly transformed into the dimension of the one-hot representation (the total number of words), and the softmax function is applied to obtain the final output

We explain the details of the RNN language model (Fig. 8.3). Consider a sequence of tokens (words): $s^0 = \text{BOS}, s^1, \ldots, s^T, s^{T+1} = \text{EOS}$.[1]

1. The input to the RNN language model is the embedding representation $\mathbf{x}^t$ of the word s^t ($t = 0, \ldots, T+1$). In other words, if $\mathbf{s}^t$ represents the one-hot representation of word s^t for $t = 0, \ldots, T+1$, then their transformation by embedding matrix $\mathbf{W}$ gives $\mathbf{x}^t = \mathbf{W}\mathbf{s}^t$.
2. The dimensions of the hidden layer and the output layer are the dimensions of the word embedding.
3. To obtain the final output as a probability distribution of words (a vector with the same dimension as the one-hot representation), the output $\mathbf{y}^t$ of the output layer is linearly transformed to $\hat{\mathbf{y}}^t = \mathbf{A}\mathbf{y}^t$, and the softmax function is applied to $\hat{\mathbf{y}}^t$ to obtain the final output.
4. Hence, the output of the RNN language model consists of a sequence of word probability distributions $\mathbf{p}^0, \mathbf{p}^1, \ldots, \mathbf{p}^T, \mathbf{p}^{T+1}$. Specifically, it is

$$\mathbf{p}^t = \sigma(\hat{\mathbf{y}}^t), \quad t = 0, \ldots, T+1.$$

The RNN language model is trained to predict the next word s^t given $s^0, \ldots, s^{t-1}$, so these are the predicted probabilities of the next token conditioned on $s^0, \ldots, s^{t-1}$ (a list of prediction probabilities for all words).

---

[1] In Sects. 8.2 and 8.3, we use superscripts as indices for sequences of random variables. When there are multiple sentences to distinguish them, we use subscript indices. Thus, we use superscript indices for indexing the sequence.

We provide additional clarification regarding the output of the RNN language model. Consider the sequence of random variables S^t, $t = 0, \ldots, T+1$, taking values as words:
$$S^0, S^1, \ldots, S^T, S^{T+1}.$$

The RNN language model defines the conditional probability of S^t given $S^0 = s^0$, $S^1 = s^1, \ldots, S^{t-1} = s^{t-1}$ as the i-th component of $\boldsymbol{\sigma}(\hat{\mathbf{y}}^t)$, when the i-th component of the one-hot representation of word s^t is 1. In other words,
$$\mathbf{p}^t = (p_1 \ p_2 \ \cdots \ p_{|V|})^T = \boldsymbol{\sigma}(\hat{\mathbf{y}}^t),$$
$$P(s^t \mid s^1, \ldots, s^{t-1}) = p^i,$$
where V is the set of all words.

We use a large corpus to train the RNN language model. Let us denote the corpus as
$$\mathcal{S} = \{\text{sent}_1, \ldots, \text{sent}_N\}, \quad \text{sent}_n = s_n^0, s_n^1, s_n^2, \ldots, s_n^{T_n}, s_n^{T_n+1},$$
where $s_n^0 = \text{BOS}$ and $s_n^{T_n+1} = \text{EOS}$. In the RNN language model, we train the model to predict one word ahead. In other words, we minimize the empirical loss:
$$L = -\sum_{n=1}^{N} \sum_{t=1}^{T_n+1} \ln P(s_n^t \mid s_n^1, \ldots, s_n^{t-1}).$$

After training, we can consider the output of the RNN as embeddings of words considering the context. Thus, by using the RNN language model, we obtain contextual word embeddings for each word in a sentence.

To summarize the properties of the RNN language model, it enables us to consider synonyms and related words through embedding representations. Theoretically, however, due to fixed-length vectors, it may miss information for distant dependencies, especially in long sentences. Also, the network tends to suffer from gradient vanishing/exploding issues due to deep word directions, making training challenging.

8.3 Sequence-to-Sequence Models

Sequence-to-sequence models (seq2seq) is a probabilistic model that converts one sequence **X** into another sequence **Y**. Essentially, sequence-to-sequence models are language models, with translation being a typical application. In this section, we introduce sequence-to-sequence models incorporating RNNs and attention mechanisms, as well as sequence-to-sequence models using Transformers.

In general, the input and output of sequence-to-sequence models are both sequences. Here, we consider the case where both input and output are language sentences. Let the input sequence be $\mathbf{X} = x^1, x^2, \ldots, x^U$, and the output sequence

8.3 Sequence-to-Sequence Models

be $\mathbf{Y} = y^0, y^1, y^2, \ldots, y^T, y^{T+1}$, where $y^0 = \text{BOS}$ and $y^{T+1} = \text{EOS}$, with BOS and EOS representing the beginning and end of sentence markers, respectively. Generally, BOS and EOS are not appended to the input. In this case, we define the sequence-to-sequence model as

$$P(\mathbf{Y} \mid \mathbf{X}) = \prod_{t=1}^{T+1} P(y^t \mid \mathbf{Y}^{0:t-1}, \mathbf{X}), \tag{8.3.1}$$

where $\mathbf{Y}^{0:t-1}$ denotes the subsequence $y^0, y^1, \ldots, y^{t-1}$. As evident from the comparison with the definition of the language generation model (8.1.1), we can consider the sequence-to-sequence model (8.3.1) as a language model conditioned on the input. Typically, the input consists of word embeddings, and the output is determined by greedy or beam search algorithms based on distributions of words.

Figure 8.4 illustrates an example of a sequence-to-sequence model utilizing RNNs and attention mechanisms [3, 24]. As shown in the figure, the sequence-to-sequence model consists of an encoder and a decoder, both composed of RNNs, along with an attention mechanism. The encoder utilizes all words in the input sentence, does not have an output layer, and the output of its hidden layer serves as the encoder's output. The decoder takes its own previous outputs (word sequences) as input and outputs one word at a time using greedy or beam search algorithms. The exchange of information between them is facilitated through the attention mechanism. At each time step, the attention mechanism computes attention by considering the output of the decoder's hidden layer as the target and the output of the encoder's hidden layer as the source.

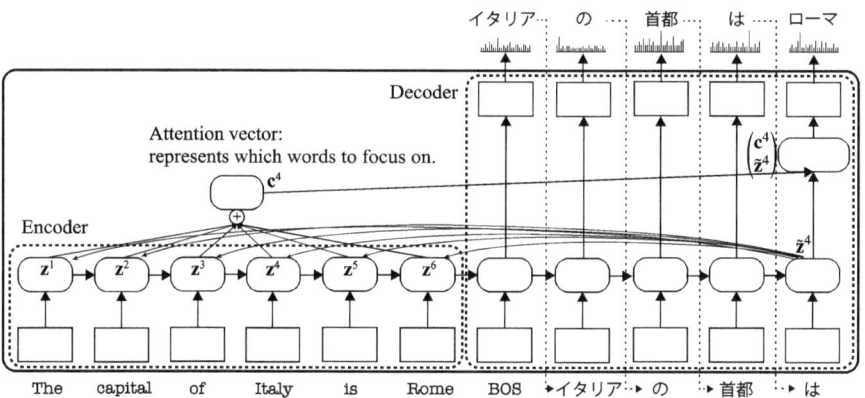

Fig. 8.4 An illustration of a sequence-to-sequence model with RNNs and attention mechanism

In Fig. 8.4, a link from a single hidden layer of the decoder to the hidden layers of the encoder represents an inner product, and the linear combination of hidden layers weighted by this inner product is denoted by ⊕, resulting in the attention (vector). It is also common to output a vector by concatenating the attention and the hidden layer's output. Figure 8.5 illustrates an example of the operation of this sequence-to-sequence model.

We discuss the details of implementing a sequence-to-sequence model. The input consists of a sequence of tokens (words) s^i, forming a sequence of sentences s^0, $s^1, \ldots, s^{T+1}$, and the output consists of a sequence of probability distributions of words in another language $\mathbf{p}^0, \ldots, \mathbf{p}^{T+1}$ (where $\mathbf{p}^0$ is the probability distribution of BOS, and $\mathbf{p}^{T+1}$ is the probability distribution of EOS). The computation of the sequence-to-sequence model proceeds as follows.

1. Represent each word s^t as a one-hot vector $\mathbf{s}^t$, for $t = 0, \ldots, T + 1$.
2. Convert the one-hot representation $\mathbf{s}^t$ into embeddings, obtaining $\mathbf{x}^t = \mathbf{W}\mathbf{s}^t$.
3. Use embeddings $\mathbf{x}^0, \mathbf{x}^1, \ldots, \mathbf{x}^{T+1}$ as inputs to the encoder.
4. Compute attention $\mathbf{c}^t$ targeting the t-th hidden layer unit output $\tilde{\mathbf{z}}^t$ of the decoder, using the output units $\mathbf{z}^1, \mathbf{z}^2, \ldots, \mathbf{z}^T$ of the encoder as the source.
5. The decoder calculates output $\mathbf{y}^t$ using $\mathbf{c}^t$ or the combined vector $\begin{pmatrix} \mathbf{c}^t \\ \tilde{\mathbf{z}}^t \end{pmatrix}$ as input to the output layer.
6. Linearly transform this to the vector with the dimension of the number of words: $\hat{\mathbf{y}}^t = \mathbf{A}\mathbf{y}^t$. The softmax function of this value (vector) yields the word distribution, i.e.,

$$\mathbf{p}^t = \sigma(\hat{\mathbf{y}}^t), \quad t = 0, \ldots, T' + 1.$$

To obtain a sequence of words, one can use either greedy search, selecting the word with the maximum probability at each $\mathbf{p}^t$, or utilize beam search on $\mathbf{p}^1, \ldots, \mathbf{p}^t$.

In sequence-to-sequence models, learning is achieved by predicting the next word in the sequence. Specifically, with a large corpus of data (pairs of original sentences, sent, and their translations, sent'), represented as follows:

$$S = \{(\text{sent}_1, \text{sent}'_1), \ldots, (\text{sent}_N, \text{sent}'_N)\},$$
$$\text{sent}_n = x_n^1, x_n^2, \ldots, x_n^{U_n},$$
$$\text{sent}'_n = y_n^1, y_n^2, \ldots, y_n^{T_n},$$

we minimize the empirical loss:

$$L = -\sum_{n=1}^{N} \sum_{t=1}^{T_n+1} \ln P(y_n^t \mid y_n^1, \ldots, y_n^{t-1}, \text{sent}_n). \tag{8.3.2}$$

8.3 Sequence-to-Sequence Models

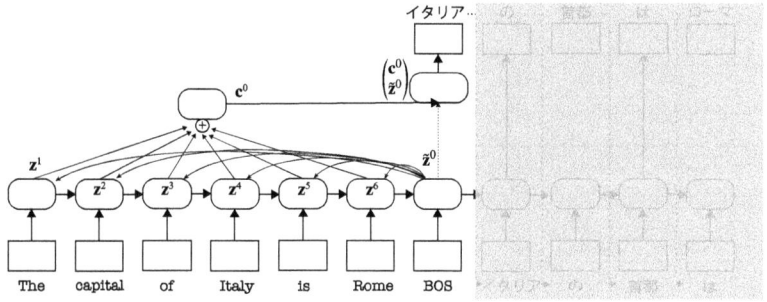

(a) Processing when the decoder reads BOS.

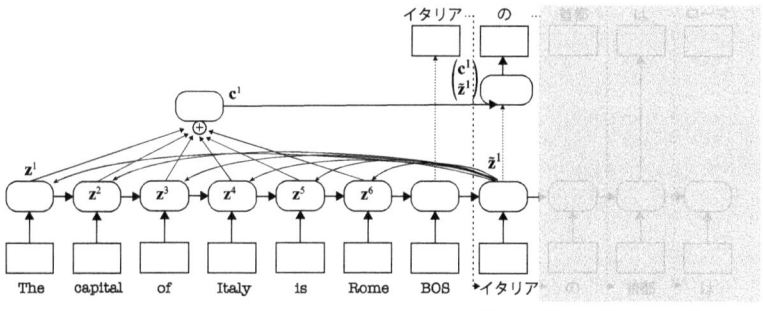

(b) Inputting BOS and the predicted word "イタリア" ("Italy") to the decoder.

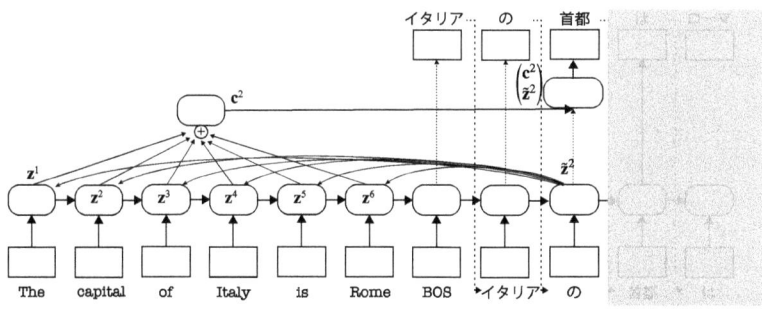

(c) Inputting BOS, the predicted word "イタリア" ("Italy"), and "の" ("of") to the decoder.

Fig. 8.5 Example of the operation of the sequence-to-sequence model with RNNs and attention mechanism

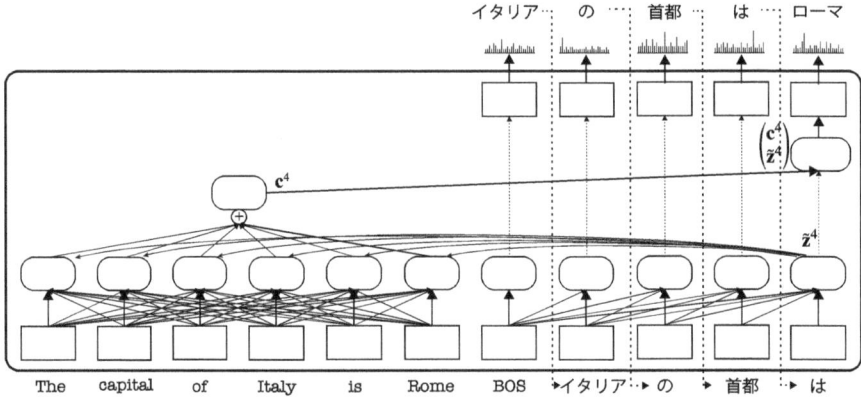

Fig. 8.6 Conceptual diagram of processing in a sequence-to-sequence model using the Transformer. The actual Transformer consists of multiple stacked blocks for both the encoder and decoder, but here, we simplify the diagram to clarify the flow of processing, emphasizing self-attention and cross-attention. Note that the decoder's self-attention is masked self-attention

Next, we explain the sequence-to-sequence model using the Transformer. We can see that the Transformer itself is the sequence-to-sequence model. Its training is performed by minimizing the empirical loss (8.3.2). Figure 8.6 illustrates the conceptual diagram of processing in a sequence-to-sequence model using the Transformer. The Transformer consists of multiple stacked blocks for both the encoder and decoder, but here, we simplify the diagram to clarify the flow of processing, emphasizing self-attention and cross-attention.[2] The fully connected links between the input and hidden layers in the encoder represent self-attention of the input. Additionally, the links between the input and hidden layers in the decoder are unidirectional "fully connected" links, indicating self-attention of a single word in the sentence and the words preceding it. Furthermore, as cross-attention, the link from a single hidden layer of the decoder to the hidden layers of the encoder represents an inner product, and the linear combination of hidden layers weighted by this inner product is denoted by ⊕. Note also that the decoder's self-attention is masked self-attention.

In a sequence-to-sequence model using the Transformer, the encoder utilizes all words in the input sentence, while the decoder predicts based on self-attention to its previous outputs (word sequences) and attention (cross-attention) to the outputs of the encoder. We employ self-attention, where words are combined in one hop, with bidirectional self-attention in the encoder and unidirectional self-attention in the decoder. Note that unlike in an RNN language model, we have no horizontal

---

[2] In the following, for simplicity, we refer to the attention mechanism as attention when we have no risk of confusion.

8.3 Sequence-to-Sequence Models

connections in the hidden layers. Figure 8.7 illustrates an example of the operation of the sequence-to-sequence model using the Transformer.

We explain the details of self-attention in the encoder based on Figs. 8.8 and 8.10. In these figures, the words "She," "seldom," "read," and "books" that constitute the input sentence are all represented as d-dimensional (here, 768-dimensional) embedding representations (vectors). The self-attention in the Transformer is implemented using multi-head attention, where the d-dimensional embeddings are split into d_k-dimensional (here, 64-dimensional) vectors per head. The number of heads is d/d_k (here, 12).[3]

Figure 8.8 illustrates the processing of self-attention for a single head. The process is as follows.

1. We apply linear transformations to the d-dimensional vectors corresponding to each word "She," "seldom," "read," and "books" using matrices $\mathbf{W}^Q$, $\mathbf{W}^K$, and $\mathbf{W}^V$ to obtain query, key, and value vectors.
2. In this illustration, we take the dot product between the "read" query vector and the key vectors of all words in the sentence, i.e., "She," "seldom," "read," and "books."
3. We use the resulting dot products, divided by $\sqrt{d_k}$, as weights to compute a linear combination of the value vectors for "She," "seldom," "read," and "books," yielding the reconstructed vector for "read" for this particular head of self-attention.

The same process is applied to "She," "seldom," and "books," resulting in reconstructed vectors for each of them for each head of self-attention. Furthermore, we show an example of the matrix calculation for self-attention in Fig. 8.9. In this figure, each row of matrices $\mathbf{Q}$, $\mathbf{K}$, and $\mathbf{V}$ corresponds to the transformed vector for each respective word after linear transformation.

Figure 8.10 illustrates the process of consolidating input embeddings split for multi-head processing for the word "read." Specifically, we compute attention for each embedded vector split into d/d_k ($= 12$) (64-dimensional vectors), and concatenate the results (vector concatenation) to create the original embedding dimension vector, which is further subjected to linear transformation. We carry out similar processing for all words constituting the sentence: "She," "seldom," "read," and "books," and create final reconstruction vectors for each.

Now, as explained in Chap. 6, for sequential data like language sentences, we encode the input positions and sum the embeddings of sequence elements (words in the case of sentences) with them to form the input. That is, for a sequence of words $\mathbf{x}_1, \mathbf{x}_2, \ldots, \mathbf{x}_l$, where the embedding of $\mathbf{x}_i$ is denoted as $\mathbf{v}_i = \mathbf{W}\mathbf{x}_i$, and the position encoding as $\mathbf{p}_i$, the input to the Transformer is formed as

$$\sqrt{d}\mathbf{v}_1 + \mathbf{p}_1, \sqrt{d}\mathbf{v}_2 + \mathbf{p}_2, \ldots, \sqrt{d}\mathbf{v}_l + \mathbf{p}_l,$$

---

[3] As mentioned in the self-attention section, due to the properties of the softmax function used for normalization of the relevance vectors, simply obtaining attention from a single vector without multi-head attention can result in one component of the normalization term being close to 1 while the other components are close to 0.

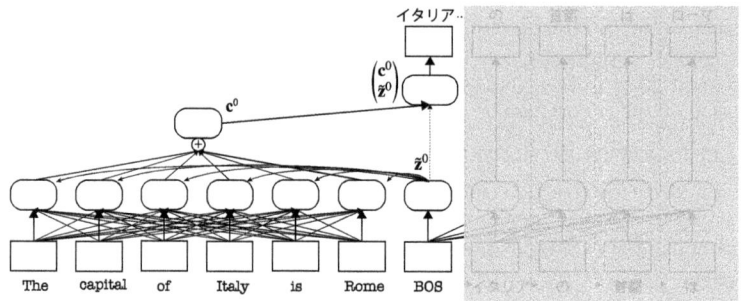

(a) Processing when the decoder reads BOS.

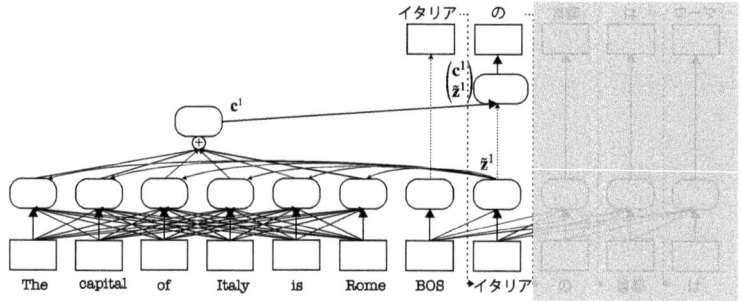

(b) Inputting BOS and the predicted word "イタリア" ("Italy") to the decoder.

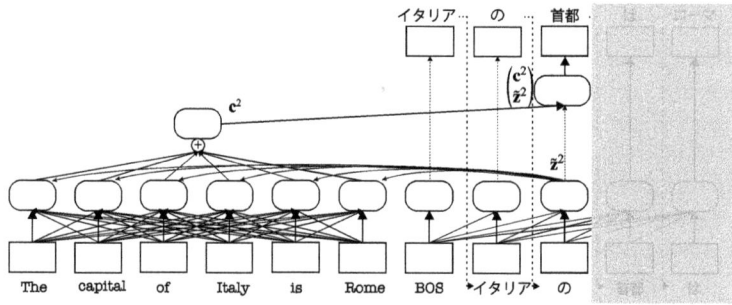

(c) Inputting BOS, the predicted word "イタリア" ("Italy"), and "の" ("of") to the decoder.

Fig. 8.7 Example of the operation of the sequence-to-sequence model using the Transformer

8.3 Sequence-to-Sequence Models

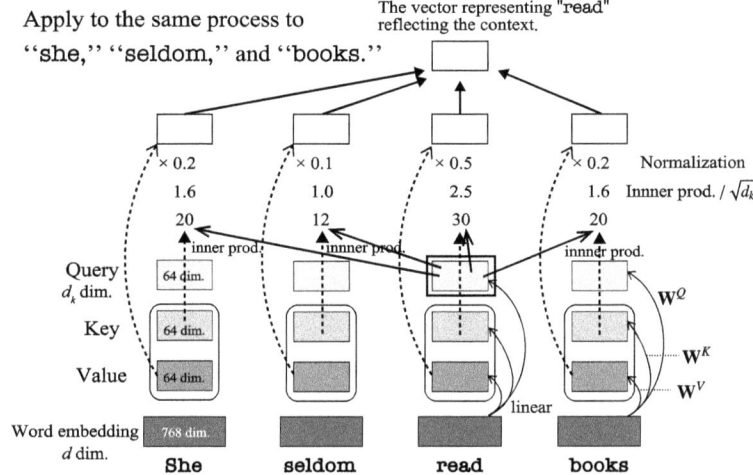

Fig. 8.8 Detailed illustration of self-attention in the encoder. Showing self-attention for a single head

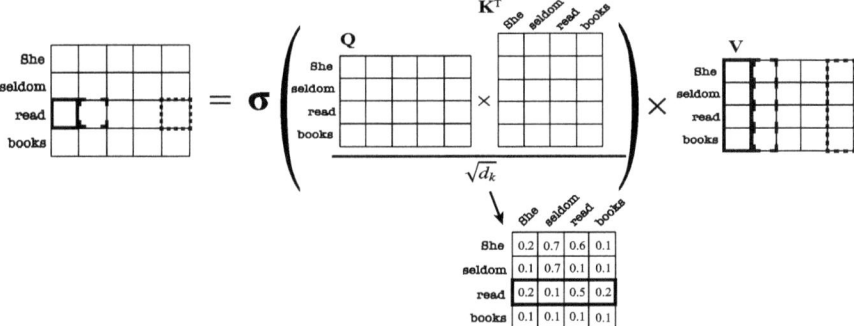

Fig. 8.9 Illustration of the matrix representation of self-attention

where d represents the dimensionality of the embedding.

Figure 8.11 illustrates the overall configuration and information flow of a sequence-to-sequence model using the Transformer architecture, assuming a translation task.

The input to the encoder is the original sentence, while the input to the decoder is the output from the encoder up to that point. The output of the decoder is the predicted next word. Both the encoder and the decoder typically consist of six layers (blocks) as a base, but implementations with 12 or 24 layers are also common.

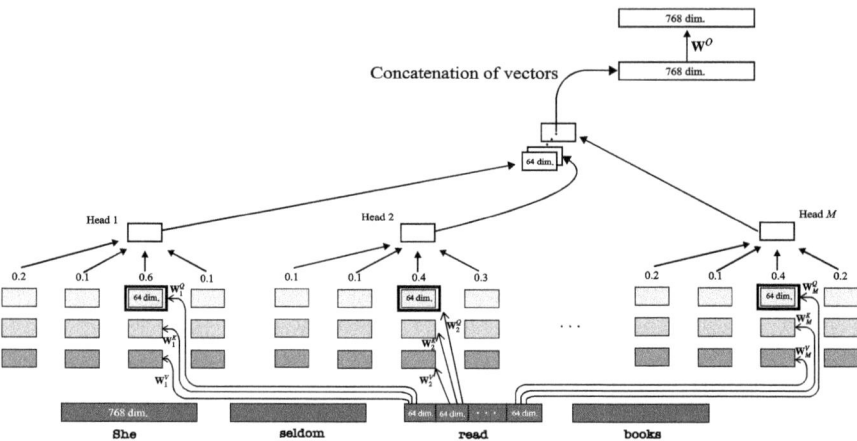

Fig. 8.10 Processing with multi-head attention. Attention computed for each head is aggregated to create the final reconstruction vector

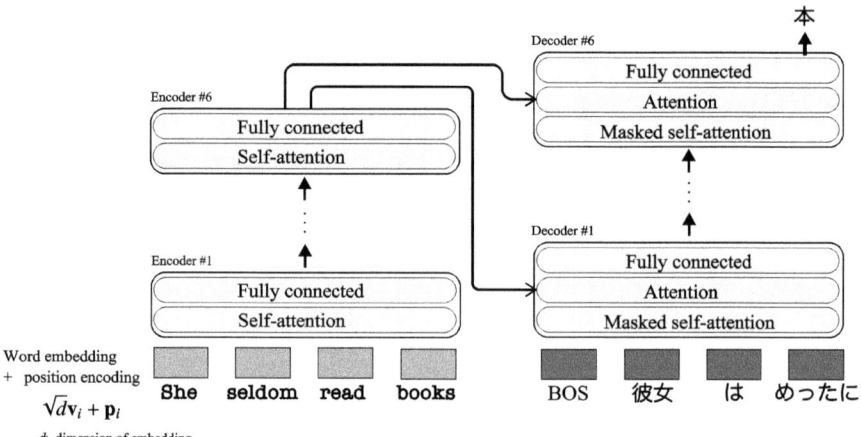

Fig. 8.11 Overall configuration and information flow of a sequence-to-sequence transformation model using the Transformer architecture, assuming a translation task

Note that the self-attention mechanism in the decoder is the *masked multi-head attention*. We discussed the necessity for the decoder's self-attention mechanism to be masked attention at the end of Chap. 6.

Chapter 9
Large-Scale Language Models

A large-scale language model generally refers to models based on Transformer architecture, such as BERT, GPT-X (X = 1, 2, 3, 3.5, 4), BART, T5, and Llama. Large-scale language models are fundamentally based on pre-training through self-supervised learning and fine-tuning for specific tasks. The aim of pre-training is to acquire general knowledge about language, and compared to pre-training, fine-tuning requires less data. Models like ChatGPT, GPT-4, Llama 2, and Llama 3, by incorporating reinforcement learning, belong to the category of large-scale language models. They are capable of generating language texts that are almost indistinguishable from those written by humans. In this book, however, we treat them separately as generative language models.

Here, we will discuss BERT and GPT-X as representative examples of large-scale language models.

9.1 BERT

BERT (bidirectional encoder representations from Transformers) [7] is composed of a bidirectional Transformer encoder that takes not only past and present but also future information as input (see Fig. 9.1). The base model of BERT consists of 12 layers (blocks), embedding dimension of 768, and 12 heads. The large model is composed of 24 layers (blocks), embedding dimension of 1024, and 16 heads. Tasks for fine-tuning BERT mainly involve word or sentence classification problems.

Due to pre-training, BERT learns general knowledge about language and the synthesis of context-aware word embeddings. Consequently, fine-tuning requires less labeled data. During BERT's pre-training, the following tasks 1 and 2 are learned concurrently (see Fig. 9.2).

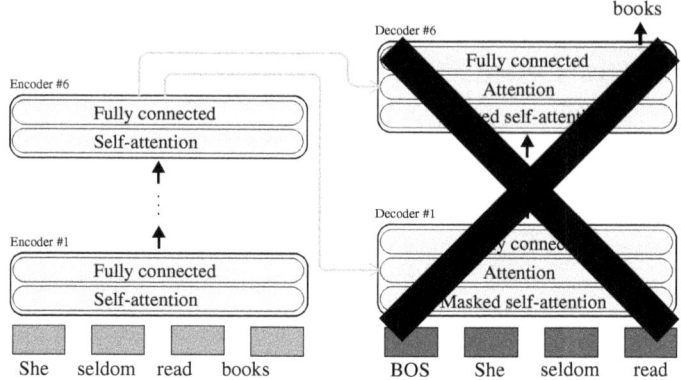

Fig. 9.1 BERT. It consists of Transformer encoders

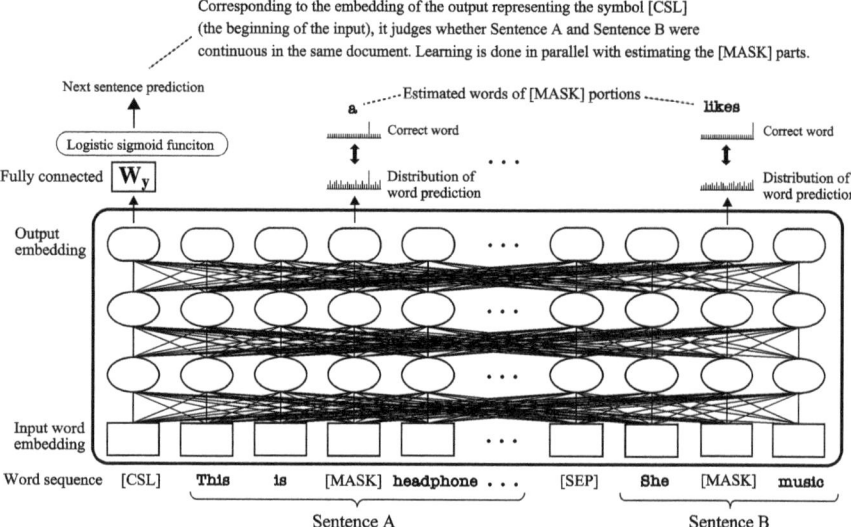

Fig. 9.2 Pre-training of BERT. Masked word reconstruction and next sentence prediction tasks are performed concurrently

1. Reconstruction of masked words.
2. Next sentence prediction, determining whether two sentences are truly consecutive in a document.

The corpora utilized for pre-training include BookCorpus (800 million words) and English Wikipedia (2,500 million words).

Fine-tuning BERT involves stacking fully connected layers designed according to the task on top of pre-trained BERT. The entire network, including internal parameters, is trained in fine-tuning.

9.1 BERT

Examples of tasks in the field of natural language processing where BERT is applied through fine-tuning include sentence pair classification problems (e.g., recognizing entailment), single-sentence classification problems (e.g., sentiment analysis), span extraction tasks (e.g., question answering), and sequence labeling tasks (e.g., named entity recognition). Below, we briefly introduce these tasks.

Entailment recognition task involves determining whether a hypothesis sentence can be inferred from a given premise sentence. For example, given the premise sentence "She is eating an apple" and the hypothesis sentence "She is eating fruit," since the premise sentence indicates that she is eating an apple, which implicitly implies that it is a type of fruit, we can judge that the hypothesis sentence is entailed by the premise sentence.

Sentiment analysis involves determining the sentiment or opinion expressed in a given text or sentence. Specifically, it aims to determine whether the text conveys a positive, negative, or neutral evaluation. Sentiment analysis is applied to various types of text data such as social media posts, product reviews, and customer feedback. The results are utilized as information to understand the reputation of a company's products or services.

Question answering tasks involve finding answers from a set of documents or sentences given a question. The types of questions vary, and some representative types are listed below. Information retrieval-type questions require answering facts or specific information. For example, answering the question "What is the capital of the United States?" with the correct answer "Washington D.C." System operation-type questions involve answering operations related to specific systems or databases. For example, responding to the question "Please tell me the inventory status of the product" with inventory information. Inference-type questions require inference or speculation to answer the question. For example, answering the question "Why is the Earth round?" using scientific knowledge or evidence.

Named entity recognition involves identifying named entities (such as person names, organization names, location names, dates, etc.) in text and classifying them into semantic categories. This analysis automatically identifies important parts of the text, which can be utilized in tasks such as information extraction and information retrieval. We provide examples of common categories identified by named entity recognition. Person names refer to the names of individuals or proper nouns related to individuals. For example, "John Smith" or "Barack Obama." Organization names refer to the names of companies, government agencies, or organizations. For example, "Google" or "United Nations." Location names refer to the names of places or facilities. For example, "Tokyo" or "Mount Everest." Dates refer to expressions representing specific dates or periods. For example, "June 8, 2023" or "every Tuesday."

We have finished with the explanation about BERT; We move on to GPT.

9.2 GPT

GPT (generative pre-training) [5, 32] is a language model trained using the decoder of the Transformer architecture (Fig. 9.3). It employs a simplified version of the decoder, omitting the attention mechanism that takes information from the encoder in the original decoder. The number of parameters for GPT is around 100 million, for GPT-2 is 1.5 billion, and for GPT-3 is 175 billion (GPT-3.5 has 355 billion).

The basic principle of pre-training in GPT involves predicting the next word, sentence, or passage (Fig. 9.4). The corpora used for pre-training include web archives called Common Crawl, as well as archives of books such as Book1 and Book2. In the pre-training of GPT-3, approximately 500 billion tokens are included.

As shown in Fig. 9.5, fine-tuning of GPT involves adding task-specific fully connected layers to the model.

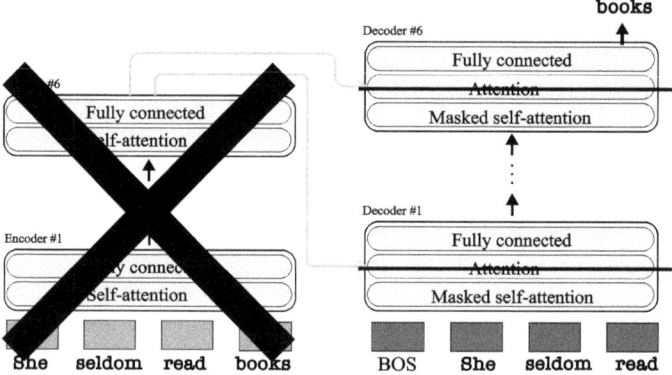

Fig. 9.3 GPT. It is composed of the decoder of the Transformer. It, however, uses a simplified block without the cross-attention mechanism

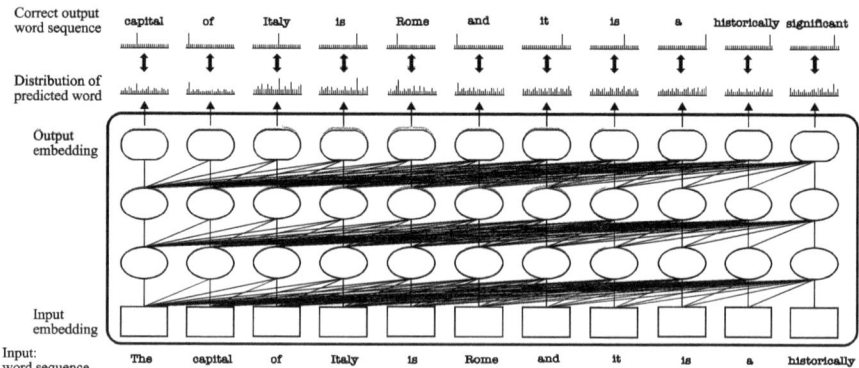

Fig. 9.4 Pre-training of GPT. In pre-training, GPT predicts the next word, sentence, or passage

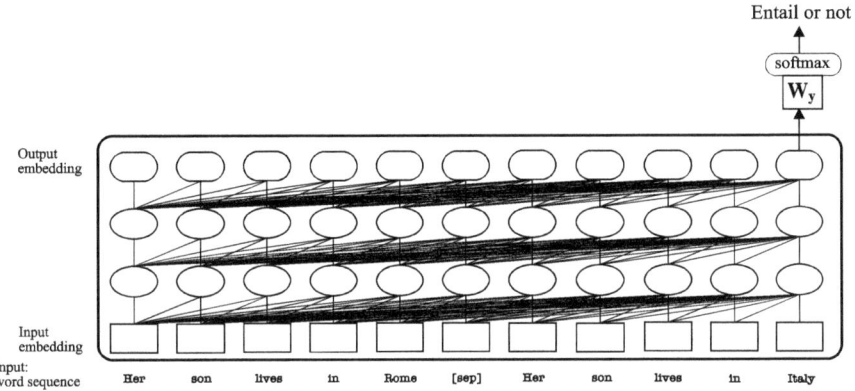

Fig. 9.5 Fine-tuning of GPT. Task-specific fully connected layers are added to the model

In general, fine-tuning large-scale models can be costly. Thus, research has been conducted to achieve desired results by crafting input texts to GPT, known as prompts, which leads to generative language models.

9.3 Towards Generative Language Models

Prompt refers to the text input provided to a language model, including instructions, questions, and example answers. Prompts can be categorized into several types. We provide some representative examples.

1. A prompt to predict words following a given text. An example of this is: `"What is the capital of Italy?"`
2. A prompt describing a task. An example of this is: `"Please answer the following question: What is the capital of Italy?"`
3. A prompt concatenating task description and example. An example of this is: `"Please answer the following question: The capital of Japan is Tokyo. What is the capital of Italy?"`

In large-scale language models, due to the high cost of fine-tuning, research has been conducted to improve task-solving abilities without fine-tuning (without adding new layers to GPT-X) through clever prompting. Particularly, zero-shot and few-shot are representative approaches. *Zero-shot* refers to the ability to make predictions or generate outputs for specific tasks without any fine-tuning, using prompts that describe the task. For example, by including a task description like `"Please answer the following question: What is the capital of Italy?"` in the prompt, the model can generate the correct answer. In contrast, *few-shot* involves including a very small number of examples (typically one to a few) in the prompt. For example, constructing a prompt by concatenating task description and examples like "Please answer the following question: The capital of Japan is Tokyo. What is the capital of Italy?"

When using zero-shot and few-shot approaches, we do not need to modify the model as long as it can predict the continuation of the text. Additionally, by providing task instructions in the text, the language model appears to behave in a generalizable manner. Compared to cases where fine-tuning is performed, however, the accuracy of task completion is often lower.

Furthermore, incorporating *chain-of-thought* in the answer examples significantly improves the performance of tasks such as arithmetic problems, common-sense reasoning, and symbolic reasoning [49]. Figure 9.6 shows an example of a prompt in the context of chain-of-thought.

Moreover, *instruction tuning* aims to improve the performance of zero-shot learning by fine-tuning on multiple tasks [6, 50]. As mentioned earlier, in regular fine-tuning of large language models, such as GPT-3, task-specific fully connected layers are added to the (simplified) decoder of the Transformer. In contrast, instruction tuning does not add fully connected layers. Instead, it creates training data for multiple tasks and performs fine-tuning based on word predictions. Particularly, existing data is supplemented with template-like instructions, and large language models are tuned to generate outputs in accordance with these instructions. Here, *instructions* refer to task directives in natural language.

For each task, instruction tuning prepares templates for building training data, converting it into the format of "prompt (instruction and example) + output," and then uses them for additional training, normal one-step-ahead word prediction, on a pre-trained language model. Figure 9.7 shows an example of the templates. Let us consider creating a prompt that asks whether a prepared "premise statement" on the left of Fig. 9.7 implies the "hypothesis statement" or not. For a template, we can generate a prompt by inserting the "premise statement" into the <premise> in

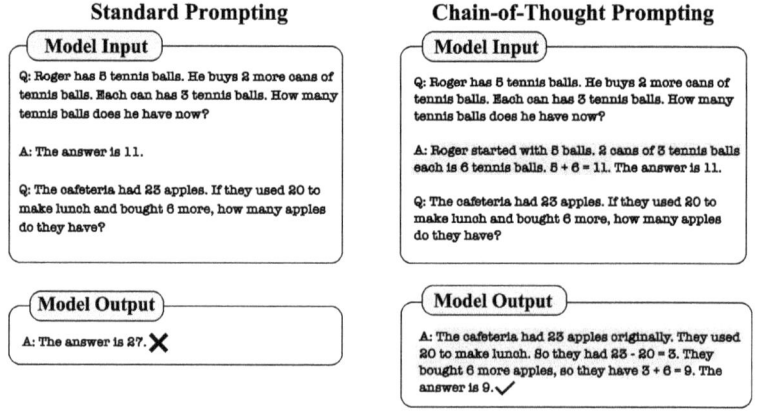

Fig. 9.6 Example prompt in the context of chain-of-thought. From Fig. 1 of [49]

9.3 Towards Generative Language Models

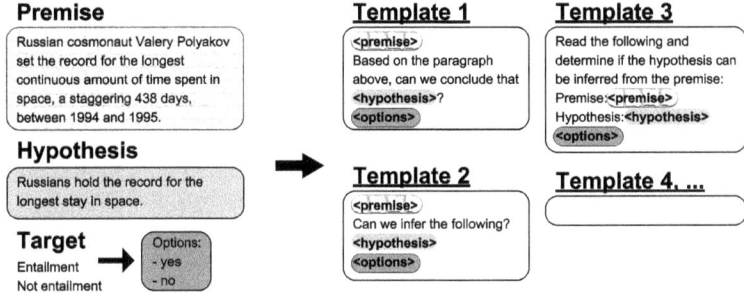

Fig. 9.7 Template for creating training data used in instruction tuning. From Fig. 4 of [50]. Used with kind permission of Jason Wei

the template, the "hypothesis statement" into the <hypothesis>, and the "options: yes or no" into the <options>. Thus, by preparing multiple templates, we can create multiple prompts in different formats from a single set of "premise statement," "hypothesis statement," and "option."[1]

In [50], they utilized LaMDA-PT, a language model with 137 billion parameters based on the Transformer decoder, and conducted experiments with 62 datasets including sentiment analysis, paraphrasing, question answering, summarization, and machine translation. In many cases, they achieved higher accuracy than GPT-3's zero-shot performance. This suggests that providing task instructions in natural language is key to success. Additionally, [6] extended the approach to over 1,800 tasks, aiming to improve performance.

However, despite employing prompt engineering approaches like the ones described above, they often did not obtain the desired output from users. Furthermore, they frequently received inaccurate answers, morally questionable answers, and biased answers. InstructGPT (referred to as the paper version of ChatGPT) uses human labels of the relative quality of model generations and fine-tunes the unsupervised language model to align with the preferences representing the types of behaviors that humans find safe and helpful through reinforcement learning. We have found that the alignment with human preferences is a key to improve the quality of generated outputs.

---

[1] In the original paper, they used ten templates created manually and targeted twelve task groups, including language inference, common-sense reasoning, and sentiment analysis, from 62 publicly available databases related to natural language processing.

9.4 Generative Language Models

The emergence of ChatGPT was met with astonishment and has had a significant impact on society. Shortly thereafter, many ChatGPT-like models such as GPT-4, Llama 2 (along with its interactive version, Llama 2-chat), and Llama 3 were developed and announced. In this book, we use the term "generative language models" to refer to models that have been aligned with the human preferences through reinforcement learning or other methods on pre-trained language models. In this section, we begin with presenting the basic structure and training of generative language models that are aligned with the human preferences through reinforcement learning. We refer a method that aligns a language model with human preferences through reinforcement learning as an *RLHF* method, or simply RLHF. As representative examples of them, we summarize the specific aspects of InstructGPT [30], which is the origin of language generation models, and Llama 2 [44], which has been partially released with its source code, although some parts remain undisclosed. Furthermore, we introduce the *direct preference optimization* (*DPO*) [35] method that directly optimizes a language model to adhere to human preferences without explicit reward modeling or reinforcement learning.

9.4.1 Basics of RLHF

The construction of generative language models starts from pre-trained models that are learned to predict the continuation of text. ChatGPT uses GPT-3.5, InstructGPT employs GPT-3 as its pre-training model, and Llama 2 utilizes a custom-built pre-training model based on the Transformer (decoder). We fine-tune the pre-training models by instruction tuning. Furthermore, by aligning fine-tuned models with the human preference through reinforcement learning, we obtain generative language models. In the learning, the (word) probability distribution of the fine-tuned model serves as the policy for reinforcement learning, where the policy is adjusted based on human feedback. Let us elaborate a bit more. RLHF constructs a generative language model by adjusting multiple pre-trained models through the following steps (see Fig. 9.8).

1. Fine-tune multiple pre-trained models with instructions (see Fig. 9.9).
2. Adjust the policy through reinforcement learning based on human feedback for the fine-tuned models. This consists of the following two steps.
    i. Construct a deep neural network (reward model) to compute the reward function through learning (see Fig. 9.10).
       The learning of the reward model involves using the outputs of multiple instruction-tuned language models as response sentences and assigning immediate rewards based on manually ranked response sentences.
    ii. Policy adjustment through reinforcement learning (see Fig. 9.11).

9.4 Generative Language Models

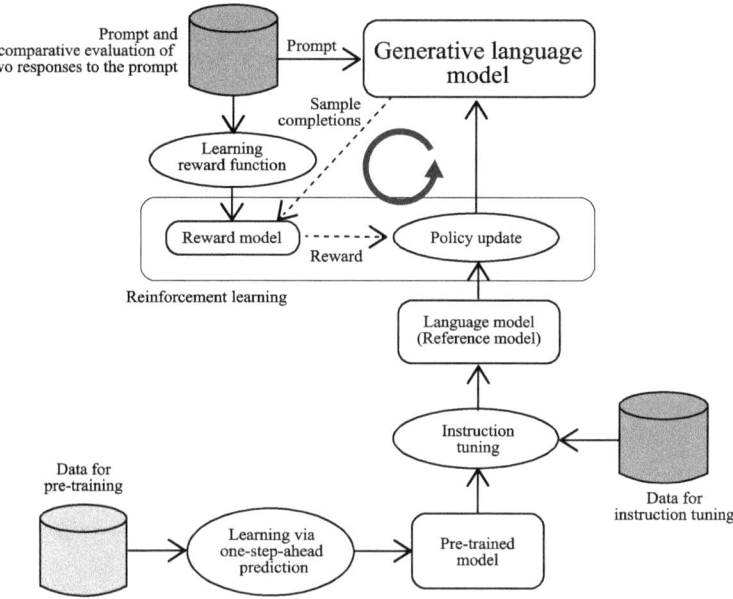

Fig. 9.8 Overview of generative language model learning through reinforcement learning (RLHF)

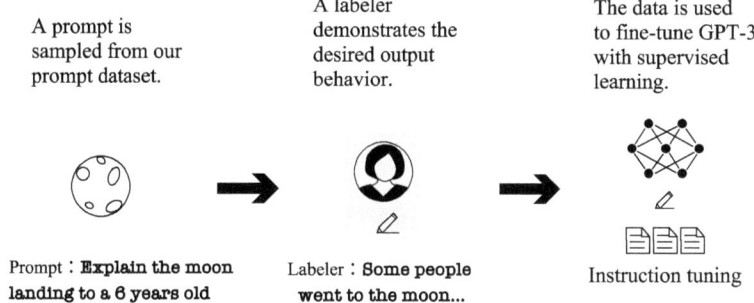

Fig. 9.9 Instruction tuning in generative language model construction. From Fig. 2 of [30]. Used with kind permission of Long Ouyang

3. Repeat steps 2-i (learning of the reward model) and 2-ii (policy adjustment through reinforcement learning).

To carry out this procedure, we must prepare the following additional training data besides the data used for training the pre-training model.

1. Training data for instruction tuning of the pre-training model. This includes newly created prompts, existing prompts, and manually created response sentences.

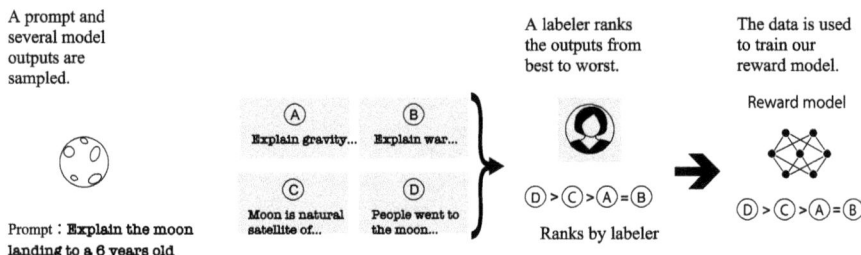

Fig. 9.10 Learning of the reward model in generative language models. From Fig. 2 of [30]. Used with kind permission of Long Ouyang

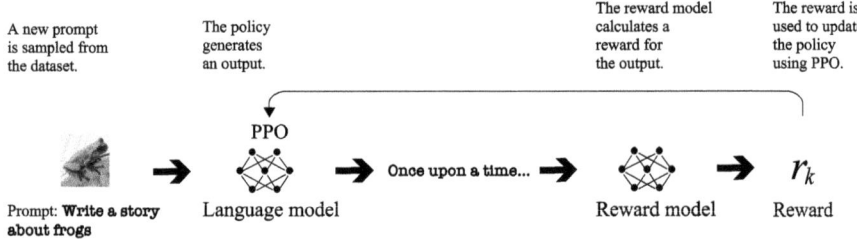

Fig. 9.11 Reinforcement learning in language generation model learning. From Fig. 2 of [30]. Used with kind permission of Long Ouyang

2. Training data for the reward model. This involves using the outputs of multiple instruction-tuned language models as response sentences and assigning immediate rewards based on manually ranked response sentences.

These data are essentially constructed manually.

We denote the output of the reward model when the response sentence to prompt x is y as $r_\theta(x, y)$. The loss function for training the reward model is given by

$$L(\theta) = -\mathbb{E}[\ln(\sigma(r_\theta(x, y_w) - r_\theta(x, y_l)))],$$

where y_w represents the response sentence that is evaluated to have a higher rank, and y_l represents the response sentence that is evaluated to have a lower rank. This directly demands that response sentences evaluated as having higher ranks by human evaluators receive larger reward values.

Moreover, policy determination in reinforcement learning is typically achieved through proximal policy optimization. The fundamental form of its objective function expresses the trade-off between updating the policy to increase rewards and not deviating too far from the policy of the instruction-tuned model. That is, it is

$$\text{objective}(\phi) = \mathbb{E}[r_\theta(x, y) - \beta \cdot \mathbb{KL}(\pi_\phi^{\text{RL}}(y \mid x) \parallel \pi^{\text{IT}}(y \mid x))], \quad (9.1)$$

where

9.4 Generative Language Models

ϕ represents the weights of the neural network that outputs the policy,
β is a constant,
$r_\theta(x, y)$ denotes the output of the reward model when the response sentence to prompt x is y,
π_ϕ^{RL} is the policy under training,
$\pi^{IT}(y \mid x)$ is the output of the instruction-tuned model from the original language model, and
$\mathbb{KL}(p(z) \parallel q(z))$ is the KL divergence[2] between probability distributions $p(z)$ and $q(z)$.

Note that $r_\theta(x, y)$ is the output of the reward model (neural network) for inputs x and y. The objective function (9.1) implicitly depends on the parameter ϕ through y. Thus, optimizing (9.1) requires the derivative of $r_\theta(x, y)$ with respect to y while holding x fixed, which can be evaluated by backpropagation in the reward model (see subsection Sect. ??: "Computing the Jacobian Matrix").

The creation of the reward model and the updating of policies through reinforcement learning are iteratively executed to improve performance.

Below, we briefly summarize distinctive features of InstructGPT and Llama 2.

9.4.1.1 InstructGPT

As mentioned earlier, while ChatGPT employs GPT-3.5 (with 355 billion parameters) as its pre-training model, InstructGPT utilizes GPT-3 (with 175 billion parameters).

In InstructGPT, there are two types of prompts for training data: one consists of prompts given to the initial version of InstructGPT, and the other consists of prompts manually created by labelers. The collected prompts cover a wide range of tasks such as text generation, question answering, dialogue, and summarization. Three prompt datasets were created for constructing instruction tuning models (13,000 prompts), reward models (33,000 prompts), and proximal policy optimization (31,000 prompts). The labelers, totaling 40 individuals, were tasked with (a) creating prompts, (b) generating desired response texts to prompts (for instruction tuning), and (c) ranking response texts to prompts (for training reward models).

The prompts created by the labelers are classified into the following three categories.

1. Plain. Labelers were asked to generate prompts arbitrarily but with sufficient diversity across various tasks.
2. Few-shot. Labelers were given instructions to create multiple question-answer pairs in response to those instructions.
3. User-based. Mimicking numerous real questions posted to OpenAI's API, labelers were tasked with creating similar questions.

---

[2] For KL divergence, see Appendix B at the end of the book.

Examples of prompts created by the labelers are provided below.

1. "Provide five ideas to regain enthusiasm for your career."
2. "Write a short story about a bear going to the beach, making friends with a seal, and then returning home."
3. "Please answer the following question: What is the shape of the Earth?

    (A) Circle
    (B) Sphere
    (C) Ellipsoid
    (D) Plane"

To be used for instruction tuning, the labelers created response sentences for 13,000 prompts. Additionally, for creating the reward model, the labelers compared 4 to 9 outputs from multiple instruction-tuned language models for 33,000 prompts and ranked each output. During the creation of the training data, labelers were instructed to prioritize response sentences that are helpful to users over sincere and non-harmful response sentences (during evaluation, however, they were instructed to prioritize sincere and non-harmful response sentences). We provide examples of ranked responses by labelers for the created data in the appendix at the end of the chapter.

In InstructGPT, we use a training dataset (13,000 instances) for instruction tuning to fine-tune GPT-3, which is referred to as supervised fine-tuning (SFT) in the original paper. This tuning involves 16 epochs, adopts cosine learning rate scheduling, and sets the unit retention rate in dropout to 0.2. For the evaluation dataset, we select the language model with the highest reward score among those instruction-tuned for scoring.

For training the reward model, we sample outputs from several ($K = 4$ to 9) language models for prompts intended for reward model creation (33,000 instances) and manually rank the outputs. These rankings serve as the training data for learning the reward function.

We denote the output of the reward model when the prompt is x and the response is y as $r_\theta(x, y)$. The loss function is defined as

$$L(\theta) = -\frac{1}{\binom{K}{2}} \mathbb{E}_{(x, y_w, y_l) \sim \mathcal{D}} [\ln(\sigma(r_\theta(x, y_w) - r_\theta(x, y_l)))],$$

where $\mathcal{D}$ is a dataset where human evaluators have ranked pairs of responses y_w (the response evaluated as higher rank) and y_l (the response evaluated as lower rank). For each prompt, there are K responses, and we consider all pairs of these responses for computing the loss. Combining them into one batch is important to avoid overfitting due to high correlation between responses for the same prompt. Dividing by the number of combinations accounts for the loss per pair. The network structure of the reward model is constructed by removing the final layer of the GPT-3 model tuned with instructions and creating a new layer that outputs a scalar value (score).

9.4 Generative Language Models

We determine the policy through proximal policy optimization. This approach consists of the following steps.

1. We select a new prompt from a prompt dataset (31,000 instances).
2. Using the policy π, we generate a response (the word sequence with the highest probability) to the prompt.
3. We calculate the reward for that response using the reward model.
4. Based on this reward, the policy is learned through proximal policy optimization.

The objective function for proximal policy optimization, called PPO-ptx, is a variant of the proximal policy optimization algorithm[3]:

$$\text{objective}(\boldsymbol{\phi}) = \mathbb{E}_{(x,\ y) \sim \mathcal{D}_{\pi_\phi^{\text{RL}}}} [r_\theta(x,\ y) - \beta \ln(\pi_\phi^{\text{RL}}(y \mid x) / \pi^{\text{IT}}(y \mid x))]$$
$$+ \gamma \mathbb{E}_{x \sim \mathcal{D}_{\text{pretrain}}} [\ln(\pi_\phi^{\text{RL}}(x))],$$

where $\boldsymbol{\phi}$ represents the weights of the neural network that outputs the policy, β and γ are constants, $r_\theta(x,\ y)$ is the output of the reward model when the prompt is x and the response is y, π_ϕ^{RL} is the policy being learned, $\pi^{\text{IT}}(y \mid x)$ is the output of the instruction-tuned language model from the original language model, $\mathcal{D}_{\pi_\phi^{\text{RL}}}$ is the dataset for reinforcement learning, and $\mathcal{D}_{\text{pretrain}}$ is the dataset for pre-training. The last term of the objective function requests the policy to be effective on the pre-training dataset to avoid performance degradation on publicly available NLP benchmark datasets.

9.4.1.2 Llama 2

Llama 2 utilizes pre-trained models (with parameter counts of 7 billion, 13 billion, 33 billion, and 66 billion) trained on a 2 trillion byte corpus, based on the Transformer architecture. Unlike the original Transformer, however, which uses layer normalization, Llama 2 employs a simpler RMSNorm (root mean square normalization) instead. Specifically, for unit i in the same layer with activation u_i, it is computed as

$$\tilde{u}_i = \gamma \frac{u_i}{\sqrt{\frac{1}{n} \sum_{i=1}^{n} u_i^2}} + \beta_i,$$

where β and γ are constants, and n is the number of units in that layer. Furthermore, while the original Transformer uses the ReLU activation function, Llama 2 adopts the SwiGLU function[4] as the activation function.

---

[3] In the original paper of InstructGPT, although it refers to it as a variant of proximal policy optimization (PPO), it would be more accurate to consider it as a variant of trust region policy optimization (TRPO), according to the original paper on proximal policy optimization algorithms by [40].

[4] SwiGLU is one of several differentiable (or smooth) functions proposed to approximate the ReLU function, as discussed in [41].

In instruction tuning (referred to as supervised fine-tuning, SFT, in the original paper, similar to the paper on InstructGPT), the process typically involves annotating existing data with instructions. Additionally, the model is further tuned using a wide-ranging, high-quality dataset of 27,000 instructions manually created.

The reward model consists of two separate types: utility reward model and safety reward model. Correspondingly, labelers ranked the outputs of two instruction-tuned models from a utility (helpfulness) and safety perspective separately, as part of creating the training data for the reward model. Rankings were done based on preference, evaluating which of the two outputs was better in terms of utility and safety. Rankings were classified into five levels: significantly better, better, slightly better, negligibly better, and unsure. The training data for the reward model was processed weekly, and the total number of ranked pairs amounted to 1.41 million.

The loss function for training the reward model is fundamentally the same as that of InstructGPT. Given the output of the reward model when the prompt x elicits response y as $r_\theta(x, y)$, the loss function is defined as

$$L(\theta) = -\mathbb{E}[\ln(\sigma(r_\theta(x, y_w) - r_\theta(x, y_l)) - m(r))],$$

where $m(r)$ represents the margin for the labeler's ranking r, where larger differences in ranking are reflected in the loss with larger margins, emphasizing greater discrepancies. y_w denotes the response ranked higher, while y_l denotes the response ranked lower.

Reinforcement learning in Llama 2 consists of two types: fine-tuning via rejection sampling and proximal policy optimization. Initially, fine-tuning via rejection sampling is conducted four times, followed by proximal policy optimization on the result of the fifth rejection sampling. Fine-tuning via rejection sampling involves sampling K outputs from the model during tuning and using the sample with the highest reward model value (referred to as the gold standard) to perform one-step-ahead prediction fine-tuning. The objective function for proximal policy optimization is defined as

$$\text{objective}(\phi) = \mathbb{E}_{(x, y) \sim \mathcal{D}_{\pi_\phi^{\text{RL}}}}[\tilde{r}_c(x, y) - \beta \cdot \mathbb{KL}(\pi_\phi^{\text{RL}}(y \mid x) \parallel \pi^0(y \mid x))],$$

where the expectation term is clipped at a threshold of 0.2. ϕ represents the weights of the neural network that outputs the policy, β is a constant, π_ϕ^{RL} is the policy being learned, $\pi^0(y \mid x)$ is the initial policy for proximal policy optimization (the policy just after fine-tuning via the fifth rejection sampling), $\mathcal{D}_{\pi_\phi^{\text{RL}}}$ is the dataset for reinforcement learning, and

$$\tilde{r}_c(x, y) = \text{norm}(\text{logit}(r_c(x, y))),$$

$$r_c(x, y) = \begin{cases} r_s(x, y), & \text{if isSafety}(x) \text{ or } r_s(x, y) < 0.15, \\ r_h(x, y), & \text{otherwise,} \end{cases}$$

where norm is the normalization function[5] that centers the data (i.e., the mean is zero) and scales it by the standard deviation. Also, logit is the logit function, defined on the domain $(0, 1)$ and the range $(-\infty, \infty)$, which is a monotonically increasing function and the inverse function of the logistic sigmoid function. Taking the logit function transforms the reward model values in $(0, 1)$ into those in $(-\infty, \infty)$. Additionally, isSafety(x) is a function that returns true if x in the data was a prompt used for ranking safety and r_s represents the safety reward model, while r_h represents the utility reward model.

In addition to the mentioned aspects, there are several other refinements in inputs, attention mechanisms, and so forth, but we have omitted them.

9.4.2 Direct Preference Optimization

As described in the previous subsections, the alignment with human preferences through reinforcement learning enables us to produce generative language models with impressive conversational and coding abilities. Reinforcement learning methods are, however, considerably more complex than supervised learning, involving training multiple language models and sampling from the language model policy in the loop of training, incurring significant computational costs.

The *direct preference optimization* (DPO) method implicitly optimizes the same objective function as RLHFs, but it trains a language model straight-forwardly without reinforcement learning. Intuitively, the DPO update increases the relative log probability of preferred to dispreferred responses, but it incorporates a dynamic, per-example importance weight that prevents the model degeneration that occurs with a naive probability ratio objective.

DPO directly aligns a language model using gradient-based techniques from human preference data without employing reinforcement learning. Specifically, it constructs a generative language model through the following steps (see Fig. 9.12).

1. Instruction-tune a pre-trained model using data for instruction tuning.
2. Using human preference data, align the instruction-tuned model built in Step 1 by optimizing an objective function equivalent to the one used in RLHFs.

For the alignment of the instruction-tuned model in Step 2, DPO minimizes the following objective function:

$$L_{\text{DPO}}(\pi_\phi; \pi_{\text{ref}}) = -\mathbb{E}_{(x, y_w, y_l) \sim \mathcal{D}_P} \left[\ln \sigma \left(\beta \ln \frac{\pi_\phi(y_w \mid x)}{\pi_{\text{ref}}(y_w \mid x)} - \beta \ln \frac{\pi_\phi(y_l \mid x)}{\pi_{\text{ref}}(y_l \mid x)} \right) \right], \quad (9.2)$$

---

[5] In the original paper, it uses "whiten" instead of "norm," which refers to a whitening function. However, whitening is an operation typically performed on multivariate data, whereas the reward model's values are scalar. Thus, we refer to it as a normalization function.

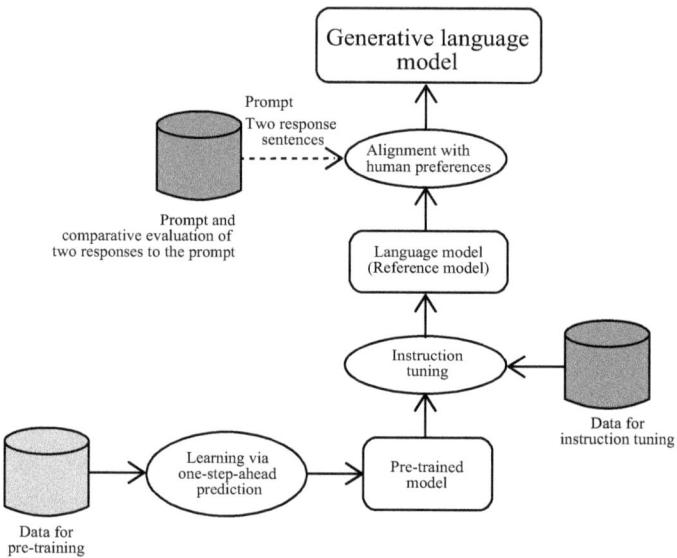

Fig. 9.12 Overview of generative language model learning through DPO

where $\mathcal{D}_p$ is a human preference dataset which consists of pairs of responses y_w (higher rank) and y_l (lower rank) that have been ranked by human evaluators for prompt x, ϕ represents the weights of the neural network that outputs the policy, β is a constant, π_ϕ is the policy under training, and $\pi_{\text{ref}}(y \mid x)$ is the output of the instruction-tuned model.

Recall that, in reinforcement learning, RLHF maximizes

$$\mathbb{E}_{x \sim \mathcal{D}_p,\, y \sim \pi_\phi(y \mid x)}[r_\theta(x, y) - \beta\, \mathbb{KL}(\pi_\phi(y \mid x) \,\|\, \pi_{\text{ref}}(y \mid x))] \tag{9.3}$$

under the reward model $r_\theta(x, y)$ that is determined by minimizing

$$L(r_\theta) = -\mathbb{E}_{(x,\, y_w,\, y_l) \sim \mathcal{D}_p}[\ln \sigma(r_\theta(x, y_w) - r_\theta(x, y_l))]. \tag{9.4}$$

We show that the minimization of (9.2) is equivalent to the maximization of (9.3) under the reward model determined by minimizing (9.4). The proof presented below holds for more general models, not limited to policy models or reward models represented by neural networks. Thus, we will omit θ and ϕ in the following description.

First, we can see that the policy π that maximizes the RLHF objective function (9.3) takes the following form:

$$\pi(y \mid x) = \frac{1}{Z(x)} \pi_{\text{ref}}(y \mid x) \exp\left(\frac{1}{\beta} r(x, y)\right),$$

9.4 Generative Language Models

where

$$Z(x) = \sum_{y} \pi_{\text{ref}}(y \mid x) \exp\left(\frac{1}{\beta} r(x, y)\right).$$

We show the derivation of this equation in the appendix at the end of this chapter. Solving this equation for $r(x, y)$ yields

$$r(x, y) = \beta \ln \frac{\pi(y \mid x)}{\pi_{\text{ref}}(y \mid x)} + \beta \ln Z(x).$$

Substituting the right-hand side of this equation into Eq. (9.4), we obtain

$$L_{\text{DPO}}(\pi; \pi_{\text{ref}}) = -\mathbb{E}_{(x, y_w, y_l) \sim D_P} \left[\ln \sigma \left(\beta \ln \frac{\pi(y_w \mid x)}{\pi_{\text{ref}}(y_w \mid x)} - \beta \ln \frac{\pi(y_l \mid x)}{\pi_{\text{ref}}(y_l \mid x)} \right) \right].$$

Note that since the training of the reward model is based on the difference in rewards, $Z(x)$, which cannot be analytically determined, is canceled out in the derivation of this equation, making the learning of the reward function unnecessary. Thus, we can align a language model with human preferences by minimizing this objective function using a standard gradient-based method.

Lastly, we summarize the benefits of DPO.

- We do not need to build a reward model.
- We do not need sentence samples for reinforcement learning.
- The implementation is simple, and parameters can be updated using backpropagation.

9.4.3 Challenges of Generative Language Models

ChatGPT demonstrates excellent performance across many tasks, enabling anyone to utilize a versatile natural language processing AI. However, there are significant challenges that need to be addressed. Let us highlight two particularly important ones.

1. Frequently, generative language models generate responses even when the model does not know the answer, leading to instances where it comfortably fabricates responses without factual basis. This issue is particularly prominent in tasks such as question answering.
2. Generative language models sometimes produce biased responses based on factors like race, religion, or gender. This bias stems from the models being trained on vast amounts of data, and the content of responses may vary depending on the language being processed.

We summarize the transition from GPT to ChatGPT. Large-scale language models adopt a strategy of pre-training and fine-tuning to predict "continuations" of text.

Additionally, the use of prompts enables language models to tackle various tasks. In other words, the utilization of prompts allows users to provide tasks as "instructions" to the model in natural language. Furthermore, the successful integration of the reinforcement learning or the direct preference optimization allows for adjustments to be made to ensure that outputs align with what humans consider appropriate.

While there are many unknown aspects regarding the structure and processing of the human brain, as seen above, we have a good understanding of the hardware configuration required to implement generative language models, as well as the structure and computations of DNNs. Furthermore, we understand the mechanisms of learning through one-step-ahead prediction and reinforcement learning. However, the fundamental question of why generative language models can perform inference and "act like humans" remains unanswered. Unfortunately, it is likely difficult to dispel this question easily because it may not be straightforward to express what exactly the model, with its vast number of parameters set to minimize loss from massive datasets, is computing.

9.5 Appendix

9.5.1 Example of Labeler Ranking in Data Creation for InstructGPT

Below is an example of how a labeler ranked responses for creating a reward model using a summary of an article. This example is from Fig. 12b of [30].

Rank 1 (best)

(A) A research group in the United States has found that parrots can imitate human speech with ease, and some of them can even do so in the same way as humans. This group studied the sounds that parrots make in their natural habitats and found that they use their tongues and breaks in ways that are strikingly ...

(B) A team of researchers from Yale University and University of California, Davis studied the vocalization patterns of several different types of parrots. They found that parrots like to mimic human speech, and can produce a wide range of sounds, such as whistles, squawks, and other types of vocalizations ...

Rank 2

(C) Parrots have been found to have the ability to understand numbers. Researchers have found that parrots can understand numbers up to six. In a series of experiments, the parrots were able to identify the amount of food items under a number of cups ...

9.5 Appendix

Rank 3

(D) Current research suggests that parrots see and hear things in a different way than humans do. While humans see a rainbow of colors, parrots only see shades of red and green. Parrots can also see ultraviolet light, which is invisible to humans. Many birds have this ability to see ultraviolet light, an ability ...

(E) Scientists have found that green-winged parrots can tell the difference between two noises that are the same except for the order in which they are heard. This is important because green-winged parrots are known to imitate sounds. This research shows that they are able to understand the difference between sounds.

Rank 5 (worst)

9.5.2 Derivation of the Policy $\pi(y \mid x)$ that Maximizes the Objective Function of RLHF

We start from the objective function of RLHF:

$$\mathbb{E}_{x \sim \mathcal{D}, \, y \sim \pi(y \mid x)}[r(x, y) - \beta \, \mathbb{KL}(\pi(y \mid x) \, \| \, \pi_{\text{ref}}(y \mid x))].$$

By the definition of KL divergence, we can rewrite this objective function into

$$\mathbb{E}_{x \sim \mathcal{D}} \mathbb{E}_{y \sim \pi(y \mid x)} \left[r(x, y) - \beta \ln \frac{\pi(y \mid x)}{\pi_{\text{ref}}(y \mid x)} \right].$$

Multiplying this by $-1/\beta$ reveals that maximizing this objective function is equivalent to minimizing the following:

$$\mathbb{E}_{x \sim \mathcal{D}} \mathbb{E}_{y \sim \pi(y \mid x)} \left[\ln \frac{\pi(y \mid x)}{\pi_{\text{ref}}(y \mid x)} - \frac{1}{\beta} r(x, y) \right].$$

Furthermore, we can transform this equation as follows.

$$\mathbb{E}_{x \sim \mathcal{D}} \mathbb{E}_{y \sim \pi(y \mid x)} \left[\ln \frac{\pi(y \mid x)}{\pi_{\text{ref}}(y \mid x)} - \frac{1}{\beta} r(x, y) \right] = \mathbb{E}_{x \sim \mathcal{D}} \mathbb{E}_{y \sim \pi(y \mid x)} \left[\ln \frac{\pi(y \mid x)}{\pi_{\text{ref}}(y \mid x)} - \ln \exp\left(\frac{1}{\beta} r(x, y)\right) \right]$$

$$= \mathbb{E}_{x \sim \mathcal{D}} \mathbb{E}_{y \sim \pi(y \mid x)} \left[\ln \frac{\pi(y \mid x)}{\pi_{\text{ref}}(y \mid x) \exp\left(\frac{1}{\beta} r(x, y)\right)} \right]$$

$$= \mathbb{E}_{x \sim \mathcal{D}} \mathbb{E}_{y \sim \pi(y \mid x)} \left[\ln \frac{\frac{1}{Z(x)} \pi(y \mid x)}{\frac{1}{Z(x)} \pi_{\text{ref}}(y \mid x) \exp\left(\frac{1}{\beta} r(x, y)\right)} \right]$$

$$= \mathbb{E}_{x \sim \mathcal{D}} \mathbb{E}_{y \sim \pi(y \mid x)} \left[\ln \frac{\pi(y \mid x)}{\frac{1}{Z(x)} \pi_{\text{ref}}(y \mid x) \exp\left(\frac{1}{\beta} r(x, y)\right)} - \ln Z(x) \right]$$

$$= \mathbb{E}_{x\sim\mathcal{D}}\left[\mathbb{E}_{y\sim\pi(y|x)}\left[\ln\frac{\pi(y|x)}{\pi^*(y|x)}\right] - \ln Z(x)\right]$$
$$= \mathbb{E}_{x\sim\mathcal{D}}[\text{KL}(\pi(y|x) \| \pi^*(y|x)) - \ln Z(x)].$$

We obtain the third equality by dividing both the numerator and denominator by

$$Z(x) = \sum_{y} \pi_{\text{ref}}(y|x) \exp\left(\frac{1}{\beta}r(x, y)\right)$$

and the fifth equality by defining

$$\pi^*(y|x) = \frac{1}{Z(x)}\pi_{\text{ref}}(y|x) \exp\left(\frac{1}{\beta}r(x, y)\right).$$

Since the rightmost expression of the above equation is minimized when the KL divergence between π and π^* is 0, we obtain

$$\pi^*(y|x) = \frac{1}{Z(x)}\pi_{\text{ref}}(y|x) \exp\left(\frac{1}{\beta}r(x, y)\right).$$

Part III
Generative Image Model

Chapter 10
Variational Autoencoder

10.1 Introduction

The *variational autoencoder* (*VAE*) is one of generative image models [21]. It is a latent variable model based on deep learning. It compresses high-dimensional data such as images into a latent space and has the ability to generate samples from the latent representation. Assuming a latent variable $\mathbf{z}$ corresponding to each data $\mathbf{x}$, a VAE computes the mean and covariance of the distribution $p(\mathbf{z}\,|\,\mathbf{x})$ as a Gaussian distribution by a neural network with $\mathbf{x}$ as input. For data generation of $\mathbf{x}$, it also assumes $p(\mathbf{x}\,|\,\mathbf{z})$ as a Gaussian distribution, and a neural network with the realization of $\mathbf{z}$ as input outputs its mean. By sampling from the Gaussian distribution $p(\mathbf{x}\,|\,\mathbf{z})$, for example, a VAE can generate new images of dogs not included in the training data.

10.2 Structure of Variational Autoencoders

In autoencoders introduced in Chap. 4, the goal is to find a code that reconstructs the input as closely as possible. Variational autoencoders take this idea further, treating both the output $\mathbf{x}$ and the code $\mathbf{z}$ as random variables, with $\mathbf{x}$ as the observed variable and $\mathbf{z}$ as the latent variable. The distribution of the latent variable $\mathbf{z}$ conditioned on the input is assumed to follow a Gaussian distribution, and the encoder is a neural network that outputs the mean and covariance matrix of that Gaussian distribution. Furthermore, the distribution of the output $\mathbf{x}$ is assumed to be an isotropic Gaussian distribution, and the decoder is a neural network that takes the realized value of $\mathbf{z}$ as input and outputs the mean of the Gaussian distribution of $\mathbf{x}$. We refine this idea further. Following convention, we denote the vector concatenating the parameters of the encoder $\mathbf{W}$ and $\mathbf{b}$ as $\boldsymbol{\phi}$, and the vector concatenating the parameters of the decoder $\tilde{\mathbf{W}}$ and $\tilde{\mathbf{b}}$ as $\boldsymbol{\theta}$.

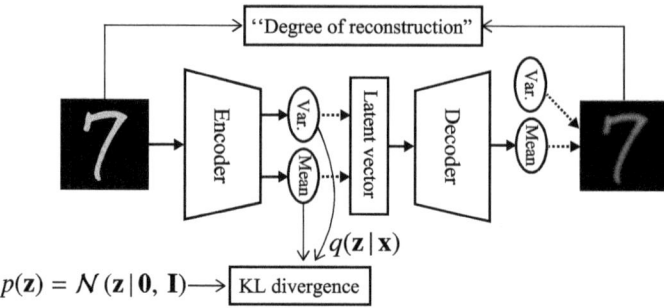

Fig. 10.1 Variational autoencoder. It consists of an encoder and a decoder. The distribution of the latent variable **z** conditioned on the input is assumed to follow a Gaussian distribution, and the encoder is a neural network that outputs the mean and covariance matrix of that Gaussian distribution. The decoder, taking the realized value of **z** as input, is also assumed to output the mean vector of **x**, which follows a Gaussian distribution. Based on https://danijar.com/building-variational-auto-encoders-in-tensorflow/. Used with kind permission of Danijar Hafner

Figure 10.1 depicts the architecture and flow of information in a VAE. First, on the decoding side of the VAE, we assume that the distribution of the output **x** conditioned on the latent variable **z** is

$$p(\mathbf{x} \mid \mathbf{z}, \boldsymbol{\theta}) = \mathcal{N}(\mathbf{x} \mid \mathbf{f}_d(\mathbf{z}; \boldsymbol{\theta}), \sigma^2 \mathbf{I}), \qquad (10.2.1)$$

where $\mathbf{f}_d$ is the decoder realized as a neural network with its weights and biases grouped into $\boldsymbol{\theta}$. The variance σ^2 is considered as a fixed parameter rather than learned during training. While we assume a Gaussian distribution here, sometimes we adopt a Bernoulli distribution depending on the context. Also, we assume that the prior distribution of the latent variable **z** is a Gaussian distribution with zero mean and identity covariance matrix:

$$p(\mathbf{z}) = \mathcal{N}(\mathbf{z} \mid \mathbf{0}, \mathbf{I}). \qquad (10.2.2)$$

On the other hand, on the encoding side of the VAE, we assume that the posterior of **z**, i.e., the distribution of the latent variable **z** conditioned on the input **x**, is

$$q(\mathbf{z} \mid \mathbf{x}, \boldsymbol{\phi}) = \mathcal{N}(\mathbf{z} \mid \mathbf{f}_{e,\mu}(\mathbf{x}; \boldsymbol{\phi}), \text{diag}(\mathbf{f}_{e,\sigma^2}(\mathbf{x}; \boldsymbol{\phi}))), \qquad (10.2.3)$$

where diag($\boldsymbol{\lambda}$) represents a diagonal matrix with the elements of vector $\boldsymbol{\lambda}$ as its diagonal elements, and $\mathbf{f}_e$ denotes the encoder realized as a neural network, which outputs the mean $\mathbf{f}_{e,\mu}$ of the distribution of latent variables and the diagonal elements $\mathbf{f}_{e,\sigma^2}$ of the assumed diagonal covariance matrix. The parameter $\boldsymbol{\phi}$ explicitly denotes the weights and biases of the network. For an input **x** to the encoder, a sample of **z** from the posterior $q(\mathbf{z} \mid \mathbf{x}, \boldsymbol{\phi})$ is inputted to the decoder.

10.3 Variational Lower Bound

In this book, we refer to the probabilistic model including the decoder on the decoding side as the *decoding model*, and the probabilistic model including the encoder on the encoding side as the *encoding model*.

To determine the parameters of the VAE, one might naturally think of maximizing the log-likelihood function $\ln p(\mathcal{D} \mid \boldsymbol{\theta}, \boldsymbol{\phi}) = \sum_{n=1}^{N} \ln p(\mathbf{x}_n \mid \boldsymbol{\theta}, \boldsymbol{\phi})$, where $\mathcal{D}$ is given data. In VAE, however, we maximize the variational lower bound instead of the log-likelihood, determining both the encoding and decoding models simultaneously. We will discuss the reason for this later. We start from the general definition of the variational lower bound.

10.3 Variational Lower Bound

In the following, for a function $f(\mathbf{x})$ of a random variable $\mathbf{x}$, we sometimes denote the expectation $\mathbb{E}_{\mathbf{x}}[f(\mathbf{x})]$ as $\mathbb{E}_{p(\mathbf{x})}[f(\mathbf{x})]$, where $p(\mathbf{x})$ is the distribution of $\mathbf{x}$.

Now, consider a probabilistic model with observed and latent variables. We denote the set of observed variables by $\mathbf{X}$ and that of latent variables by $\mathbf{Z}$. Let $p(\mathbf{X}, \mathbf{Z})$ denote the joint distribution of $\mathbf{X}$ and $\mathbf{Z}$, and $q(\mathbf{Z})$ denote the distribution of $\mathbf{Z}$. The *variational lower bound* (*evidence lower bound*; *ELBO*) is defined as a function of the distributions $q(\mathbf{Z})$ and $p(\mathbf{X}, \mathbf{Z})$:

$$\mathcal{L}(q, p) \equiv \mathbb{E}_{q(\mathbf{Z})}\left[\ln \frac{p(\mathbf{X}, \mathbf{Z})}{q(\mathbf{Z})}\right] = \int q(\mathbf{Z}) \ln \frac{p(\mathbf{X}, \mathbf{Z})}{q(\mathbf{Z})} d\mathbf{Z}. \quad (10.3.1)$$

Precisely, the variational lower bound $\mathcal{L}(q, p)$ is a functional[1] on the sets $\{q\}$ and $\{p\}$ of distributions[2] of the random variable $\mathbf{Z}$. That is, in the definition (10.3.1), q and p are variables over the sets of distributions.

Since the function $-\ln x$ is convex, we obtain the following equation by Jensen's inequality:

$$\mathbb{E}_{q(\mathbf{Z})}\left[\ln \frac{p(\mathbf{X}, \mathbf{Z})}{q(\mathbf{Z})}\right] \leq \ln \int q(\mathbf{Z}) \frac{p(\mathbf{X}, \mathbf{Z})}{q(\mathbf{Z})} d\mathbf{Z}$$
$$= \ln p(\mathbf{X}).$$

---

[1] While ordinary functions map sets of numbers (such as real or complex numbers) to numbers, functionals map sets of functions to numbers. For example, the mapping that assigns the definite integral $F[f(x)] = \int_a^b f(x)\,dx$ to a function $f(x)$ is a functional. The entropy of a random variable X, as well as the KL divergence between distributions $p(x)$ and $q(x)$, are also functionals.

[2] We must distinguish clearly between a random variable and its distribution. For simplicity, we consider a finite probability space, which is defined by the pair of a sample space Ω and a probability measure P. A random variable is a function from Ω to $\mathbf{R}$. Thus, if $P \neq P'$, the random variable $Z : \Omega \to \mathbf{R}$ on (Ω, P) has a different distribution from that of the same random variable $Z : \Omega \to \mathbf{R}$ on (Ω, P').

This equation shows that if p is the distribution of data, the variational lower bound is a lower bound on the log-likelihood function (for Jensen's inequality and the definition of a lower bound of a function, see Appendices A and B.1 at the end of the book).

We here show a case when we use the variational lower bound as the objective function for optimization. Consider a model that has the set of observed variables $\mathbf{X}$, the corresponding latent variables $\mathbf{Z}$, and the set of parameters $\mathbf{\Theta}$. Generally, to obtain the likelihood function of the model, we must integrate out the latent variables as follows[3]:

$$p(\mathbf{X} \mid \mathbf{\Theta}) = \int p(\mathbf{X} \mid \mathbf{Z}, \mathbf{\Theta}) p(\mathbf{Z}) \, d\mathbf{Z},$$

where $p(\mathbf{Z})$ is the prior distribution of $\mathbf{Z}$. We often, however, find the integral analytically infeasible or computationally impossible. In such cases, instead of the likelihood, we can sometimes use the variational lower bound.

For example, in the EM algorithm, which we use when the posterior probability of the latent variables can be expressed in a simple form and the expectation of the joint probability of the observed and latent variables with respect to the posterior probability can be obtained explicitly, we alternate between maximizing the variational lower bound with respect to the distribution of the latent variables and maximizing with respect to the parameters. Within the framework of Bayesian inference, we also treat the parameters as latent variables, restrict the posterior distribution of the latent variables to a certain family, and then find the distribution within that family that maximizes the variational lower bound.

We discuss the reason why we use the variational lower bound as the objective function for optimization. We present an important equation that characterizes the variational lower bound, which serves as the basis for maximizing the variational lower bound instead of maximizing the likelihood. This equation is expressed as the following decomposition formula of the log-likelihood $\ln p(\mathbf{X} \mid \mathbf{\Theta})$:

$$\ln p(\mathbf{X} \mid \mathbf{\Theta}) = \mathcal{L}(q, p; \mathbf{\Theta}) + \mathbb{KL}(q \parallel p; \mathbf{\Theta}), \qquad (10.3.2)$$

where

$$\mathcal{L}(q, p; \mathbf{\Theta}) = \sum_{\mathbf{Z}} q(\mathbf{Z}) \ln \left\{ \frac{p(\mathbf{X}, \mathbf{Z} \mid \mathbf{\Theta})}{q(\mathbf{Z})} \right\}$$

is the variational lower bound and

$$\mathbb{KL}(q \parallel p; \mathbf{\Theta}) = - \sum_{\mathbf{Z}} q(\mathbf{Z}) \ln \left\{ \frac{p(\mathbf{Z} \mid \mathbf{X}, \mathbf{\Theta})}{q(\mathbf{Z})} \right\}$$

---

[3] Typically, the notation $p(x \mid \theta)$ indicates that θ represents parameters characterizing the distribution of the random variable x. However, in the following context, we take a broader view and include parameters on which the model depends when estimating the distribution of x, such as the weights in a neural network.

is the KL divergence[4] between the distributions $q(\mathbf{Z})$ and $p(\mathbf{Z}\,|\,\mathbf{X},\,\Theta)$ that is a posterior distribution of $\mathbf{Z}$ (refer to the appendix at end of this chapter on the derivation of the decomposition formula (10.3.2)). The decomposition formula (10.3.2) holds even when we represent model parameters as latent variables, considering Θ is the empty set.

Here, we consider the case where $p(\mathbf{X},\,\mathbf{Z}\,|\,\Theta)$ is a specific fixed distribution and thus, the variational lower bound is a functional of $q(\mathbf{Z})$ alone for fixed Θ. Note first that the formula (10.3.2) holds for any distribution of $\mathbf{Z}$. Note also that for fixed Θ, the left hand of the formula (10.3.2) is a constant for a given data $\mathbf{X}$. Thus, maximizing the variational lower bound $\mathcal{L}(q;\,\Theta)$ with respect to q is minimizing KL divergence $\mathbb{KL}(q\,\|\,p;\,\Theta)$, which means finding the distribution $q(\mathbf{Z})$ that is "closest" to the posterior probability $p(\mathbf{Z}\,|\,\mathbf{X},\,\Theta)$. From the Bayesian inference standpoint, the posterior probability serves as the most preferable distribution for latent variables, and thus maximizing the variational lower bound is justified in that regard.

We comment on the variables of the variational lower bound at the end of this section. For example, as mentioned above, in variational inference, we introduce an approximate posterior distribution $q(\mathbf{Z})$ and aim to make it as close as possible to the true posterior distribution. In this case, $p(\mathbf{X},\,\mathbf{Z})$ is a specific joint distribution of $\mathbf{X}$ and $\mathbf{Z}$, which includes model parameters, and the variational lower bound is a functional of $q(\mathbf{Z})$ alone. In contrast, in the training of the diffusion model introduced in Sect. 11.4, since $q(\mathbf{Z})$ for the latent variable $\mathbf{Z}$ is a given distribution, the variational lower bound is a functional of $p(\mathbf{X},\,\mathbf{Z}\,|\,\Theta)$ alone. In the training of a VAE, described shortly, the variational lower bound is a functional of both the distribution $q(\mathbf{Z})$ represented by the encoder's output and the distribution $p(\mathbf{X},\,\mathbf{Z}\,|\,\Theta)$ represented by the decoder's output.

10.4 Learning of Variational Autoencoders

10.4.1 Training of Variational Autoencoders

Let the data be denoted as $\mathcal{D} = \{\mathbf{x}_1,\,\ldots,\,\mathbf{x}_N\}$. For ease of notation, we denote $p(\mathbf{x}\,|\,\mathbf{z},\,\boldsymbol{\theta})$ as $p_\theta(\mathbf{x}\,|\,\mathbf{z})$ and $q(\mathbf{z}\,|\,\mathbf{x},\,\boldsymbol{\phi})$ as $q_\phi(\mathbf{z}\,|\,\mathbf{x})$, using the parameters as subscripts. In a VAE, since the variational lower bound is a function of parameters $\boldsymbol{\theta}$ and $\boldsymbol{\phi}$, denoting it explicitly, we define the variational lower bound for a given single data $\mathbf{x}$ as

$$L(\boldsymbol{\theta},\,\boldsymbol{\phi}\,|\,\mathbf{x}) \equiv \int q_\phi(\mathbf{z}\,|\,\mathbf{x}) \ln \frac{p_\theta(\mathbf{x},\,\mathbf{z})}{q_\phi(\mathbf{z}\,|\,\mathbf{x})}\,d\mathbf{z}$$
$$= \mathbb{E}_{q_\phi(\mathbf{z}\,|\,\mathbf{x})}[\ln p_\theta(\mathbf{x},\,\mathbf{z}) - \ln q_\phi(\mathbf{z}\,|\,\mathbf{x})], \qquad (10.4.1)$$

---

[4] For KL divergence, see Appendix B at the end of the book.

where $p_\theta(\mathbf{x}, \mathbf{z}) = p_\theta(\mathbf{x}\,|\,\mathbf{z})p(\mathbf{z})$ (here, we use the letter "L," the initial of the word "lower," to represent the variational lower bound. Note, thus, that L does not stand for "loss").

We can rewrite Eq. (10.4.1) as follows:

$$\begin{aligned}
L(\boldsymbol{\theta}, \boldsymbol{\phi}\,|\,\mathbf{x}) &= \mathbb{E}_{q_\phi(\mathbf{z}|\mathbf{x})}[\ln p_\theta(\mathbf{x}, \mathbf{z}) - \ln q_\phi(\mathbf{z}\,|\,\mathbf{x})] \\
&= \mathbb{E}_{q_\phi(\mathbf{z}|\mathbf{x})}[\ln p_\theta(\mathbf{x}\,|\,\mathbf{z})] + \mathbb{E}_{q_\phi(\mathbf{z}|\mathbf{x})}[\ln p(\mathbf{z})] - \mathbb{E}_{q_\phi(\mathbf{z}|\mathbf{x})}[\ln q_\phi(\mathbf{z}\,|\,\mathbf{x})] \\
&= \mathbb{E}_{q_\phi(\mathbf{z}|\mathbf{x})}[\ln p_\theta(\mathbf{x}\,|\,\mathbf{z})] + \mathbb{E}_{q_\phi(\mathbf{z}|\mathbf{x})}\left[\ln\left(\frac{p(\mathbf{z})}{q_\phi(\mathbf{z}\,|\,\mathbf{x})}\right)\right] \\
&= \mathbb{E}_{q_\phi(\mathbf{z}|\mathbf{x})}[\ln p_\theta(\mathbf{x}\,|\,\mathbf{z})] - \mathbb{KL}(q_\phi(\mathbf{z}\,|\,\mathbf{x})\,\|\,p(\mathbf{z})),
\end{aligned} \qquad (10.4.2)$$

where $\mathbb{E}_{q_\phi(\mathbf{z}|\mathbf{x})}[\ln p_\theta(\mathbf{x}\,|\,\mathbf{z})]$ represents the expectation of $\ln p_\theta(\mathbf{x}\,|\,\mathbf{z})$ with respect to the posterior distribution of $\mathbf{z}$, and $\mathbb{KL}(q_\phi(\mathbf{z}\,|\,\mathbf{x})\,\|\,p(\mathbf{z}))$ represents the KL divergence between the posterior distribution and the prior distribution of $\mathbf{z}$.

We maximize Eq. (10.4.2) with respect to $\boldsymbol{\theta}$ and $\boldsymbol{\phi}$. Maximizing the first term on the right-hand side means adjusting the parameters so that the probability of generating the data point $\mathbf{x}$ is generally higher. In other words, it adjusts the parameters to fit the data ("Degree of reconstruction" in Fig. 10.1). On the other hand, the (negative) KL divergence term acts as a regularization term, ensuring that the posterior distribution of $\mathbf{z}$ does not deviate too far from the prior distribution (KL divergence term in Fig. 10.1).

Now, our goal is to maximize the following objective function by determining the parameters:

$$L(\boldsymbol{\theta}, \boldsymbol{\phi}\,|\,\mathcal{D}) \equiv \sum_{n=1}^{N} L(\boldsymbol{\theta}, \boldsymbol{\phi}\,|\,\mathbf{x}_n).$$

To achieve this, we use stochastic gradient descent, computing gradients for each mini-batch or each individual data point. For simplicity of notation, we compute the gradient of the variational lower bound (10.4.2) for a single data point:

$$\nabla_{\{\boldsymbol{\theta},\boldsymbol{\phi}\}} L(\boldsymbol{\theta}, \boldsymbol{\phi}\,|\,\mathbf{x}) = \nabla_{\{\boldsymbol{\theta},\boldsymbol{\phi}\}} \mathbb{E}_{q_\phi(\mathbf{z}|\mathbf{x})}\left[\ln p_\theta(\mathbf{x}\,|\,\mathbf{z})\right] - \nabla_\phi \mathbb{KL}(q_\phi(\mathbf{z}\,|\,\mathbf{x})\,\|\,p(\mathbf{z})). \qquad (10.4.3)$$

First, note that the gradient $\nabla_\phi \mathbb{KL}(q_\phi(\mathbf{z}\,|\,\mathbf{x})\,\|\,p(\mathbf{z}))$ is independent of the decoder. Since $q_\phi(\mathbf{z}\,|\,\mathbf{x})$ and $p(\mathbf{z})$ are Gaussian distributions, we can calculate the KL divergence term in Eq. (10.4.3) analytically and represent it as a function of the encoder's output. That is, let L be the dimensionality of the latent vector $\mathbf{z}$, then we have

$$\mathbb{KL}(q_\phi(\mathbf{z}\,|\,\mathbf{x})\,\|\,p(\mathbf{z})) = -\frac{1}{2}\sum_{l=1}^{L}[1 - \sigma_l^2 - \mu_l^2 + \ln \sigma_l^2],$$

where μ_l is the l-th component of $\mathbf{f}_{e,\mu}(\mathbf{x}; \boldsymbol{\phi})$, and σ_l^2 is the l-th diagonal component of $\mathbf{f}_{e,\sigma^2}(\mathbf{x}; \boldsymbol{\phi})$, which are the outputs of the encoder units (see the appendix at the

10.4 Learning of Variational Autoencoders

end of the chapter). Thus, if we use the identity function as the activation function for the encoder output units, the "errors" of the encoder output units can be obtained by differentiating the right-hand side of the above equation with respect to σ_l^2 and μ_l. Then, the "errors" of the remaining units in the encoder can be obtained using backpropagation (see Sect. 1.1.2.5).

Next, we focus on the first term of Eq. (10.4.3): $\nabla_{\{\theta, \phi\}} \mathbb{E}_{q_\phi(\mathbf{z}|\mathbf{x})}[\ln p_\theta(\mathbf{x}|\mathbf{z})]$. We divide it into the following:

$$\nabla_{\{\theta, \phi\}} \mathbb{E}_{q_\phi(\mathbf{z}|\mathbf{x})}[\ln p_\theta(\mathbf{x}|\mathbf{z})] = \begin{cases} \nabla_\theta \mathbb{E}_{q_\phi(\mathbf{z}|\mathbf{x})}[\ln p_\theta(\mathbf{x}|\mathbf{z})], \\ \nabla_\phi \mathbb{E}_{q_\phi(\mathbf{z}|\mathbf{x})}[\ln p_\theta(\mathbf{x}|\mathbf{z})]. \end{cases}$$

The former:

$$\nabla_\theta \mathbb{E}_{q_\phi(\mathbf{z}|\mathbf{x})}[\ln p_\theta(\mathbf{x}|\mathbf{z})] = \int q_\phi(\mathbf{z}|\mathbf{x}) \frac{\partial}{\partial \theta} \ln p_\theta(\mathbf{x}|\mathbf{z}) \, d\mathbf{z}$$

is the expectation of $\frac{\partial}{\partial \theta} \ln p_\theta(\mathbf{x}|\mathbf{z})$ with respect to the distribution $q_\phi(\mathbf{z}|\mathbf{x})$. We can commonly use sampling techniques to approximate expectations. That is, generally, according to the law of large numbers, the expected value of a function $f(\mathbf{x})$ of a random variable $\mathbf{x}$ can be approximated by using samples (realizations) $\hat{\mathbf{x}}_1, \ldots, \hat{\mathbf{x}}_M$ of $\mathbf{x}$ as

$$\mathbb{E}_\mathbf{x}[f(\mathbf{x})] \approx \frac{1}{M} \sum_{m=1}^M f(\hat{\mathbf{x}}_m).$$

By inputting samples of $\mathbf{z}$ from $q_\phi(\mathbf{z}|\mathbf{x})$, which is a Gaussian distribution,[5] to the decoder, we can consider $\ln p_\theta(\mathbf{x}|\mathbf{z})$ as a function of the decoder's output. This is because given an input $\mathbf{x}$, $\ln p_\theta(\mathbf{x}|\mathbf{z})$ is the logarithm of the density function value of the Gaussian distribution with the mean that the decoder outputs. Thus, we can approximate $\nabla_\theta \mathbb{E}_{q_\phi(\mathbf{z}|\mathbf{x})}[\ln p_\theta(\mathbf{x}|\mathbf{z})]$ through backpropagation. For this calculation, we can expect that we obtain a relatively good approximation with a small number of samples of $\mathbf{z}$. This is because, for samples from the distribution of $\mathbf{z}$ conditioned on $\mathbf{x}$, the values of $p(\mathbf{x}|\mathbf{z})$ are expected to be relatively large.

The calculation of the latter:

$$\nabla_\phi \mathbb{E}_{q_\phi(\mathbf{z}|\mathbf{x})}[\ln p_\theta(\mathbf{x}|\mathbf{z})] = \int \frac{\partial q_\phi(\mathbf{z}|\mathbf{x})}{\partial \phi} \ln p_\theta(\mathbf{x}|\mathbf{z}) \, d\mathbf{z}$$

requires some consideration. With respect to the parameters ϕ of the encoding model, the derivative of $q_\phi(\mathbf{z}|\mathbf{x})$ multiplied by $\ln p_\theta(\mathbf{x}|\mathbf{z})$ forms an integral, and this integral is not an expectation calculation. This is because the derivative of $q_\phi(\mathbf{z}|\mathbf{x})$ with respect to ϕ is generally not a probabilistic distribution. Thus, we cannot approximate it using the realized values of $\mathbf{z}$.

---

[5] See Appendix C at the end of the book for a sampling method from a Gaussian distribution.

To address this issue, we utilize a technique called *reparameterization*, which is used to transform one set of parameters into another, making calculations or optimizations easier. In this case, specifically, considering that the posterior probability $q_\phi(\mathbf{z}|\mathbf{x})$ is a Gaussian distribution with mean $\mathbf{f}_{e,\mu}(\mathbf{x};\phi)$ and covariance matrix $\mathrm{diag}(\mathbf{f}_{e,\sigma^2}(\mathbf{x};\phi))$, we introduce a random variable $\boldsymbol{\varepsilon} \sim \mathcal{N}(\mathbf{0}, \mathbf{I})$, then we express $\mathbf{z}$ as follows:

$$\mathbf{z} = \mathbf{f}_{e,\mu}(\mathbf{x};\phi) + \mathbf{f}^{1/2}_{e,\sigma^2}(\mathbf{x};\phi) \odot \boldsymbol{\varepsilon},$$

where $\mathbf{x} \odot \mathbf{y}$ represents the element-wise product of vectors $\mathbf{x}$ and $\mathbf{y}$ (the Hadamard product), and $\mathbf{f}^{1/2}_{e,\sigma^2}(\mathbf{x};\phi)$ is a vector obtained by taking the positive square root of each component of $\mathbf{f}_{e,\sigma^2}(\mathbf{x};\phi)$. This expression of $\mathbf{z}$ leads us to

$$\nabla_\phi \mathbb{E}_{q_\phi(\mathbf{z}|\mathbf{x})}[\ln p_\theta(\mathbf{x}|\mathbf{z})] = \nabla_\phi \mathbb{E}_{\boldsymbol{\varepsilon}} \left[\ln p_\theta(\mathbf{x}|\mathbf{f}_{e,\mu}(\mathbf{x};\phi) + \mathbf{f}^{1/2}_{e,\sigma^2}(\mathbf{x};\phi) \odot \boldsymbol{\varepsilon})\right].$$
(10.4.4)

Note that the left-hand side takes the expectation with respect to the distribution $q_\phi(\mathbf{z}|\mathbf{x})$, which is related to the variable ϕ being differentiated, whereas the right-hand side takes the expectation with respect to $\boldsymbol{\varepsilon}$, which is independent of ϕ. Thus, we can approximate the right-hand side of Eq. (10.4.4) using samples of $\boldsymbol{\varepsilon}$.

During the training of a VAE, the expectation on the right-hand side of Eq. (10.4.4) is approximated by sampling only one sample $\hat{\boldsymbol{\varepsilon}}$ from the distribution of $\boldsymbol{\varepsilon}$ which is $\mathcal{N}(\mathbf{0}, \mathbf{I})$. That is, we compute the output of the decoder in the following.

1. For an input $\mathbf{x}$, we use forward propagation to compute $\mathbf{f}_{e,\mu}(\mathbf{x};\phi)$ and $\mathbf{f}_{e,\sigma^2}(\mathbf{x};\phi)$ with the encoder having the current parameters ϕ.
2. We generate a sample $\hat{\boldsymbol{\varepsilon}}$ of $\boldsymbol{\varepsilon}$ to set:

$$\hat{\mathbf{z}} = \mathbf{f}_{e,\mu}(\mathbf{x};\phi) + \mathbf{f}^{1/2}_{e,\sigma^2}(\mathbf{x};\phi) \odot \hat{\boldsymbol{\varepsilon}}.$$

3. Using this $\hat{\mathbf{z}}$ as input to the decoder (with current parameters θ), we obtain the output of the decoder (the mean of the Gaussian distribution). Thus, given an input $\mathbf{x}$, we can consider $\ln p_\theta(\mathbf{x}|\hat{\mathbf{z}})$ as a function of the decoder's output, which enables us to use backpropagation for the calculation of (10.4.4).

Note that for an input $\mathbf{x}$, $\mathbf{f}_{e,\mu}(\mathbf{x};\phi)$ and $\mathbf{f}_{e,\sigma^2}(\mathbf{x};\phi)$ are the outputs of the encoder, and their linear combination, $\hat{\mathbf{z}}$, serves as the input to the decoder. The entire system, therefore, can be regarded as a single neural network, allowing the gradients to be calculated through backpropagation. For numerical stability, encoders often output the logarithm of the variance $\gamma_l = \ln \sigma_l^2$ in practice.

10.4.2 Why Maximizing Variational Lower Bound?

In VAE, to determine the parameters, we optimize the variational lower bound instead of maximizing the likelihood function:

$$p(\mathbf{x} \mid \boldsymbol{\theta}) = \int p(\mathbf{x} \mid \mathbf{z}, \boldsymbol{\theta}) p(\mathbf{z}) \, d\mathbf{z}.$$

The function $p(\mathbf{x} \mid \mathbf{z}, \boldsymbol{\theta})$ in the integrand of the likelihood is a Gaussian distribution, but it is a non-linear function of the latent variable $\mathbf{z}$ determined by the encoder's output. Thus, we cannot expect to express the integral analytically, even assuming a simple isotropic Gaussian distribution as the prior $p(\mathbf{z})$. Instead, sampling from $\mathbf{z}$ might be used to approximate the integral calculation for the likelihood function. Many samples from $p(\mathbf{z})$, however, have very small values for the probability $p(\mathbf{x} \mid \mathbf{z})$, requiring an extremely large number of samples of $\mathbf{z}$ to achieve sufficiently accurate integration. These facts lead us to face a challenge in determining the decoder's parameter $\boldsymbol{\theta}$ through likelihood maximization.

The situation where an analytical solution cannot be obtained is the same for maximizing the first term of the variational lower bound (10.4.2). In VAE training, we address this difficulty in integral calculation by reparameterization and sampling. In particular, samples from the posterior probability $q(\mathbf{z} \mid \mathbf{x})$ rather than the prior probability $p(\mathbf{z})$ can be expected to yield relatively large values for the probability $p(\mathbf{x} \mid \mathbf{z})$, making the expected value (integral) of $p(\mathbf{x} \mid \mathbf{z})$ under $q(\mathbf{z} \mid \mathbf{x})$ a good approximation with a small number of samples.

Note, first of all, and finally, that the likelihood is independent of the encoder's parameter $\boldsymbol{\phi}$, we cannot determine $\boldsymbol{\phi}$ by maximizing the likelihood.

10.5 Features of VAE

10.5.1 VAE as a Generative Model

The biggest advantage of VAE is its ability to generate new data from random noise. This is achieved because the decoder of VAE is trained to map random points in the latent space to appropriate outputs. Specifically, by passing a realization of $\mathbf{z}$ sampled from the Gaussian prior distribution $\mathcal{N}(\mathbf{z} \mid \mathbf{0}, \mathbf{I})$ through the decoder, we can obtain $\mathbb{E}[\mathbf{x} \mid \mathbf{z}] = \mathbf{f}_d(\mathbf{z}; \boldsymbol{\theta})$. Figure 10.2 illustrates face images generated by VAE when trained on the CelebA dataset.[6] Figure 10.2a shows examples of face images used for training, while Fig. 10.2b displays the generated face images.

10.5.2 Operations in Latent Space

Latent variable models enable the generation of new samples by a method called *latent space interpolation*, where the "features" of two different inputs are interpolated to create new samples. For instance, given two images $\mathbf{x}_1$ and $\mathbf{x}_2$, let

---

[6] Source: https://mmlab.ie.cuhk.edu.hk/projects/CelebA.html.

(a) Examples of training images.   (b) Generated images.

Fig. 10.2 Out of 202,599 images in the CelebA dataset, 162,080 images were resized to 64 × 64 for training data. Used with kind permission of Ziwei Liu. The encoder consists of an input layer, 5 convolutional layers, and a fully connected layer, while the decoder comprises a fully connected layer and 6 convolutional layers. The dimension of the latent variables is set to 128

$z_1 = \mathbb{E}_{q(\mathbf{z}|\mathbf{x}_1)}[\mathbf{z}]$ and $z_2 = \mathbb{E}_{q(\mathbf{z}|\mathbf{x}_2)}[\mathbf{z}]$ be their respective encodings. Then, by linearly interpolating their latent vectors to create $\mathbf{z} = \lambda \mathbf{z}_1 + (1-\lambda)\mathbf{z}_2$, where $0 \leq \lambda \leq 1$, and decoding it using $\mathbb{E}[\mathbf{x}|\mathbf{z}]$, new images can be generated. Figure 10.3 illustrates face images generated by interpolating latent variables obtained from two images at both ends.

Furthermore, latent variable models allow for enhancing or attenuating attributes of data through operations in latent space. Consider attributes such as a person wearing sunglasses, having piercings, or being blonde in facial images. We denote the set of images with attribute i as $\mathbf{X}_i^+$ and the set of images without this attribute as $\mathbf{X}_i^-$. Correspondingly, we define $\mathbf{Z}_i^+$ and $\mathbf{Z}_i^-$ as the sets in the corresponding latent space, and $\bar{\mathbf{z}}^+$ and $\bar{\mathbf{z}}^-$ as their respective means. Introducing an offset vector $\Delta = \bar{\mathbf{z}}^+ - \bar{\mathbf{z}}^-$, we can add positive multiples of this offset vector to a new point $\mathbf{z}$, resulting in an increase in the attribute i, and subtracting multiples of Δ would decrease the attribute i. This operation enables transforming, for example, facial images of men without sunglasses into images of the same men wearing sunglasses. Thus, latent

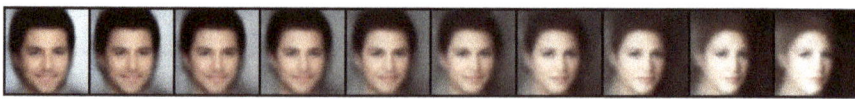

Fig. 10.3 The images depict face images generated based on linearly interpolated latent variables in the latent space, starting from the latent variables of the face image on the left and ending with those of the face image on the right. The parameter λ is varied from 1 to 0 from left to right

variable models allow for increasing or decreasing attributes through vector addition and subtraction in latent space.

10.6 Appendix

10.6.1 Computation of $\mathrm{KL}(q_\phi(\mathbf{z}\,|\,\mathbf{x}) \,\|\, p(\mathbf{z}))$

We define the prior distribution of latent variable $\mathbf{z}$ as a Gaussian distribution with mean $\mathbf{0}$ and covariance matrix $\mathbf{I}$:

$$p(\mathbf{z}) = \mathcal{N}(\mathbf{z}\,|\,\mathbf{0},\,\mathbf{I}).$$

Additionally, on the encoder side, let the distribution of latent variable $\mathbf{z}$ conditioned on input $\mathbf{x}$ be

$$q_\phi(\mathbf{z}\,|\,\mathbf{x}) = \mathcal{N}(\mathbf{z}\,|\,\boldsymbol{\mu},\,\boldsymbol{\Sigma}),$$

where $\boldsymbol{\Sigma}$ is a diagonal matrix. Then, we will show

$$\mathrm{KL}(q_\phi(\mathbf{z}\,|\,\mathbf{x}) \,\|\, p(\mathbf{z})) = \frac{1}{2}\sum_{i=1}^{L}[\sigma_i^2 + \mu_i^2 - \ln \sigma_i^2 - 1]$$

in the following steps.

(1) We obtain the expected value of the inner product $\mathbf{z}^\mathrm{T}\mathbf{z}$ with respect to $q_\phi(\mathbf{z}\,|\,\mathbf{x})$.
(2) We compute the expected value of the quadratic form $(\mathbf{z}-\boldsymbol{\mu})^\mathrm{T}\boldsymbol{\Sigma}^{-1}(\mathbf{z}-\boldsymbol{\mu})$ with respect to $q_\phi(\mathbf{z}\,|\,\mathbf{x})$.
(3) We show that $\mathrm{KL}(q_\phi(\mathbf{z}\,|\,\mathbf{x}) \,\|\, p(\mathbf{z})) = -\frac{1}{2}\sum_{i=1}^{L}\left[1 - \sigma_i^2 - \mu_i^2 + \ln \sigma_i^2\right]$, where L is the dimension of the latent vector $\mathbf{z}$, μ_l is the l-th component of $\boldsymbol{\mu}$, and σ_l^2 is the l-th diagonal component of $\boldsymbol{\Sigma}$.

We start by demonstrating (1).

1. Let $\mathbf{y} = \mathbf{z} - \boldsymbol{\mu}$. Then, we have

$$\mathbb{E}_{q_\phi(\mathbf{z}|\mathbf{x})}[\mathbf{z}^T\mathbf{z}] = \frac{1}{(2\pi)^{L/2}} \frac{1}{|\boldsymbol{\Sigma}|^{1/2}} \int \exp\left\{-\frac{1}{2}(\mathbf{z}-\boldsymbol{\mu})^T \boldsymbol{\Sigma}^{-1}(\mathbf{z}-\boldsymbol{\mu})\right\} \mathbf{z}^T\mathbf{z}\, d\mathbf{z}$$

$$= \frac{1}{(2\pi)^{L/2}} \frac{1}{|\boldsymbol{\Sigma}|^{1/2}} \int \exp\left\{-\frac{1}{2}\mathbf{y}^T \boldsymbol{\Sigma}^{-1}\mathbf{y}\right\} (\mathbf{y}+\boldsymbol{\mu})^T(\mathbf{y}+\boldsymbol{\mu})\, d\mathbf{y}$$

$$= \mathbb{E}_{\mathbf{y}\sim\mathcal{N}(0,\boldsymbol{\Sigma})}[\mathbf{y}^T\mathbf{y}] - 2\mathbb{E}_{\mathbf{y}\sim\mathcal{N}(0,\boldsymbol{\Sigma})}[\boldsymbol{\mu}^T\mathbf{y}] + \mathbb{E}_{\mathbf{y}\sim\mathcal{N}(0,\boldsymbol{\Sigma})}[\boldsymbol{\mu}^T\boldsymbol{\mu}].$$

We calculate the three expectations in the above expression in order.

(a) $\mathbb{E}_{\mathbf{y}\sim\mathcal{N}(0,\boldsymbol{\Sigma})}[\mathbf{y}^T\mathbf{y}]$.

$$\mathbb{E}_{\mathbf{y}\sim\mathcal{N}(0,\boldsymbol{\Sigma})}[\mathbf{y}^T\mathbf{y}] = \frac{1}{(2\pi)^{L/2}} \frac{1}{|\boldsymbol{\Sigma}|^{1/2}} \int \cdots \int \exp\left\{-\sum_{k=1}^L \frac{y_k^2}{2\sigma_k^2}\right\} \left(\sum_{i=1}^L y_i^2\right) dy_1 \cdots dy_L$$

$$= \sum_{i=1}^L \left(\frac{1}{(2\pi)^{1/2}} \frac{1}{\sigma_i} \int y_i^2 \exp\left\{-\frac{y_i^2}{2\sigma_i^2}\right\} dy_i\right) = \sum_{i=1}^L \sigma_i^2.$$

Here, σ_k^2 is the k-th diagonal element of $\boldsymbol{\Sigma}$. The second and third equalities are obtained by noting that $|\boldsymbol{\Sigma}| = \sigma_1^2 \cdots \sigma_L^2$ and

$$\frac{1}{(2\pi)^{1/2}\sigma_k} \int \exp\left\{-\frac{y_k^2}{2\sigma_k^2}\right\} dy_k = 1,$$

and by using the fact that

$$\frac{1}{(2\pi)^{L/2}} \frac{1}{|\boldsymbol{\Sigma}|^{1/2}} \int \cdots \int y_i^2 \exp\left\{-\sum_{k=1}^L \frac{y_k^2}{2\sigma_k^2}\right\} dy_1 \cdots dy_L$$

$$= \frac{1}{(2\pi)^{1/2}} \frac{1}{\sigma_i} \int y_i^2 \exp\left(-\frac{y_i^2}{2\sigma_i^2}\right) dy_i \times \frac{\int \cdots \int \exp\left\{-\sum_{k\neq i} \frac{y_k^2}{2\sigma_k^2}\right\} dy_1 \cdots d_{i-1}d_{i+1}dy_L}{(2\pi)^{(L-1)/2}\sigma_1 \cdots \sigma_{i-1}\sigma_{i+1} \cdots \sigma_L}$$

$$= \frac{1}{(2\pi)^{1/2}} \frac{1}{\sigma_i} \int y_i^2 \exp\left(-\frac{y_i^2}{2\sigma_i^2}\right) dy_i \times \prod_{k\neq i} \frac{1}{(2\pi)^{1/2}\sigma_k} \int \exp\left\{-\frac{y_k^2}{2\sigma_k^2}\right\} dy_k$$

$$= \frac{1}{(2\pi)^{1/2}} \frac{1}{\sigma_i} \int y_i^2 \exp\left(-\frac{y_i^2}{2\sigma_i^2}\right) dy_i = \sigma_i^2.$$

(b) $\mathbb{E}_{\mathbf{y}\sim\mathcal{N}(0,\boldsymbol{\Sigma})}[\boldsymbol{\mu}^T\mathbf{y}]$.
Since $\mathbf{y}$ is symmetric about the origin, we have $\mathbb{E}_{\mathbf{y}\sim\mathcal{N}(0,\boldsymbol{\Sigma})}[\boldsymbol{\mu}^T\mathbf{y}] = 0$.

(c) $\mathbb{E}_{\mathbf{y}\sim\mathcal{N}(0,\boldsymbol{\Sigma})}[\boldsymbol{\mu}^T\boldsymbol{\mu}]$.
Since $\boldsymbol{\mu}$ is a constant (vector), $\mathbb{E}_{\mathbf{y}\sim\mathcal{N}(0,\boldsymbol{\Sigma})}[\boldsymbol{\mu}^T\boldsymbol{\mu}] = \boldsymbol{\mu}^T\boldsymbol{\mu} = \sum_{i=1}^L \mu_i^2$ holds.
Thus, we have

$$\mathbb{E}_{q_\phi(\mathbf{z}|\mathbf{x})}[\mathbf{z}^T\mathbf{z}] = \sum_{i=1}^L \sigma_i^2 + \sum_{i=1}^L \mu_i^2.$$

10.6 Appendix

Next, we show (2). Let $\mathbf{y} = \mathbf{z} - \boldsymbol{\mu}$. Then, we have

$$\begin{aligned}
&\mathbb{E}_{q_\phi(\mathbf{z}|\mathbf{x})}[(\mathbf{z}-\boldsymbol{\mu})^\mathrm{T}\boldsymbol{\Sigma}^{-1}(\mathbf{z}-\boldsymbol{\mu})] \\
&= \frac{1}{(2\pi)^{L/2}}\frac{1}{|\boldsymbol{\Sigma}|^{1/2}}\int \exp\left\{-\frac{1}{2}(\mathbf{z}-\boldsymbol{\mu})^\mathrm{T}\boldsymbol{\Sigma}^{-1}(\mathbf{z}-\boldsymbol{\mu})\right\}(\mathbf{z}-\boldsymbol{\mu})^\mathrm{T}\boldsymbol{\Sigma}^{-1}(\mathbf{z}-\boldsymbol{\mu})\,d\mathbf{z} \\
&= \frac{1}{(2\pi)^{L/2}}\frac{1}{|\boldsymbol{\Sigma}|^{1/2}}\int \exp\left\{-\frac{1}{2}\mathbf{y}^\mathrm{T}\boldsymbol{\Sigma}^{-1}\mathbf{y}\right\}\mathbf{y}^\mathrm{T}\boldsymbol{\Sigma}^{-1}\mathbf{y}\,d\mathbf{y} \\
&= \frac{1}{(2\pi)^{L/2}}\frac{1}{|\boldsymbol{\Sigma}|^{1/2}}\int\cdots\int \exp\left\{-\sum_{k=1}^{L}\frac{y_k^2}{2\sigma_k^2}\right\}\left(\sum_{i=1}^{L}\frac{y_i^2}{\sigma_i^2}\right)dy_1\cdots dy_L \\
&= \sum_{i=1}^{L}\left(\frac{1}{(2\pi)^{1/2}}\frac{1}{\sigma_i}\int y_i^2\exp\left\{-\frac{y_i^2}{2\sigma_i^2}\right\}dy_i \times \frac{1}{\sigma_i^2}\right) = \sum_{i=1}^{L}\sigma_i^2\frac{1}{\sigma_i^2} = L.
\end{aligned}$$

Finally, we show (3). From (1) and (2), with noting that $\ln|\boldsymbol{\Sigma}| = \sum_{i=1}^{L}\sigma_i^2$ and $\ln|\mathbf{I}| = \ln 1 = 0$ hold, we obtain

$$\begin{aligned}
\mathbb{KL}(q_\phi(\mathbf{z}|\mathbf{x}) \parallel p(\mathbf{z})) &= \int q_\phi(\mathbf{z}|\mathbf{x})\ln\left(\frac{q_\phi(\mathbf{z}|\mathbf{x})}{p(\mathbf{z})}\right)d\mathbf{z} \\
&= \mathbb{E}_{q_\phi(\mathbf{z}|\mathbf{x})}[\ln q_\phi(\mathbf{z}|\mathbf{x})] - \mathbb{E}_{q_\phi(\mathbf{z}|\mathbf{x})}[\ln p(\mathbf{z})] \\
&= \mathbb{E}_{q_\phi(\mathbf{z}|\mathbf{x})}\left[-\frac{1}{2}(\mathbf{z}-\boldsymbol{\mu})^\mathrm{T}\boldsymbol{\Sigma}^{-1}(\mathbf{z}-\boldsymbol{\mu})\right] - \frac{L}{2}\ln(2\pi) - \frac{1}{2}\ln|\boldsymbol{\Sigma}| \\
&\quad - \mathbb{E}_{q_\phi(\mathbf{z}|\mathbf{x})}\left[-\frac{1}{2}\mathbf{z}^\mathrm{T}\mathbf{z}\right] + \frac{L}{2}\ln(2\pi) + \frac{1}{2}\ln|\mathbf{I}| \\
&= \frac{1}{2}\sum_{i=1}^{L}[\sigma_i^2 + \mu_i^2 - \ln\sigma_i^2 - 1].
\end{aligned}$$

10.6.2 Proof of Decomposition Formula of the Likelihood

In this appendix, we derive the decomposition formula of the likelihood $p(\mathbf{X}\mid\boldsymbol{\Theta})$:

$$\ln p(\mathbf{X}\mid\boldsymbol{\Theta}) = \mathcal{L}(q, p; \boldsymbol{\Theta}) + \mathbb{KL}(q \parallel p; \boldsymbol{\Theta}),$$

where

$$\mathcal{L}(q, p; \boldsymbol{\Theta}) = \sum_{\mathbf{Z}} q(\mathbf{Z})\ln\left\{\frac{p(\mathbf{X}, \mathbf{Z}\mid\boldsymbol{\Theta})}{q(\mathbf{Z})}\right\} \tag{10.6.1}$$

and

$$\mathbb{KL}(q \parallel p; \boldsymbol{\Theta}) = -\sum_{\mathbf{Z}} q(\mathbf{Z})\ln\left\{\frac{p(\mathbf{Z}\mid\mathbf{X}, \boldsymbol{\Theta})}{q(\mathbf{Z})}\right\}. \tag{10.6.2}$$

Substituting the definition of the conditional distribution:

$$\ln p(\mathbf{X},\, \mathbf{Z} \mid \Theta) = \ln p(\mathbf{Z} \mid \mathbf{X},\, \Theta) + \ln p(\mathbf{X} \mid \Theta)$$

into the right-hand side of Eq. (10.6.1), we obtain

$$\begin{aligned}
\mathcal{L}(q,\, p;\, \Theta) &= \sum_{\mathbf{Z}} q(\mathbf{Z}) \ln \left\{ \frac{p(\mathbf{X},\, \mathbf{Z} \mid \Theta)}{q(\mathbf{Z})} \right\} \\
&= \sum_{\mathbf{Z}} q(\mathbf{Z}) \ln \left\{ \frac{p(\mathbf{Z} \mid \mathbf{X},\, \Theta) p(\mathbf{X} \mid \Theta)}{q(\mathbf{Z})} \right\} \\
&= \sum_{\mathbf{Z}} q(\mathbf{Z}) \left(\ln \left\{ \frac{p(\mathbf{Z} \mid \mathbf{X},\, \Theta)}{q(\mathbf{Z})} \right\} + \ln p(\mathbf{X} \mid \Theta) \right) \\
&= -\mathbb{KL}(q \parallel p;\, \Theta) + \ln p(\mathbf{X} \mid \Theta).
\end{aligned}$$

The final equality uses the fact that $q(\mathbf{Z})$ is a distribution, so the sum of $q(\mathbf{Z})$ over $\mathbf{Z}$ is 1.

Chapter 11
Diffusion Model

11.1 Overview of Diffusion Model

Diffusion model (or *diffusion probability model*) [17, 42] is a generative model using latent variables inspired by non-equilibrium thermodynamics. The diffusion model is a Markov chain trained with variational inference to generate samples from data, gradually replacing signals with noise in the reverse direction of the diffusion process, restoring signals from noisy signals (Fig. 11.1). In the following, we describe the details of the diffusion model. To avoid complexity, we defer the computation details to the appendix at the end of the chapter. We begin with the Markov process.

11.2 Markov Process (Markov Chain)

We call a sequence of random variables $x_0, x_1, \ldots, x_T$ a *stochastic process*. A stochastic process satisfying the following condition is called a *Markov process* (or *Markov chain*):

$$p(x_t \mid x_0, \ldots, x_{t-1}) = p(x_t \mid x_{t-1}), \quad t = 1, \ldots, T. \tag{11.2.1}$$

Considering the index t as time and the values taken by the random variable x_t as states, as implied by Eq. (11.2.1), we can see a Markov chain as a sequence of random variables where the conditional probability at time t conditioned on all past states depends only on the immediate past state. We can show Eq. (11.2.1) to be equivalent to the following:

$$p(x_t, \ldots, x_T \mid x_0, \ldots, x_{t-1}) = p(x_t, \ldots, x_T \mid x_{t-1}), \quad t = 1, \ldots, T. \tag{11.2.2}$$

Furthermore, in a Markov chain, we can express the joint probability of the sequence as

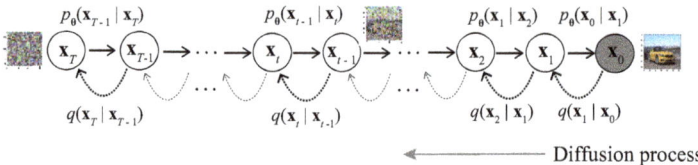

Fig. 11.1 The Bayesian network of the diffusion model. Based on Fig. 2 of [17]

$$p(\mathbf{x}_0, \ldots, \mathbf{x}_T) = p(\mathbf{x}_T \mid \mathbf{x}_{T-1}) \cdots p(\mathbf{x}_2 \mid \mathbf{x}_1) p(\mathbf{x}_1 \mid \mathbf{x}_0) p(\mathbf{x}_0). \tag{11.2.3}$$

This follows easily from the definition of conditional probability:

$$p(\mathbf{x}_0, \ldots, \mathbf{x}_T) = p(\mathbf{x}_T \mid \mathbf{x}_0, \ldots, \mathbf{x}_{T-1}) \cdots p(\mathbf{x}_2 \mid \mathbf{x}_0, \mathbf{x}_1) p(\mathbf{x}_1 \mid \mathbf{x}_0) p(\mathbf{x}_0)$$

and Eq. (11.2.1). Conversely, if we can represent the joint probability as in Eq. (11.2.3), it implies Eq. (11.2.1). We demonstrate the equivalence of the defining Eqs. (11.2.1), (11.2.2), and (11.2.3) in the appendix at the end of the chapter.

Let $\mathbf{x}_0, \mathbf{x}_1, \ldots, \mathbf{x}_T$ be a stochastic process. Then, we define the *inverse process* (or *reverse process*) of it as $\mathbf{x}_T, \mathbf{x}_{T-1}, \ldots, \mathbf{x}_0$. If a stochastic process is a Markov process, then its inverse process is also a Markov process (see the appendix at the end of the chapter for details).

11.2.1 Origin of the Diffusion Model

Consider a long, thin, uniform wire, and let $u(x, t)$ denote the temperature at position x at time t. It is known that $u(x, t)$ satisfies the well-known diffusion equation:

$$\frac{\partial u(x, t)}{\partial t} = \alpha^2 \frac{\partial^2 u(x, t)}{\partial x^2}, \tag{11.2.4}$$

where α^2 is a constant called the diffusion coefficient, determined by the material of the wire. Many diffusion phenomena in nature also satisfy this equation. On the other hand, in the continuous-time limit of a discrete-time Markov process with small time intervals, under the assumption that at time τ, the state (position) is ξ, we can show that the conditional probability $p_{t,\tau}(x \mid \xi)$ of being at state (position) x at time $t > \tau$ satisfies the diffusion Eq. (11.2.4) under the constraint that as $t - \tau$ becomes small, so does $|x - \xi|$ (see the appendix at the end of the chapter for details). Furthermore, taking the Gaussian distribution

$$\frac{1}{2\alpha\sqrt{\pi(t-\tau)}} \exp\left\{-\frac{(x-\xi)^2}{4\alpha^2(t-\tau)}\right\}$$

as the distribution $p_{t,\tau}(x \mid \xi)$, we can easily see that this distribution is a solution to the diffusion Eq. (11.2.4).

The continuous-time Markov process described above is called a *diffusion process*. This is the origin of the name of the diffusion model introduced in this chapter. In the diffusion model, we assume that there is a Markov chain with small state changes in transitions. Furthermore, as mentioned earlier, the inverse process of a Markov chain is also a Markov chain. If the state changes in transitions of the Markov chain are small, then it is reasonable to assume that the conditional transition distribution of the chain follows a Gaussian distribution, and the same applies to its inverse process. In the diffusion model, we assume that the transition distribution of the inverse process follows a Gaussian distribution, and this distribution is represented by neural networks.

11.3 Formulation of Diffusion Model

Let $q(\mathbf{x})$ denote the unknown distribution from which the data is generated, and let $\mathbf{x}_0$ be a data sampled from $q(\mathbf{x}_0)$. We consider vectors $\mathbf{x}_1, \ldots, \mathbf{x}_T$ of the same dimensionality as $\mathbf{x}_0$ as latent variables that have the distribution $q(\mathbf{x})$, and denote $\mathbf{x}_{0:T}$ as shorthand for $\{\mathbf{x}_0, \ldots, \mathbf{x}_T\}$. Also, let θ represent the set of weight parameters of the neural network used to estimate the inverse process. We define $p_\theta(\mathbf{x}_{0:T})$ as the joint probability estimated by the neural network for $\mathbf{x}_0, \ldots, \mathbf{x}_T$.

We can obtain the likelihood of the data $\mathbf{x}_0$ by marginalization:

$$p_\theta(\mathbf{x}_0) = \int p_\theta(\mathbf{x}_{0:T}) \, d\mathbf{x}_{1:T}.$$

Furthermore, we assume that in the inverse process, the initial value $\mathbf{x}_T$ follows the distribution $p(\mathbf{x}_T) = \mathcal{N}(\mathbf{x}_T \mid \mathbf{0}, \mathbf{I})$, where $\mathcal{N}(\mathbf{x}_T \mid \mathbf{0}, \mathbf{I})$ denotes a multivariate Gaussian distribution with mean $\mathbf{0}$ and identity covariance matrix $\mathbf{I}$.

The forward process (diffusion process) of the diffusion model proceeds gradually from $\mathbf{x}_0$ to $\mathbf{x}_T$ by adding noise in each step of a Markov chain (see Fig. 11.2). Specifically, we assume the transition probabilities $q(\mathbf{x}_t \mid \mathbf{x}_{t-1})$, $t = 1, \ldots, T$, to be

$$q(\mathbf{x}_t \mid \mathbf{x}_{t-1}) = \mathcal{N}(\mathbf{x}_t \mid \sqrt{1 - \beta_t}\mathbf{x}_{t-1}, \beta_t \mathbf{I}), \tag{11.3.1}$$

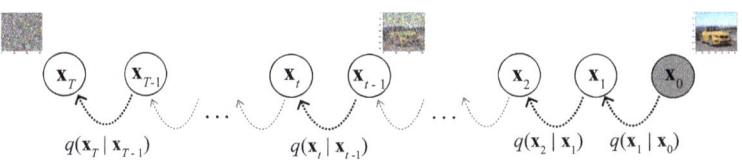

Fig. 11.2 Diffusion model: forward process. Based on Fig. 2 of [17]

where $0 < \beta_1 < \cdots < \beta_T < 1$ are parameters called the *variance schedule*. Due to the Markov property, the joint probability of $\mathbf{x}_{1:T}$ conditioned on $\mathbf{x}_0$ is

$$q(\mathbf{x}_{1:T} \mid \mathbf{x}_0) = \prod_{i=1}^{T} q(\mathbf{x}_t \mid \mathbf{x}_{t-1}). \tag{11.3.2}$$

In the Bayesian framework, the forward process corresponds to the inference of the distribution of latent variables. In the diffusion model, however, we do not need to infer the distribution of latent variables because we have them from the beginning. Generally, in generative models, we need to infer the distribution of latent variables given the data. This inference is one of the challenging aspects of Bayesian inference. In the diffusion model, since we have the fixed inference, we can avoid the difficulties of Bayesian inference.

In general, since we do not know the distribution $q(\mathbf{x}_0)$ from which the data $\mathbf{x}_0$ is sampled, we cannot obtain $q(\mathbf{x}_1)$ in a simple form even if $q(\mathbf{x}_1 \mid \mathbf{x}_0)$ is a Gaussian distribution. Also, we cannot obtain $q(\mathbf{x}_t)$ in a simple form either. By contrast, the distribution of $\mathbf{x}_t$ conditioned on $\mathbf{x}_0$ is a Gaussian distribution. We demonstrate this below.

First, let us define

$$\alpha_t \equiv 1 - \beta_t, \quad \bar{\alpha}_t \equiv \prod_{i=1}^{t} \alpha_i \tag{11.3.3}$$

and introduce independent and identically distributed (i.i.d.) Gaussian noise vectors $\epsilon_t \sim \mathcal{N}(\mathbf{0}, \mathbf{I})$, $t = 1, \ldots, T$. Then, we can express

$$\mathbf{x}_t = \sqrt{\alpha_t} \mathbf{x}_{t-1} + \sqrt{1 - \alpha_t} \epsilon_t.$$

Furthermore, note that if we introduce constants σ_t and σ_{t-1}, we have

$$\epsilon'_{t-1} \equiv \sigma_t \epsilon_t + \sigma_{t-1} \epsilon_{t-1} \sim \mathcal{N}(\mathbf{0}, (\sigma_t^2 + \sigma_{t-1}^2)\mathbf{I}).$$

With this in mind, we can recursively express $\mathbf{x}_t$ as

$$\mathbf{x}_t = \sqrt{\alpha_t} \mathbf{x}_{t-1} + \sqrt{1 - \alpha_t} \epsilon_t = \sqrt{\alpha_t \alpha_{t-1}} \mathbf{x}_{t-2} + \sqrt{1 - \alpha_t \alpha_{t-1}} \epsilon_{t-1} = \cdots$$
$$= \sqrt{\bar{\alpha}_t} \mathbf{x}_0 + \sqrt{1 - \bar{\alpha}_t} \epsilon_1,$$

where we have rewritten ϵ'_{t-1} as ϵ_{t-1}. Thus, we obtain

$$q(\mathbf{x}_t \mid \mathbf{x}_0) = \mathcal{N}(\mathbf{x}_t \mid \sqrt{\bar{\alpha}_t} \mathbf{x}_0, (1 - \bar{\alpha}_t)\mathbf{I}). \tag{11.3.4}$$

Taking the limit as T approaches infinity, we have $\lim_{T \to \infty} \bar{\alpha}_T = 0$ and $\lim_{T \to \infty} 1 - \bar{\alpha}_T = 1$, so we obtain

$$q(\mathbf{x}_\infty \mid \mathbf{x}_0) = \mathcal{N}(\mathbf{x}_\infty \mid \mathbf{0}, \mathbf{I}).$$

11.4 Learning of Diffusion Models

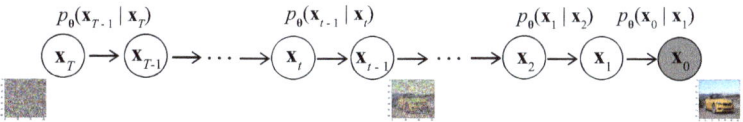

Fig. 11.3 Diffusion model: reverse process. Based on Fig. 2 of [17]

This implies that in the forward process, as time T increases, $\mathbf{x}_T$ becomes a Gaussian noise image.

Next, we formulate the reverse process of the diffusion model (see Fig. 11.3). We estimate the transition probabilities in the reverse process using a neural network as

$$p_\theta(\mathbf{x}_{t-1} \mid \mathbf{x}_t) = \mathcal{N}(\mathbf{x}_{t-1} \mid \boldsymbol{\mu}_\theta(\mathbf{x}_t, t), \boldsymbol{\Sigma}_\theta(\mathbf{x}_t, t)), \tag{11.3.5}$$

where $\boldsymbol{\mu}_\theta(\mathbf{x}_t, t)$ and $\boldsymbol{\Sigma}_\theta(\mathbf{x}_t, t)$ represent the mean and covariance matrix of a Gaussian distribution, respectively, expressed as outputs of the neural network. The distribution of the initial value $\mathbf{x}_T$ is given by

$$p(\mathbf{x}_T) = \mathcal{N}(\mathbf{x}_T \mid \mathbf{0}, \mathbf{I}). \tag{11.3.6}$$

Then, the joint probability (estimated) of $\mathbf{x}_{0:T}$ in the reverse process is given by

$$p_\theta(\mathbf{x}_{0:T}) = p(\mathbf{x}_T) \prod_{t=1}^{T} p_\theta(\mathbf{x}_{t-1} \mid \mathbf{x}_t). \tag{11.3.7}$$

The implementation of the diffusion model comes with various options and variations. For example, in the forward process, we can choose to determine the variance schedule through learning or keep it fixed. Similarly, in the reverse process, we have options regarding the selection of the neural network architecture. We treat these choices as hyperparameters. For simplicity, in the following, we consider the variance schedule to be fixed.

11.4 Learning of Diffusion Models

Now we move on to the learning of diffusion models. In learning the diffusion model, we determine the weights of a neural network that computes the reverse process $p_\theta(\mathbf{x}_{t-1} \mid \mathbf{x}_t)$ while keeping the diffusion process $q(\mathbf{x}_t \mid \mathbf{x}_{t-1})$ fixed. The likelihood for data $\mathbf{x}_0$ is given by

$$p_\theta(\mathbf{x}_0) = \int p_\theta(\mathbf{x}_{0:T}) \, d\mathbf{x}_{1:T}.$$

The integral on the right-hand side of this equation cannot be solved analytically and maximizing the likelihood is challenging. Instead of maximizing the likelihood, we minimize the variational upper bound (negative variational lower bound).

11.4.1 Variational Upper Bound

Let $\mathbf{X}$ be the set of observed variables and $\mathbf{Z}$ be the set of corresponding latent variables. Also, let $p(\mathbf{X}, \mathbf{Z})$ denote the joint distribution of $\mathbf{X}$ and $\mathbf{Z}$, and $q(\mathbf{Z})$ denote the distribution of $\mathbf{Z}$. Recall the definition of the variational lower bound (10.3.1):

$$\mathcal{L}(q, p) \equiv \mathbb{E}_{q(\mathbf{Z})}\left[\ln \frac{p(\mathbf{X}, \mathbf{Z})}{q(\mathbf{Z})}\right] \leq \ln p(\mathbf{X}),$$

which is defined as a functional of the distributions $q(\mathbf{Z})$ and $p(\mathbf{X}, \mathbf{Z})$. The variational upper bound is the reverse of the sign of the variational lower bound:

$$\mathbb{E}_{q(\mathbf{Z})}\left[-\ln \frac{p(\mathbf{X}, \mathbf{Z})}{q(\mathbf{Z})}\right] \geq -\ln p(\mathbf{X}).$$

Following the original paper, we consider the minimization of the variational upper bound instead of the maximization of the variational lower bound.

We assume that the observed data $\mathbf{X}_0 = \{\mathbf{x}_0^{(1)}, \mathbf{x}_0^{(2)}, \ldots, \mathbf{x}_0^{(N)}\}$ are independently generated from the same distribution. In the diffusion model, for a single data $\mathbf{x}_0$, we define the variational upper bound $L_{\mathbf{x}_0}$ as

$$L_{\mathbf{x}_0} = \mathbb{E}_{q(\mathbf{x}_{1:T} \mid \mathbf{x}_0)}\left[-\ln \frac{p_\theta(\mathbf{x}_{0:T})}{q(\mathbf{x}_{1:T} \mid \mathbf{x}_0)}\right] \geq -\ln p_\theta(\mathbf{x}_0).$$

Note that since $q(\mathbf{x}_{1:T} \mid \mathbf{x}_0)$ is given by Eq. (11.3.2), the variational upper bound $L_{\mathbf{x}_0}$ is a functional of $p_\theta(\mathbf{x}_{0:T})$ alone. For all data $\mathbf{X}_0$, the variational upper bound is

$$L(\theta) = \sum_{n=1}^{N} L_{\mathbf{x}_0^{(n)}} \geq \sum_{n=1}^{N} \left(-\ln p_\theta(\mathbf{x}_0^{(n)})\right) = -\ln p_\theta(\mathbf{X}_0).$$

The goal is to find θ that minimizes $L(\theta)$. Hereafter, when there is no risk of confusion, we denote $L_{\mathbf{x}_0}$ as L.

Here, we provide some comments on the variational upper bound in diffusion models.

1. In diffusion models, $\mathbf{x}_0$ is the only observed variable, and $\mathbf{x}_1$ through $\mathbf{x}_T$ are latent variables. In the variational upper bound:

11.4 Learning of Diffusion Models

$$L = \mathbb{E}_{q(\mathbf{x}_{1:T} \mid \mathbf{x}_0)} \left[-\ln \frac{p_\theta(\overbrace{\mathbf{x}_0}^{\text{observed}}, \overbrace{\mathbf{x}_{1:T}}^{\text{latent}})}{\underbrace{q(\mathbf{x}_{1:T} \mid \mathbf{x}_0)}_{\text{latent}}} \right],$$

the denominator inside the expectation is the distribution conditioned on $\mathbf{x}_0$, which is the posterior joint distribution of $\mathbf{x}_1$ through $\mathbf{x}_T$ given by Expression (11.3.4).

2. a. In likelihood maximization, we set $p_\theta(\mathbf{x}_0)$ as an approximation to the distribution of the data $q(\mathbf{x}_0)$. That is, likelihood maximization aims to minimize the KL divergence[1] between $q(\mathbf{x}_0)$ and $p_\theta(\mathbf{x}_0)$:

$$-\int q(\mathbf{x}_0) \ln \frac{p_\theta(\mathbf{x}_0)}{q(\mathbf{x}_0)} d\mathbf{x}_0 = -\mathbb{E}_{q(\mathbf{x}_0)} \left[\ln \frac{p_\theta(\mathbf{x}_0)}{q(\mathbf{x}_0)} \right],$$

which is approximated by the law of large numbers as

$$-\frac{1}{N} \sum_{n=1}^{N} \ln \frac{p_\theta(\mathbf{x}_0^{(n)})}{q(\mathbf{x}_0^{(n)})},$$

i.e., the maximization of

$$\frac{1}{N} \sum_{n=1}^{N} \ln p_\theta(\mathbf{x}_0^{(n)})$$

since $q(\mathbf{x}_0^{(n)})$ is independent of the parameters θ.

b. In contrast, minimizing the variational upper bound here involves a trade-off between bringing the fixed posterior probability $q(\mathbf{x}_{1:T} \mid \mathbf{x}_0)$ closer to $p_\theta(\mathbf{x}_{1:T} \mid \mathbf{x}_0)$ and increasing the log-likelihood. This can be understood from the following transformation of the variational upper bound:

$$\begin{aligned}
L_{\mathbf{x}_0} &= \mathbb{E}_{q(\mathbf{x}_{1:T} \mid \mathbf{x}_0)} \left[-\ln \frac{p_\theta(\mathbf{x}_{0:T})}{q(\mathbf{x}_{1:T} \mid \mathbf{x}_0)} \right] \\
&= \mathbb{E}_{q(\mathbf{x}_{1:T} \mid \mathbf{x}_0)} \left[-\ln \frac{p_\theta(\mathbf{x}_{1:T} \mid \mathbf{x}_0) \cdot p_\theta(\mathbf{x}_0)}{q(\mathbf{x}_{1:T} \mid \mathbf{x}_0)} \right] \\
&= \mathbb{E}_{q(\mathbf{x}_{1:T} \mid \mathbf{x}_0)} \left[-\ln \frac{p_\theta(\mathbf{x}_{1:T} \mid \mathbf{x}_0)}{q(\mathbf{x}_{1:T} \mid \mathbf{x}_0)} \right] - \mathbb{E}_{q(\mathbf{x}_{1:T} \mid \mathbf{x}_0)} \left[\ln p_\theta(\mathbf{x}_0) \right] \\
&= \mathbb{KL} \left(q(\mathbf{x}_{1:T} \mid \mathbf{x}_0) \parallel p_\theta(\mathbf{x}_{1:T} \mid \mathbf{x}_0) \right) - \ln p_\theta(\mathbf{x}_0).
\end{aligned}$$

From the rightmost expression in this equation, we see that the KL divergence $\mathbb{KL}(q(\mathbf{x}_{1:T} \mid \mathbf{x}_0) \parallel p_\theta(\mathbf{x}_{1:T} \mid \mathbf{x}_0))$ serves as a regularization term in the minimization of the variational upper bound.

---

[1] For more information on KL divergence, see Appendix B at the end of the book.

3. a. Regarding the relationship between the expected value of the variational upper bound and all the data, by the law of large numbers, we have

$$L(\boldsymbol{\theta}) = \sum_{n=1}^{N} L_{\mathbf{x}_0^{(n)}} \approx \mathbb{E}_{q(\mathbf{x}_0)}[L_{\mathbf{x}_0}].$$

b. Ideally, we would like to determine the parameters by minimizing the expected value of the variational upper bound. However, since we cannot calculate that value analytically, as presenting later, we use the stochastic gradient descent algorithm based on the above relationship.

c. Hereafter, we will consider the minimization of the variational upper bound for a single data point $\mathbf{x}_0$:

$$L_{\mathbf{x}_0} = \mathbb{E}_{q(\mathbf{x}_{1:T}\mid \mathbf{x}_0)}\left[-\ln \frac{p_\theta(\mathbf{x}_{0:T})}{q(\mathbf{x}_{1:T}\mid \mathbf{x}_0)}\right].$$

11.4.2 Temporal Decomposition of Variational Upper Bound

Now, to minimize the variational upper bound, we decompose it temporally. Through this decomposition, we can replace the overall optimization by optimization at each time step. We start from

$$L = \mathbb{E}_{q(\mathbf{x}_{1:T}\mid \mathbf{x}_0)}\left[-\ln \frac{p_\theta(\mathbf{x}_{0:T})}{q(\mathbf{x}_{1:T}\mid \mathbf{x}_0)}\right] = \mathbb{E}_{q(\mathbf{x}_{1:T}\mid \mathbf{x}_0)}\left[-\ln p(\mathbf{x}_T) - \sum_{t\geq 1}\ln \frac{p_\theta(\mathbf{x}_{t-1}\mid \mathbf{x}_t)}{q(\mathbf{x}_t\mid \mathbf{x}_{t-1})}\right].$$

From this expression, we can derive the following decomposition:

$$L = L_0 + L_1 + \cdots + L_{T-1} + L_T,$$

where

$$L_0 = -\mathbb{E}_{q(\mathbf{x}_1\mid \mathbf{x}_0)}[\ln p_\theta(\mathbf{x}_0\mid \mathbf{x}_1)],$$
$$L_{t-1} = \mathbb{E}_{q(\mathbf{x}_t\mid \mathbf{x}_0)}[\mathbb{KL}(q(\mathbf{x}_{t-1}\mid \mathbf{x}_t, \mathbf{x}_0) \parallel p_\theta(\mathbf{x}_{t-1}\mid \mathbf{x}_t))], \quad t = 2, \ldots, T,$$
$$L_T = \mathbb{KL}(q(\mathbf{x}_T\mid \mathbf{x}_0) \parallel p(\mathbf{x}_T)).$$

We describe a proof of the decomposition in the appendix at the end of this chapter. Note that in the original L, we take the expectation over the distribution $q(\mathbf{x}_{1:T}\mid \mathbf{x}_0)$, whereas in L_0 and L_{t-1}, we take the expectation over the distribution $q(\mathbf{x}_t\mid \mathbf{x}_0)$. If the variance schedule β_t is not learned but fixed, then,

$$L_T = \mathbb{KL}(q(\mathbf{x}_T\mid \mathbf{x}_0) \parallel p(\mathbf{x}_T))$$

11.4 Learning of Diffusion Models

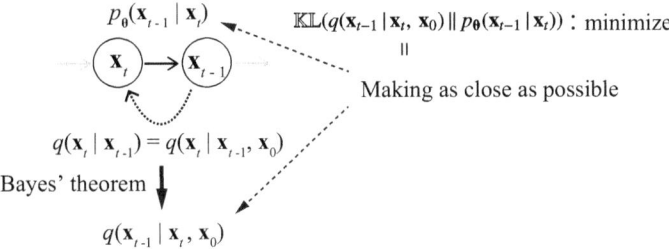

Fig. 11.4 Learning details: minimization of L_{t-1}. This minimization implies making the transition probabilities of the reverse diffusion process conditioned on data $\mathbf{x}_0$, as close as possible on average, to the estimated transition probabilities of the reverse diffusion process through a neural network

becomes a constant and thus, it is irrelevant to learning. Thus, minimizing the variational upper bound boils down to individually minimizing $L_0, L_1, L_2, \ldots, L_{T-1}$.

Looking at the term in the decomposition expression:

$$L_{t-1} = \mathbb{E}_{q(\mathbf{x}_t \mid \mathbf{x}_0)}[\mathbb{KL}(q(\mathbf{x}_{t-1} \mid \mathbf{x}_t, \mathbf{x}_0) \parallel p_\theta(\mathbf{x}_{t-1} \mid \mathbf{x}_t))],$$

we see that its minimization implies making the estimated transition probabilities of the reverse diffusion process:

$$p_\theta(\mathbf{x}_{t-1} \mid \mathbf{x}_t)$$

as close as possible, on average, to the estimated transition probabilities of the reverse diffusion process:

$$q(\mathbf{x}_{t-1} \mid \mathbf{x}_t, \mathbf{x}_0)$$

conditioned on $\mathbf{x}_0$ (Fig. 11.4).

We calculate the minimization of L_{t-1}. For simplicity, we assume $\Sigma_\theta(\mathbf{x}_t, t) = \sigma_t^2 \mathbf{I}$, $\sigma_t^2 = \beta_t$. Then, we have

$$p_\theta(\mathbf{x}_{t-1} \mid \mathbf{x}_t) = \mathcal{N}(\mathbf{x}_{t-1} \mid \boldsymbol{\mu}_\theta(\mathbf{x}_t, t), \sigma_t^2 \mathbf{I}).$$

First, we find the transition probability of the inverse diffusion process:

$$q(\mathbf{x}_{t-1} \mid \mathbf{x}_t)$$

by reversing $\mathbf{x}_t$ and $\mathbf{x}_{t-1}$ of the diffusion process:

$$q(\mathbf{x}_t \mid \mathbf{x}_{t-1}) = \mathcal{N}(\mathbf{x}_t \mid \sqrt{1 - \beta_t} \mathbf{x}_{t-1}, \beta_t \mathbf{I})$$

using Bayes' theorem. This, however, is not straightforward to compute. Thus, using the conditional independence of $\mathbf{x}_0$ given $\mathbf{x}_{t-1}$, which follows from the Markov property, we express

$$q(\mathbf{x}_t \mid \mathbf{x}_{t-1}) = q(\mathbf{x}_t \mid \mathbf{x}_{t-1}, \mathbf{x}_0)$$

and then apply Bayes' theorem. That is, considering Eq. (11.3.4):

$$q(\mathbf{x}_t \mid \mathbf{x}_0) = \mathcal{N}(\mathbf{x}_t \mid \sqrt{\bar{\alpha}_t}\mathbf{x}_0, \ (1-\bar{\alpha}_t)\mathbf{I})$$

and applying Bayes' theorem with respect to the conditional probability:

$$q(\mathbf{x}_t \mid \mathbf{x}_{t-1}, \mathbf{x}_0) = q(\mathbf{x}_t \mid \mathbf{x}_{t-1}) = \mathcal{N}(\mathbf{x}_t \mid \sqrt{1-\beta_t}\mathbf{x}_{t-1}, \ \beta_t \mathbf{I}),$$

we obtain

$$q(\mathbf{x}_{t-1} \mid \mathbf{x}_t, \mathbf{x}_0) \propto q(\mathbf{x}_t \mid \mathbf{x}_{t-1}, \mathbf{x}_0) \cdot q(\mathbf{x}_{t-1} \mid \mathbf{x}_0)$$
$$= \mathcal{N}(\mathbf{x}_{t-1} \mid \tilde{\boldsymbol{\mu}}_t(\mathbf{x}_t, \mathbf{x}_0), \ \tilde{\beta}_t \mathbf{I}),$$

where

$$\tilde{\boldsymbol{\mu}}_t(\mathbf{x}_t, \mathbf{x}_0) \equiv \frac{\sqrt{\bar{\alpha}_{t-1}}\beta_t}{1-\bar{\alpha}_t}\mathbf{x}_0 + \frac{\sqrt{\alpha_t}(1-\bar{\alpha}_{t-1})}{1-\bar{\alpha}_t}\mathbf{x}_t \qquad (11.4.1)$$

and

$$\tilde{\beta}_t \equiv \frac{1-\bar{\alpha}_{t-1}}{1-\bar{\alpha}_t}\beta_t,$$

where $\bar{\alpha}_t$ is as defined in Eq. (11.3.3). We provide specific calculations in the appendix of the chapter. Note that while the transition probability of the inverse process $q(\mathbf{x}_{t-1} \mid \mathbf{x}_t)$ is not easy to compute directly, $q(\mathbf{x}_{t-1} \mid \mathbf{x}_t, \mathbf{x}_0)$ conditioned on $\mathbf{x}_0$ can be analytically derived. Note also that the notation $\tilde{\boldsymbol{\mu}}_t(\mathbf{x}_t, \mathbf{x}_0)$ indicates that $\tilde{\boldsymbol{\mu}}_t$ is a function of $\mathbf{x}_t$ and $\mathbf{x}_0$.

We can compute the KL divergence between Gaussian distributions. Ignoring constant terms irrelevant to $\boldsymbol{\theta}$ with the assumption $\sigma_t^2 = \beta_t$, we obtain

$$L_{t-1} = \mathbb{E}_{q(\mathbf{x}_t \mid \mathbf{x}_0)}[\mathbb{KL}(q(\mathbf{x}_{t-1} \mid \mathbf{x}_t, \mathbf{x}_0) \parallel p_{\boldsymbol{\theta}}(\mathbf{x}_{t-1} \mid \mathbf{x}_t))]$$
$$= \mathbb{E}_{q(\mathbf{x}_t \mid \mathbf{x}_0)}\left[\frac{1}{2\sigma_t^2}\|\tilde{\boldsymbol{\mu}}_t(\mathbf{x}_t, \mathbf{x}_0) - \boldsymbol{\mu}_{\boldsymbol{\theta}}(\mathbf{x}_t, t)\|^2\right]$$

(see the appendix at the end of the chapter). Minimizing L_{t-1} means making the output of the neural network $\boldsymbol{\mu}_{\boldsymbol{\theta}}(\mathbf{x}_t, t)$ as close as possible, on average, to $\tilde{\boldsymbol{\mu}}_t(\mathbf{x}_t, \mathbf{x}_0)$ determined by Eq. (11.4.1), with respect to

$$q(\mathbf{x}_t \mid \mathbf{x}_0) = \mathcal{N}(\mathbf{x}_t \mid \sqrt{\bar{\alpha}_t}\mathbf{x}_0, \ (1-\bar{\alpha}_t)\mathbf{I}).$$

We can achieve the minimization by approximating the expectation through sampling $\mathbf{x}_t$ from the distribution $q(\mathbf{x}_t \mid \mathbf{x}_0)$. Experiments, however, suggest that this strategy does not lead to successful learning. Possible reasons for this include the following. (a) The mean and variance of the distribution $q(\mathbf{x}_t \mid \mathbf{x}_0)$ vary at each time step t, leading to significant variations in the input range of the neural network computing $\boldsymbol{\mu}_{\boldsymbol{\theta}}(\mathbf{x}_t, t)$. (b) The values of $\tilde{\boldsymbol{\mu}}_t(\mathbf{x}_t, \mathbf{x}_0)$ that need to be approximated also

11.4 Learning of Diffusion Models

change with each time step t. Consequently, the learning process may lack stability. These factors contribute to the inability of the model to effectively minimize the objective function.

Thus, by decomposing $\mathbf{x}_t$, we can rewrite L_{t-1} as follows. Given Eq. (11.3.4):

$$q(\mathbf{x}_t \mid \mathbf{x}_0) = \mathcal{N}(\mathbf{x}_t \mid \sqrt{\bar{\alpha}_t}\mathbf{x}_0, (1-\bar{\alpha}_t)\mathbf{I}),$$

we express $\mathbf{x}_t$ using $\epsilon \sim \mathcal{N}(\mathbf{0}, \mathbf{I})$ as

$$\mathbf{x}_t(\mathbf{x}_0, \epsilon) = \sqrt{\bar{\alpha}_t}\mathbf{x}_0 + \sqrt{1-\bar{\alpha}_t}\epsilon, \tag{11.4.2}$$

which is a function of $\mathbf{x}_0$ and ϵ. From Eq. (11.4.2), we can derive

$$\mathbf{x}_0 = \frac{1}{\sqrt{\bar{\alpha}_t}}\left(\mathbf{x}_t(\mathbf{x}_0, \epsilon) - \sqrt{1-\bar{\alpha}_t}\epsilon\right).$$

Combining this with Eq. (11.4.1), we obtain

$$L_{t-1} = \mathbb{E}_\epsilon\left[\frac{1}{2\sigma_t^2}\left\|\tilde{\mu}_t\left(\mathbf{x}_t(\mathbf{x}_0, \epsilon), \frac{1}{\sqrt{\bar{\alpha}_t}}\left(\mathbf{x}_t(\mathbf{x}_0, \epsilon) - \sqrt{1-\bar{\alpha}_t}\epsilon\right)\right) - \mu_\theta(\mathbf{x}_t(\mathbf{x}_0, \epsilon), t)\right\|^2\right]$$

$$= \mathbb{E}_\epsilon\left[\frac{1}{2\sigma_t^2}\left\|\frac{1}{\sqrt{\alpha_t}}\left(\mathbf{x}_t(\mathbf{x}_0, \epsilon) - \frac{\beta_t}{\sqrt{1-\bar{\alpha}_t}}\epsilon\right) - \mu_\theta(\mathbf{x}_t(\mathbf{x}_0, \epsilon), t)\right\|^2\right].$$

Note that the expectation is taken with respect to ϵ instead of $q(\mathbf{x}_t \mid \mathbf{x}_0)$.

The expression (11.4.2) corresponds to a decomposition representation of $\mathbf{x}_t$ in the diffusion process into a signal ($\mathbf{x}_0$) and added noise (ϵ). That is, the mean $\tilde{\mu}_t$ of the inverse diffusion process is expressed in terms of the signal $\mathbf{x}_0$ and the noise ϵ, with $\mathbf{x}_0$ being given as data. Thus, we shift the objective of the neural network from estimating the mean $\tilde{\mu}_t$ to estimating ϵ. To achieve this, we introduce $\epsilon_\theta(\mathbf{x}_t, t)$ as an estimator for ϵ. Given that the original mean to be estimated is

$$\left(\tilde{\mu}_t(\mathbf{x}_t, \mathbf{x}_0) =\right) \tilde{\mu}_t(\mathbf{x}_t, \epsilon) = \frac{1}{\sqrt{\alpha_t}}\left(\mathbf{x}_t - \frac{\beta_t}{\sqrt{1-\bar{\alpha}_t}}\epsilon\right), \tag{11.4.3}$$

we define $\epsilon_\theta(\mathbf{x}_t, t)$ in the following equation:

$$\mu_\theta(\mathbf{x}_t, t) = \frac{1}{\sqrt{\alpha_t}}\left(\mathbf{x}_t - \frac{\beta_t}{\sqrt{1-\bar{\alpha}_t}}\epsilon_\theta(\mathbf{x}_t, t)\right).$$

Then, we rewrite L_{t-1} as

$$L_{t-1} = \mathbb{E}_\epsilon\left[\frac{\beta_t^2}{2\sigma_t^2\alpha_t(1-\bar{\alpha}_t)}\left\|\epsilon - \epsilon_\theta(\sqrt{\bar{\alpha}_t}\mathbf{x}_0 + \sqrt{1-\bar{\alpha}_t}\epsilon, t)\right\|^2\right]. \tag{11.4.4}$$

The above definition of $\epsilon_\theta(\mathbf{x}_t, t)$ is equivalent to defining it such that the expression obtained by substituting $\epsilon_\theta(\mathbf{x}_t, t)$ for ϵ in the right-hand side of Eq. (11.4.3) equals the estimated mean $\boldsymbol{\mu}_\theta(\mathbf{x}_t, t)$, i.e.,

$$\boldsymbol{\mu}_\theta(\mathbf{x}_t, t) = \tilde{\boldsymbol{\mu}}_t(\mathbf{x}_t, \boldsymbol{\epsilon}).$$

This may make the interpretation of $\epsilon_\theta(\mathbf{x}_t, t)$ easier to understand.

We can minimize Eq. (11.4.4) by sampling ϵ from $\mathcal{N}(\mathbf{0}, \mathbf{I})$ (refer to Appendix C at the end of the book for sampling from a multivariate Gaussian distribution). Since we sample from a standard Gaussian distribution for all time steps t, the range of values that the neural network needs to compute is limited, leading to stable learning.

Next is the minimization of $L_0 = -\mathbb{E}_{q(\mathbf{x}_1 | \mathbf{x}_0)}[\ln p_\theta(\mathbf{x}_0 | \mathbf{x}_1)]$. The diffusion model generates an image $\mathbf{x}_0$ at the final step of the inverse process. Learning at this generation stage involves maximizing the likelihood $p_\theta(\mathbf{x}_0 | \mathbf{x}_1)$. Since images consist of integer pixel values, it requires some adjustments to compute the discrete log-likelihood. We assume that pixels take values $0, 1, \ldots, 255$, which are then scaled to the range $[-1, 1]$. That is, if we denote the i-th component of $\mathbf{x}_0$ as $x_0^{(i)}$, it takes discrete values within $[-1, 1]$:

$$\mathbf{x}_0 = (x_0^{(1)} \, x_0^{(2)} \, \cdots \, x_0^{(D)})^\mathrm{T}, \quad x_0^{(i)} \in [-1, 1].$$

See Fig. 11.5 for an illustration of the minimization of L_0, where pixels are scaled to $[-1, 1]$.

We generate the image $\mathbf{x}_0$ as a decoding of independent discrete values ranging from -1 to 1 for each pixel based on $\mathbf{x}_1$. Specifically, generating the i-th component of $\mathbf{x}_0$ from a Gaussian distribution with the i-th component $\mu_\theta^{(i)}(\mathbf{x}_1, 1)$ of the neural network output $\boldsymbol{\mu}_\theta(\mathbf{x}_1, 1)$ as the mean, we maximize the likelihood:

$$p_\theta(\mathbf{x}_0 | \mathbf{x}_1) = \prod_{i=1}^{D} \int_{\delta_-(x_0^{(i)})}^{\delta_+(x_0^{(i)})} \mathcal{N}(x | \mu_\theta^{(i)}(\mathbf{x}_1, 1), \sigma_1^2) \, dx,$$

where

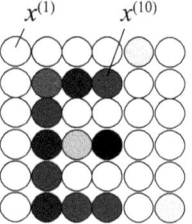

Fig. 11.5 Minimization of L_0. Pixels are scaled to $[-1, 1]$

11.4 Learning of Diffusion Models

Fig. 11.6 Training algorithm for the diffusion model

Algorithm: Training
repeat
  $x_0 \sim q(x_0)$
  $t \sim \text{Uniform}(\{1, \ldots, T\})$
  $\epsilon \sim \mathcal{N}(0, I)$
  Take gradient descent step on
    $\nabla_\theta \|\epsilon - \epsilon_\theta(\sqrt{\bar{\alpha}_t} x_0 + \sqrt{1 - \bar{\alpha}_t}\epsilon, t)\|^2$
until converged

Fig. 11.7 Generation algorithm for the diffusion model

Algorithm: Sampling
$x_T \sim \mathcal{N}(0, I)$
for $t = T, \ldots, 1$ **do**
  $z \sim \mathcal{N}(0, I)$ if $t > 1$, else $z = 0$
  $x_{t-1} = \frac{1}{\sqrt{\alpha_t}} \left(x_t - \frac{1-\alpha_t}{\sqrt{1-\bar{\alpha}_t}} \epsilon_\theta(x_t, t) \right) + \sigma_t z$
end for
return x_0

$$\delta_+(x) = \begin{cases} \infty, & \text{if } x = 1, \\ x + \frac{1}{255}, & \text{if } x < 1, \end{cases}$$

$$\delta_-(x) = \begin{cases} -\infty, & \text{if } x = -1, \\ x - \frac{1}{255}, & \text{if } x > -1. \end{cases}$$

Indeed, in the diffusion model, for $t > 1$, rather than directly calculating $\mu_\theta(x_t, t)$, we compute the error estimate $\epsilon_\theta(x_t, t)$. This aims to remove noise added in the forward process.

We provide an algorithm for minimizing the variational upper bound. Instead of sequentially reversing time from T for each data point, we minimize L_0 and L_{t-1} by stochastic gradient descent, randomly selecting data x_0, time t, and noise ϵ. A detailed algorithm is shown in Fig. 11.6.

Next, we provide the generation algorithm. At step $t > 1$, since

$$p_\theta(x_{t-1} \mid x_t) = \mathcal{N}(x_{t-1} \mid \mu_\theta(x_t, t), \sigma_t^2 I),$$

$$\mu_\theta(x_t, t) = \frac{1}{\sqrt{\alpha_t}} \left(x_t - \frac{\beta_t}{\sqrt{1-\bar{\alpha}_t}} \epsilon_\theta(x_t, t) \right)$$

hold, we obtain samples from $p_\theta(x_{t-1} \mid x_t)$ by sampling from $\mathcal{N}(0, I)$ and using

$$x_{t-1} = \frac{1}{\sqrt{\alpha_t}} \left(x_t - \frac{1-\alpha_t}{\sqrt{1-\bar{\alpha}_t}} \epsilon_\theta(x_t, t) \right) + \sigma_t z, \quad z \sim \mathcal{N}(0, I).$$

The details of the generation algorithm are shown in Fig. 11.7.

11.5 Implementation of Diffusion Models

Many systems implement diffusion models, such as DALLE-2, DALLE-3, Imagen, and Stable diffusion. In this section, we focus on Stable diffusion as an example of implementing a diffusion model. In image generation, it is common to compress images, extract features, and then enlarge them. Stable diffusion also performs image compression and enlargement processes using VAE.

Before describing Stable diffusion, we present the basic network architecture for image generation as described in the original paper on diffusion models [17] (Fig. 11.8). It follows an architecture based on U-net [37], which consists of a left part resembling the letter "U" performing image compression via pooling, and a right part enlarging the image through transposed convolutions.[2] Convolutions are applied in each part of the U-shaped structure, and the arrows from the left to the right at the same level represent skip connections. While the original U-net employs weight normalization, diffusion models use group normalization. U-net may sound like a special network, but it is essentially stacking residual blocks, arranged in a U-shaped configuration, thus earning the name U-net. This configuration makes skip connections between compression and enlargement explicit.

Note that at each time step t, the sinusoidal positional encoding of time t are added to each residual block and self-attention block. At time t, for an input "image"

$$\mathbf{x}_t(\mathbf{x}_0, \epsilon) = \sqrt{\bar{\alpha}_t}\mathbf{x}_0 + \sqrt{1-\bar{\alpha}_t}\epsilon,$$

where ϵ is a sample generated from $\mathcal{N}(\mathbf{0}, \mathbf{I})$, this U-shaped network accepts the input:

$$\mathbf{x}_t(\mathbf{x}_0, \epsilon) + \tilde{t},$$

where $\tilde{t}$ is the time-step positional encoding, and it outputs the noise estimation:

$$\epsilon_\theta(\mathbf{x}_t, t).$$

We use the difference between $\epsilon_\theta(\mathbf{x}_t, t)$ and sampled ϵ as the error for training.

The original and generated images in Fig. 11.8 are relatively small, each being 32 × 32 pixels, making both training and generation feasible. As the image size increases, however, the number of residual blocks also increases, leading to significantly longer training times.

---

[2] For a general explanation of image size enlargement through transposed convolution, refer to Appendix D at the end of the book.

11.5 Implementation of Diffusion Models

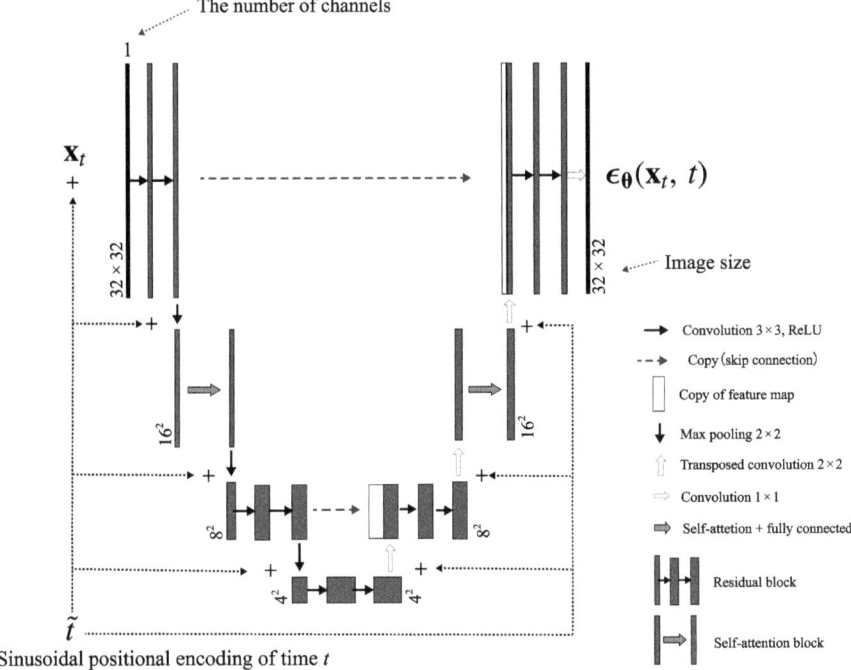

Fig. 11.8 Neural network adhering to U-net. Example architecture of the network for image generation by diffusion models. Based on Fig. 1 of [37]. Used with kind permission of Olaf Ronneberger

11.5.1 Stable Diffusion

Stable diffusion [36][3] is a method that initially compresses 512×512 input images into 8×8 images using the encoder of a variational autoencoder (VAE). The compressed images then undergo diffusion modeling. During image generation, the 8×8 images computed through the inverse diffusion process are transformed into 512×512 images using the decoder of the VAE (see Fig. 11.9). In essence, this approach applies diffusion and inverse diffusion processes to small images, aiming to reduce computational complexity.

Furthermore, Stable diffusion can generate images conditioned on text or images. Figure 11.9 shows an example of an image generated conditioned on the text "Sushi-chef-like cat." To generate images conditioned on text, Stable diffusion employs a text encoder that converts text into embeddings in the latent space (the space of image representations). Additionally, during the denoising step, an attention mechanism is inserted after the residual block processing. This attention mechanism takes the output of the residual blocks as the source Q and the output of the text encoder as the key-value pair (K, V), transforming the text prompt

---

[3] https://huggingface.co/blog/stable_diffusion.

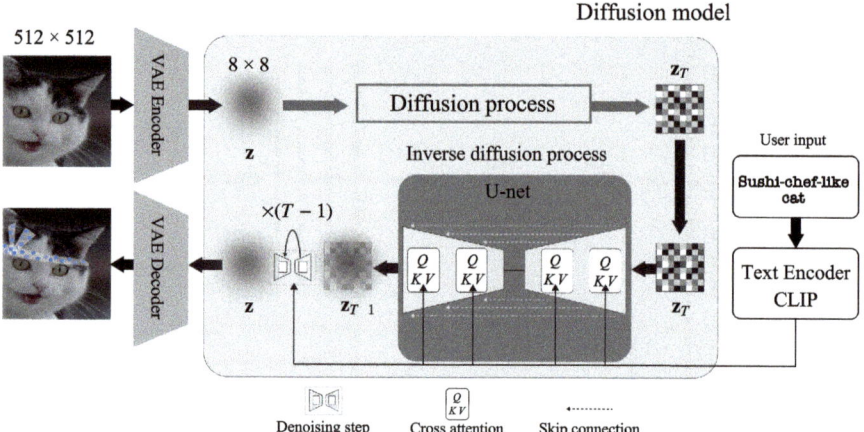

Fig. 11.9 Network architecture of Stable diffusion. Input images are compressed to 8 × 8 using the encoder of a VAE, followed by diffusion modeling on the compressed images. During image generation, 8 × 8 images computed through the inverse diffusion process are transformed into 512 × 512 images using the decoder of the VAE. Text-conditioned images can also be generated (note that the image of the cat wearing a headband in the figure is for illustration purposes and not generated by Stable diffusion). Based on Fig. 3 of [36]. Used under license from IEEE

into embeddings and using these embeddings as the output of the residual blocks in the inverse diffusion process. This enables the generation of images conditioned on text (see Fig. 11.10). The text encoder used is a Transformer-based pre-trained model called CLIPTextModel. CLIPTextModel is part of CLIP, an image classification model trained on a dataset of 400 million image-text pairs collected from the Internet and used for natural language supervision [33].

The Stable diffusion model primarily utilizes two subsets of the LAION-5B dataset, consisting of 5.85 billion image-caption pairs.

1. LAION2B-EN. This subset contains 2.3 billion images with English captions. The images are of low resolution, typically 256 × 256 pixels.
2. LAION-High-Resolution. This subset comprises 170 million images that have higher resolutions than 1024 × 1024 pixels, which are downsampled to 512 × 512 pixels.

These subsets are mainly used for the initial training of the model [4].

11.6 Appendix

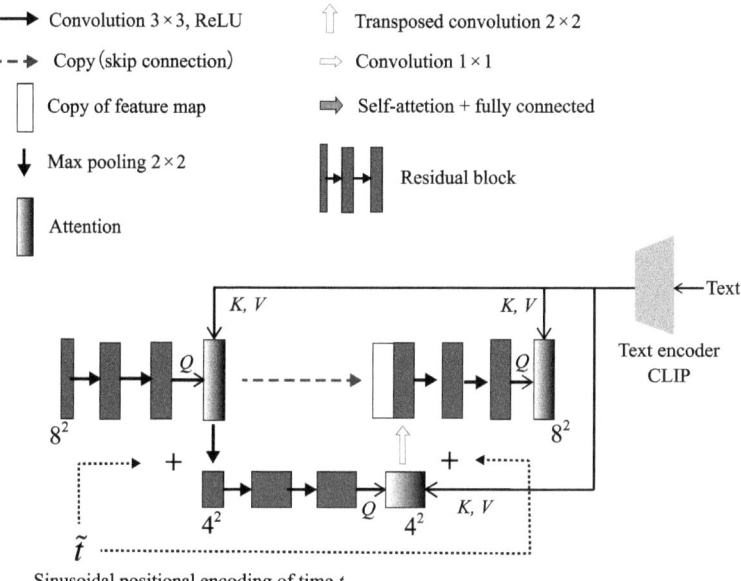

Fig. 11.10 Text conditioning in Stable diffusion. A text encoder converts the conditioning text into embeddings in the latent space of images, and an attention mechanism after the residual blocks

11.6 Appendix

11.6.1 Equivalence of Definitions for Markov Processes

Three equations characterizing a Markov process, for $t = 1, \ldots, T$, are

$$p(\mathbf{x}_t \mid \mathbf{x}_0, \ldots, \mathbf{x}_{t-1}) = p(\mathbf{x}_t \mid \mathbf{x}_{t-1}), \quad (11.6.1)$$

$$p(\mathbf{x}_t, \ldots, \mathbf{x}_T \mid \mathbf{x}_0, \ldots, \mathbf{x}_{t-1}) = p(\mathbf{x}_t, \ldots, \mathbf{x}_T \mid \mathbf{x}_{t-1}), \quad (11.6.2)$$

$$p(\mathbf{x}_0, \ldots, \mathbf{x}_T) = p(\mathbf{x}_T \mid \mathbf{x}_{T-1}) \cdots p(\mathbf{x}_2 \mid \mathbf{x}_1) p(\mathbf{x}_1 \mid \mathbf{x}_0) p(\mathbf{x}_0). \quad (11.6.3)$$

We demonstrate their equivalence.

First, we show the equivalence between Eqs. (11.6.1) and (11.6.3). Assume that Eq. (11.6.1) holds. From this assumption and the definition of conditional probability

$$p(\mathbf{x}_0, \ldots, \mathbf{x}_T) = p(\mathbf{x}_T \mid \mathbf{x}_0, \ldots, \mathbf{x}_{T-1}) \cdots p(\mathbf{x}_2 \mid \mathbf{x}_0, \mathbf{x}_1) p(\mathbf{x}_1 \mid \mathbf{x}_0) p(\mathbf{x}_0), \quad (11.6.4)$$

the derivation of Eq. (11.6.3) is trivial. Conversely, assume that Eq. (11.6.3) holds. Then, eliminating $\mathbf{x}_T$ by integral from both sides of this equation, we have

$$p(\mathbf{x}_0, \ldots, \mathbf{x}_{T-1}) = p(\mathbf{x}_{T-1} \mid \mathbf{x}_{T-2}) \cdots p(\mathbf{x}_2 \mid \mathbf{x}_1) p(\mathbf{x}_1 \mid \mathbf{x}_0) p(\mathbf{x}_0). \quad (11.6.5)$$

Decomposing the left-hand side of Eq. (11.6.3) by the definition of conditional probability and expressing the right-hand side similarly, we obtain

$$p(\mathbf{x}_T \mid \mathbf{x}_0, \ldots, \mathbf{x}_{T-1}) \cdot p(\mathbf{x}_0, \ldots, \mathbf{x}_{T-1}) = p(\mathbf{x}_T \mid \mathbf{x}_{T-1}) \cdots p(\mathbf{x}_2 \mid \mathbf{x}_1) p(\mathbf{x}_1 \mid \mathbf{x}_0) p(\mathbf{x}_0)$$
$$= p(\mathbf{x}_T \mid \mathbf{x}_{T-1}) \cdot p(\mathbf{x}_0, \ldots, \mathbf{x}_{T-1}).$$

Thus, we have

$$p(\mathbf{x}_T \mid \mathbf{x}_0, \ldots, \mathbf{x}_{T-1}) = p(\mathbf{x}_T \mid \mathbf{x}_{T-1}).$$

Multiplying both sides by $p(\mathbf{x}_{T-1} \mid \mathbf{x}_{T-2})$ and eliminating $\mathbf{x}_T$ by integral lead us to

$$p(\mathbf{x}_{T-1} \mid \mathbf{x}_{T-2}) = p(\mathbf{x}_{T-1} \mid \mathbf{x}_0, \ldots, \mathbf{x}_{T-2}).$$

Similarly, we have

$$p(\mathbf{x}_t \mid \mathbf{x}_{t-1}) = p(\mathbf{x}_t \mid \mathbf{x}_0, \ldots, \mathbf{x}_{t-1}),$$

which is Eq. (11.6.1).

Next, we demonstrate the equivalence between Eqs. (11.6.1) and (11.6.2). First, assume that Eq. (11.6.2) holds. Eliminating $\mathbf{x}_{t+1}, \ldots, \mathbf{x}_T$ by integral from both sides of this equation, we have

$$p(\mathbf{x}_t \mid \mathbf{x}_0, \ldots, \mathbf{x}_{t-1}) = p(\mathbf{x}_t \mid \mathbf{x}_{t-1}),$$

which is Eq. (11.6.1). Conversely, assuming Eq. (11.6.1), we prove Eq. (11.6.2) by induction. For $t = T$, Equation (11.6.2) holds trivially. Assume Eq. (11.6.2) holds for $t = k$. That is,

$$p(\mathbf{x}_k, \ldots, \mathbf{x}_T \mid \mathbf{x}_0, \ldots, \mathbf{x}_{k-1}) = p(\mathbf{x}_k, \ldots, \mathbf{x}_T \mid \mathbf{x}_{k-1}).$$

With this assumption and Eq. (11.6.1), for $t = k - 1$, we have

$$p(\mathbf{x}_{k-1}, \ldots, \mathbf{x}_T \mid \mathbf{x}_0, \ldots, \mathbf{x}_{k-2}) = p(\mathbf{x}_k, \ldots, \mathbf{x}_T \mid \mathbf{x}_0, \ldots, \mathbf{x}_{k-1}) \cdot p(\mathbf{x}_{k-1} \mid \mathbf{x}_0, \ldots, \mathbf{x}_{k-2})$$
$$= p(\mathbf{x}_k, \ldots, \mathbf{x}_T \mid \mathbf{x}_{k-1}) \cdot p(\mathbf{x}_{k-1} \mid \mathbf{x}_{k-2})$$
$$= p(\mathbf{x}_k, \ldots, \mathbf{x}_T \mid \mathbf{x}_{k-1}, \mathbf{x}_{k-2}) \cdot p(\mathbf{x}_{k-1} \mid \mathbf{x}_{k-2})$$
$$= p(\mathbf{x}_{k-1}, \mathbf{x}_k, \ldots, \mathbf{x}_T \mid \mathbf{x}_{k-2}).$$

Thus, Eq. (11.6.2) holds again.

11.6.2 Markov Property of the Inverse Process

Let $\mathbf{x}_0, \ldots, \mathbf{x}_T$ be a Markov random process. We show that its inverse process $\mathbf{x}_T, \ldots, \mathbf{x}_0$ is also a Markov process. First, from the Markov property of $\mathbf{x}_0, \ldots, \mathbf{x}_T$, we have

$$p(\mathbf{x}_T, \ldots, \mathbf{x}_t \mid \mathbf{x}_{t-1}) = p(\mathbf{x}_T, \ldots, \mathbf{x}_t \mid \mathbf{x}_{t-1}, \ldots, \mathbf{x}_0).$$

Using the definition of conditional probability, this becomes

$$\frac{p(\mathbf{x}_T, \ldots, \mathbf{x}_t, \mathbf{x}_{t-1})}{p(\mathbf{x}_{t-1})} = \frac{p(\mathbf{x}_T, \mathbf{x}_{T-1}, \ldots, \mathbf{x}_0)}{p(\mathbf{x}_{t-1}, \ldots, \mathbf{x}_0)}.$$

Multiplying both sides by $\dfrac{p(\mathbf{x}_{t-1}, \ldots, \mathbf{x}_0)}{p(\mathbf{x}_T, \ldots, \mathbf{x}_t, \mathbf{x}_{t-1})}$ yields

$$\frac{p(\mathbf{x}_{t-1}, \ldots, \mathbf{x}_0)}{p(\mathbf{x}_{t-1})} = \frac{p(\mathbf{x}_T, \mathbf{x}_{T-1}, \ldots, \mathbf{x}_0)}{p(\mathbf{x}_T, \ldots, \mathbf{x}_{t-1})}.$$

Again, using the definition of conditional probability, we have

$$p(\mathbf{x}_{t-2}, \ldots, \mathbf{x}_0 \mid \mathbf{x}_{t-1}) = p(\mathbf{x}_{t-2}, \ldots, \mathbf{x}_0 \mid \mathbf{x}_T, \ldots, \mathbf{x}_{t-1}).$$

This demonstrates that the inverse process is also a Markov chain.

11.6.3 Derivation of Diffusion Equation from a Markov Chain

We denote the conditional probability that at time $t > \tau$, the state (position) is y given that it was at state x at time τ as $p_{t,\tau}(y \mid x)$. We assume that both the time intervals and the intervals of probability values are sufficiently small. In the limit of reducing the time interval of a discrete-time Markov process to infinitesimally small intervals, leading to a continuous-time Markov process, we aim to demonstrate that under the constraint that $t - \tau$ is small implies $|y - x|$ is also small, the conditional probability $p_{t,\tau}(y \mid x)$ satisfies the diffusion equation. For simplicity, we show that $p_{t,\tau}(y \mid x)$ serves as a solution to the so-called "backward equation" of the diffusion equation, considering $p_{t,\tau}(y \mid x)$ as a function of x. (Note: we can also demonstrate that $p_{t,\tau}(y \mid x)$ serves as a solution to the "forward equation" of the diffusion equation, considering $p_{t,\tau}(y \mid x)$ as a function of y, but it requires additional assumptions and leads to a more complex derivation.)

We begin with the Chapman-Kolmogorov equation, which holds in a Markov chain. That is, considering the meaning of a Markov chain, we obtain the equation, for any arbitrary time s satisfying $\tau < s < t$,

$$p_{t,\tau}(y\,|\,x) = \sum_v p_{s,\tau}(v\,|\,x) p_{t,s}(y\,|\,v),$$

where the sum extends over all possible states at time s. Choosing an appropriate h, from the Chapman-Kolmogorov equation above, we have

$$\begin{aligned} p_{t,\tau-h}(y\,|\,x) - p_{t,\tau}(y\,|\,x) &= \sum_v p_{s,\tau-h}(v\,|\,x) p_{t,s}(y\,|\,v) - p_{t,\tau}(y\,|\,x) \\ &= \sum_v p_{s,\tau-h}(v\,|\,x) p_{t,s}(y\,|\,v) - \sum_v p_{s,\tau-h}(v\,|\,x) p_{t,\tau}(y\,|\,x) \\ &= \sum_v p_{s,\tau-h}(v\,|\,x)(p_{t,s}(y\,|\,v) - p_{t,\tau}(y\,|\,x)). \end{aligned}$$

In the second equality, we utilized the fact that $p_{t,\tau}(y\,|\,x)$ is independent of the sum over v, and also that $\sum_v p_{s,\tau-h}(v\,|\,x) = 1$. Now, considering $s - \tau$ to be small, and thus $|v - x|$ to be sufficiently small, we can approximate

$$p_{t,s}(y\,|\,v) - p_{t,\tau}(y\,|\,x) \approx \frac{\partial p_{t,\tau}(y\,|\,x)}{\partial x}(v-x) + \frac{1}{2}\frac{\partial^2 p_{t,\tau}(y\,|\,x)}{\partial x^2}(v-x)^2.$$

Hence, in this approximation, we have

$$p_{t,\tau-h}(y\,|\,x) - p_{t,\tau}(y\,|\,x) \approx \sum_v p_{s,\tau-h}(v\,|\,x)\left(\frac{\partial p_{t,\tau}(y\,|\,x)}{\partial x}(v-x) + \frac{1}{2}\frac{\partial^2 p_{t,\tau}(y\,|\,x)}{\partial x^2}(v-x)^2\right). \quad (11.6.6)$$

Here, we make the following assumptions. As $h \to 0$, $v - x$ approaches zero sufficiently quickly, and the expected value of $v - x$ with respect to $p_{s,\tau-h}(v\,|\,x)$ also does:

$$\lim_{h\to 0} \frac{1}{h} \sum_v p_{s,\tau-h}(v\,|\,x)(v-x) = 0,$$

and, furthermore, the expected value of the second-order moment of $v - x$ divided by h approaches a constant ($2\alpha^2$):

$$\lim_{h\to 0} \frac{1}{h} \sum_v p_{s,\tau-h}(v\,|\,x)(v-x)^2 = 2\alpha^2.$$

Under these assumptions, dividing both sides of Eq. (11.6.6) by h and letting $h \to 0$, we obtain

$$\frac{\partial p_{t,\tau}(y\,|\,x)}{\partial \tau} = \lim_{h\to 0} \frac{p_{t,\tau-h}(y\,|\,x) - p_{t,\tau}(y\,|\,x)}{h} \approx \alpha^2 \frac{\partial^2 p_{t,\tau}(y\,|\,x)}{\partial x^2}.$$

This is the diffusion equation.

11.6 Appendix

11.6.4 Time-Wise Decomposition of Variational Upper Bound

Let us denote the expectation $\mathbb{E}_{q(\mathbf{x}_{1:T} \mid \mathbf{x}_0)}[\cdot]$ as $\mathbb{E}_q[\cdot]$ for brevity. We can decompose the variational upper bound L:

$$L = \mathbb{E}_q\left[-\ln \frac{p_\theta(\mathbf{x}_{0:T})}{q(\mathbf{x}_{1:T} \mid \mathbf{x}_0)}\right] = \mathbb{E}_q\left[-\ln p(\mathbf{x}_T) - \sum_{t \geq 1} \ln \frac{p_\theta(\mathbf{x}_{t-1} \mid \mathbf{x}_t)}{q(\mathbf{x}_t \mid \mathbf{x}_{t-1})}\right]$$

as follows:

$$L = L_0 + L_1 + \cdots + L_{T-1} + L_T,$$

where

$$L_0 = -\mathbb{E}_{q(\mathbf{x}_1 \mid \mathbf{x}_0)}[\ln p_\theta(\mathbf{x}_0 \mid \mathbf{x}_1)],$$
$$L_{t-1} = \mathbb{E}_{q(\mathbf{x}_t \mid \mathbf{x}_0)}[\mathbb{KL}(q(\mathbf{x}_{t-1} \mid \mathbf{x}_t, \mathbf{x}_0) \parallel p_\theta(\mathbf{x}_{t-1} \mid \mathbf{x}_t))], \quad t = 2, \ldots, T,$$
$$L_T = \mathbb{KL}(q(\mathbf{x}_T \mid \mathbf{x}_0) \parallel p(\mathbf{x}_T)).$$

Now, we show this decomposition. That is,

$$\begin{aligned}
L &= \mathbb{E}_q\left[-\ln \frac{p_\theta(\mathbf{x}_{0:T})}{q(\mathbf{x}_{1:T} \mid \mathbf{x}_0)}\right] \\
&= \mathbb{E}_q\left[-\ln p(\mathbf{x}_T) - \sum_{t \geq 1} \ln \frac{p_\theta(\mathbf{x}_{t-1} \mid \mathbf{x}_t)}{q(\mathbf{x}_t \mid \mathbf{x}_{t-1})}\right] \\
&= \mathbb{E}_q\left[-\ln p(\mathbf{x}_T) - \sum_{t > 1} \ln \frac{p_\theta(\mathbf{x}_{t-1} \mid \mathbf{x}_t)}{q(\mathbf{x}_t \mid \mathbf{x}_{t-1})} - \ln \frac{p_\theta(\mathbf{x}_0 \mid \mathbf{x}_1)}{q(\mathbf{x}_1 \mid \mathbf{x}_0)}\right] \\
&= \mathbb{E}_q\left[-\ln p(\mathbf{x}_T) - \sum_{t > 1} \ln \left(\frac{p_\theta(\mathbf{x}_{t-1} \mid \mathbf{x}_t)}{q(\mathbf{x}_{t-1} \mid \mathbf{x}_t, \mathbf{x}_0)} \cdot \frac{q(\mathbf{x}_{t-1} \mid \mathbf{x}_0)}{q(\mathbf{x}_t \mid \mathbf{x}_0)}\right) - \ln \frac{p_\theta(\mathbf{x}_0 \mid \mathbf{x}_1)}{q(\mathbf{x}_1 \mid \mathbf{x}_0)}\right] \\
&= \mathbb{E}_q\left[-\ln \frac{p(\mathbf{x}_T)}{q(\mathbf{x}_T \mid \mathbf{x}_0)} - \sum_{t > 1} \ln \frac{p_\theta(\mathbf{x}_{t-1} \mid \mathbf{x}_t)}{q(\mathbf{x}_{t-1} \mid \mathbf{x}_t, \mathbf{x}_0)} - \ln p_\theta(\mathbf{x}_0 \mid \mathbf{x}_1)\right] \\
&= \mathbb{KL}(q(\mathbf{x}_T \mid \mathbf{x}_0) \parallel p(\mathbf{x}_T)) + \sum_{t > 1} \mathbb{E}_{q(\mathbf{x}_t \mid \mathbf{x}_0)}[\mathbb{KL}(q(\mathbf{x}_{t-1} \mid \mathbf{x}_t, \mathbf{x}_0) \parallel p_\theta(\mathbf{x}_{t-1} \mid \mathbf{x}_t))] \\
&\quad - \mathbb{E}_{q(\mathbf{x}_1 \mid \mathbf{x}_0)}[\ln p_\theta(\mathbf{x}_0 \mid \mathbf{x}_1)].
\end{aligned}$$

The second equality follows from

$$\begin{cases} p_\theta(\mathbf{x}_{0:T}) = p(\mathbf{x}_T)\prod_{t=1}^{T} p_\theta(\mathbf{x}_{t-1} \mid \mathbf{x}_t), \\ q(\mathbf{x}_{1:T} \mid \mathbf{x}_0) = \prod_{t=1}^{T} q(\mathbf{x}_t \mid \mathbf{x}_{t-1}) \end{cases}$$

and the fourth equality follows from Bayes' theorem and the conditional independence due to the Markov property:

$$q(\mathbf{x}_t \mid \mathbf{x}_{t-1}) = q(\mathbf{x}_t \mid \mathbf{x}_{t-1}, \mathbf{x}_0).$$

Also, the last equality can be shown as follows. Consider, for example, the second term within the sum:

$$\mathbb{E}_{q(\mathbf{x}_{1:T} \mid \mathbf{x}_0)} \left[\ln \frac{p_\theta(\mathbf{x}_{t-1} \mid \mathbf{x}_t)}{q(\mathbf{x}_{t-1} \mid \mathbf{x}_t, \mathbf{x}_0)} \right].$$

Expanding this using the definition of the expectation, we have

$$\mathbb{E}_{q(\mathbf{x}_{1:T} \mid \mathbf{x}_0)} \left[\ln \frac{p_\theta(\mathbf{x}_{t-1} \mid \mathbf{x}_t)}{q(\mathbf{x}_{t-1} \mid \mathbf{x}_t, \mathbf{x}_0)} \right] = \int q(\mathbf{x}_{1:T} \mid \mathbf{x}_0) \ln \frac{p_\theta(\mathbf{x}_{t-1} \mid \mathbf{x}_t)}{q(\mathbf{x}_{t-1} \mid \mathbf{x}_t, \mathbf{x}_0)} d\mathbf{x}_1 \cdots d\mathbf{x}_T$$

$$= \int q(\mathbf{x}_{t-1}, \mathbf{x}_t \mid \mathbf{x}_0) \ln \frac{p_\theta(\mathbf{x}_{t-1} \mid \mathbf{x}_t)}{q(\mathbf{x}_{t-1} \mid \mathbf{x}_t, \mathbf{x}_0)} d\mathbf{x}_{t-1} d\mathbf{x}_t$$

$$= \int q(\mathbf{x}_t \mid \mathbf{x}_0) q(\mathbf{x}_{t-1} \mid \mathbf{x}_t, \mathbf{x}_0) \ln \frac{p_\theta(\mathbf{x}_{t-1} \mid \mathbf{x}_t)}{q(\mathbf{x}_{t-1} \mid \mathbf{x}_t, \mathbf{x}_0)} d\mathbf{x}_{t-1} d\mathbf{x}_t$$

$$= \int q(\mathbf{x}_t \mid \mathbf{x}_0) \left(\int q(\mathbf{x}_{t-1} \mid \mathbf{x}_t, \mathbf{x}_0) \ln \frac{p_\theta(\mathbf{x}_{t-1} \mid \mathbf{x}_t)}{q(\mathbf{x}_{t-1} \mid \mathbf{x}_t, \mathbf{x}_0)} d\mathbf{x}_{t-1} \right) d\mathbf{x}_t$$

$$= \mathbb{E}_{q(\mathbf{x}_t \mid \mathbf{x}_0)} [\mathbb{KL}(q(\mathbf{x}_{t-1} \mid \mathbf{x}_t, \mathbf{x}_0) \parallel p_\theta(\mathbf{x}_{t-1} \mid \mathbf{x}_t))].$$

The second equality holds by integrating out $\mathbf{x}_1$ to $\mathbf{x}_{t-2}$ and $\mathbf{x}_{t+1}$ to $\mathbf{x}_T$. This completes the demonstration.

11.6.5 Distribution of $\mathbf{x}_{t-1}$ Conditioned on $\mathbf{x}_0$ and $\mathbf{x}_t$

If we have

$$q(\mathbf{x}_t \mid \mathbf{x}_{t-1}, \mathbf{x}_0) = \mathcal{N}(\mathbf{x}_t \mid \sqrt{1-\beta_t}\mathbf{x}_{t-1}, \beta_t \mathbf{I}) \text{ and}$$
$$q(\mathbf{x}_{t-1} \mid \mathbf{x}_0) = \mathcal{N}(\mathbf{x}_{t-1} \mid \sqrt{\bar{\alpha}_{t-1}}\mathbf{x}_0, (1-\bar{\alpha}_{t-1})\mathbf{I}),$$

then we obtain

$$q(\mathbf{x}_{t-1} \mid \mathbf{x}_t, \mathbf{x}_0) = \mathcal{N}(\mathbf{x}_{t-1} \mid \tilde{\boldsymbol{\mu}}_t(\mathbf{x}_t, \mathbf{x}_0), \tilde{\beta}_t \mathbf{I}),$$

11.6 Appendix

where

$$\tilde{\mu}_t(\mathbf{x}_t, \mathbf{x}_0) \equiv \frac{\sqrt{\bar{\alpha}_{t-1}}\beta_t}{1-\bar{\alpha}_t}\mathbf{x}_0 + \frac{\sqrt{\alpha_t}(1-\bar{\alpha}_{t-1})}{1-\bar{\alpha}_t}\mathbf{x}_t, \quad \tilde{\beta}_t \equiv \frac{1-\bar{\alpha}_{t-1}}{1-\bar{\alpha}_t}\beta_t,$$

where $\alpha_t \equiv 1 - \beta_t, \bar{\alpha}_t \equiv \prod_{i=1}^{t}\alpha_i$. To show this, by noting that, from Bayes' theorem,

$$q(\mathbf{x}_{t-1}\,|\,\mathbf{x}_t, \mathbf{x}_0) \propto q(\mathbf{x}_t\,|\,\mathbf{x}_{t-1}, \mathbf{x}_0) \cdot q(\mathbf{x}_{t-1}\,|\,\mathbf{x}_0)$$

holds, we directly apply Bayes' theorem for multivariate Gaussian distributions with conditional and marginal distributions: if

$$p(\mathbf{x}) = \mathcal{N}(\mathbf{x}\,|\,\boldsymbol{\mu}, \boldsymbol{\Lambda}^{-1}) \text{ and } p(\mathbf{y}\,|\,\mathbf{x}) = \mathcal{N}(\mathbf{y}\,|\,\mathbf{A}\mathbf{x} + \mathbf{b}, \mathbf{L}^{-1})$$

hold, then we have

$$p(\mathbf{x}\,|\,\mathbf{y}) = \mathcal{N}(\mathbf{x}\,|\,\boldsymbol{\Sigma}_{\mathbf{x}|\mathbf{y}}\{\mathbf{A}^{\mathrm{T}}\mathbf{L}(\mathbf{y} - \mathbf{b}) + \boldsymbol{\Lambda}\boldsymbol{\mu}\}, \boldsymbol{\Sigma}_{\mathbf{x}|\mathbf{y}}),$$

where $\boldsymbol{\Sigma}_{\mathbf{x}|\mathbf{y}} = (\boldsymbol{\Lambda} + \mathbf{A}^{\mathrm{T}}\mathbf{L}\mathbf{A})^{-1}$.

To achieve this, we can correspond the variables in the theorem to those in the equation that we aim to prove as follows:

$$\mathbf{y} \mapsto \mathbf{x}_t, \quad \mathbf{x} \mapsto \mathbf{x}_{t-1}.$$

Through this correspondence, the constants in the expressions representing the mean and covariance in the theorem correspond to those in the expressions we prove as follows:

$$\boldsymbol{\mu} \mapsto \sqrt{\bar{\alpha}_{t-1}}\mathbf{x}_0, \quad \boldsymbol{\Lambda}^{-1} \mapsto (1 - \bar{\alpha}_{t-1})\mathbf{I},$$
$$\mathbf{A} \mapsto \sqrt{1 - \beta_t}\mathbf{I}, \quad \mathbf{b} \mapsto \mathbf{0}, \quad \mathbf{L}^{-1} \mapsto \beta_t\mathbf{I},$$

where $\mathbf{I}$ denotes the identity matrix. Additionally, noting that $\bar{\alpha}_t = \alpha_t\bar{\alpha}_{t-1}$ from $\bar{\alpha}_t \equiv \prod_{i=1}^{t}\alpha_i$ and $\alpha_t \equiv 1 - \beta_t$ implies $\alpha_t + \beta_t = 1$, we can calculate the correspondence of $\boldsymbol{\Sigma}_{\mathbf{x}|\mathbf{y}}$ as follows:

$$\boldsymbol{\Sigma}_{\mathbf{x}|\mathbf{y}} \mapsto \left((1 - \bar{\alpha}_{t-1})^{-1}\mathbf{I} + (1 - \beta_t)/\beta_t\mathbf{I}\right)^{-1}$$
$$= \frac{1 - \bar{\alpha}_{t-1}}{\beta_t + (1 - \bar{\alpha}_{t-1})\alpha_t}\beta_t\mathbf{I} = \frac{1 - \bar{\alpha}_{t-1}}{1 - \bar{\alpha}_t}\beta_t\mathbf{I}.$$

Similarly, applying the correspondence, we obtain

$$\Sigma_{\mathbf{x}|\mathbf{y}}\{\mathbf{A}^\mathsf{T}\mathbf{L}(\mathbf{y}-\mathbf{b})+$$

boldsymbol$\Lambda\mu\}$

$$\mapsto \frac{1-\bar{\alpha}_{t-1}}{1-\bar{\alpha}_t}\beta_t\mathbf{I}\left(\sqrt{1-\beta_t}\mathbf{I}^\mathsf{T}\beta_t^{-1}\mathbf{I}\mathbf{x}_t + (1-\bar{\alpha}_{t-1})^{-1}\sqrt{\bar{\alpha}_{t-1}}\mathbf{I}\mathbf{x}_0\right)$$

$$=\frac{\sqrt{\bar{\alpha}_{t-1}}\beta_t}{1-\bar{\alpha}_t}\mathbf{x}_0 + \frac{\sqrt{\alpha_t}(1-\bar{\alpha}_{t-1})}{1-\bar{\alpha}_t}\mathbf{x}_t.$$

11.6.6 KL Divergence Between Gaussian Distributions

Let $\mathbf{x}$ be a D-dimensional vector, and consider the following Gaussian distributions:

$$p(\mathbf{x}) \sim \mathcal{N}(\boldsymbol{\mu}_0, \boldsymbol{\Sigma}_0), \quad q(\mathbf{x}) \sim \mathcal{N}(\boldsymbol{\mu}_1, \boldsymbol{\Sigma}_1).$$

Then, the Kullback-Leibler (KL) divergence is given by

$$\mathbb{KL}(p(\mathbf{x}) \| q(\mathbf{x})) = \int p(\mathbf{x}) \ln \frac{p(\mathbf{x})}{q(\mathbf{x})} d\mathbf{x}$$

$$= \int p(\mathbf{x})[\ln p(\mathbf{x}) - \ln q(\mathbf{x})] d\mathbf{x}$$

$$= \int p(\mathbf{x}) \left[-\frac{D}{2}\ln 2\pi - \frac{1}{2}\ln|\boldsymbol{\Sigma}_0| - \frac{1}{2}(\mathbf{x}-\boldsymbol{\mu}_0)^\mathsf{T}\boldsymbol{\Sigma}_0^{-1}(\mathbf{x}-\boldsymbol{\mu}_0) \right.$$
$$\left. +\frac{D}{2}\ln 2\pi + \frac{1}{2}\ln|\boldsymbol{\Sigma}_1| + \frac{1}{2}(\mathbf{x}-\boldsymbol{\mu}_1)^\mathsf{T}\boldsymbol{\Sigma}_1^{-1}(\mathbf{x}-\boldsymbol{\mu}_1) \right] d\mathbf{x}$$

$$= \frac{1}{2}\ln\frac{|\boldsymbol{\Sigma}_1|}{|\boldsymbol{\Sigma}_0|} - \frac{1}{2}\mathbb{E}_{p(\mathbf{x})}[(\mathbf{x}-\boldsymbol{\mu}_0)^\mathsf{T}\boldsymbol{\Sigma}_0^{-1}(\mathbf{x}-\boldsymbol{\mu}_0)] + \frac{1}{2}\mathbb{E}_{p(\mathbf{x})}[(\mathbf{x}-\boldsymbol{\mu}_1)^\mathsf{T}\boldsymbol{\Sigma}_1^{-1}(\mathbf{x}-\boldsymbol{\mu}_1)]$$

$$= \frac{1}{2}\ln\frac{|\boldsymbol{\Sigma}_1|}{|\boldsymbol{\Sigma}_0|} - \frac{1}{2}D + \frac{1}{2}\mathbb{E}_{p(\mathbf{x})}[(\mathbf{x}-\boldsymbol{\mu}_1)^\mathsf{T}\boldsymbol{\Sigma}_1^{-1}(\mathbf{x}-\boldsymbol{\mu}_1)]$$

$$= \frac{1}{2}\ln\frac{|\boldsymbol{\Sigma}_1|}{|\boldsymbol{\Sigma}_0|} - \frac{1}{2}D + \frac{1}{2}\mathbb{E}_{p(\mathbf{x})}[(\mathbf{x}-\boldsymbol{\mu}_0+\boldsymbol{\mu}_0-\boldsymbol{\mu}_1)^\mathsf{T}\boldsymbol{\Sigma}_1^{-1}(\mathbf{x}-\boldsymbol{\mu}_0+\boldsymbol{\mu}_0-\boldsymbol{\mu}_1)]$$

$$= \frac{1}{2}\ln\frac{|\boldsymbol{\Sigma}_1|}{|\boldsymbol{\Sigma}_0|} - \frac{1}{2}D + \frac{1}{2}\mathbb{E}_{p(\mathbf{x})}[(\mathbf{x}-\boldsymbol{\mu}_0)^\mathsf{T}\boldsymbol{\Sigma}_1^{-1}(\mathbf{x}-\boldsymbol{\mu}_0)] + \frac{1}{2}\mathbb{E}_{p(\mathbf{x})}[(\boldsymbol{\mu}_0-\boldsymbol{\mu}_1)^\mathsf{T}\boldsymbol{\Sigma}_1^{-1}(\boldsymbol{\mu}_0-\boldsymbol{\mu}_1)]$$

$$= \frac{1}{2}\left[\ln\frac{|\boldsymbol{\Sigma}_1|}{|\boldsymbol{\Sigma}_0|} - D + \mathrm{Tr}(\boldsymbol{\Sigma}_1^{-1}\boldsymbol{\Sigma}_0) + (\boldsymbol{\mu}_1-\boldsymbol{\mu}_0)^\mathsf{T}\boldsymbol{\Sigma}_1^{-1}(\boldsymbol{\mu}_1-\boldsymbol{\mu}_0)\right].$$

In the fifth equality, we utilize $\mathbf{x}^\mathsf{T}\mathbf{A}\mathbf{x} = \mathrm{Tr}(\mathbf{A}\mathbf{x}\mathbf{x}^\mathsf{T})$ to obtain

$$\mathbb{E}_{p(\mathbf{x})}[(\mathbf{x}-\boldsymbol{\mu}_0)^\mathsf{T}\boldsymbol{\Sigma}_0^{-1}(\mathbf{x}-\boldsymbol{\mu}_0)] = \mathrm{Tr}(\boldsymbol{\Sigma}_0^{-1}\mathbb{E}_{p(\mathbf{x})}[(\mathbf{x}-\boldsymbol{\mu}_0)(\mathbf{x}-\boldsymbol{\mu}_0)^\mathsf{T}])$$
$$= \mathrm{Tr}(\boldsymbol{\Sigma}_0^{-1}\boldsymbol{\Sigma}_0) = D.$$

In the seventh equality, we use $\mathbb{E}_{p(\mathbf{x})}[\mathbf{x}-\boldsymbol{\mu}_0] = 0$, and in the last equality, we again use $\mathbf{x}^\mathsf{T}\mathbf{A}\mathbf{x} = \mathrm{Tr}(\mathbf{A}\mathbf{x}\mathbf{x}^\mathsf{T})$ and $\mathbb{E}_{p(\mathbf{x})}[(\mathbf{x}-\boldsymbol{\mu}_0)(\mathbf{x}-\boldsymbol{\mu}_0)^\mathsf{T}] = \boldsymbol{\Sigma}_0$.

Chapter 12
GAN: Generative Adversarial Network

12.1 Basics of GAN

Generative Adversarial Network (*GAN*) [11] is one of the deep generative models, where the final artifact is a generator that generates new data (fake data) following the distribution of real data from noise (seeds) (Fig. 12.1). GAN consists of a generator (*G*) that constructs the desired generator separately and a discriminator (*D*) that outputs the probability that the input received is real data. Both the generator *G* and the discriminator *D* are composed of multi-layer perceptrons. During training, the generator *G* learns to deceive (mislead) the discriminator *D*, while the discriminator *D* learns not to be fooled (to correctly classify) (Fig. 12.2).

Let the output of the generator for random noise $\mathbf{z}$ be denoted as $G(\mathbf{z})$.[1] Also, let $D(\mathbf{x})$ represent the probability that the discriminator assigns to $\mathbf{x}$ being generated from the distribution of real data (the probability that the discriminator assigns to $\mathbf{x}$ being fake data generated by the generator G is $1 - D(\mathbf{x})$). In this context, GAN learns such that the evaluation function (objective function)[2]

$$L(D, G) = \mathbb{E}_{\mathbf{x} \sim p(\mathbf{x})}[\ln D(\mathbf{x})] + \mathbb{E}_{\mathbf{z} \sim q(\mathbf{z})}[\ln(1 - D(G(\mathbf{z})))] \quad (12.1.1)$$

is maximized with respect to D and minimized with respect to G. Here, $p(\mathbf{x})$ represents the distribution of real data, and $q(\mathbf{z})$ represents a distribution from which sampling is easily performed, such as uniform or Gaussian distribution. In other words, we can express GAN optimization as

$$\min_{G} \max_{D} L(D, G).$$

---

[1] Originally, since it outputs a vector, it should be denoted as **G** in bold, but here we follow convention and use $G(\mathbf{z})$.

[2] The evaluation function (12.1.1) is not a loss function, but here we simply denote it as L.

© The Author(s), under exclusive license to Springer Nature Singapore Pte Ltd. 2025
T. Okadome, *Essentials of Generative AI*,
https://doi.org/10.1007/978-981-96-0029-8_12

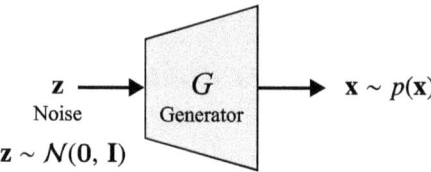

Fig. 12.1 Generator as the final artifact of GAN

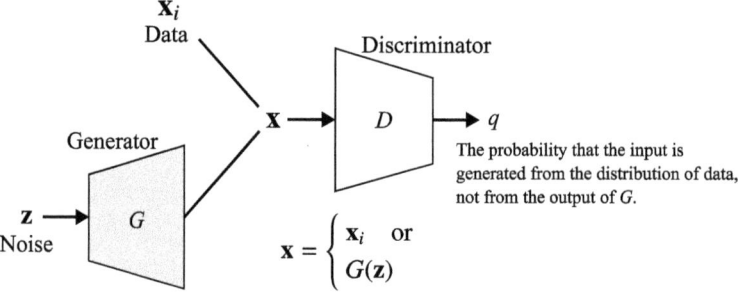

Fig. 12.2 Basic idea of GAN training

In actual training, given real data samples $x_1, \ldots, x_N$, and samples $z_1, \ldots, z_M$ drawn from distribution $q(z)$, we maximize

$$\sum_{n=1}^{N} \ln D(x_n) + \sum_{m=1}^{M} \ln(1 - D(G(z_m)))$$

with respect to D and minimize with respect to G. The first term in this equation is the negative cross-entropy error when the input to the discriminator D is real data, and the second term is the negative cross-entropy error when the input to the discriminator D is the output of the generator G (fake data).

We examine some properties of the optimal solution for GAN. Firstly, we show that the optimal solution following the above learning strategy is also optimal for the discriminator in the sense of Bayesian estimation. Let us rewrite the evaluation function (12.1.1) with the data generating distribution as $p_{dt}(x)$ and the generator's output distribution as $p_{gen}(x)$.[3] Then, we have

$$L(D, G) = \int \big(p_{dt}(x) \ln D(x) + p_{gen}(x) \ln(1 - D(x))\big) dx.$$

The optimal solution for the discriminator D under the condition of fixing the generator G is a variational problem to find $D(x)$ that maximizes the functional

---

[3] The distribution $q(z)$ represents the distribution of samples inputted into the generator, whereas $p_{gen}(x)$ represents the distribution of the generator's output.

12.1 Basics of GAN

$F[D] = L(G, D)$. To solve this variational problem, we define $g(D(\mathbf{x}))$ as

$$g(D(\mathbf{x})) = p_{dt}(\mathbf{x}) \ln D(\mathbf{x}) + p_{gen}(\mathbf{x}) \ln(1 - D(\mathbf{x})).$$

By setting the variation of $g(D(\mathbf{x}))$ with respect to $D(\mathbf{x})$ to zero, we can obtain the optimal solution. That is, the optimal solution satisfies

$$\frac{\delta g(D)}{\delta D} = 0 \iff \frac{p_{dt}(\mathbf{x}) - (p_{dt}(\mathbf{x}) + p_{gen}(\mathbf{x}))D(\mathbf{x})}{D(\mathbf{x})(1 - D(\mathbf{x}))} = 0.$$

Thus, the optimal solution for the evaluation function (12.1.1) is

$$D^*(\mathbf{x}) = \frac{p_{dt}(\mathbf{x})}{p_{dt}(\mathbf{x}) + p_{gen}(\mathbf{x})}.$$

Here, we consider the case where real and fake data are randomly inputted to the discriminator with a probability of 1/2 each. We introduce a random variable c taking values in $\{0, 1\}$, where $c = 0$ when the input is the output of the generator (fake data) and $c = 1$ when the input is real data. Then, we have $p(c = 1) = p(c = 0) = 1/2$, and $p(\mathbf{x} \mid c)$ represents the probability of input $\mathbf{x}$ to the discriminator given c:

$$\begin{cases} p(\mathbf{x} \mid c = 0) = p_{gen}(\mathbf{x}), \\ p(\mathbf{x} \mid c = 1) = p_{dt}(\mathbf{x}). \end{cases}$$

If we denote the distribution of inputs to the discriminator as $p_{D_{in}}(\mathbf{x})$, then we have

$$p_{D_{in}}(\mathbf{x}) = p(\mathbf{x} \mid c = 0)p(c = 0) + p(\mathbf{x} \mid c = 1)p(c = 1) = \frac{1}{2}(p_{gen}(\mathbf{x}) + p_{dt}(\mathbf{x})).$$

The optimal solution in the context of Bayesian estimation for a classification problem is the posterior probability $p(c = 1 \mid \mathbf{x})$. We can derive it as

$$p(c = 1 \mid \mathbf{x}) = \frac{p(\mathbf{x} \mid c = 1)p(c = 1)}{p(\mathbf{x})} = \frac{p_{dt}(\mathbf{x})}{p_{dt}(\mathbf{x}) + p_{gen}(\mathbf{x})} = D^*(\mathbf{x}).$$

Thus, it matches the optimal solution of the evaluation function (12.1.1). On the other hand, if the output distribution of the generator p_{gen} perfectly matches the distribution of real data p_{dt}, i.e., $p_{gen}(\mathbf{x}) = p_{dt}(\mathbf{x})$, then this is the optimal generator. In this case, we have

$$D^*(\mathbf{x}) = \frac{1}{2}.$$

This implies that in the presence of a perfect generator, the discriminator would be ineffective, as it cannot distinguish between real and fake data.

Next, we show that when the discriminator is optimal, the evaluation function $L(D^*, G)$ is essentially equivalent to the JS divergence between p_{dt} and p_{gen}. The *JS divergence* between distributions p and q is a measure of divergence between distributions, defined as

$$\mathbb{JS}(p \parallel q) \equiv \frac{1}{2}\left(\mathbb{KL}\left(p \,\bigg\|\, \frac{p+q}{2}\right) + \mathbb{KL}\left(q \,\bigg\|\, \frac{p+q}{2}\right)\right),$$

where $\mathbb{KL}(p \parallel q)$ is the KL divergence[4] between probability distributions p and q. Unlike the KL divergence, the JS divergence satisfies the properties of a distance metric. For example, consider probability distributions δ_x and δ_y that are certain to be points **x** and **y**, respectively (as illustrated in Fig. 12.3). The KL divergence between them is

$$\mathbb{KL}(\delta_x \parallel \delta_y) = \begin{cases} 1 \cdot \ln(1/1) = 0, & \text{if } \mathbf{x} = \mathbf{y}, \\ 1 \cdot \ln(1/0) + 0 \cdot \ln(0/1) = \infty, & \text{otherwise}, \end{cases}$$

while the JS divergence is

$$\mathbb{JS}(\delta_x \parallel \delta_y) = \begin{cases} 0, & \text{if } \mathbf{x} = \mathbf{y}, \\ \ln 2, & \text{otherwise}, \end{cases}$$

since when $\mathbf{x} = \mathbf{y}$, we have

$$\frac{1}{2}\left(\mathbb{KL}(\delta_x \parallel \delta_x) + \mathbb{KL}(\delta_x \parallel \delta_x)\right) = 0,$$

and when $\mathbf{x} \neq \mathbf{y}$, we have

$$\frac{1}{2}\left(\mathbb{KL}\left(\delta_x \,\bigg\|\, \frac{\delta_x + \delta_y}{2}\right) + \mathbb{KL}\left(\delta_y \,\bigg\|\, \frac{\delta_x + \delta_y}{2}\right)\right) = \frac{1}{2}\left(1 \cdot \ln\left(\frac{1}{1/2}\right) + 1 \cdot \ln\left(\frac{1}{1/2}\right)\right) = \ln 2.$$

JS divergence takes a finite value even when the distributions have no overlap. JS (and KL) divergence, however, may be discontinuous and have no gradient in areas where there is no overlap between the two distributions. Additionally, in cases like this example, the JS divergence between point distributions is a constant outside of the discontinuous points, resulting in zero gradient.

Now, we directly compute the JS divergence between distributions $p_{dt}(\mathbf{x})$ and $p_{gen}(\mathbf{x})$. That is,

$$\mathbb{JS}(p_{dt} \parallel p_{gen}) = \frac{1}{2}\mathbb{KL}\left(p_{dt} \,\bigg\|\, \frac{p_{dt} + p_{gen}}{2}\right) + \frac{1}{2}\mathbb{KL}\left(p_{gen} \,\bigg\|\, \frac{p_{dt} + p_{gen}}{2}\right)$$

---

[4] For KL divergence, see Appendix B at the end of the book.

12.1 Basics of GAN

Fig. 12.3 Probability distributions δ_x and δ_y that are certain to be points **x** and **y**, respectively

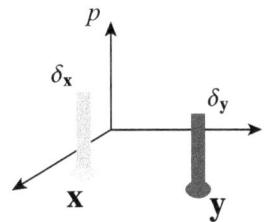

$$= \frac{1}{2}\left(\int p_{dt}(\mathbf{x}) \ln \frac{2 p_{dt}(\mathbf{x})}{p_{dt}(\mathbf{x}) + p_{gen}(\mathbf{x})} d\mathbf{x}\right)$$
$$+ \frac{1}{2}\left(\int p_{gen}(\mathbf{x}) \ln \frac{2 p_{gen}(\mathbf{x})}{p_{dt}(\mathbf{x}) + p_{gen}(\mathbf{x})} d\mathbf{x}\right)$$
$$= \frac{1}{2}\left(\int p_{dt}(\mathbf{x}) \ln 2\, d\mathbf{x} + \int p_{dt}(\mathbf{x}) \ln \frac{p_{dt}(\mathbf{x})}{p_{dt}(\mathbf{x}) + p_{gen}(\mathbf{x})} d\mathbf{x}\right)$$
$$+ \frac{1}{2}\left(\int p_{gen}(\mathbf{x}) \ln 2\, d\mathbf{x} + \int p_{gen}(\mathbf{x}) \ln \frac{p_{gen}(\mathbf{x})}{p_{dt}(\mathbf{x}) + p_{gen}(\mathbf{x})} d\mathbf{x}\right)$$
$$= \frac{1}{2}(\ln 4 + L(D^*, G)).$$

In the last step, we used the fact that p_{dt} and p_{gen} are probability distributions, so their integrals equal 1. Thus, when the discriminator is optimal, minimizing the evaluation function $L(D^*, G)$ with respect to G is essentially equivalent to minimizing the distance (JS divergence) between the distribution of the data and the output distribution of the generator.

In actual optimization, the generator G and the discriminator D are alternately optimized sequentially as follows:

$$D_{t+1} = \arg\max_D L(D, G_t),$$
$$G_{t+1} = \arg\min_G L(D_t, G).$$

During the initial stages of training, the generator G produces outputs that are close to random, and the discriminator D can make correct judgments. However, $1 - D(G(\mathbf{z}))$ approaches 1 very closely, causing the gradient to vanish, which hinders further learning. To mitigate this issue of gradient vanishing during the initial stages of training, instead of $L(D, G)$, we often use the evaluation function $L'(D, G)$ defined as

$$L'(D, G) = \mathbb{E}_{\mathbf{x}\sim p(\mathbf{x})}[\ln D(\mathbf{x})] - \mathbb{E}_{\mathbf{z}\sim q(\mathbf{z})}[\ln D(G(\mathbf{z}))].$$

Furthermore, we compute $D(G(\mathbf{z}))$ using a concatenated network composed of the networks that compute G and D. Consequently, the parameter learning of the generator G relies on the error propagated from D, and the output distribution (likelihood) of G is unnecessary for its learning. This is one of the advantages of GANs.

We list the disadvantages of GANs.

- Throughout the training process, we need to balance the performance of the generator and the discriminator.
- Gradient vanishing occurs during the initial stages of training. Additionally, as mentioned earlier, the JS divergence is constant in regions where there is no overlap between the two distributions. Consequently, gradient vanishing can occur even in regions where there is no overlap between the output distribution of the generator and the input distribution of the discriminator.
- Ideally, we want to sample widely from the data generation distribution. However, the generator G only needs to produce samples that can fool the discriminator D. Once such samples are found, we do not need to generate new samples (known as *mode collapse*).

Due to these issues, it is difficult to achieve stable learning with the basic GAN framework, and generating images of resolution 64×64 was the limit. Various advanced forms of GANs have been proposed with the aim of achieving stable learning and increasing the resolution of generated images.

We provide some examples of advanced forms of GANs. Before that, we clarify the issue of mode collapse mentioned earlier. First, in the JS divergence between distributions p_{dt} and p_{gen}:

$$\mathrm{JS}(p_{dt} \| p_{gen}) = \frac{1}{2} \left(\mathrm{KL}\left(p_{dt} \;\middle\|\; \frac{p_{dt} + p_{gen}}{2} \right) + \mathrm{KL}\left(p_{gen} \;\middle\|\; \frac{p_{dt} + p_{gen}}{2} \right) \right),$$

we fix $p_{dt}(\mathbf{x})$. Thus, we vary only $p_{gen}(\mathbf{x})$ to minimize the JS divergence. Of the two terms in the JS divergence,

$$\mathrm{KL}\left(p_{dt} \;\middle\|\; \frac{p_{dt} + p_{gen}}{2} \right)$$

is the standard KL divergence, while

$$\mathrm{KL}\left(p_{gen} \;\middle\|\; \frac{p_{dt} + p_{gen}}{2} \right)$$

is the reverse KL divergence. For multimodal distributions, it is known that minimizing the KL divergence typically leads to the average of modes as the solution, whereas minimizing the reverse KL divergence tends to find one of the modes as the solution. In many cases, the distribution p_{dt} of real data is multimodal. Thus, when minimizing the JS divergence, the varied p_{gen} might fall into a local minimum of the

12.2 Development of GANs

reverse KL divergence term, approximating one of the peaks of p_{dt}. This provides a theoretical interpretation of mode collapse.

Now we introduce some examples of advanced forms of GANs, such as PGGAN, conditional GANs, and Wasserstein GANs.

12.2 Development of GANs

The generator in the original GAN stacked fully connected layers. However, in the development of GANs such as DCGAN [34], the generator began to stack convolutional layers instead of fully connected layers, gradually increasing the image size to generate the final image.

12.2.1 PGGAN and Conditional GAN

PGGAN (progressive growing GAN) [19] starts with a 4 × 4 resolution and gradually increases the resolution of the training data. Additionally, both the generator and discriminator in PGGAN increase the resolution through upsampling,[5] ultimately obtaining images of size 1024 × 1024 (see Fig. 12.4). PGGAN normalizes an image pixel-wise according to the equation:

$$b^{(i)}_{x,y} = \frac{a^{(i)}_{x,y}}{\sqrt{\frac{1}{N}\sum_{j=0}^{N-1}\left(a^{(j)}_{x,y}\right)^2 + \epsilon}}, \quad i = 0, \ldots, N-1,$$

where $\epsilon = 10^{-8}$, N is the number of feature maps, and $a^{(i)}_{x,y}$ and $b^{(i)}_{x,y}$ represent the i-th element of the original and normalized feature vector in pixel (x, y), respectively. Figure 12.5 shows examples of images generated by PGGAN.

The original GAN generates a single new data instance for a given noise vector **z**. Thus, for example, in generating face images, whether a male or female face image is generated depends on **z**. *Conditional GAN* (conditional generative adversarial network) [27] introduces additional information **a** to control the characteristics of the generated image. The generator is constructed as $G(\mathbf{z}, \mathbf{a})$, and the discriminator as $D(\mathbf{x}, \mathbf{a})$, both being functions of two variables (see Fig. 12.6). In the case of male and female face images, **a** represents the gender label, taking values such as $(0\ 1)^T$ for male and $(1\ 0)^T$ for female. The generator G takes $(\mathbf{z}^T\ \mathbf{a}^T)^T$ as input to generate new

---

[5] For a general explanation of image size enlargement, refer to Appendix D at the end of the book.

Fig. 12.4 Image enlargement generation by upsampling in PGGAN

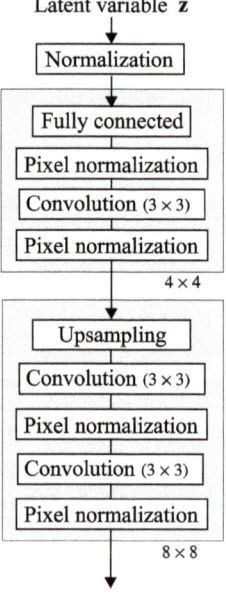

Fig. 12.5 Example of images generated by PGGAN. From Fig. 5 of [19]. Used with kind permission of Samuli Laine

data, while the discriminator D, under the specification of $\mathbf{a}$, outputs the probability that the input $\mathbf{x}$ was generated from the data distribution $p(\mathbf{x})$. The objective function is defined as

$$L(D, G) = \mathbb{E}_{\mathbf{x} \sim p(\mathbf{x})}[\ln D(\mathbf{x}, \mathbf{a})] + \mathbb{E}_{\mathbf{z} \sim q(\mathbf{z})}[\ln(1 - D(G(\mathbf{z}, \mathbf{a}), \mathbf{a}))],$$

and the optimization is performed as

$$\min_G \max_D L(D, G).$$

This optimization trains the neural network weights.

12.2 Development of GANs

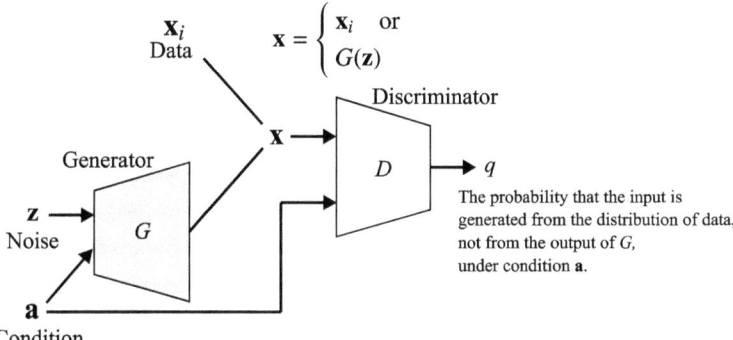

Fig. 12.6 Conditional GAN. It introduces additional information **a** to control the characteristics of the generated image

12.2.2 Wasserstein GAN

Wasserstein GAN (WGAN) [1] utilizes the evaluation function:

$$\mathbb{E}_{\mathbf{x}\sim p(\mathbf{x})}[D(\mathbf{x})] - \mathbb{E}_{\mathbf{z}\sim q(\mathbf{z})}[D(G(\mathbf{z}))],$$

which is equivalent to

$$\mathbb{E}_{\mathbf{x}\sim p_{dt}(\mathbf{x})}[D(\mathbf{x})] - \mathbb{E}_{\mathbf{x}\sim p_{gen}(\mathbf{x})}[D(\mathbf{x})]. \qquad (12.2.1)$$

We can show that the following optimizations are equivalent.

1. Optimizing this evaluation function (12.2.1).
2. Optimizing the distance between the data generation distribution and the output distribution of the generator G (instead of the JS divergence) with adopting the Wasserstein distance as the distance measure.

This avoids the gradient vanishing problem of JS divergence that occurs when there is no overlap between the two distributions. The Wasserstein distance is defined based on the optimal transport problem, providing a meaningful measure even when the distributions being compared have no overlap. The application of the optimal transport problem is broad and deserves its own discussion. We summarize the key points about these concepts.

Optimal Transport Problem and Wasserstein Distance

We provide an intuitive explanation of the optimal transport distance between two probability distributions before diving into a formal definition. Imagine two probability distributions. To transform one distribution into the other, we shave off parts of the first distribution until it vanishes, then move these shaved parts to align with the

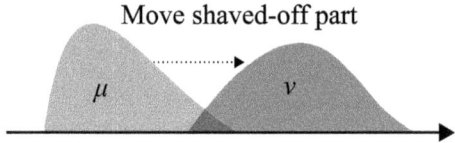

Fig. 12.7 Intuitive explanation of optimal transport distance between two distributions

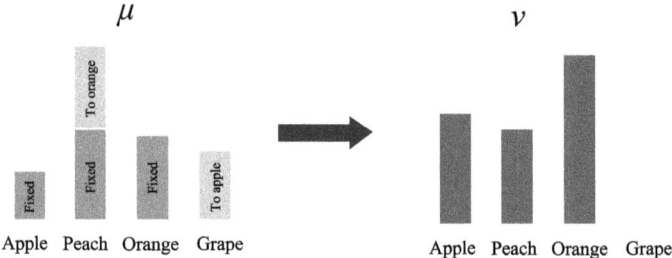

Fig. 12.8 Optimal transport distance between two histograms

Fig. 12.9 Comparison of two distributions by KL divergence only considers the size of bins at the same position

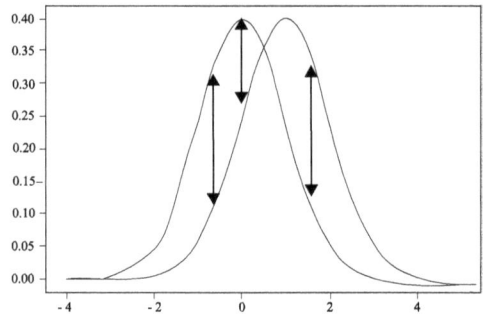

second distribution. The minimum cost incurred during this process is considered the distance between the distributions, known as the *Wasserstein distance* (see Fig. 12.7). The Wasserstein distance is also referred to as the Earth Mover's distance.

For instance, consider comparing two histograms μ and ν as shown in Fig. 12.8. Initially, we manually assign costs to move bins from one class to another. For example, if we know that moving from "peaches" to "oranges" costs less than moving from "peaches" to "apples," we utilize this insight. Then, we aim to align the bins of μ to match ν. The minimum cost incurred during this operation is the optimal transport distance between the histograms μ and ν.

By the way, as mentioned earlier, we can view the optimization of the evaluation function of GANs as the optimization of JS divergence. Remember that JS divergence is defined as the average of KL divergence and reverse KL divergence. When considering KL divergence as a distance measure, it has several drawbacks. First, the KL divergence between discrete distributions $p = (p_1, \ldots, p_M)$ and $q = (q_1, \ldots, q_M)$ is

12.2 Development of GANs

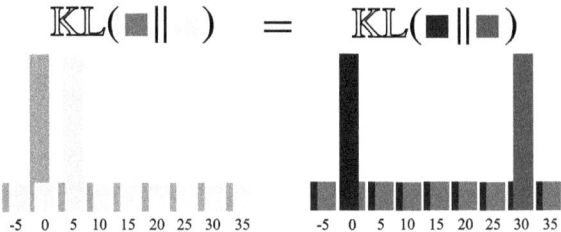

Fig. 12.10 Drawback of KL divergence. Generally, the histograms of temperatures at distant points differ significantly, while at nearby points, the histograms of temperatures tend to be similar. However, in this figure, the KL divergence is the same for both the left and right cases

Fig. 12.11 KL divergence is inappropriate as a distance measure for two point clouds

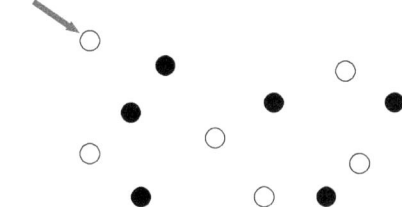

$$\mathbb{KL}(p \parallel q) \equiv \sum_i p_i \cdot \ln\left(\frac{p_i}{q_i}\right).$$

It only considers the size of bins at the same position and does not consider the proximity or distance between positions i and j (see Fig. 12.9).

For example, therefore, when trying to classify regions based on differences in temperature distributions, inconveniences arise (see Fig. 12.10). Furthermore, KL divergence has the drawback that it cannot be used when the support of two distributions (where density values are non-zero) does not overlap. This is because the value of KL divergence becomes infinite where there is no overlap.

An example where this is problematic is when the distance between two point clouds exists (see Fig. 12.11). That is, in multidimensional space, there are two sets of points (n white points and m black points), and each white point is assigned a probability of $1/n$ as the distribution on the white point set, and each black point is assigned a probability of $1/m$ as the distribution on the black point set. In this case, using KL divergence as a distribution "distance" measure is inappropriate.

On the contrary, in optimal transport, we can consider the distance between i and j in histograms. For example, as shown in Fig. 12.12, while KL divergence cannot distinguish between distributions with similar shapes as in the left figure, the KL divergence of the distributions with significantly different shapes in the right figure becomes larger than that of the similar temperature distributions in the left figure.

Furthermore, in optimal transport, it is acceptable even if the supports do not overlap. As can be understood from the above explanation, the optimal transport distance is suitable when a natural distance can be introduced to the object. That is,

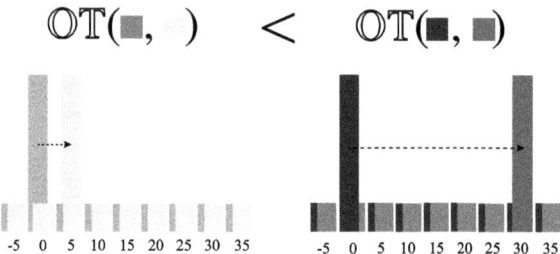

Fig. 12.12 The optimal transport distance between the two histograms in the right figure becomes larger than that between the two histograms in the left figure. $OT(\mathbf{a}, \mathbf{b})$ denotes the optimal transport distance between histograms $\mathbf{a}$ and $\mathbf{b}$

when dealing with regression or classification subjects with ordinal scales such as temperature or humidity, or for example, in fruit classification, when there is a scale such as "grapefruit" and "orange" being closer than "grape" and "orange," or when handling point clouds (sets of points) in Euclidean space, using the optimal transport distance is appropriate.

Now, we formulate the optimal transport distance for histograms. Let $\mathbf{a} = (a_i)$ and $\mathbf{b} = (b_j)$ be normalized histograms to compare, represented as n-dimensional vectors, and let $\mathbf{C} = (c_{ij})$ be an $n \times n$ matrix representing the distance between bins. In this case, the optimal transport distance is defined as the total cost:

$$\min_{\mathbf{P}} \sum_{i=1}^{n} \sum_{j=1}^{n} c_{ij} P_{ij},$$

where $\mathbf{P} = (P_{ij})$ is an $n \times n$ matrix satisfying the following.

$$P_{ij} \geq 0, \quad i, j = 1, \ldots, n,$$

$$\sum_{j=1}^{n} P_{ij} = a_i, \quad i = 1, \ldots, n,$$

$$\sum_{i=1}^{n} P_{ij} = b_j, \quad j = 1, \ldots, n.$$

The decision variables P_{ij} represent the amount transported from bin i to bin j, including the amount "leaving" bin i to itself. The first condition means that the transport amount is non-negative, the second ensures that each bin does not send more than it has, and the third ensures that each bin does not receive more than it needs. The problem of finding the optimal transport amount is a linear programming problem because the objective function is linear with respect to $\mathbf{P}$, and all constraints regarding $\mathbf{P}$ are also linear. We can find the optimal transport amount using well-known linear programming methods.

As an application of this definition, we consider the harvest quantities of (apples, peaches, oranges, grapes) in California and New York, represented as normalized histograms:

12.2 Development of GANs

$$a = \begin{pmatrix} 0.2 \\ 0.5 \\ 0.2 \\ 0.1 \end{pmatrix}, \quad b = \begin{pmatrix} 0.3 \\ 0.3 \\ 0.4 \\ 0.0 \end{pmatrix}.$$

Also, we assume the distances between bins are given by the matrix:

$$C = \begin{pmatrix} 0 & 2 & 2 & 2 \\ 2 & 0 & 1 & 2 \\ 2 & 1 & 0 & 2 \\ 2 & 2 & 2 & 0 \end{pmatrix}.$$

In this case, solving the optimal transport amount using linear programming yields

$$P^* = \arg\min_P \sum_{i=1}^n \sum_{j=1}^n c_{ij} P_{ij} = \begin{pmatrix} 0.2 & 0 & 0 & 0 \\ 0 & 0.3 & 0.2 & 0 \\ 0 & 0 & 0.2 & 0 \\ 0.1 & 0 & 0 & 0 \end{pmatrix}.$$

Thus,

$$C \odot P^* = \begin{pmatrix} 0 & 0 & 0 & 0 \\ 0 & 0 & 0.2 & 0 \\ 0 & 0 & 0 & 0 \\ 0.2 & 0 & 0 & 0 \end{pmatrix},$$

where $\odot$ denotes the Hadamard product (element-wise multiplication). The optimal transport distance, therefore, is

$$\min_P \sum_{i=1}^n \sum_{j=1}^n c_{ij} P_{ij} = 0.2 + 0.2 = 0.4.$$

As mentioned earlier, the optimal transport distance is a distance measure that avoids the drawbacks of KL divergence as a distance between distributions. Despite being labeled as a "distance," however, the optimal transport distance may not satisfy the distance axioms depending on the configuration of the cost matrix.

Wasserstein Distance

The Wasserstein distance is defined using the optimal transport distance and satisfies the distance axioms. We fix one distance function on the set X as $d : X \times X \to \mathbf{R}$, and introduce the distance $C(x, y) \equiv d(x, y)^p$ between points in X using a real number $p \geq 1$. Let us denote the optimal transport distance between distributions μ and ν on X as $OT(\mu, \nu, C)$. Then, we define the *p-Wasserstein distance* as

$$W_p(\mu, \nu) = (OT(\mu, \nu, C))^{1/p}.$$

In particular, we commonly use the 1-Wasserstein distance $C(x, y) = \|x - y\|_2$ and the 2-Wasserstein distance $C(x, y) = \|x - y\|_2^2$.

The Wasserstein distance between probability distributions $\delta_\mathbf{x}$ and $\delta_\mathbf{y}$, where $\mathbf{x}$ and $\mathbf{y}$ are points in $\mathbf{R}^d$, is

$$W_1(\delta_\mathbf{x}, \delta_\mathbf{y}) = \|\mathbf{x} - \mathbf{y}\|_2.$$

This means that the Euclidean distance in d-dimensional space is the distance between distributions (see Fig. 12.13). This is in contrast to KL divergence, which becomes infinite when $\mathbf{x} \neq \mathbf{y}$, and JS divergence, which is a constant ($\ln 2$).

Wasserstein Distance Minimization as WGAN

We revisit the optimal transport distance for normalized histograms $\mathbf{a} = (a_i)$ and $\mathbf{b} = (b_j)$. Since both are normalized, we have

$$\sum_{i=1}^n a_i = 1, \quad \sum_{j=1}^n b_j = 1.$$

From these and the constraints:

$$\sum_{j=1}^n P_{ij} = a_i, \quad i = 1, \ldots, n,$$

$$\sum_{i=1}^n P_{ij} = b_j, \quad j = 1, \ldots, n,$$

it follows that

Fig. 12.13 Wasserstein distance between probability distributions $\delta_\mathbf{x}$ and $\delta_\mathbf{y}$, where $\mathbf{x}$ and $\mathbf{y}$ are points in $\mathbf{R}^d$

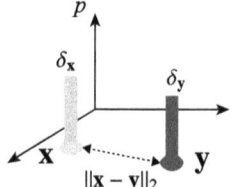

12.2 Development of GANs

$$\sum_{i=1}^{n}\sum_{j=1}^{n} P_{ij} = 1.$$

Since $P_{ij} \geq 0$, we can interpret the matrix $\mathbf{P} = (P_{ij})$ as a probability distribution (a normalized 2D histogram). Under this interpretation, the optimal transport distance:

$$\min_{\mathbf{P}} \sum_{i=1}^{n}\sum_{j=1}^{n} c_{ij} P_{ij}$$

is the minimization of the expected value of the cost $\mathbf{C} = (c_{ij})$ with respect to the distribution $\mathbf{P} = (P_{ij})$. In other words, the optimal transport distance between distributions $\mathbf{a} = (a_i)$ and $\mathbf{b} = (b_j)$ is

$$\min_{\mathbf{P}} \mathbb{E}_{\mathbf{P}}[c_{ij}].$$

If we set c_{ij} to be the Euclidean distance between i and j, the above expression is

$$\min_{\mathbf{P}} \mathbb{E}_{\mathbf{P}}[\|i-j\|_2] = \min_{\mathbf{P}} \sum_{i=1}^{n}\sum_{j=1}^{n} P_{ij}\|i-j\|_2. \qquad (12.2.2)$$

This is the 1-Wasserstein distance.

As we will describe in the following subsection, the primal form of the linear programming

$$\underset{\mathbf{P}}{\text{minimize}} \sum_{i=1}^{n}\sum_{j=1}^{n} P_{ij}\|i-j\|_2 \text{ subject to } \begin{cases} P_{ij} \geq 0, & i,j=1,\ldots,n, \\ \sum_{j=1}^{n} P_{ij} = a_i, & i=1,\ldots,n, \\ \sum_{i=1}^{n} P_{ij} = b_j, & j=1,\ldots,n \end{cases}$$

(12.2.3)

has a dual form

$$\underset{\|f\|_L \leq 1}{\text{maximize}} \{\mathbb{E}_{\mathbf{a}}[f(z)] - \mathbb{E}_{\mathbf{b}}[f(z)]\},$$

where $\|f\|_L \leq 1$ implies that the function f is a continuous function satisfying the 1-Lipschitz condition, meaning that f is an abbreviation for a continuous function that satisfies $|f(i) - f(j)| \leq \|i-j\|_2$ for all i and j. By replacing the distribution $\mathbf{a}$ with $p_{dt}(\mathbf{x})$ and $\mathbf{b}$ with $p_{gen}(\mathbf{x})$, we obtain the optimization problem for Wasserstein GAN:

$$\underset{D(\mathbf{x})}{\text{maximize}} \{\mathbb{E}_{\mathbf{x} \sim p_{dt}(\mathbf{x})}[D(\mathbf{x})] - \mathbb{E}_{\mathbf{x} \sim p_{gen}(\mathbf{x})}[D(\mathbf{x})]\}.$$

Note that because the strong duality holds in the linear programming, if the primary problem (12.2.3) has the optimal solution, then the dual problem also has the optimal solution, and their optimal values coincide (see Appendix E at the end of the book).

WGAN as Dual Representation

To align with the description in Appendix E at the end of the book, we replace occurrences of $n \times n$ matrices with $l \times l$ matrices, and n-dimensional vectors with l-dimensional vectors. We also replace the vectors **a** and **b** with **q** and **r**. That is, **P** is an $l \times l$ matrix, we have $\mathbf{q} = (q_1 \cdots q_l)$ and $\mathbf{r} = (r_1 \cdots r_l)$, and thus, the primary problem of the linear programming (12.2.3) is replaced with

$$\underset{\mathbf{P}}{\text{minimize}} \sum_{i=1}^{l}\sum_{j=1}^{l} P_{ij}\|i-j\|_2 \quad \text{subject to} \begin{cases} P_{ij} \geq 0, \quad i, j = 1, \ldots, l, \\ \sum_{j=1}^{l} P_{ij} = q_i, \quad i = 1, \ldots, l, \\ \sum_{i=1}^{l} P_{ij} = r_j, \quad j = 1, \ldots, l. \end{cases} \quad (12.2.4)$$

We show that the dual form associated with the problem (12.2.4) is

$$\underset{\|f\|_L \leq 1}{\text{maximize}} \{\mathbb{E}_\mathbf{q}[f(z)] - \mathbb{E}_\mathbf{r}[f(z)]\}, \quad (12.2.5)$$

where $\|f\|_L \leq 1$ implies that the function f is a continuous function satisfying the 1-Lipschitz condition, meaning that f is an abbreviation for a continuous function that satisfies $|f(i) - f(j)| \leq \|i - j\|_2$ for all i and j.

First, letting $m = 2l$ and $n = l^2$, we transform the linear programming (12.2.4) into a canonical primal form:

$$\underset{\mathbf{x} \in R^n}{\text{minimize}} \ \mathbf{c}^T\mathbf{x} \quad \text{subject to} \begin{cases} \mathbf{A}\mathbf{x} = \mathbf{b}, \\ \mathbf{x} \geq \mathbf{0}, \end{cases} \quad (12.2.6)$$

where **A** is an $m \times n$ matrix, **b** is an m-dimensional vector, and **c** is an n-dimensional vector. For carrying out this transformation, we define an n-dimensional ($= l^2$-dimensional) vector **x** by vectorizing the matrix $\mathbf{P} = (\mathbf{p}_1 \cdots \mathbf{p}_l)$ as follows:

$$\mathbf{x} \equiv \begin{pmatrix} \mathbf{p}_1 \\ \vdots \\ \mathbf{p}_l \end{pmatrix}.$$

We also define an n-dimensional vector **c** that represents the distance between the positions i and j as follows:

12.2 Development of GANs

$$\mathbf{c} \equiv \begin{pmatrix} \|1-1\|_2 \\ \|1-2\|_2 \\ \|1-3\|_2 \\ \vdots \\ \|i-j\|_2 \\ \vdots \\ \|l-(l-1)\|_2 \\ \|l-l\|_2 \end{pmatrix} = \begin{pmatrix} 0 \\ 1 \\ 2 \\ \vdots \\ |i-j| \\ \vdots \\ 1 \\ 0 \end{pmatrix},$$

that is, the distance of the pair (i, j) is the $(i \times (l-1) + j)$-th component. Then, by defining the $m \times n$ ($= 2l \times l^2$) matrix $\mathbf{A}$ as

$$\mathbf{A} = \begin{pmatrix} 1\,1\,\cdots\,1 & 0\,0\,\cdots\,0 & \cdots & 0\,0\,\cdots\,0 \\ 0\,0\,\cdots\,0 & 1\,1\,\cdots\,1 & \cdots & 0\,0\,\cdots\,0 \\ \vdots\,\vdots\,\ddots\,\vdots & \vdots\,\vdots\,\ddots\,\vdots & \cdots & \vdots\,\vdots\,\ddots\,\vdots \\ 0\,0\,\cdots\,0 & 0\,0\,\cdots\,0 & \cdots & 1\,1\,\cdots\,1 \\ \hline 1\,0\,\cdots\,0 & 1\,0\,\cdots\,0 & \cdots & 1\,0\,\cdots\,0 \\ 0\,1\,\cdots\,0 & 0\,1\,\cdots\,0 & \cdots & 0\,1\,\cdots\,0 \\ \vdots\,\vdots\,\ddots\,\vdots & \vdots\,\vdots\,\ddots\,\vdots & \cdots & \vdots\,\vdots\,\ddots\,\vdots \\ 0\,0\,\cdots\,1 & 0\,0\,\cdots\,1 & \cdots & 0\,0\,\cdots\,1 \end{pmatrix},$$

and the m-dimensional ($= 2l$-dimensional) vector $\mathbf{b}$ as

$$\mathbf{b} = \begin{pmatrix} \mathbf{q} \\ \mathbf{r} \end{pmatrix},$$

you can see a canonical form of the linear programming (12.2.4).

For the primal form of the linear programming (12.2.6), as we describe in Appendix E at the end of the book, we have the following dual form:

$$\underset{\mathbf{y} \in R^m}{\text{maximize}} \; \mathbf{b}^T \mathbf{y} \;\; \text{subject to} \; \mathbf{A}^T \mathbf{y} \leq \mathbf{c}.$$

Let us divide $\mathbf{y}$ into two m-dimensional vectors $\mathbf{f}$ and $\mathbf{g}$, that is,

$$\mathbf{y} = \begin{pmatrix} \mathbf{f} \\ \mathbf{g} \end{pmatrix},$$

where $\mathbf{f} = (f_1 \cdots f_m)^T$ and $\mathbf{g} = (g_1 \cdots g_m)^T$. Then, we have the objective of the dual form

$$\mathbf{b}^T \mathbf{y} = \mathbf{q}^T \mathbf{f} + \mathbf{r}^T \mathbf{g}. \tag{12.2.7}$$

We also have the constraints of the dual form

$$f_i + g_j \le c_{i,j},$$

where $c_{i,j}$ is the $(i \times (l-1) + j)$-th component of **c**. When $i = j$ holds, we have $g_i \le -f_i$ for all i because of $c_{i,i} = 0$. Thus, since **q** and **r** are probability distributions, the objective (12.2.7) is bounded above by

$$\sum_{i=1}^{m}(f_i + g_i).$$

The maximum value of this sum is 0, which is attained when $\mathbf{g} = -\mathbf{f}$ holds. Hence, the maximum value of the objective (12.2.7) is 0, which is also attained when $\mathbf{g} = -\mathbf{f}$ holds, because **q** and **r** are non-negative.

Here, by rewriting the vectors **f** and **g** as values the functions f and g, for $\mathbf{g} = -\mathbf{f}$, the constraints are represented by

$$f(z)|_{z=i} - f(z)|_{z=j} \le c_{i,j} \quad \text{and} \quad f(z)|_{z=i} - f(z)|_{z=j} \ge -c_{i,j}.$$

If we see the value $f(z)|_{z=i}$ as connected with line segments, the above inquires represent that the upward and the downward slope of these segments is bounded. These slope bounds are 1 and -1 because we use the Euclidean distance. We call these constraints *Lipschitz continuity* with Lipschitz constant 1 and write $\|f\|_{L \le 1}$. Thus, we have the dual form:

$$\underset{\|f\|_L \le 1}{\text{maximize}} \ \{\mathbb{E}_{\mathbf{q}}[f(z)] - \mathbb{E}_{\mathbf{r}}[f(z)]\}.$$

Appendix A
Basic Terminology of Optimization Problems

We summarize some basic terms on the optimization of functions. Let S be a subset of R^n, $S \subset R^n$, and f a function on S, $f(\mathbf{x}): S \to R$.

A *lower bound* of a function f on a set S is a real value L such that $f(\mathbf{x}) \geq L$ for all $\mathbf{x}$ in S.

The *infimum* of a function f on a set S is the greatest lower bound of the function on that set. Symbolically, it is denoted as $\inf_{\mathbf{x} \in S} f(\mathbf{x})$. In essence, it is the lowest value that the function approaches within the set, but it does not necessarily have to attain this value.

The *minimum value* of a function is the infimum that the function actually takes on within the set S. Symbolically, it is denoted as $\min_{\mathbf{x} \in S} f(\mathbf{x})$.

The *minimum* of a function refers to the point $\mathbf{x}^*$ such that $f(\mathbf{x}^*)$ takes the minimum value.[1] It is denoted as $\arg\min_{\mathbf{x} \in S} f(\mathbf{x})$ symbolically.[2]

A function $f(\mathbf{x})$ is *bounded below* on a set S if there exists a real number m such that $f(\mathbf{x}) \geq m$ for all $\mathbf{x}$ in S.

From the definition of the real numbers, we can prove that there always exists the infimum of a function if it is bounded below. On the other hand, there does not necessarily exist the minimum value of a function. If there exists the minimum value of a function, it coincides with its infimum.

For instance, consider the function $f(x) = x^2$ on the close interval $[0, 1]$. On this interval, -1 is a lower bound of $f(x)$ and 0 is another lower bound of $f(x)$. The infimum of $f(x)$ on $[0, 1]$ is 0 and the minimum value of $f(x)$ on $[0, 1]$ is also 0, thus in this case, they coincide. However, if we consider the same function on the open interval $(0, 1)$, then the infimum is 0, but the lower bound is not attained, as

---

[1] More specifically, these points are called the *local* or *global minimum*, depending on whether they are the lowest points in their respective neighborhoods or in the entire domain of the function. The plural of "minimum" is "*minima*."

[2] If there are two or more minima, it represents one of them.

$f(x)$ can get arbitrarily close to 0 but never actually reaches it for $x > 0$. Thus, we have no minimum value of $f(x)$.

We can similarly define the concepts of upper bound, supremum, maximum value, maximum, and bounded above for a function by considering the opposite order.

A *upper bound* of a function f on a set S is a real value U such that $f(\mathbf{x}) \leq U$ for all $\mathbf{x}$ in S.

The *supremum* of a function f on a set S is the least upper bound of the function on that set. Symbolically, it is denoted as $\sup_{\mathbf{x} \in S} f(\mathbf{x})$. In essence, it is the greatest value that the function approaches within the set, but it does not necessarily have to attain this value.

The *maximum value* of a function is the supremum that the function actually takes on within the set S. Symbolically, it is denoted as $\max_{\mathbf{x} \in S} f(\mathbf{x})$.

The *maximum* of a function refers to the point $\mathbf{x}^*$ such that $f(\mathbf{x}^*)$ takes the maximum value.[3] It is denoted as $\arg\max_{\mathbf{x} \in S} f(\mathbf{x})$ symbolically.[4]

A function $f(\mathbf{x})$ is *bounded above* on a set S if there exists a real number m such that $f(\mathbf{x}) \leq m$ for all $\mathbf{x}$ in S.

There always exists the supremum of a function if it is bounded above. On the other hand, there does not necessarily exist the maximum value of a function. If there exists the maximum value of a function, it coincides with its supremum.

A set C is *convex* if the line segment between any two points in C lies in C, i.e., if for any $x_1, x_2 \in C$ and any θ with $0 \leq \theta \leq 1$, we have

$$\theta x_1 + (1 - \theta) x_2 \in C.$$

In other words, a set is convex if it contains the line segment connecting any two of its points. We can simply prove that the intersection of two convex sets is also convex.

Let the domain of a function $f : \mathbf{R}^n \to \mathbf{R}$ be convex. The function f is convex if, for any two points within its domain (convex), the line segment connecting those points lies above or on the graph of the function. That is, f is *convex* if the domain of f is a convex set and if all $\mathbf{x}, \mathbf{y}$ in the domain of f, and θ with $0 \leq \theta \leq 1$, we have

$$f(\theta \mathbf{x} + (1 - \theta) \mathbf{y}) \leq \theta f(\mathbf{x}) + (1 - \theta) f(\mathbf{y}).$$

In other words, a function is convex if its graph does not lie above the chord connecting any two points within its domain. For example, constant functions and the function x^2 are convex over their entire domains, while the functions $x \ln x$ and $-\ln x$ are convex for $x > 0$. Also, f is *strictly convex* if the domain of f is a convex set and if all $\mathbf{x}, \mathbf{y}$ in the domain of f, and θ with $0 \leq \theta \leq 1$, we have

---

[3] More specifically, these points are called the *local* or *global maximum*, depending on whether they are the heighest points in their respective neighborhoods or in the entire domain of the function. The plural of "maximum" is "*maxima*."

[4] If there are two or more maxima, it represents one of them.

Appendix A: Basic Terminology of Optimization Problems

$$f(\theta \mathbf{x} + (1-\theta)\mathbf{y}) < \theta f(\mathbf{x}) + (1-\theta) f(\mathbf{y}).$$

Assume that a function f is twice differentiable. Then it is strictly convex if its second derivative is strictly positive: $f''(x) > 0$ over its entire domain. For example, the function $-\ln x$ is strictly convex for $x > 0$.

By contrast a function is concave if, for any two points within its domain, the line segment connecting those points lies below or on the graph of the function. That is, f is *concave* if the domain of f is a convex set and if all $\mathbf{x}, \mathbf{y}$ in the domain of f, and θ with $0 \leq \theta \leq 1$, we have

$$f(\theta \mathbf{x} + (1-\theta)\mathbf{y}) \geq \theta f(\mathbf{x}) + (1-\theta) f(\mathbf{y}).$$

Also, f is *strictly concave* if the domain of f is a convex set and if all $\mathbf{x}, \mathbf{y}$ in the domain of f, and θ with $0 \leq \theta \leq 1$, we have

$$f(\theta \mathbf{x} + (1-\theta)\mathbf{y}) > \theta f(\mathbf{x}) + (1-\theta) f(\mathbf{y}).$$

Appendix B
Kullback-Leibler Divergence

In this appendix, we will discuss the Kullback-Leibler divergence, which measures the "distance" between two distributions. To demonstrate the positivity of the Kullback-Leibler divergence, we will first introduce Jensen's inequality, which is highly useful and powerful.

B.1 Jensen's Inequality

The function f is *convex*[5] if, for any two points within its domain (convex), the line segment connecting those points lies above or on the graph of the function. For example, constant functions and the function x^2 are convex over their entire domains, while the functions $x \ln x$ and $-\ln x$ are convex for $x > 0$.

Let a function $f(\mathbf{x})$ be convex. Then, for any $M \geq 2$ and any $0 \leq \lambda_i \leq 1$, $i = 1, \ldots, M$, where $\lambda_1 + \cdots + \lambda_M = 1$, the following inequality

$$f\left(\sum_{i=1}^{M} \lambda_i \mathbf{x}_i\right) \leq \sum_{i=1}^{M} \lambda_i f(\mathbf{x}_i) \tag{B.1.1}$$

holds. We can show this inequality using mathematical induction. For the base case of mathematical induction, $M = 2$, this equation is the very definition of a convex function. Assume the inequality holds for $M = k$. For $\lambda_i \geq 0$ such that $\sum_{i=1}^{k+1} \lambda_i = 1$, let $\Lambda_k = \sum_{j=1}^{k} \lambda_j$, then

---

[5] For the precise definition of a convex function, see Appendix A.

$$\sum_{i=1}^{k+1} \lambda_i f(\mathbf{x}_i) = \sum_{i=1}^{k} \lambda_i f(\mathbf{x}_i) + \lambda_{k+1} f(\mathbf{x}_{k+1})$$

$$= \Lambda_k \sum_{i=1}^{k} \frac{\lambda_i}{\Lambda_k} f(\mathbf{x}_i) + \lambda_{k+1} f(\mathbf{x}_{k+1})$$

$$\geq \Lambda_k f \left(\sum_{i=1}^{k} \frac{\lambda_i}{\Lambda_k} \mathbf{x}_i \right) + \lambda_{k+1} f(\mathbf{x}_{k+1})$$

$$\geq f \left(\sum_{i=1}^{k+1} \lambda_i \mathbf{x}_i \right).$$

The first inequality holds because $\sum_{i=1}^{k} \frac{\lambda_i}{\Lambda_k} = 1$ allows the use of the induction hypothesis. The second inequality follows from $\Lambda_k + \lambda_{k+1} = \left(\sum_{i=1}^{k} \lambda_i \right) + \lambda_{k+1} = 1$ and the convexity of $f(\mathbf{x})$. This completes the proof.

Since λ_i satisfies $0 \leq \lambda_i \leq 1$ and $\lambda_1 + \cdots + \lambda_M = 1$, λ_i can be interpreted as the probability distribution of a discrete random variable $\mathbf{x}$ over the set $\{\mathbf{x}_1, \ldots, \mathbf{x}_M\}$ when each $\mathbf{x}_i$ is fixed at some value. Under this interpretation, Eq. (B.1.1) can be expressed as

$$f(\mathbb{E}[\mathbf{x}]) \leq \mathbb{E}[f(\mathbf{x})]. \tag{B.1.2}$$

It can also be shown that equation (B.1.2) holds for continuous random variables $\mathbf{x}$, and using the definition of expectation with integrals, we can write

$$f \left(\int \mathbf{x} p(\mathbf{x}) \, d\mathbf{x} \right) \leq \int f(\mathbf{x}) p(\mathbf{x}) d\mathbf{x}. \tag{B.1.3}$$

Inequalities (B.1.1), (B.1.2), and (B.1.3) are collectively referred to as *Jensen's inequality*.

B.2 Kullback-Leibler Divergence

Consider a coin with the probability of getting heads being $p = 0.5$. Naturally, the probability of getting tails is also $1 - p = 0.5$. Suppose that, by some method, the probability of getting heads is estimated to be $q_1 = 0.4$ and the probability of getting tails is estimated to be $1 - q_1 = 0.6$. Additionally, by another method, the probability of getting heads is estimated to be $q_2 = 0.3$ and the probability of getting tails is estimated to be $1 - q_2 = 0.7$. Clearly, the first estimation result is closer to the true probability p of getting heads. In such cases, as a measure of closeness

Appendix B: Kullback-Leibler Divergence

between two Bernoulli distributions where the probability of taking 1 is p and q, one might consider using squared error $(p - q)^2 + ((1 - p) - (1 - q))^2$ or absolute error $|p - q| + |(1 - p) - (1 - q)|$. As a measure of this closeness, we consider here the expected value of the difference in logarithms, namely,

$$p \cdot (\ln p - \ln q) + (1 - p) \cdot (\ln(1 - p) - \ln(1 - q)).$$

In general, the *Kullback-Leibler divergence* (abbreviated as *KL divergence*) between two probability distributions p and q is defined for discrete distributions as

$$\mathbb{KL}(p \| q) \equiv \sum_i p_i \cdot (\ln p_i - \ln q_i) = \sum_i p_i \cdot \ln\left(\frac{p_i}{q_i}\right) \quad (B.2.1)$$

and for continuous distributions as

$$\mathbb{KL}(p \| q) \equiv \int p(\mathbf{x}) \cdot (\ln p(\mathbf{x}) - \ln q(\mathbf{x}))\, d\mathbf{x} = \int p(\mathbf{x}) \cdot \ln\left(\frac{p(\mathbf{x})}{q(\mathbf{x})}\right) d\mathbf{x}. \quad (B.2.2)$$

The KL divergence is also known as *relative entropy*.

KL divergence is not a distance in the mathematical sense[6] but is often used as a measure of closeness between distributions. The reason why KL divergence is valid as a measure of closeness lies in its important properties:

(a) $\mathbb{KL}(p \| q) \geq 0$ (non-negativity), and
(b) equality, $\mathbb{KL}(p \| q) = 0$, holds if and only if $p(\mathbf{x}) = q(\mathbf{x})$ holds (identity).

Using Jensen's inequality, we can prove the non-negativity of KL divergence as follows. Let the function $h(x)$ be convex. Applying Jensen's inequality (B.1.2) to the composite function $h(g(\mathbf{x}))$ yields

$$h\left(\mathbb{E}[g(\mathbf{x})]\right) \leq \mathbb{E}[h(g(\mathbf{x}))].$$

Since the function $-\ln x$ is convex, letting $h(x) = -\ln x$ and $g(\mathbf{x}) = \frac{q(\mathbf{x})}{p(\mathbf{x})}$, and using the above inequality, we obtain

$$\mathbb{KL}(p \| q) = \int p(\mathbf{x}) \ln\left(\frac{p(\mathbf{x})}{q(\mathbf{x})}\right) d\mathbf{x} = \int p(\mathbf{x}) \cdot \left(-\ln\left(\frac{q(\mathbf{x})}{p(\mathbf{x})}\right)\right) d\mathbf{x}$$

$$\geq -\ln \int p(\mathbf{x}) \frac{q(\mathbf{x})}{p(\mathbf{x})} d\mathbf{x} = -\ln \int q(\mathbf{x})\, d\mathbf{x} = -\ln 1 = 0.$$

---

[6] A real-valued function of two variables $d(x, y) \geq 0$ on a non-empty set X is a *distance* on X if it satisfies: (1) identity: for any $x, y \in X$, if $d(x, y) = 0$ then $x = y$, and conversely if $x = y$ then $d(x, y) = 0$, (2) symmetry: for any $x, y \in X$, $d(x, y) = d(y, x)$, (3) triangle inequality: for any $x, y, z \in X$, $d(x, z) \leq d(x, y) + d(y, z)$. KL divergence $\mathbb{KL}(p \| q)$ satisfies (1) but is not symmetric with respect to p and q, and does not satisfy the triangle inequality.

Here, the second-to-last equality uses the fact that $q(\mathbf{x})$ is a distribution. This demonstrates that the KL divergence is non-negative.

However, while the above proof of non-negativity serves as a typical application of Jensen's inequality, this approach cannot establish the identity property. To show the identity property of the KL divergence, namely that $\mathbb{KL}(p \parallel q) = 0$ if and only if $p(\mathbf{x}) = q(\mathbf{x})$, we need a different approach.

First, consider the function $f(z) = z - 1 - \ln z$ $(z > 0)$. We will show that $f(z) \geq 0$, and equality holds if and only if $z = 1$. Differentiating the function $f(z) = z - 1 - \ln z$ $(z > 0)$, we obtain

$$f'(z) = 1 - \frac{1}{z} \begin{cases} < 0, & 0 < z < 1, \\ = 0, & z = 1, \\ > 0, & z > 1. \end{cases}$$

Furthermore, finding the second derivative of $f(z)$, we obtain

$$f''(z) = \frac{1}{z^2} > 0.$$

Hence, $f(z)$ is strictly convex for $z > 0$, and it is strictly decreasing for $0 < z < 1$ with $f(z) > 0$, attaining its minimum value of 0 at $z = 1$, and it is strictly increasing for $z > 1$ with $f(z) > 0$. In other words, $f(z) \geq 0$, and equality holds if and only if $z = 1$.

Next, assume that the two distributions $p(\mathbf{x})$ and $q(\mathbf{x})$ are positive and continuous over the domain of interest. Let $z = \dfrac{q(\mathbf{x})}{p(\mathbf{x})}$ and substitute this into $f(z)$. Then, we obtain

$$\frac{q(\mathbf{x})}{p(\mathbf{x})} - 1 - \ln \frac{q(\mathbf{x})}{p(\mathbf{x})} \geq 0.$$

Multiplying this equation by $p(\mathbf{x})$ leads us to

$$q(\mathbf{x}) - p(\mathbf{x}) - p(\mathbf{x}) \cdot \ln \frac{q(\mathbf{x})}{p(\mathbf{x})} \geq 0. \tag{B.2.3}$$

Integrating this equation over $\mathbf{x}$, and noting that $p(\mathbf{x})$ and $q(\mathbf{x})$ are distributions, hence $\int p(\mathbf{x}) \, d\mathbf{x} = \int q(\mathbf{x}) \, d\mathbf{x} = 1$, we obtain

$$- \int p(\mathbf{x}) \ln \frac{q(\mathbf{x})}{p(\mathbf{x})} \, d\mathbf{x} \geq 0.$$

The left-hand side of this is $\mathbb{KL}(p \parallel q)$; thus, again, we have shown that $\mathbb{KL}(p \parallel q) \geq 0$.

Moreover, if $p(\mathbf{x}) = q(\mathbf{x})$ over the entire domain, it is clear that $\mathbb{KL}(p \parallel q) = 0$. Now, suppose there exists some $\mathbf{x}$ within the domain where $p(\mathbf{x}) \neq q(\mathbf{x})$. Then,

Appendix B: Kullback-Leibler Divergence

at that point, the left-hand side of equation (B.2.3) is positive (not zero). Since $p(\mathbf{x})$ and $q(\mathbf{x})$ are continuous by assumption, the left-hand side is also continuous. Therefore, the integral of this term is positive. Hence, $\mathbb{KL}(p \parallel q) = 0$ holds if and only if $p(\mathbf{x}) = q(\mathbf{x})$ holds over the entire domain.

Appendix C
Sampling from Gaussian Distributions

C.1 Linear Congruential Method: Sampling from a Uniform Distribution

For a positive integer M, the *linear congruential method* is a simple way to generate uniformly distributed random numbers between 0 and M. It involves choosing constants $a > 0$ and $c \geq 0$ ($M > a$), setting an initial value X_0, and then generating the sequence $X_1, X_2, \ldots$ according to the recurrence relation:

$$X_{n+1} = aX_n + c \pmod{M}, \quad n \geq 1,$$

where $X \bmod M$ represents the remainder when X is divided by M. For example, if $X_0 = 2$, $a = 3$, $c = 2$, and $M = 7$, then we have

$$\begin{aligned} X_1 &= aX_0 + c \pmod{M} \\ &= 3 \times 2 + 2 \pmod 7 \\ &= 8 \pmod 7 \\ &= 1 \pmod 7. \end{aligned}$$

Similarly, $X_2 = 5$, $X_3 = 3$, $X_4 = 4$, and so on. If M is taken to be a large number, dividing the sequence obtained by adding a small number to the generated sequence by M yields uniformly distributed random numbers in the interval $(0, 1)$.

Fig. C.1 In the Marsaglia method, two samples z_1 and z_2 are first generated from a uniform distribution on $(-1, 1)$, and only those within the unit circle are accepted

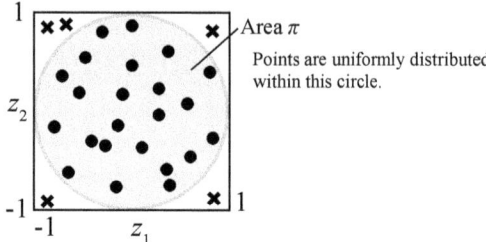

C.2 Marsaglia Method: Sampling from the Standard Gaussian Distribution

The *Marsaglia method* is a technique for generating random numbers following the standard Gaussian distribution (a Gaussian distribution with mean 0 and variance 1) (see Fig. C.1). The procedure is as follows.

1. Generate a pair of random numbers z'_1 and z'_2 following the (0, 1) uniform distribution.
2. Transform the variables by $z_i = 2z'_i - 1$, for $i = 1, 2$. This ensures $z_1, z_2 \in (-1, 1)$.
3. If $z_1^2 + z_2^2 > 1$, go back to step 1.
4. Compute the following to obtain two samples, y_1 and y_2:

$$r^2 = z_1^2 + z_2^2,$$

$$y_1 = z_1 \cdot \left(\frac{-2 \ln r^2}{r^2}\right)^{\frac{1}{2}}, \quad y_2 = z_2 \cdot \left(\frac{-2 \ln r^2}{r^2}\right)^{\frac{1}{2}}.$$

Steps 1 to 3 generate random numbers following the distribution $p(z_1, z_2) = 1/\pi$. Note that the probability of falling outside the circle in step 3 is 21.5%.

We can sample from a multivariate Gaussian distribution with mean $\boldsymbol{\mu}$ and covariance $\boldsymbol{\Sigma}$ as follows.

1. Perform Cholesky decomposition[7] on the covariance matrix $\boldsymbol{\Sigma}$ to obtain $\boldsymbol{\Sigma} = \mathbf{L}\mathbf{L}^T$, where $\mathbf{L}$ is a lower triangular matrix.
2. Generate a vector $\mathbf{z} = (z_1 \cdots z_D)^T$, where each component z_i follows an independent standard Gaussian distribution.
3. Sample each component of $\mathbf{z}$ using the Marsaglia method and then transform it to $\mathbf{y} = \boldsymbol{\mu} + \mathbf{L}\mathbf{z}$.

The resulting vector $\mathbf{y}$ will be the desired random sample. This is because

---

[7] Any positive definite symmetric matrix $\mathbf{A}$ can be decomposed into the product of a lower triangular matrix $\mathbf{L}$ with all positive diagonal elements (where all elements above the diagonal are zero) and its transpose $\mathbf{L}^T$: $\mathbf{A} = \mathbf{L}\mathbf{L}^T$. The proof is provided in most textbooks on linear algebra.

Appendix C: Sampling from Gaussian Distributions

$$\mathbb{E}[\mathbf{y}] = \mathbb{E}[\boldsymbol{\mu} + \mathbf{L}\mathbf{z}] = \boldsymbol{\mu} + \mathbf{0} = \boldsymbol{\mu},$$
$$\begin{aligned}
\mathrm{cov}[\mathbf{y}] &= \mathbb{E}[\mathbf{y}\mathbf{y}^\mathsf{T}] - \mathbb{E}[\mathbf{y}]\mathbb{E}[\mathbf{y}^\mathsf{T}] \\
&= \mathbb{E}[(\boldsymbol{\mu} + \mathbf{L}\mathbf{z})(\boldsymbol{\mu} + \mathbf{L}\mathbf{z})^\mathsf{T}] - \boldsymbol{\mu}\boldsymbol{\mu}^\mathsf{T} \\
&= \mathbb{E}[\boldsymbol{\mu}\boldsymbol{\mu}^\mathsf{T}] + \mathbb{E}[2\mathbf{L}\mathbf{z}\boldsymbol{\mu}^\mathsf{T}] + \mathbb{E}[\mathbf{L}\mathbf{z}\mathbf{z}^\mathsf{T}\mathbf{L}^\mathsf{T}] - \boldsymbol{\mu}\boldsymbol{\mu}^\mathsf{T} \\
&= \boldsymbol{\mu}\boldsymbol{\mu}^\mathsf{T} + 2\mathbf{L}\mathbb{E}[\mathbf{z}]\boldsymbol{\mu}^\mathsf{T} + \mathbf{L}\mathbb{E}[\mathbf{z}\mathbf{z}^\mathsf{T}]\mathbf{L}^\mathsf{T} - \boldsymbol{\mu}\boldsymbol{\mu}^\mathsf{T} \\
&= \mathbf{L}\mathbf{L}^\mathsf{T} = \boldsymbol{\Sigma}.
\end{aligned}$$

In the above, the fourth equality uses the fact that $\mathbb{E}[\mathbf{z}\mathbf{z}^\mathsf{T}] = \mathbf{I}$ because $\mathbf{z}$ follows a standard Gaussian distribution.

C.3 Verification of the Marsaglia Method

We verify that the random numbers y_1 and y_2 generated by the Marsaglia method independently follow the standard Gaussian distribution. First, we convert the variables z_1 and z_2 to polar coordinates r and θ:

$$z_1 = r\cos\theta, \quad z_2 = r\sin\theta \qquad (r^2 = z_1^2 + z_2^2).$$

Then, we further transform r and θ to y_1 and y_2:

$$y_1 = z_1 \cdot \left(\frac{-2\ln r^2}{r^2}\right)^{\frac{1}{2}} = \left(-2\ln r^2\right)^{\frac{1}{2}} \cos\theta,$$

$$y_2 = z_2 \cdot \left(\frac{-2\ln r^2}{r^2}\right)^{\frac{1}{2}} = \left(-2\ln r^2\right)^{\frac{1}{2}} \sin\theta,$$

where we derive an expression needed for the calculation of the Jacobian determinant by squaring and summing the above two equations:

$$y_1^2 + y_2^2 = \left(-2\ln r^2\right)\cos^2\theta + \left(-2\ln r^2\right)\sin^2\theta = -2\ln r^2.$$

From this, we obtain

$$r^2 = \exp\left(-\frac{y_1^2 + y_2^2}{2}\right), \tag{C.3.1}$$

as the relationship between r^2 and $y_1^2 + y_2^2$.

We calculate the Jacobian determinant. First, we have

$$\left|\frac{\partial(z_1, z_2)}{\partial(r, \theta)}\right| = \left|\begin{matrix} \cos\theta & -r\sin\theta \\ \sin\theta & r\cos\theta \end{matrix}\right| = r\cos^2\theta - (-r\sin^2\theta) = r.$$

Furthermore, we obtain

$$\left|\frac{\partial(y_1, y_2)}{\partial(r, \theta)}\right| = \left|\begin{matrix} -2(-2\ln r^2)^{-1/2} r^{-1} \cos\theta & -(-2\ln r^2)^{1/2} \sin\theta \\ -2(-2\ln r^2)^{-1/2} r^{-1} \sin\theta & (-2\ln r^2)^{1/2} \cos\theta \end{matrix}\right|$$

$$= -2r^{-1}\cos^2\theta - 2r^{-1}\sin^2\theta = -\frac{2}{r}.$$

From these, we have

$$\left|\frac{\partial(z_1, z_2)}{\partial(y_1, y_2)}\right| = \left|\frac{\partial(z_1, z_2)}{\partial(r, \theta)}\right| \left|\frac{\partial(y_1, y_2)}{\partial(r, \theta)}\right|^{-1} = -\frac{r^2}{2} = -\frac{1}{2}\exp\left(-\frac{1}{2}(y_1^2 + y_2^2)\right).$$

Substituting this into the formula for the transformation of probability variables, we obtain

$$p(y_1, y_2) = p(z_1, z_2) \left\|\frac{\partial(z_1, z_2)}{\partial(y_1, y_2)}\right\| = \frac{1}{\pi} \left|-\frac{1}{2}\exp\left(-\frac{1}{2}(y_1^2 + y_2^2)\right)\right|$$

$$= \frac{1}{\pi}\frac{1}{2}\exp\left(-\frac{1}{2}(y_1^2 + y_2^2)\right)$$

$$= \left[\frac{1}{\sqrt{2\pi}}\exp\left(-\frac{y_1^2}{2}\right)\right]\left[\frac{1}{\sqrt{2\pi}}\exp\left(-\frac{y_2^2}{2}\right)\right].$$

Thus, the validity of the Marsaglia method is demonstrated.

Appendix D
Enlargement of Image Size

This appendix explains two representative methods for enlarging image size: upsampling and transposed convolution.

Upsampling is an enlargement method where the pixel values x_{ij} of the image are arranged at intervals of r pixels, and the pixel values between them are interpolated (see Fig. D.1). The interpolation method is, however, not unique, and we have no guarantee that the interpolation method used is optimal for the data.

Transposed convolution is a method of enlarging the size of an image by applying the transpose of the matrix $\mathbf{W}_h$, which represents convolution (see Fig. D.2a), to the image. Here, $\mathbf{W}_h$ is the matrix representation of convolution performed using matrix operations (see Fig. D.2b).

Since transposed convolution is a simple linear operation, we can implement it in neural networks. Furthermore, the elements of the matrix can be determined from the data through training, ensuring optimality. We now describe a detailed explanation of transposed convolution using an example.

First, we review convolution on images and introduce the matrix representation of convolution using image filters. Convolution of a $W \times W$ image $\mathbf{X} = (x_{ij})$ with a $H \times H$ filter $\mathbf{H} = (h_{pq})$ is expressed as

$$u_{ij} = \sum_{p=0}^{H-1} \sum_{q=0}^{H-1} x_{i+p, j+q} h_{pq}, \quad i, j = 0, \ldots, W-1.$$

Figure D.3 shows an example of convolving a 4×4 image with a 3×3 filter, resulting in a 2×2 image. In this convolution, the (1, 1) element of the resulting image is obtained by overlaying the top-left 3×3 portion of the image with the filter, taking the element-wise product, and summing them up. Similarly, the (1, 2) element corresponds to the computation involving the top-right 3×3 portion of the image, the (2, 1) element involves the bottom-left 3×3 portion, and the (2, 2) element involves the bottom-right 3×3 portion (Fig. D.4). In the following, albeit confusing, we also refer convolutional operations as convolutions of the results (images).

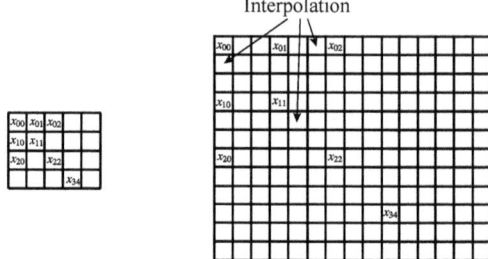

Fig. D.1 Upsampling

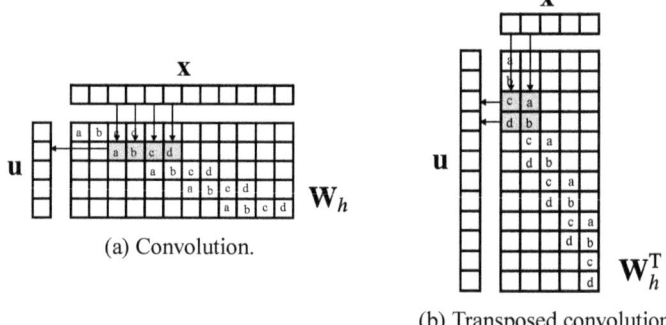

Fig. D.2 Illustration of convolution and transposed convolution represented by matrix-vector multiplication

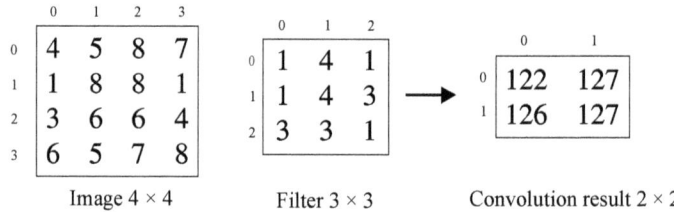

Fig. D.3 Example of convolution with an image filter

We express convolution with image filters in matrix form. First, we represent the image to be convolved as a vector (Fig. D.5). Specifically, we stack the rows of the image vertically to form a 16-dimensional vector (referred to as the image vector), concatenating each row successively. In this image vector, for example, the corresponding elements to the top-left 3×3 sub-image are the 1st, 2nd, 3rd, 5th, 6th, 7th, 9th, 10th, and 11th elements; elements 4th, 8th, 12th, 13th, 14th, 15th, and 16th are irrelevant (Note that the indices written outside the vector (and matrix) start from 0 and differ from the indices representing the elements of the vector (matrix), which start from 1).

Appendix D: Enlargement of Image Size

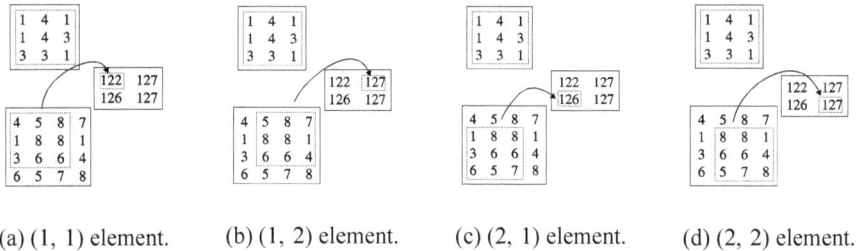

(a) (1, 1) element. (b) (1, 2) element. (c) (2, 1) element. (d) (2, 2) element.

Fig. D.4 Detailed computation of convolution with image filter

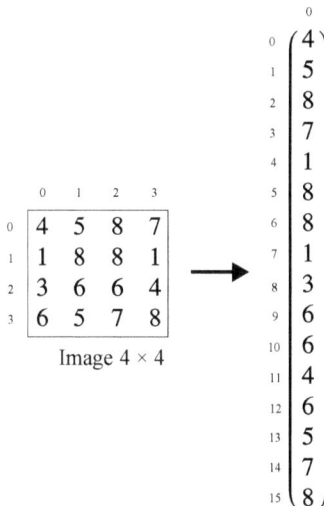

Vector representation of image 16 × 1

Fig. D.5 Representation of the image as a vector

Next, we construct the convolution matrix from the filter (Fig. D.6). The convolution matrix and the image vector will result in the convolution operation. That is, the dimension of the row vector of the convolution matrix is the same as that of the image vector, and the dimension of the column vector corresponds to the number of elements in the resulting convolution. The product of each row of the convolution matrix with the image vector corresponds to the elements of the convolution result: the first row with the image vector yields the (1, 1) element of the convolution, the second row yields the (1, 2) element, the third row yields the (2, 1) element, and the fourth row yields the (2, 2) element.

We construct the convolution matrix so that the convolution operation becomes the product of the convolution matrix and the image vector. Specifically, we obtain each element of the convolution, such as the (1, 1) element, by summing the products of the components of the first row of the convolution matrix and the corresponding

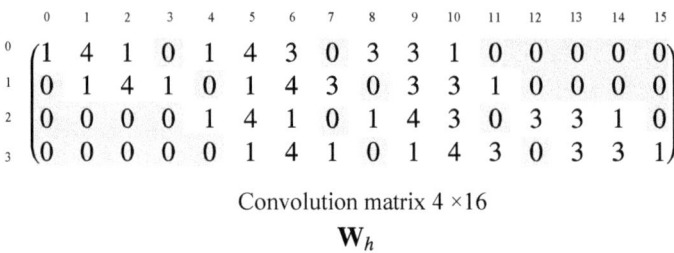

Convolution matrix 4 ×16

$\mathbf{W}_h$

Fig. D.6 Convolution matrix: matrix representation of the filter

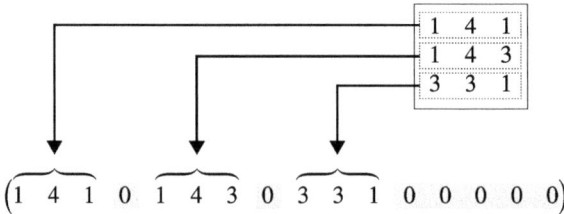

Fig. D.7 Construction of the convolution matrix. This figure illustrates the construction of the first row of the convolution matrix from the filter, where zeros are inserted in the positions corresponding to irrelevant parts of the image in the top-left 3 × 3 area

components of the image vector corresponding to the top-left 3 × 3 part of the image. We construct the convolution matrix by arranging the components of the filter's first, second, and third rows and placing zeros in the positions corresponding to irrelevant parts of the 3 × 3 area (Fig. D.7). Similarly, for the (1, 2) element of the convolution, we arrange the components of the filter's first, second, and third rows to sum with the corresponding components of the image vector corresponding to the top-right 3 × 3 part of the image, with zeros placed in the positions corresponding to irrelevant parts. We repeat this process for the third and fourth rows of the convolution matrix.

Figure D.8 illustrates the convolution operation using the image vector and the convolution matrix. Figures D.9 and D.10 show, respectively, the first and third components of the convolution operation, as well as the partial vectors (corresponding to parts of the convolution matrix and the image vector) involved in the dot product calculation. In the example, the image vector being convolved is 16-dimensional, and the convolution matrix is of size 4 × 16, resulting in a convolution of 4 dimensions after multiplying the image vector.

Appendix D: Enlargement of Image Size

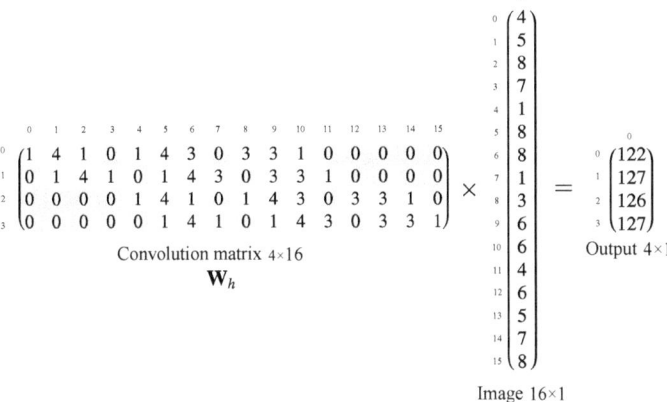

Fig. D.8 Matrix representation of convolution operation

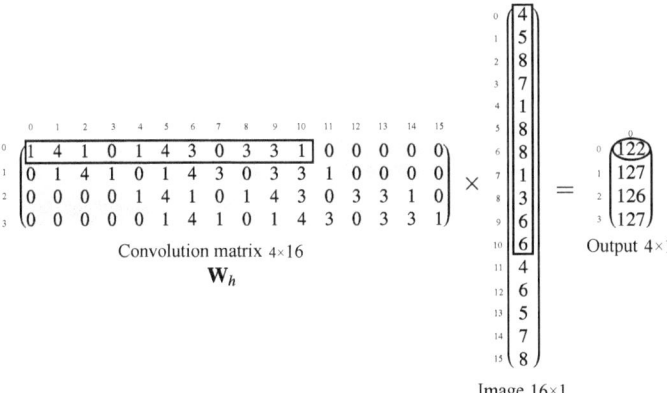

Fig. D.9 First component of convolution operation and the corresponding partial vector involved in the dot product calculation (part of the convolution matrix and the image vector)

Finally, we introduce transpose convolution, which aims to "reconstruct" the original-sized image from the convolved image (see Fig. D.11). Here, "reconstruct" is used because the resulting image may not be identical to the original (convolved) image. The transpose convolution operation enlarges the image by applying the transpose of the convolution matrix to the target (enlarged) image vector (see Fig. D.12). Since the resulting "image" is represented as a vector, it needs to be reshaped into

$$\underbrace{\begin{pmatrix} 1 & 4 & 1 & 0 & 1 & 4 & 3 & 0 & 3 & 3 & 1 & 0 & 0 & 0 & 0 & 0 \\ 0 & 1 & 4 & 1 & 0 & 1 & 4 & 3 & 0 & 3 & 3 & 1 & 0 & 0 & 0 & 0 \\ 0 & 0 & 0 & 0 & \boxed{1} & 4 & 1 & 0 & 1 & 4 & 3 & 0 & 3 & 3 & \boxed{1} & 0 \\ 0 & 0 & 0 & 0 & 0 & 1 & 4 & 1 & 0 & 1 & 4 & 3 & 0 & 3 & 3 & 1 \end{pmatrix}}_{\text{Convolution matrix } 4\times 16,\ \mathbf{W}_h} \times \underbrace{\begin{pmatrix} 4 \\ 5 \\ 8 \\ 7 \\ 1 \\ 8 \\ 8 \\ 1 \\ 3 \\ 6 \\ 6 \\ 4 \\ 6 \\ 5 \\ 7 \\ 8 \end{pmatrix}}_{\text{Image } 16\times 1} = \underbrace{\begin{pmatrix} 122 \\ 127 \\ \textcircled{126} \\ 127 \end{pmatrix}}_{\text{Output } 4\times 1}$$

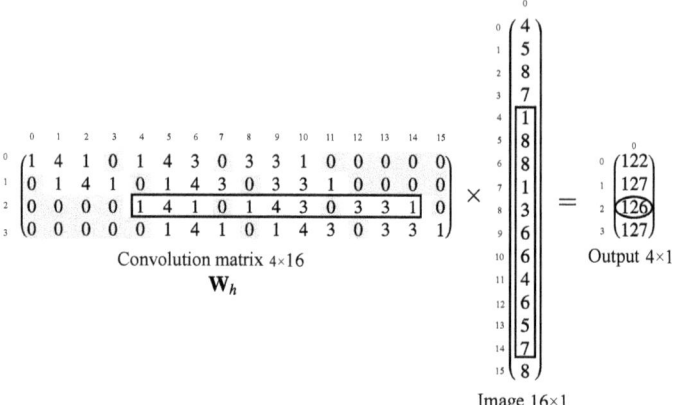

Fig. D.10 Third component of convolution operation and the corresponding partial vector involved in the dot product calculation (part of the convolution matrix and the image vector)

(a) (1, 1) element. (b) (1, 2) element. (c) (2, 1) element. (d) (2, 2) element.

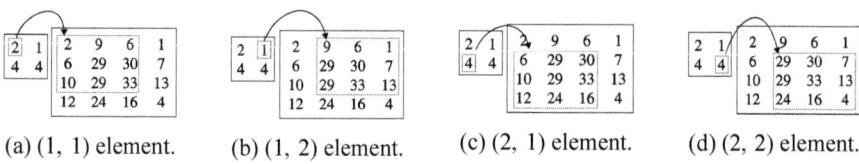

Fig. D.11 Illustration of transpose convolution. Enlargement of the image using the inverse operation of convolution

Fig. D.12 Matrix representation of transpose convolution

$$\underbrace{\begin{pmatrix} 1 & 0 & 0 & 0 \\ 4 & 1 & 0 & 0 \\ 1 & 4 & 0 & 0 \\ 0 & 1 & 0 & 0 \\ 1 & 0 & 1 & 0 \\ 4 & 1 & 4 & 1 \\ 3 & 4 & 1 & 4 \\ 0 & 3 & 0 & 1 \\ 3 & 0 & 1 & 0 \\ 3 & 3 & 4 & 1 \\ 1 & 3 & 3 & 4 \\ 0 & 1 & 0 & 3 \\ 0 & 0 & 3 & 0 \\ 0 & 0 & 3 & 3 \\ 0 & 0 & 1 & 3 \\ 0 & 0 & 0 & 1 \end{pmatrix}}_{\text{Transposed convolution matrix } 16\times 4,\ \mathbf{W}_h^{\mathrm{T}}} \times \underbrace{\begin{pmatrix} 2 \\ 1 \\ 4 \\ 4 \end{pmatrix}}_{\text{Image } 4\times 1} = \underbrace{\begin{pmatrix} 2 \\ 9 \\ 6 \\ 1 \\ 6 \\ 29 \\ 30 \\ 7 \\ 10 \\ 29 \\ 33 \\ 13 \\ 12 \\ 24 \\ 16 \\ 4 \end{pmatrix}}_{\text{Output } 16\times 1}$$

a 2D format to be viewed as a conventional image. In the previous examples, the transpose convolution matrix was 16×4, and multiplying it by a 4-dimensional image vector (representing a 2×2 image) results in a 16-dimensional image vector (representing a 4×4 image).

Appendix E
Strong Duality in Linear Programming

In this chapter, we define equality and inequality between two vectors based on their component-wise relations. For example, for $\mathbf{x} = (x_1 \ldots x_n)$ and $\mathbf{y} = (y_1 \ldots y_n)$, $\mathbf{x} \leq \mathbf{y}$ means $x_1 \leq y_1, \ldots, y_n \leq y_n$. For basic terms such as the infimum and supremum of a function, refer to Appendix A.

E.1 Primary Problem

Let D be a subset of $\mathbf{R}^n$, $D \subset \mathbf{R}^n$, and $f(\mathbf{x}), h_1(\mathbf{x}), \ldots, h_l(\mathbf{x})$, and $r_1(\mathbf{x}), \ldots, r_m(\mathbf{x})$ be functions on D. We use the following notation

$$\underset{\mathbf{x} \in D}{\text{minimize}}\ f(\mathbf{x}) \quad \text{subject to} \quad \begin{cases} h_i(\mathbf{x}) \leq 0, & i = 1, \ldots, l, \\ r_j(\mathbf{x}) = 0, & j = 1, \ldots, m \end{cases} \quad \text{(E.1.1)}$$

to describe the problem of finding an $\mathbf{x}$ that minimizes $f(\mathbf{x})$ among all $\mathbf{x}$ that satisfy the conditions $h_i(\mathbf{x}) \leq 0, i = 1, \ldots, l,$ and $r_j(\mathbf{x}) = 0, j = 1, \ldots, m$. We call the function $f(\mathbf{x})$ the *objective function*, and $h_i(\mathbf{x}) \leq 0, i = 1, \ldots, l,$ the *inequality constraints*, and $r_j(\mathbf{x}) = 0, j = 1, \ldots, m,$ the *equality constraints*. In the following, for simplicity, we write $h_i(\mathbf{x}) \leq 0$ and $r_j(\mathbf{x}) = 0$ instead of $h_1(\mathbf{x}) \leq 0, \ldots, h_l(\mathbf{x}) \leq 0$ and $r_1(\mathbf{x}) = 0, \ldots, r_m(\mathbf{x}) = 0$, respectively.

The set
$$F = \{\mathbf{x} \in D \mid h_i(\mathbf{x}) \leq 0,\ r_j(\mathbf{x}) = 0\}$$

is called the *feasible* set. If F is non-empty, the optimization problem is called *feasible*.

The value $\inf_{\mathbf{x} \in F} f(\mathbf{x})$, the infimum of $f(\mathbf{x})$ on F, is called the *optimal value* of the optimization problem (E.1.1). Also, the set of the *optimal solutions* or the *optimals* of the optimization problem (E.1.1) is

$$X^* = \{\mathbf{x} \in D \mid f(\mathbf{x}) = \inf_{\mathbf{y} \in D} f(\mathbf{y})\}$$
$$= \{\mathbf{x} \in F \mid f(\mathbf{x}) = \inf_{\mathbf{y} \in F} f(\mathbf{y})\}.$$

In other words, the set of the optimal solutions is that of the minima in the feasible set. Note that generally, we have multiple values of $\mathbf{x}$ at which a function $f(\mathbf{x})$ attains its minimum value.

In the following, we assume that there exists the optimal value for the optimization problem (E.1.1).

E.2 Dual Problem

For this optimization problem (referred to as the *primary problem*), we define the following function $g : \mathbf{R}^l \times \mathbf{R}^m \to [-\infty, \infty)$:

$$g(\boldsymbol{\lambda}, \boldsymbol{\nu}) = \inf_{\mathbf{x} \in D} L(\mathbf{x}, \boldsymbol{\lambda}, \boldsymbol{\nu}), \tag{E.2.1}$$

which is called the *Lagrangian dual function*. Here,

$$L(\mathbf{x}, \boldsymbol{\lambda}, \boldsymbol{\nu}) \equiv f(\mathbf{x}) + \sum_{i=1}^{l} \lambda_i h_i(\mathbf{x}) + \sum_{j=1}^{m} \nu_j r_j(\mathbf{x}) \tag{E.2.2}$$

is the *Lagrangian function*, where $\boldsymbol{\lambda} = (\lambda_1 \cdots \lambda_l)^{\mathrm{T}}$ and $\boldsymbol{\nu} = (\nu_1 \cdots \nu_m)^{\mathrm{T}}$. The variables λ_j and ν_j of the function g are called *Lagrange multipliers*.

For the primary problem (E.1.1), the following form of the optimization problem:

$$\text{maximize } g(\boldsymbol{\lambda}, \boldsymbol{\nu}) \quad \text{subject to } \boldsymbol{\lambda} \geq \mathbf{0} \tag{E.2.3}$$

is called the *dual problem*. Here, $\boldsymbol{\lambda} \geq \mathbf{0}$ means $\lambda_1 \geq 0, \ldots, \lambda_l \geq 0$.

Theorem 1 (Weak duality) *Let p^* be the optimal value of a primary problem (E.1.1). That is,*

$$p^* = \inf_{\mathbf{x} \in F_p} f(\mathbf{x}), \tag{E.2.4}$$

where $F_p = \{\mathbf{x} \in D \mid h_i(\mathbf{x}) \leq 0, r_j(\mathbf{x}) = 0\}$. Also, let d^* be that of its dual problem. That is,

$$d^* = \sup_{\boldsymbol{\lambda} \geq \mathbf{0},\, \boldsymbol{\nu} \in \mathbf{R}^m} g(\boldsymbol{\lambda}, \boldsymbol{\nu}). \tag{E.2.5}$$

Then, we have
$$d^* \leq p^*.$$

Appendix E: Strong Duality in Linear Programming

Proof Note first that F_p is the feasible set of the primary problem. Thus, for all $\boldsymbol{\lambda} \geq \mathbf{0}$, $\boldsymbol{v} \in \boldsymbol{R}^m$, $\mathbf{x} \in F_p$, we have

$$L(\mathbf{x}, \boldsymbol{\lambda}, \boldsymbol{v}) \equiv f(\mathbf{x}) + \sum_{i=1}^{l} \lambda_i h_i(\mathbf{x}) + \sum_{j=1}^{m} v_j r_j(\mathbf{x}) \leq f(\mathbf{x}).$$

This is because when $\mathbf{x} \in F_p$, if $\boldsymbol{\lambda} \geq \mathbf{0}$, $\sum_{i=1}^{l} \lambda_i h_i(\mathbf{x}) \leq 0$ and $\sum_{j=1}^{m} v_j r_j(\mathbf{x}) = 0$ hold. Hence, we obtain

$$\inf_{\mathbf{x} \in F_p} L(\mathbf{x}, \boldsymbol{\lambda}, \boldsymbol{v}) \leq \inf_{\mathbf{x} \in F_p} f(\mathbf{x}) = p^*.$$

Thus, for all $\boldsymbol{\lambda} \geq \mathbf{0}, \boldsymbol{v} \in \boldsymbol{R}^m$,

$$g(\boldsymbol{\lambda}, \boldsymbol{v}) = \inf_{\mathbf{x} \in D} L(\mathbf{x}, \boldsymbol{\lambda}, \boldsymbol{v}) \leq \inf_{\mathbf{x} \in F_p} L(\mathbf{x}, \boldsymbol{\lambda}, \boldsymbol{v}) \leq p^*$$

holds. This leads us to $d^* \leq p^*$. End of proof.

E.3 Convex Optimization Problem

A function is convex if, for any two points within its domain, the line segment connecting those points lies above or on the graph of the function. By contrast a function is concave if, for any two points within its domain, the line segment connecting those points lies below or on the graph of the function.[8]

In this context, the following theorem holds.

Theorem 2 *The Lagrangian dual function $g(\boldsymbol{\lambda}, \boldsymbol{v})$ is a concave function on $\boldsymbol{R}^l \times \boldsymbol{R}^m$.*

Proof The Lagrangian function $L(\mathbf{x}, \boldsymbol{\lambda}, \boldsymbol{v})$ is a linear function of $\boldsymbol{\lambda}$ and $\boldsymbol{v}$ for all $\mathbf{x} \in D$. In particular, it is linear even with respect to $\mathbf{x}$ that satisfies $\inf_{\mathbf{x} \in D} L$. Linear functions are concave, thus $g(\boldsymbol{\lambda}, \boldsymbol{v})$ is concave. End of proof.

A set is convex if, for any two points within the set, the line segment connecting those points lies entirely within the set.[9] We can simply prove that the intersection of two convex sets is also convex.

Now, let D be a convex set of $\boldsymbol{R}^n$, $f(\mathbf{x}), h_1(\mathbf{x}), \ldots, h_l(\mathbf{x})$ convex functions on D, and $r_j(\mathbf{x}) = \mathbf{a}_j^T \mathbf{x} + b_j$, $j = 1, \ldots, m$, where $\mathbf{a}_j$ and b_j are constant vectors. Then, the optimization problem:

---

[8] For the precise definition of a convex (concave) function, see Appendix A.
[9] For the precise definition of a convex set, see also Appendix A.

$$\underset{\mathbf{x}\in D}{\text{minimize}}\ f(\mathbf{x}) \text{ subject to } \begin{cases} h_i(\mathbf{x}) \leq 0, & i = 1, \ldots, l, \\ r_j(\mathbf{x}) = \mathbf{a}_j^T\mathbf{x} + b_j = 0, & j = 1, \ldots, m \end{cases} \qquad (\text{E.3.1})$$

is called the *convex optimization problem*. Also, if $f(\mathbf{x})$ is concave and $h_1(\mathbf{x}), \ldots, h_l(\mathbf{x})$ convex, the problem:

$$\underset{\mathbf{x}\in D}{\text{maximize}}\ f(\mathbf{x}) \text{ subject to } \begin{cases} h_i(\mathbf{x}) \leq 0, & i = 1, \ldots, l, \\ r_j(\mathbf{x}) = \mathbf{a}_j^T\mathbf{x} + b_j = 0, & j = 1, \ldots, m \end{cases} \qquad (\text{E.3.2})$$

is called the *concave optimization problem*.

From Theorem 2, we can see that a dual problem is always a concave optimization problem even if the corresponding primary problem is not a convex optimization problem (Note that $\boldsymbol{\lambda} \geq \mathbf{0}$ is equivalent to $-\boldsymbol{\lambda} \leq \mathbf{0}$ and $h(\boldsymbol{\lambda}) = -\boldsymbol{\lambda}$ is a convex function).

Theorem 3 *For a convex optimization problem (E.3.1)*,

1. *the feasible set F is convex, and*
2. *the set of the optimum solutions:*

$$X^* = \{\mathbf{x} \in F \mid f(\mathbf{x}) = \inf_{\mathbf{y}\in F} f(\mathbf{y})\}$$

is convex.

Proof 1. The sets $\{\mathbf{x} \in \mathbf{R}^n \mid h_i(\mathbf{x}) \leq 0\}$ are convex and the sets $\{\mathbf{x} \in \mathbf{R}^n \mid r_j(\mathbf{x}) = 0\}$ are convex. By assumption, D is also convex. Because the feasible set is the intersection of them, it is also convex.

2. If $X^* = \emptyset$, it is trivial. Assume $X^* \neq \emptyset$. Let $p^* = \inf_{\mathbf{x}\in F} f(\mathbf{x})$. Then, using p^*, we can rewrite the set of the solutions of the primary problem as follows:

$$X^* = \{\mathbf{x} \in D \mid f(\mathbf{x}) \leq p^*\} \cap F.$$

The sets of the right-hand side of this equation are convex, thus we obtain X^* is convex.
End of proof.

A property similar to Theorem 3 also holds for concave optimization problems. From Theorem 3(2), we can conclude that the convex (also concave) optimization problem does not have a local minimum, which is a solution that are optimal within a specific neighborhood or region of the solution space, but may not necessarily be the globally optimal solution.

Appendix E: Strong Duality in Linear Programming

E.4 Linear Programming

Consider the following primary problem:

$$\underset{\mathbf{x} \in R^n}{\text{minimize }} \mathbf{c}^T \mathbf{x} \quad \text{subject to} \quad \begin{cases} \mathbf{Ax} = \mathbf{b}, \\ \mathbf{x} \geq \mathbf{0}, \end{cases} \quad (E.4.1)$$

where $\mathbf{A}$ is an $m \times n$ matrix, $\mathbf{b}$ is an m-dimensional vector, and $\mathbf{c}$ is an n-dimensional vector. We call this primary problem as a *linear programming*. Note that in a linear programming, the objective function, the inequality constraints and the equality constraints are all linear. This linearity leads us to a conclusion that the linear programming is a convex optimization problem.

For the primal form of the linear programming (E.4.1), we have the following dual form:

$$\underset{\mathbf{y} \in R^m}{\text{maximize }} \mathbf{b}^T \mathbf{y} \quad \text{subject to} \quad \mathbf{A}^T \mathbf{y} \leq \mathbf{c}. \quad (E.4.2)$$

Let us derive the dual form (E.4.2) from the primal form (E.4.1). First, we construct the Lagrangian function from the primal form. It is

$$L(\mathbf{x}, \boldsymbol{\lambda}, \mathbf{y}) = \mathbf{c}^T \mathbf{x} + \boldsymbol{\lambda}^T(-\mathbf{x}) + \mathbf{y}^T(\mathbf{b} - \mathbf{Ax}),$$

where $\boldsymbol{\lambda} = (\lambda_1 \cdots \lambda_n)^T$ and $\mathbf{y} = (y_1 \cdots y_m)^T$ are the Lagrange multipliers. Rearranging the right-hand side of this equation, we have

$$L(\mathbf{x}, \boldsymbol{\lambda}, \mathbf{y}) = (\mathbf{c} - \boldsymbol{\lambda} - \mathbf{A}^T \mathbf{y})^T \mathbf{x} + \mathbf{b}^T \mathbf{y}.$$

If, for some i, i-th component of $\mathbf{c} - \boldsymbol{\lambda} - \mathbf{A}^T \mathbf{y}$ is less than 0, we have $\lim_{x_i \to \infty} L(\mathbf{x}, \boldsymbol{\lambda}, \mathbf{y}) = -\infty$. On the other hand, if $\mathbf{c} - \boldsymbol{\lambda} - \mathbf{A}^T \mathbf{y} \geq \mathbf{0}$ holds, we have the optimum solution $\mathbf{x}^* = \mathbf{0}$. Hence, we obtain the following Lagrangian dual function:

$$g(\mathbf{y}, \boldsymbol{\lambda}) = \underset{\mathbf{x} \in R^n}{\inf} L(\mathbf{x}, \boldsymbol{\lambda}, \mathbf{y}) = \begin{cases} \mathbf{b}^T \mathbf{y}, & \mathbf{c} - \boldsymbol{\lambda} - \mathbf{A}^T \mathbf{y} \geq \mathbf{0}, \\ -\infty, & \text{otherwise.} \end{cases}$$

From this, we have the dual problem:

$$\underset{\mathbf{y} \in R^m, \boldsymbol{\lambda} \geq 0}{\text{maximize }} g(\mathbf{y}, \boldsymbol{\lambda}) = \underset{\mathbf{y} \in R^m, \boldsymbol{\lambda} \geq 0}{\text{maximize }} \mathbf{b}^T \mathbf{y} \quad \text{subject to} \quad \mathbf{A}^T \mathbf{y} + \boldsymbol{\lambda} \leq \mathbf{c}.$$

This is equivalent to

$$\underset{\mathbf{y} \in R^m}{\text{maximize }} \mathbf{b}^T \mathbf{y} \quad \text{subject to} \quad \mathbf{A}^T \mathbf{y} \leq \mathbf{c}.$$

E.5 Strong Duality

Note that for linear programming, Theorems 1, 2, and 3 hold and, in particular, we can show the weak duality, Theorem 1, straightforwardly as follows:

$$p^* = \mathbf{c}^T\mathbf{x}^* \geq (\mathbf{y}^*)^T\mathbf{A}\mathbf{x}^* = (\mathbf{y}^*)^T\mathbf{b} = d^*,$$

where p^* is the optimal value of the primary problem and d^* is that of the dual problem, which are given by Eqs. (E.2.4) and (E.2.5), respectively, and $\mathbf{x}^*$ and $\mathbf{y}^*$ are the optimum solutions to the primary and the dual problems.

In this section, we demonstrate the *strong duality*: $p^* = d^*$ that holds in linear programming. Proving it requires Farkas theorem.

Lemma 1 (Farkas theorem) *Let $\mathbf{A}$ be an $m \times n$ matrix, $\mathbf{b}$ an m-dimensional vector, and $\mathbf{c}$ an n-dimensional vector. Then, exactly one of the following holds.*

1. *There exists $\mathbf{x} \in \mathbf{R}^n$ such that $\mathbf{A}\mathbf{x} = \mathbf{b}$ and $\mathbf{x} \geq \mathbf{0}$.*
2. *There exists $\mathbf{y} \in \mathbf{R}^m$ such that $\mathbf{A}^T\mathbf{y} \leq \mathbf{0}$ and $\mathbf{b}^T\mathbf{y} > 0$.*

Proof We regard the columns of the matrix $\mathbf{A}$ as column vectors $\mathbf{a}_1, \ldots, \mathbf{a}_n$, $\mathbf{a}_i \in \mathbf{R}^m$. That is,

$$\mathbf{A} = (\mathbf{a}_1 \; \mathbf{a}_2 \; \cdots \; \mathbf{a}_n).$$

Consider a convex cone with its apex at the origin that is generated by $\mathbf{a}_1, \ldots, \mathbf{a}_n$, that is, the set of all possible linear combinations of these vectors with non-negative coefficients:

$$\{x_1\mathbf{a}_1 + \cdots + x_n\mathbf{a}_n \mid x_1 \geq 0, \ldots, x_n \geq 0\}.$$

For the vector $\mathbf{b}$, there are two possibilities. That is, either $\mathbf{b}$ is contained in the convex cone, or not. In the former case, $\mathbf{A}\mathbf{x} = \mathbf{b}$ holds for some $\mathbf{x} \geq \mathbf{0}$, $\mathbf{x} \in \mathbf{R}^n$. Assume that $\mathbf{b}$ is not contained in the convex cone. Then, we can find a hyperplane h that goes through the origin and lies between the convex cone and $\mathbf{b}$. Let $\mathbf{y} \in \mathbf{R}^m$ be the normal vector of the hyperplane h. Note that $\mathbf{b}$ lies in opposite half-space with respect to h compared to all vectors $\mathbf{a}_i$. Let $\mathbf{v}$ be a vector in $\mathbf{R}^m$. If the vector $\mathbf{v}$ lies on h, we have $\mathbf{v}^T\mathbf{y} = 0$, if $\mathbf{v}$ does not lie on h and it does on the same side as $\mathbf{y}$, we have $\mathbf{v}^T\mathbf{y} > 0$, and if $\mathbf{v}$ does not lie on h and it does on the opposite side as $\mathbf{y}$, we have $\mathbf{v}^T\mathbf{y} < 0$. Now, without loss of generality, we can assume that $\mathbf{y}$ lies on the same side as $\mathbf{b}$ with respect to h. Because $\mathbf{b}$ lies in opposite half-space with respect to h compared to all vectors $\mathbf{a}_i$, we have $\mathbf{a}_i^T\mathbf{y} \leq 0$ and $\mathbf{b}^T\mathbf{y} > 0$. This is, $\mathbf{A}^T\mathbf{y} \leq \mathbf{0}$ and $\mathbf{b}^T\mathbf{y} > 0$. End of proof.

Now we describe the strong duality in linear programing. Note that we have groball y optimal solutions from Theorem 3.

Theorem 4 (Strong Duality) *Let p^* be the optimal value of the primary form in linear programming (E.4.1) and d^* is that of the dual form (E.4.2), which are given*

Appendix E: Strong Duality in Linear Programming

by Equations (E.2.4) and (E.2.5), respectively. Then, if the primal problem has the solution, we also have the optimal solution to the dual problem and $d^* = p^*$ holds.

Proof Let $\mathbf{x}^*$ be a optimal solution to the primal problem. That is, $p^* = \mathbf{c}^T\mathbf{x}^*$. By extending $\mathbf{A}$ and $\mathbf{b}$, we define the $(m+1) \times n$ matrix $\hat{\mathbf{A}}$ and the $(m+1)$-dimensional vector $\hat{\mathbf{b}}_\varepsilon$ as follows:

$$\hat{\mathbf{A}} \equiv \begin{pmatrix} \mathbf{A} \\ -\mathbf{c}^T \end{pmatrix}, \quad \hat{\mathbf{b}}_\varepsilon \equiv \begin{pmatrix} \mathbf{b} \\ -p^* + \varepsilon \end{pmatrix},$$

where $\varepsilon, \alpha \in R$. If $\varepsilon = 0$, we have Farkas case 1 because of $\hat{\mathbf{A}}\mathbf{x}^* = \hat{\mathbf{b}}_0$, which is derived from the equality constraint of the original primary form. For $\varepsilon > 0$, we have no non-negative optimum solution because p^* is the minimum value of the original linear programming, thus we have Farkas case 2. Hence, there exist a vector $\mathbf{y} \in R^m$ and $\alpha \in R$ that satisfy

$$\begin{pmatrix} \mathbf{A} \\ -\mathbf{c}^T \end{pmatrix}^T \begin{pmatrix} \mathbf{y} \\ \alpha \end{pmatrix} = (\mathbf{A}^T \ -\mathbf{c}) \begin{pmatrix} \mathbf{y} \\ \alpha \end{pmatrix} \leq 0, \quad \begin{pmatrix} \mathbf{b} \\ -p^* + \varepsilon \end{pmatrix}^T \begin{pmatrix} \mathbf{y} \\ \alpha \end{pmatrix} = (\mathbf{b}^T \ -p^* + \varepsilon) \begin{pmatrix} \mathbf{y} \\ \alpha \end{pmatrix} > 0. \tag{E.5.1}$$

These are equivalent to

$$\mathbf{A}^T\mathbf{y} \leq \alpha\mathbf{c}, \quad \mathbf{b}^T\mathbf{y} > \alpha(p^* - \varepsilon). \tag{E.5.2}$$

We also define $\hat{\mathbf{y}}$ as

$$\hat{\mathbf{y}} \equiv \begin{pmatrix} \mathbf{y} \\ \alpha \end{pmatrix}.$$

As the normal vector of a hyperplane, $\hat{\mathbf{y}}$ satisfies $\hat{\mathbf{b}}_0^T \hat{\mathbf{y}} = 0$. This is because

1. from the second inequality of (E.5.1), we have $\hat{\mathbf{b}}_\varepsilon^T \hat{\mathbf{y}} > 0$ for all $\varepsilon > 0$,
2. the vector $\hat{\mathbf{b}}_0$ lies within or on the surface of the convex cone that is generated by

$$\begin{pmatrix} \mathbf{a}_1 \\ -c_1 \end{pmatrix}, \ldots, \begin{pmatrix} \mathbf{a}_n \\ -c_n \end{pmatrix}$$

because of $\hat{\mathbf{A}}\mathbf{x}^* = \hat{\mathbf{b}}_0$, which leads us to $\hat{\mathbf{b}}_0^T \hat{\mathbf{y}} \leq 0$,
3. the vector $\hat{\mathbf{b}}_\varepsilon$ and also the inner product $\hat{\mathbf{b}}_\varepsilon^T \hat{\mathbf{y}}$ are continuous with respect to ε, and, in particular, they are continuous at $\varepsilon = 0$, and
4. hence, we have $\hat{\mathbf{b}}_0^T \hat{\mathbf{y}} = 0$, which means that the vector $\hat{\mathbf{b}}_0$ lies on the surface of the convex cone.

For this $\hat{\mathbf{y}}$, we have $\mathbf{b}^T\mathbf{y} = \alpha p^*$. Also, for this $\hat{\mathbf{y}}$, we have $\mathbf{b}^T\mathbf{y} > \alpha(p^* - \varepsilon)$ from the second inequality of (E.5.2). From these two relations, we obtain $\alpha\varepsilon > 0$, which leads us to $\alpha > 0$. Furthermore, we can freely scale $\hat{\mathbf{y}}$ to any magnitude greater than 0 because, again, it is the normal vector of the hyperplane. Thus, setting $\alpha = 1$, we obtain

$$\mathbf{A}^\mathrm{T}\mathbf{y} \leq \mathbf{c}, \quad \mathbf{b}^\mathrm{T}\mathbf{y} > p^* - \varepsilon.$$

For any $\varepsilon > 0$, therefore,

$$d^* \geq \mathbf{b}^\mathrm{T}\mathbf{y} > p^* - \varepsilon$$

holds because d^* is the supremum of the feasible set of the dual problem. Also, $d^* \leq p^*$ holds from the weak duality. We have $\varepsilon > 0$, which is arbitrary; hence, we obtain $\mathbf{b}^\mathrm{T}\mathbf{y} = d^* = p^*$, and we conclude this $\mathbf{y}$ is the optimal solution to the dual problem. End of proof.

References

1. Arjovsky, M., Chintala, S., & Bottou, L. (2017). Wasserstein generative adversarial networks. *ICML 2017 PMLR, 70*, 214–223.
2. Ba, J. L., Kiros, J. R., & Hinton, G. E. (2016). Layer normalization. arXiv:1607.06450.
3. Bahdanau, D., Cho, K., & Bengio, Y. (2015). Neural machine translation by jointly learning to align and translate. *ICLR 2014*. arXiv:1409.0473.
4. Baio, A. (2022). https://waxy.org/2022/08/exploring-12-million-of-the-images-used-to-train-stable-diffusions-image-generator
5. Brown, T. B., et al. (2020). Language models are few-shot learners. *NeurIPS 2020*, 1877–1901.
6. Chung, H. W., et al. (2022). Scaling instruction-finetuned language models. *Journal of Machine Learning Research, 25*, 1–53 (2024). arXiv:2210.11416.
7. Devlin, J., et al. (2018). BERT: Pre-training of deep bidirectional Transformers for language understanding. *NAACL-HLT 2019* 4171–4186. arXiv:1810.04805.
8. Duchi, J., Hazan, E., & Singer, Y. (2011). Adaptive subgradient methods for online learning and stochastic optimization. *Journal of Machine Learning Research, 12*, 2121–2159.
9. Elman, J. L. (1990). Finding structure in time. *Cognitive Science, 14*, 179–211.
10. Glorot, X., Bordes, A., & Bengio, Y. (2011). Deep sparse rectifier neural networks. *AISTATS 2011*, 315–323.
11. Goodfellow, I. J., et al. (2014). Generative adversarial nets. *NIPS 2014*, 2672–2680.
12. Gullapalli, V. (1990). A stochastic reinforcement learning algorithm for learning real-valued functions. *Neural Networks, 3*, 671–692.
13. Hahnloser, R. H. R., et al. (2000). Digital selection and analogue amplification coexist in a cortex-inspired silicon circuit. *Nature, 405*, 947–951.
14. He, K., et al. (2015). Deep residual learning for image recognition. *CVPR 2016*, 770–778. arXiv:1512.03385.
15. Hinton, G. E., & Salakhutdinov, R. R. (2006). Reducing the dimensionality of data with neural networks. *Science, 313*(5786), 504–507.
16. Hinton, G., Srivastava, N., & Swersky, K. (2020). Lecture 6a: Overview of Mini-Batch Gradient Descent. https://www.cs.toronto.edu/~tijmen/csc321/slides/lecture_slides_lec6.pdf.
17. Ho, J., Jain, A., & Abbeel, P. (2020). Denoising diffusion probabilistic models. *NeurIPS 2020*, 6840–6851. arXiv:2006.11239.
18. Ioffe, S., & Szegedy, C. (2015). Batch normalization: Accelerating deep network training by reducing internal covariate shift. *ICML 2015*, 448–456. arXiv:1502.03167.

19. Karras, T., et al. (2017). Progressive growing of GANs for improved quality, stability, and variation. *ICLR 2018*. arXiv:1710.10196.
20. Kingma, D. P., & Ba, J. (2014). Adam: A method for stochastic optimization. *ICLR 2015*. arXiv:1412.6980.
21. Kingma, D. P., & Welling, M. (2014). Auto-encoding variational Bayes. *ICLR 2013*. arXiv:1312.6114.
22. Labaien, J., et al. (2023). Diagnostic spatio-temporal transformer with faithful encoding. *Knowledge-Based Systems, 274*, 110639.
23. Lang, K. J., Waibel, A. H., & Hinton, G. E. (1990). A time-delay neural network architecture for isolated word recognition. *Neural Networks, 3*, 23–43.
24. Luong, T., Pham, H., & Manning, C. D. (2015). Effective approaches to attention-based neural machine translation. *EMNLP 2015*, 1412–1421.
25. Mikolov, T., et al. (2010). Recurrent neural network based language model. *INTERSPEECH, 2010*, 1045–1048.
26. Mikolov, T., et al. (2013). ICLR: Efficient estimation of word representations in vector space. *ICLR2013*. arXiv:1301.3781.
27. Mirza, M., & Osindero, S. (2014). Conditional generative adversarial nets. arXiv:1411.1784.
28. Mnih, V., et al. (2013). Playing Atari with deep reinforcement learning. arXiv:1312.5602.
29. Nair, V., & Hinton, G. E. (2010). Rectified linear units improve restricted Boltzmann machines. *ICML 2010*, 807–814.
30. Ouyang, L., et al. (2022). Training language models to follow instructions with human feedback. *NeurIPS 2022*. arXiv:2203.02155.
31. Polyak, B. T. (1964). Some methods of speeding up the convergence of iteration methods. *USSR Computational Mathematics and Mathematical Physics, 4*, 1–17.
32. Radford, A., et al. (2018). Improving language understanding by generative pre-training. https://cdn.openai.com/research-covers/language-unsupervised/language_understanding_paper.pdf.
33. Radford, A., et al. (2021). Learning transferable visual models from natural language supervision. *PMLR 139*, 8748–8763. arXiv:2103.00020.
34. Radford, A., Metz, L., & Chintala, S. (2015). Unsupervised representation learning with deep convolutional generative adversarial networks. *ICLR 2016*. arXiv:1511.06434.
35. Rafailov, R., et al. (2023). Direct preference optimization: Your language model is secretly a reward model. *NeurIPS 2023*.
36. Rombach, R., et al. (2022). High-resolution image synthesis with latent diffusion models. *CVPR 2022*, 10674–10685. arXiv:2112.10752.
37. Ronneberger, O., Fischer, P., & Brox, T. (2015). U-net: convolutional networks for biomedical image segmentation. *MICCAI 2015*, 234–241. arXiv:1505.04597.
38. Rosenblatt, F. (1961). *Principles of Neurodynamics: Perceptrons and the Theory of Brain Mechanisms* (p. 313). Cornell AeroNautical Laboratory, Inc.
39. Schulman, J., et al. (2015). Trust region policy optimization. *PMLR, 37*, 1889–1897. arXiv:1502.05477.
40. Schulman, J., et al. (2017). Proximal policy optimization algorithms. arXiv:1707.06347.
41. Shazeer, N. (2020). GLU variants improve Transformer. arXiv:2002.05202.
42. Sohl-Dickstein, J., et al. (2015). Deep unsupervised learning using nonequilibrium thermodynamics. *ICML 2015*, 2256–2265. arXiv:1503.03585.
43. Sutton, R. S., et al. (1999). Policy gradient methods for reinforcement learning with function approximation. *NIPS 1999*, 1057–1063.
44. Touvron, H., et al. (2023). Llama 2: Open foundation and fine-tuned chat models. arXiv:2307.09288.
45. Ulyanov, D., Vedaldi, A., & Lempitsky, V. (2016). Instance normalization: The missing ingredient for fast stylization. CoRR, July 2016. arXiv:1607.08022.
46. Vaswani, A., et al. (2017). Attention is all you need. *NIPS 2017*, 5998–6008.
47. Watkins, C. J. C. H. (1989). Learning from delayed rewards. Ph.D. thesis, King's College, Cambridge.

48. Watkins, C. J. C. H., & Dayan, P. (1992). Technical note: Q-learning. *Machine Learning, 8*, 279–292.
49. Wei, J., et al. (2022). Chain-of-thought prompting elicits reasoning in large language models. *NIPS 2022*, 24824–24837. arXiv:2201.11903.
50. Wei, J., et al. (2022). Finetuned language models are zero-shot learners. *ICLR2022*.
51. Werbos, P. J. (1990). Backpropagation through time: What it does and how to do it. *Proceedings of the IEEE, 78*, 1550–1560.
52. Williams, R. J. (1992). Simple statistical gradient-following algorithms for connectionist reinforcement learning. *Machine Learning, 8*, 229–256.
53. Wu, Y., & He, K. (2018). Group normalization. *ECCV 2018*. arXiv:1803.08494.
54. Zeiler, M. D. (2012). ADADELTA: An adaptive learning rate method. arXiv:1212.5701.

Index

A
Action, 82
Action policy, 83
Action value function, 87
Activation, 4
Activation function, 5
Adadelta, 27
AdaGrad, 26
Adam, 28
Additive attention, 69
Advantage function, 92
Agent, 82
Attention, 68
Attention function, 71
Attention mechanism, 67
Autoencoder (AE), 51, 53
Average reward, 92

B
Backpropagation, 11
Backpropagation formula, 14
Backpropagation through time, 48
Baseline function, 93
Batch normalization, 32
Beam search, 104, 105
Beam width, 105
Bellman equation, 87
Bias parameter, 4
Bidirectional Encoder Representations from Transformers (BERT), 117
Bottleneck, 31
Bounded above, 196
Bounded below, 195

C
Chain-of-thought, 122
Code, 53
Concave, 197, 219
Concave optimization problem, 220
Conditional GAN, 183
Content-based attention, 69
Context vector, 58
Convex, 196, 199, 219
Convex optimization problem, 220
Cumulative reward, 82, 83

D
Data sparsity, 103
Decoder, 51, 53
Decoding, 53
Decoding model, 141
Deep learning, 3
Deep neural network, 3
Deep Q-Network (DQN), 86, 89, 90
Differential action-value function, 94
Diffusion model, 153
Diffusion probability model, 153
Diffusion process, 155
Direct Preference Optimization (DPO), 124, 131
Discounted cumulative reward, 83
Discounted present value, 83
Discount factor, 83
Distance, 201
Distributional hypothesis, 56
Dot product attention, 68
Dual problem, 218

E
Embedding matrix, 57
Empirical loss function, 7
Encoder, 51, 53
Encoding, 53
Encoding model, 141
Entailment recognition, 119
Episode, 85
Epoch, 9
Epoch count, 9
ε-greedy, 89
Equality constraint, 217
Ergodicity, 93
Error, 11
Error backpropagation formula, 14
Error function, 7
Evidence Lower Bound (ELBO), 141
Experience replay, 91
Exponential moving average, 33

F
Farkas theorem, 222
Feasible, 217
Feature, 54
Few-shot, 121
Fine-tuning, 20
Fully connected, 4

G
Generative Adversarial Network (GAN), 177
Generative Pre-Training (GPT), 120
Global maximum, 196
Global minimum, 195
Gradient clipping, 91
Greedy, 89
Greedy search, 104, 105
Group normalization, 37

H
Hidden layer, 3
Hyperbolic tangent function, 6

I
Immediate reward, 82, 83
Inequality constraint, 217
Infimum, 195
Input layer, 3
Instance normalization, 36
Instruction, 122

Instruction tuning, 122
Intermediate layer, 3
Inverse process, 154

J
Jacobian, 16
Jensen's inequality, 200
JS divergence, 180

K
Key, 69
KL divergence, 201
Kullback-Leibler divergence, 201

L
Lagrange multiplier, 218
Lagrangian dual function, 218
Lagrangian function, 218
Latent space interpolation, 147
Layer normalization, 35
Layer-wise normalization, 35
Learning rate, 26
Linear congruential method, 205
Linear programming, 221
Link, 3
Lipschitz continuity, 194
Local maximum, 196
Local minimum, 195
Logistic sigmoid function, 5
Loss function, 7
Lower bound, 195

M
Markov chain, 153
Markov decision process, 84
Markov process, 153
Marsaglia method, 206
Masked multi-head attention, 80, 116
Maxima, 196
Maximum, 196
Maximum value, 196
Middle layer, 3
Mini-batch learning, 9
Minima, 195
Minimum, 195
Minimum value, 195
Mode collapse, 182
Momentum, 24
Momentum method, 24
Momentum stochastic gradient descent, 24

Index 231

Multi-head attention, 72
Multi-layer perceptron, 3
Multiplicative attention, 69

N
Named entity recognition, 119
Negative sampling, 62
Neural network, 3

O
Objective function, 217
One-hot representation (vector), 7
Optimal, 217
Optimal action value function, 87
Optimal solution, 217
Optimal value, 217
Output layer, 3

P
Policy, 82, 83
Policy gradient method, 86, 93
Policy gradient theorem, 93
Position-based attention, 69
Pre-training, 21
Primary problem, 218
Progressive Growing GAN (PGGAN), 183
Prompt, 121
Proximal Policy Optimization (PPO), 86, 96
p-Wasserstein distance, 190

Q
Q-function, 87
Q-learning, 86, 88
Query, 67
Question answering, 119

R
Recurrent Neural Network (RNN), 45
Reinforcement Learning (RLHF), 124
REINFORCE method, 94
Relatedness vector, 68
Relative entropy, 201
ReLU function, 29
Reparameterization, 146
Representation learning, 20, 55
Residual block, 31
Residual connection, 30
Reverse process, 154
Reward, 82

Reward function, 83
RMSProp, 27
RNN language model, 106

S
Self-attention, 73
Sentiment analysis, 119
Seq2seq, 108
Sequence-to-sequence model, 108
Skip connection, 31
Softmax function, 6
Source, 67
Stable diffusion, 167
State, 82
State transition probability, 82
Stationary, 93
Stochastic process, 82, 153
Strictly concave, 197
Strictly convex, 196
Strong duality, 222
Subdifferential, 44
Supervised Fine-Tuning (SFT), 128, 130
Supremum, 196

T
Target, 67
Tensor, 33
Token, 73
Transfer learning, 20
Transformer, 75
Transformer block, 72
Transposed convolution, 209
Trust Region Policy Optimization (TRPO), 86, 96

U
Undiscounted cumulative reward, 83
Unit, 3
Unsupervised learning, 53
Upper bound, 196
Upsampling, 209

V
Value, 69
Value function (V-function), 91
Variance schedule, 156
Variational Autoencoder (VAE), 139
Variational lower bound, 141

W
Wasserstein distance, 186
Wasserstein GAN, 185
Weak duality, 218, 222
Word embedding, 55

Word vector representation, 55

Z
Zero-shot, 121

GPSR Compliance

The European Union's (EU) General Product Safety Regulation (GPSR) is a set of rules that requires consumer products to be safe and our obligations to ensure this.

If you have any concerns about our products, you can contact us on

ProductSafety@springernature.com

In case Publisher is established outside the EU, the EU authorized representative is:

Springer Nature Customer Service Center GmbH
Europaplatz 3
69115 Heidelberg, Germany

www.ingramcontent.com/pod-product-compliance
Ingram Content Group UK Ltd.
Pitfield, Milton Keynes, MK11 3LW, UK
UKHW021343170625
459763UK00001B/12